AF804652

AMERICAN FOREIGN POLICY IDEOLOGY AND THE INTERNATIONAL RULE OF LAW

American engagement with international law has long been framed by commitment to the 'international rule of law' that persists even across divergent political and historical eras. Yet, despite appeals to legal ideals, American international law policy is consistently criticised as fraught with contradiction and distorted by beliefs in 'exceptionalism'. These contested claims of fidelity to law are the subject of this book: what does the 'international rule of law' mean for American legal policymakers even as they advocate competing commitments to international legal order? Answers are found in extensive evidence that American policymakers receive international law through established foreign policy ideologies that correspond with divisions in both legal scholarship and diplomatic history. Using the case of the International Criminal Court, the book demonstrates that the very meaning of the international rule of law is structured by competing ideological beliefs; between American policymakers and global counterparts, and among American policymakers themselves.

MALCOLM JORGENSEN is a Fellow at the Berlin Potsdam Research Group 'International Law: Rise or Decline?'. He holds a PhD in International Law and American Foreign Policy from the University of Sydney, where he was a Research Associate at the United States Studies Centre and remains an Associate of the Sydney Centre for International Law. He formerly served in the Australian foreign ministry.

AMERICAN FOREIGN POLICY IDEOLOGY AND THE INTERNATIONAL RULE OF LAW

Contesting Power through the International Criminal Court

MALCOLM JORGENSEN
Humboldt University of Berlin

CAMBRIDGE
UNIVERSITY PRESS

CAMBRIDGE
UNIVERSITY PRESS

University Printing House, Cambridge CB2 8BS, United Kingdom

One Liberty Plaza, 20th Floor, New York, NY 10006, USA

477 Williamstown Road, Port Melbourne, VIC 3207, Australia

314–321, 3rd Floor, Plot 3, Splendor Forum, Jasola District Centre, New Delhi – 110025, India

79 Anson Road, #06–04/06, Singapore 079906

Cambridge University Press is part of the University of Cambridge.

It furthers the University's mission by disseminating knowledge in the pursuit of education, learning, and research at the highest international levels of excellence.

www.cambridge.org
Information on this title: www.cambridge.org/9781108481434
DOI: 10.1017/9781108630658

© Malcolm Andrew Jorgensen 2020

This publication is in copyright. Subject to statutory exception and to the provisions of relevant collective licensing agreements, no reproduction of any part may take place without the written permission of Cambridge University Press.

First published 2020

Printed in the United Kingdom by TJ International Ltd, Padstow Cornwall

A catalogue record for this publication is available from the British Library.

Library of Congress Cataloging-in-Publication Data
Names: Jorgensen, Malcolm Andrew, 1982– author.
Title: American foreign policy ideology and the international rule of law : contesting power through the International Criminal Court / Malcolm Jorgensen, Humboldt-Universität zu Berlin
Description: Cambridge, United Kingdom ; New York, NY, USA Cambridge University Press, 2020 | Based on author's thesis (doctoral – University of Sydney, Faculty of Law, 2015). | Includes bibliographical references and index.
Identifiers: LCCN 2019028644 (print) | LCCN 2019028645 (ebook) | ISBN 9781108481434 (hardback) | ISBN 9781108630658 (epub)
Subjects: LCSH: International law – United States. | International criminal law – United States. | United States – Foreign relations – 1945–1989. | United States – Foreign relations – 1989– | International Criminal Court – History.
Classification: LCC KZ3410 .J67 2019 (print) | LCC KZ3410 (ebook) | DDC 345/.01–dc23
LC record available at https://lccn.loc.gov/2019028644
LC ebook record available at https://lccn.loc.gov/2019028645

ISBN 978-1-108-48143-4 Hardback

DAMAGED

Cambridge University Press has no responsibility for the persistence or accuracy of URLs for external or third-party internet websites referred to in this publication and does not guarantee that any content on such websites is, or will remain, accurate or appropriate.

CONTENTS

TABLES

FOREWORD

It is an honour to write the foreword for Malcolm Jorgensen's fine book. I have long been a believer in the need for comparative scholarship about international law. International lawyers from different states, regions and geopolitical groupings often have distinct backgrounds, influences, opportunities, incentives, networks and spheres of influence. Instead of constituting a single, uniform field, international law is produced from an amalgamation of multiple, partially overlapping fields and communities. If we truly want to understand our field, we need to be aware of what international law looks like from diverse perspectives and through different eyes.

Comparative international law often focuses attention on divisions among international lawyers located in, coming from or educated in different states, regions or geopolitical groupings. In this sense, it is often horizontal in nature, drawing comparisons across states. But to develop a really sophisticated understanding of how international law is approached within a single state, we also need vertical studies that unpack differences within a particular state. American international lawyers as a group certainly differ from Chinese or French international lawyers, but they are also not homogenous and often differ from each other. The trick is being aware of differences both across and within states.

It is this difficult horizontal and vertical work that Jorgensen achieves so brilliantly in this volume. He starts from the horizontal observation that international lawyers from inside and outside the United States often have different perspectives on America's engagement with the international rule of law. Is America a champion of the international rule of law or a flouter of it? Jorgensen then proceeds to skilfully unpack what different types of US international lawyers mean when they proclaim fidelity to the international rule of law. In doing so, he sheds light on both an internal/external disconnect and the variation within America's internal make-up. If we had more studies like this of different countries, our understanding of different national approaches to international law and foreign policy would be greatly improved.

Jorgensen's sophisticated work takes the skill of an insider/outsider. Jorgensen has read deeply in the American literature and met and interviewed many key international lawyers, so he is able to discuss US approaches with nuance and credibility. He approaches the subject with empathy, seeking to understand what international law looks like from within the US prism. He critically analyses what he finds without seeking to condemn or dismiss. He also has the advantage of looking at American international lawyers with the eye of an outsider. This makes it possible for him to observe some aspects that American international lawyers might be unable to detect because they are rendered natural or inevitable. Not himself wanting to work for the US government, Jorgensen can also speak more freely than some of his subjects, who often rotate in and out of government and academia.

Jorgensen analyses competing conceptions of American exceptionalism and suggests breaking down US international law foreign policy approaches based on two axes. The first concerns governance: how internationalist versus nationalist is the international law policy approach? The second concerns values: how liberal versus illiberal are the values that are pursued? These questions produce four ideal types: liberal internationalism, illiberal internationalism, liberal nationalism and illiberal nationalism. While some famous US international lawyers (including Harold Koh and Anne-Marie Slaughter) are clearly liberal internationalists, this typology provides a useful way to understand the approaches of President Trump and advisers such as John Bolton who seem much more illiberal nationalist in their inclinations. America's approach to international law often represents the push and pull of actors in these different ideal types, as Jorgensen shows with respect to US policy toward the International Criminal Court.

I was asked to write a foreword for this book, *American Foreign Policy Ideology and the International Rule of Law*, at the same time as I was asked to write a blurb for Professor Congyan Cai's new book, *The Rise of China and International Law: Taking Chinese Exceptionalism Seriously*.[1] In some ways, the books could be understood as bookends.

[1] Congyan Cai, *The Rise of China and International Law: Taking Chinese Exceptionalism Seriously* (Oxford University Press, 2019).

One seeks to take a deep dive into international law's most significant existing great power, while the other takes a look at the approach of international law's most significant rising (or returning) great power. Both look at national claims to exceptionalism. Given the emerging US–China rivalry internationally, it would behove all international scholars to read both books so that they can better appreciate the distinctive approaches of these two great powers whose relationship will significantly influence the development of international law and relations in the coming decades.

In my work on China and the United States, I have often been struck by the way in which they can make similar statements but mean utterly different things by them. Invocations of democracy and the rule of law are a case in point. The United States has been a strong advocate for democracy on the international stage, but by this it means that it supports states (including China) becoming democratic on a national level. In terms of international relations, however, the United States has been decidedly undemocratic in its approach to lawmaking. Far from accepting a one-state-one-vote or one-individual-one-vote approach to international lawmaking, the United States has been happy to enjoying the lawmaking advantages that have come with being the world's only superpower.

China is the exact opposite. As an authoritarian state, China has strongly resisted calls by other states (including the United States) for it or other nondemocratic states to become or be made to become democratic. This viewpoint lies behind China's rejection of calls to embrace values such as human rights and doctrines such as unilateral humanitarian intervention, as well as its professed loyalty to principles such as the sovereign equality of states and the doctrine of non-intervention. At the same time, China has resisted the legitimacy of Western and US hegemony in international lawmaking, insisting (in principle, though not always in practice) that all states should be involved in lawmaking without the strong being able to impose their will on the weak. China's emphasis on sovereign equality, including equality in lawmaking, is sometimes characterised as a belief in 'democracy between states' as opposed to 'democracy within states'.[2]

When the United States calls internationally for democracy, it often means democracy at home but hegemony abroad. By contrast, when

[2] Julian Ku, 'What Does China Mean When It Celebrates the "International Rule of Law"?', *Opinio Juris*, 29 October 2014, http://opiniojuris.org/2014/10/29/china-mean-celebrates-international-rule-law.

China calls internationally for democracy, it seems to be embracing some concept of democracy abroad but hegemony at home. One adopts a national level of analysis; the other an international level. It would be easy to stand in the shoes of one state and simply dismiss the other state's invocation of these terms as opportunistic. But it is probably more useful to examine what policymakers in each state mean when they invoke these terms, being aware of the differences between them and the internal inconsistencies within each position. Critique is useful, but understanding is a necessary first step.

In reading both books, it was striking to me that Cai's book on China's approach to international law is replete with references to the United States, but Jorgensen's book on US approaches to international law contains only one reference to China. This observation does not amount to a critique of the book; instead, the asymmetry reflects the way in which our field has been constructed to date. One cannot be an international lawyer without knowing a lot about America. However, it has long been possible to be an international lawyer whilst writing – and, for some, even knowing – little about China. America has been central, but China has been peripheral. Knowledge of the United States has been required; knowledge of China has often been treated as optional.

Here, Jorgensen's career trajectory provides a fascinating example of how individual agendas and field dynamics are interwoven. His PhD thesis, on which this book is based, was focused on America. Yet his current writings have moved towards exploring the way in which China is seeking to craft 'geolegal orders' in areas such as the law of the sea.[3] Geopolitical power has shifted and, with that, so has the field's scholarship. Jorgensen's work in both areas represents a form of comparative international law, focusing on distinctive approaches to international law both within and among states, with a particular focus on great powers. His ability to do a deep vertical dive into one state in this book and then shift tacks and do a horizontal assessment across states reflects the versatility of his comparative approach.

[3] See e.g. Malcolm Jorgensen, 'Equilibrium & Fragmentation in the International Rule of Law: The Rising Chinese Geolegal Order' (November 2018) No. 21 *KFG Working Paper Series*, https://ssrn.com/abstract=3283626; Malcolm Jorgensen, 'Internationalizing the Monroe Doctrine: From Venezuela to Golan Heights and Back Around', *Just Security*, 4 June 2019, www.justsecurity.org/64397/internationalizing-the-monroe-doctrine-from-venezuela-to-golan-heights-and-back-around/.

I recommend that readers read this book as well as Jorgensen's related body of work. He is a very promising young scholar with much to add to our understanding of great powers and their relationships. I have learnt a lot from reading his work and from the conversations we have had. I hope others feel the same way once they have read this book.

Anthea Roberts
August 2019

ACKNOWLEDGEMENTS

This book has been written in an era when civility of political debate in established democracies is faltering over a particular hurdle: reluctance among political opponents to acknowledge when competing norms and values are not merely rhetoric to mask self-serving interests, but represent good faith commitment to sincerely held beliefs. Assuming the calculated hypocrisy of one's opponents establishes an insurmountable barrier to constructive dialogue towards a better politics. So it is with global legal order, where recognition of competing yet sincere commitment to rule of law ideals becomes the baseline for any meaningful discourse over the rules and institutions organising international life. As in politics, learning to see through the eyes of others is not to surrender one's own conception of rightful conduct but to take seriously and engage with alternative worldviews. The people and institutions I thank here have together taught me to undertake this critical task, both in the book that follows and when looking to the world beyond.

I give thanks foremost to the Berlin Potsdam Research Group 'International Law: Rise or Decline?' and its members, whose commitment to scholarship on the politics and future of international law has made this book possible. In particular I am indebted to the leadership of Professors Georg Nolte, Heike Krieger and Andreas Zimmermann, whose innovative work I have long followed and from whom it has been an honour to learn and grow as an international lawyer during my years in Berlin. Every colleague at the group has contributed to and improved my scholarship in innumerable ways, including Professor Campbell McLachlan in furnishing me with comments during a roundtable discussion of the book, Dr Nina Reiners for reviewing draft chapters, my office mate for two years Dr Velimir Zivkovic, Dr Dana Burchardt, Dr Felix Lange, Dr James Devaney, Julian Kulaga and, finally, Kerstin Schuster and all the administrative staff and students who have provided so much support.

I also owe deep gratitude to the United States Studies Centre at the University of Sydney for its many years of scholarly, financial and personal support, without which the original research would not have been possible. I thank every one of the countless staff, students and visitors I was able to engage with, each of whom contributed to my intellectual enrichment as a scholar of American politics and foreign policy. I do single out former CEO Professor Bates Gill for his unqualified and ongoing support from the beginning, my associate PhD supervisor Dr David Smith, whose judgement and advice was impeccable every time, and, most especially, Craig Purcell, whose professionalism and friendship in equal measure always made the difference. I also thank the many other staff of the USSC who gave support in specific ways, including former CEO Professor Geoffrey Garrett, Associate Professor Brendon O'Connor, Dr Rebecca Sheehan, Dr Sarah Graham, Dr Gorana Grgic, Dr Nina Silove, Dr Thomas Adams, Dr Rob Rakove, Dr Niki Hemmer, Dr Marc-William Palen, Dr Benjamin Kahan, Dr Lizzie Ingleson, Dr Rodney Taveira, Dr Aaron Nyerges, Tom Switzer, Amelia Trial, Susan Beale, Max Halden, Jonathan Bradley, Nina Fudala, Nicole Phillips, Meghan Walters, Melissa Grah-McIntosh and Cindy Tang.

I give further thanks to the Faculty of Law at the University of Sydney and its academic staff, whose doors were always open to me as a student and colleague, and continue to be so as an Associate of the Sydney Centre for International Law. My highest thanks are reserved for Professor Tim Stephens, who was enthusiastic about my research from the first day I informally ran it past him, to seeing me through as my PhD supervisor. His ongoing collegial support is deeply appreciated. The evolution of the book owes much to Professor Anthea Roberts of the Australian National University, who early on recognised complementarities in our thinking on comparative international law and has been supportive ever since, up to and including writing the foreword to this book. I also offer thanks to other colleagues and mentors in the international law world who have read over and provided comments on my developing ideas. These include, among others, Professors David Weisbrot, Fleur Johns, Ben Saul, Shirley Scott, Charlotte Ku, John Noyes, Harlan Cohen, Madeleine Morris and Associate Professor Douglas Guilfoyle. My final academic thanks are given to Professors Anthony Cassimatis of the TC Beirne School of Law at the University of Queensland and William Tow of the Australian National University, who, respectively, were my first teachers in public international law and American foreign policy and who conveyed a passion for the subjects that remains with me.

I thank the colleagues with whom I have worked as a legal practitioner and especially those in the Legal Division of the Australian Department of Foreign Affairs and Trade in Canberra, under the leadership of then Senior Legal Advisor Katrina Cooper, where I was able to refine my first-hand understanding of the role and worldview of the international legal policymaker. I am particularly indebted to former Australian Senior Legal Advisor Richard Rowe, who provided such wise advice when making the difficult decision to leave the foreign ministry in order to complete this book. I also thank Justice Peter Applegarth of the Supreme Court of Queensland, for whom I had the honour of clerking and who continues to keep an eye over my career as one of his associate 'children'.

I owe many thanks to the numerous former United States government officials who generously gave their time to answering my questions, both on and off the record. It was from these conversations with American international lawyers that I confirmed my sense of a genuine commitment to the ideal of the international rule of law, but one that diverged systematically from conceptions of global counterparts in ways that demanded investigation. These policymakers include, but are certainly not limited to, William Taft IV, John Bellinger III, Stephen Rapp, Edwin Meese III, Ben Rhodes, as well as Professors Michael Matheson, John Moore and Detlev Vagts. I also acknowledge the assistance of Professor Walter Russell Mead for discussing my adaptation of his foreign policy traditions to international legal scholarship.

Finally, I have been privileged in having so many magnificent friends and family in Berlin, Canberra, Sydney, Brisbane, New Zealand, the United States and beyond, who have spent so many years supporting my endeavours, and occasional misadventures, during the long years of writing this thesis and book. I am forever indebted to my parents Stephen and Elvira, who taught me from childhood to think critically about the world and always to recognise the perspectives of others. That lesson has been practised and refined ever since with my siblings Timothy, Phillip, Hugh and Astrid and, I hope one day, with my nieces and nephew Charlotte, Daniel, Vivienne and Ingrid. On behalf of all of them, the book is dedicated to my grandmothers, Chen Siu June and Rosa Elisabetta Jorgensen, née Caccioppoli, whose lives represent the sacrifice and promise that we all enjoy today. These were two strong women who could not have hailed from more different backgrounds, yet committed themselves to passing on the core values and respect for education that have allowed succeeding generations to experience privileges they never could in their own lifetimes.

ABBREVIATIONS

ASP	Assembly of States Parties
ASPA	*American Service-Members' Protection Act* (2002)
Bush 41	George H. W. Bush, 41st President of the United States of America
Bush 43	George W. Bush, 43rd President of the United States of America
CCFR	Chicago Council on Foreign Relations
CI	cooperative internationalism
CICC	Coalition for the International Criminal Court
EU	European Union
FPA	Foreign Policy Analysis
FPLP	Foreign Policy Leadership Project
ICC	International Criminal Court
ICJ	International Court of Justice
ICTR	International Criminal Tribunal for Rwanda
ICTY	International Criminal Tribunal for the Former Yugoslavia
IL	international law
ILC	International Law Commission
IR	International Relations
LMS	like-minded states
MI	militant internationalism
NATO	North Atlantic Treaty Organization
NGO	non-governmental organisation
NSS	National Security Strategy
OTP	Office of the Prosecutor
P5	Permanent Five Members of the United Nations Security Council
SOFA	Status of Force Agreement
UK	United Kingdom of Great Britain and Northern Ireland
UN	United Nations
UNCLOS	*United Nations Convention on the Law of the Sea* (1982)
UNGA	United Nations General Assembly
UNSC	United Nations Security Council

US	United States
VCDR	*Vienna Convention on Diplomatic Relations* (1961)
VCLT	*Vienna Convention on the Law of Treaties* (1969)
WWI	World War I
WWII	World War II

Introduction

Contesting the International Rule of Law

In the closing years of World War II, German jurist and diplomat Wilhelm Grewe wrote: 'After this war has ended, a newly founded, politically balanced world order will also bring forth a new international legal order.'[1] Grewe was then undertaking the formidable task of periodising 'epochs' of international law (IL) defined by the rise and decline of great powers.[2] As Spain, France and Britain in turn enjoyed global predominance, so each was shown to mould prevailing international legal doctrines according to distinctive national ideologies. An 'American century'[3] thus seemed on the rise in the post-war years, in which the United States articulated a new legal order defined by 'the rule of law' in international affairs.[4] President Truman, in authorising the 1950 Korean War, argued: 'A return to the rule of force in international affairs would have far-reaching effects. The United States will continue to uphold the rule of law.'[5] President Eisenhower, in his 1959 State of the Union address, expressed hope that 'the rule of law may replace the rule of force in the affairs of nations'.[6] Perhaps most memorably, in his 1991

1 Cited in Bardo Fassbender, 'Stories of War and Peace on Writing the History of International Law in the "Third Reich" and After' (2002) 13 *European Journal of International Law* 479, p. 482.

2 Wilhelm G. Grewe, *The Epochs of International Law: Translated and Revised by Michael Byers* (Walter de Gruyter, 2000). The original book manuscript was completed in Germany during 1944 and has been criticised for being influenced by that ideological context: See Martti Koskenniemi, 'Book Reviews: *The Epochs of International Law*. By Wilhelm Grewe. Translated and Revised by Michael Byers' (2002) 51 *International and Comparative Law Quarterly* 746.

3 Henry R. Luce, 'The American Century' (1941) 17 February *Life Magazine* 61.

4 For an early review of these pronouncements see William W. Bishop, 'The International Rule of Law' (1961) 59 *Michigan Journal of International Law* 553, pp. 554–5 & 562–3.

5 Harry S. Truman, 'Statement by the President on the Situation in Korea', 27 June 1950, www.presidency.ucsb.edu/node/230845.

6 Dwight D. Eisenhower, 'Annual Message to the Congress on the State of the Union', 9 January 1959, www.presidency.ucsb.edu/node/235339.

national address at the commencement of the Persian Gulf War, President Bush envisioned 'the opportunity to forge for ourselves and for future generations a new world order – a world where the rule of law, not the law of the jungle, governs the conduct of nations'.[7] This book explains how commitments to 'the international rule of law' are informed by long-established and competing American foreign policy ideologies that structure profoundly contested meanings between American policymakers and their global counterparts and among American policymakers themselves.

The puzzling aspect of these presidential statements is that they set a benchmark inviting systematic charges of hypocrisy: that America has failed to honour the ideal of the international rule of law, with practice instead fraught with contradiction and distorted by beliefs in 'exceptionalism'. The standard inventory starts with the United States presenting itself as architect and chief advocate of the League of Nations after World War I (WWI) and then failing to join the organisation. After World War II (WWII) it again assumed this leadership role in the creation of the United Nations (UN), this time as a founding member. Yet the United States has subsequently become a conspicuous critic of the institution and was the greatest defaulter on UN dues by the close of the twentieth century. The United States has repeatedly used military force outside of UN prohibitions, including notoriously in the 2003 Iraq War, and has withdrawn consent to jurisdiction before the International Court of Justice (ICJ) in part for ruling to that effect.[8] More broadly, the United States has occupied a central role in efforts to create the International Criminal Court (ICC), ban anti-personnel landmines[9] and establish the *United Nations Convention on the Law of the Sea* (1982), while in each case failing to ratify the relevant treaties. Conversely, ratification of the 2015 Paris Climate Agreement served only to highlight apparent fickleness when the United States declared its intention to withdraw a mere nine months later.[10]

In *Lawless World*, British jurist Philippe Sands launched an influential critique of contemporary American legal policy by asking the question:

[7] George H. W. Bush, 'Address to the Nation Announcing Allied Military Action in the Persian Gulf', 16 January 1991, www.presidency.ucsb.edu/node/265756.

[8] See *Military and Paramilitary Activities in and Against Nicaragua (Nicaragua* v. *United States of America)* (1984) *ICJ Rep* 392.

[9] *Convention on the Prohibition of the Use, Stockpiling, Production and Transfer of Anti-Personnel Mines and on their Destruction* (1999).

[10] Concluded under *The United Nations Framework Convention on Climate Change* (1994).

'How could it be that a country as profoundly attached to the rule of law and principles of constitutionality as the United States could have so little regard for international law?'[11] Reviewing US rejection of the founding statute of the ICC, Sands charged that US policy came down to a question of: 'When can brute political power override the rule of law and legal processes?'[12] For Michael Mandel, references to the rule of law in American ICC policy constitute mere 'hypocrisy' in the sense that the United States 'claims to be acting for some principled reason, but in fact has something less noble in mind'.[13] Criticism between lawyers is no less intense within the United States itself. Then legal adviser to the Department of State William Taft IV argued that America's use of force in the 2003 Iraq War 'was and is lawful',[14] yet in the same period Taft's eventual successor Harold Koh characterised the Iraq policy as a violation of IL that set the United States against its historical vision for 'a multilateral world under law'.[15] These contested claims of fidelity to law form the puzzle animating this book: What does the 'international rule of law' mean for American legal policymakers even as they advocate competing commitments to international legal order?

Ideology in International Law

Critiques in the form levelled by Sands and Mandel establish a binary opposition between the legal ideal of the international rule of law and the political interests of states: contradictions in American IL policy ultimately reflect a contest between law and power. Sands characterises his examples of contradictory US legal behaviour 'as conflicts, between political values and legal rules, between competing conceptions as to the hierarchy of moral choices, between different interpretations of what the rules require'.[16] The underlying conception presents the international rule of law as a normative ideal independent of the ideological commitments and political identity of states in which 'politics is an external

11 Philippe Sands, *Lawless World: Making and Breaking Global Rules* (Viking, 2006), p. xv.

12 Ibid., p. 58.

13 Michael Mandel, *How America Gets Away with Murder: Illegal Wars, Collateral Damage and Crimes Against Humanity* (Pluto Press, 2004), pp. 215 & 219.

14 William H. Taft IV & Todd F. Buchwald, 'Preemption, Iraq and International Law' (2003) 97 *American Journal of International Law* 557, p. 557.

15 Harold H. Koh, 'A Better Way to Deal with Iraq', *Hartford Courant*, 20 October 2002, www.courant.com/news/connecticut/hc-xpm-2002-10-20-0210200607-story.htm.

16 Sands, *Lawless World*, p. xvi.

spectre threatening to undo its good works'.[17] In this influential view, American engagement with IL reveals the consistent logic of calculated state interests causing inconsistent compliance with legal ideals. American policymakers show tactical deference to the international rule of law where it aligns with US interests, but override its constraints wherever political expedience demands. The consequence from a legal perspective is 'continued schizophrenia about global rules and foreign policies'.[18]

This book offers a reconsideration of the relationship between law and politics, by uncovering the commitments of American legal policymakers to distinctive conceptions of the international rule of law drawn from American foreign policy ideology. Disputes between the United States and its global counterparts are thus read as a power contest fought through competing conceptions of the very meaning of the international rule of law. Foreign policy ideology crystallises political interests and cultural beliefs in interpretations of legal principle, such that contradictions are best explained as opposition at the level of competing legal ideals. These divisions extend outward between American legal policymakers and their global counterparts and inward between American legal policymakers themselves. That story is told through the history of the ICC, where divergent global interests have become more intractable than a mere political contest: they are constitutive of IL. Ideological structure thus sets predictable limits on US accommodation of international rule of law ideals advanced even by close allies, thereby offering actors who comprehend that structure a capacity to respond strategically and to plan legal affairs with greater certainty.[19]

The book's exploration of ideology is amplified by an increasingly conspicuous gap between existing accounts of American international legal practice and questions being asked by legal scholars and practitioners following the 2016 election of US President Donald Trump, including: What kind of IL is envisioned by a nationalist 'America first' foreign policy?[20] The task of getting inside the worldview of American

[17] Gerry J. Simpson, *Law, War & Crime: War Crimes, Trials and the Reinvention of International Law* (Polity, 2007), p. 11.

[18] Sands, *Lawless World*, p. 252.

[19] Being a generally agreed advantage of the rule of law: Friedrich A. Hayek, *The Road to Serfdom* (University of Chicago Press, 1944), pp. 54 & 72–5.

[20] Donald J. Trump, 'Inaugural Address: Remarks of President Donald J. Trump', 20 January 2017, www.whitehouse.gov/inaugural-address.

legal policymakers highlights a silence in legal scholarship on the influence of foreign policy ideology over the design and development of IL. Philip Bobbitt, in his sweeping account of international legal history *The Shield of Achilles*, raises the notion that legal policy in each state is inevitably

> formed by a particular view of law, and what law ought to be, and how it ought to be enforced. Every leadership of every state has such a view – self-interested, culturally idiosyncratic, haunted by historical threats, excited by historic visions – that is its own view of international law.[21]

This book makes the case that, far from being unprecedented, the views of IL now emanating from Washington have a pedigree deeply rooted in the intellectual history of American foreign policy. Contradictions in American legal practice exhibit a clear ideological structure that goes well beyond tactical modifications to law, emerging, instead, from conflicts between alternative but internally coherent conceptions of the international rule of law. Following Martti Koskenniemi, the book accepts that international legal rules and institutions cannot be apolitical, but are understood 'only by reference to substantive ideals about the political good we wish to pursue'. In short: 'Institutions do not *replace* politics, but *enact* them.'[22] IL is thus a site for contesting international power according to competing ideologies.

For the explanation of politics consciously displacing law to be true, it must be asserted that international lawyers, employed to develop and advise on American legal compliance, systematically disregard recognised legal ideals. If American lawyers were indeed engaged in subversion of an agreed conception of the rule of law, then repeated expressions of commitment to the principle must be interpreted as consciously 'bogus'.[23] The Trump administration conducted airstrikes on Syria in April of 2017 and 2018, generally considered to be contrary to IL, and yet justified its actions as legitimate in circumstances where 'civilized nations [had] joined together to ban chemical warfare',[24] such that alleged acts of

[21] Philip Bobbitt, *The Shield of Achilles: War, Peace and the Course of History* (Penguin, 2003), p. 356.

[22] Martti Koskenniemi, *The Gentle Civilizer of Nations 1870–1960* (Cambridge University Press, 2001), p. 177, original emphasis.

[23] Paris noted recurrent use of this word by critics of American ICC policy: Erna Paris, *The Sun Climbs Slow: The International Criminal Court and the Struggle for Justice* (Seven Stories Press, 2009), p. 75.

[24] Donald J. Trump, 'Statement by President Trump on Syria', 13 April 2018, www.whitehouse.gov/briefings-statements/statement-president-trump-syria/.

President Bashar al-Assad were 'prohibited by international law'.[25] Conscious legal hypocrisy is a possible interpretation of what is happening, but not one that accords with the 'direct historical evidence – of which there is a great deal – of the actual motivations' of policymakers[26] and beliefs that a government legal adviser's 'key role is to promote the rule of law based on principle, not politics'.[27] More broadly, the evidence suggests that the United States genuinely 'conceives of itself as a nation dedicated to the rule of law, both at home and abroad'.[28] This is therefore not a straightforward story of political power challenging legal principle, but, rather, one of competing understandings of power constituting multiple meanings of the rule of law.

The implication for the ICC is that political interests are imbued into the law such that even principled commitment to a court designed in accordance with the 'international rule of law' will mean different things to differently situated legal policymakers. Entreaties for the United States to abandon parochialism and accept a court design guided by the rule of law rely on an artificial account of the nature of legal ideals. This observation is not to make a normative claim, that is, that, because US policymakers' divergent legal conceptions demonstrate that IL is radically contested, legal scholars and practitioners should yield to American conceptions. Rather, the book advocates that legal scholars and practitioners should take seriously the proposition that American IL policy is often guided by sincerely held beliefs about the nature of IL and its role in global governance, but that these conceptions systematically diverge according to national context. The book therefore moves beyond the many legal accounts of US omissions and failures, instead employing the ideological perspective of US legal policymakers in order to articulate substantive principles and doctrines that do comprise American conceptions of and contributions to IL. These are principles capable of

[25] Jim Mattis, 'Statement by Secretary of Defense Jim Mattis on the U.S. Military Response to the Syrian Government's Use of Chemical Weapons', 10 April 2017, www.defense.gov/News/News-Releases/News-Release-View/Article/1146758/statement-by-secretary-of-defense-jim-mattis-on-the-us-military-response-to-the/.

[26] David M. Golove, 'Leaving Customary International Law Where It Is: Goldsmith and Posner's *The Limits of International Law*' (2005) 34 *Georgia Journal of International and Comparative Law* 333, p. 348.

[27] Harold H. Koh, cited in Michael P. Scharf & Paul R. Williams, *Shaping Foreign Policy in Times of Crisis: The Role of International Law and the State Department Legal Adviser* (Cambridge University Press, 2010), p. xiii.

[28] David Wippman, 'The International Criminal Court', in Christian Reus-Smit (ed.), *The Politics of International Law* (Cambridge University Press, 2004), p. 162.

informing global counterparts about the type of international legal system envisioned by its most powerful voice and how to respond in a systematic way. Constructing global legal order is refocused when advocates appreciate that asserting a universal conception of the rule of law is limited not merely by preponderant American power but also by the transformation of power into legal ideals.

International Law Policy

The book's object of analysis is American *international law policy*. This original concept refers to the specific form of foreign policy concerned with the conception of and strategies taken in relation to international legal rules and institutions.[29] Foreign policy more generally has been defined as actions of governments 'directed towards objectives, conditions and actors – both governmental and non-governmental – which they want to affect and which lie beyond their territorial legitimacy'[30] and 'the strategy or approach chosen by the national government to achieve its goals in its relations with external entities'.[31] IL policy falls within these definitions as a compound concept concerned with the structure of *political* ideas about *legal* obligation. The concept necessarily weakens the conceptual bright-line between law and politics, but a distinction can nevertheless be maintained. Harold Lasswell, a cofounder of the New Haven School of jurisprudence, memorably defined politics as the determination of 'who gets what, when, how'.[32] In that sense, IL is undeniably a form of politics, since its rules and institutions represent the ongoing bargains between states about how to allocate international rights and resources. What distinguishes IL policy from general foreign policy, however, is an ongoing commitment to reconciling policy with obligations established by predetermined legal ideals, including those embodied in rules and institutions.

[29] For references to 'Soviet' and 'Russia's international law policy' see respectively: Theodor Schweisfurth, 'The Acceptance by the Soviet Union of the Compulsory Jurisdiction of the ICJ for Six Human Rights Conventions' (1991) 2 *European Journal of International Law* 110, p. 117; George Ginsburgs, *From Soviet to Russian International Law: Studies in Continuity and Change* (Martinus Nijhoff Publishers, 1998), p. i.

[30] Walter Carlsnaes, 'Foreign Policy', in Walter Carlsnaes, Thomas Risse & Beth A. Simmons (eds.), *Handbook of International Relations* (SAGE Publications, 2002), p. 335.

[31] Valerie M. Hudson, 'The History and Evolution of Foreign Policy Analysis', in Steve Smith, Amelia Hadfield & Tim Dunne (eds.), *Foreign Policy: Theories, Actors, Cases* (Oxford University Press, 2008), p. 12.

[32] Harold D. Lasswell, *Politics, Who Gets What, When, How* (Peter Smith, 1950).

The lens of ideology may cause policymakers to receive the reach and depth of obligations in sharply divergent ways. But commitment to foreign policy that makes its terms with processes of the international legal system remains the necessary foundation for any conception of the international rule of law. Conversely, truly lawless foreign policy is that where policymakers lack any conception of international legal obligations and any commitment to engaging on those terms.

Interdisciplinary Research

The IL policy concept is inherently interdisciplinary, strengthening legal analysis through the empirical insights of political science. IL and International Relations (IR) are prime examples of disciplines that share an overlapping 'territory' but are separated by distinct 'tribal cultures'.[33] The shared territory is a basic concern about forms of governance in the international system, but, as historical cycles of convergence and divergence demonstrate, IL and IR remain 'distinct disciplines because their fundamental objectives differ. In international relations, the objective is to understand behaviour. In international law, the objective is to direct behaviour.'[34] Legal scholars are tasked with identifying and articulating which norms have attained the status of law, while leaving explanations of state behaviour to the realm of IR. This book informs debates within and across the two disciplines but, for reasons of both analytical substance and academic convention, remains foremost a work of legal scholarship, being concerned with questions about legal norms and obligations guiding American policymakers.

The real value of interdisciplinary research is where legal scholarship is assessed on its own terms and deficiencies are revealed in areas addressed by political science. A driving purpose of legal scholarship is to identify the rights and obligations of states in order to influence policymakers towards an international rule of law. In conventional terms, this entails increasing IL 'compliance', in the sense of 'a state of conformity or identity between an actor's behaviour and a specified rule'.[35] The

[33] Tony Becher & Paul Trowler, *Academic Tribes and Territories: Intellectual Inquiry and the Cultures of Disciplines* (Open University Press, 2001), pp. 25 & 60.

[34] Charlotte Ku, *International Law, International Relations, and Global Governance* (Routledge, 2012), p. 26.

[35] Kal Raustiala & Anne-Marie Slaughter, 'International Law, International Relations and Compliance', in Walter Carlsnaes, Thomas Risse & Beth A. Simmons (eds.), *Handbook of International Relations* (SAGE Publications, 2002), p. 539.

necessary correlative of this task is that legal scholars possess some understanding of how norms are actually received within a named state and what status they hold for legal policymakers. For a universal conception of the international rule of law to be fully realised, it would require that all states internalise its constitutive norms in identical form, as part of their own commitments, and that foreign policies promote this ideal domestically and internationally. The rapidly developing field of 'comparative international law' well demonstrates that states, to the extent to which they internalise rule of law norms, do so not in a theoretically pure form but, rather, through their particular interests, culture, historical experience and ideology.[36] For this reason, Henkin reminded that IL:

> is not a self-contained abstraction, or even a distant star for nations to steer by. It affords a framework, a pattern, a fabric for international society, grown out of relations in turn. The law that is made or left unmade reflects the political forces effective in the system. Law that is made is a force in international affairs, but its influence can be understood only in the context of other forces governing the behaviour of nations and their governments.[37]

Uncovering the meaning of the international rule of law embedded in worldviews of US policymakers transforms a theoretical question, about doctrine, into an empirical analysis of the real forces of American foreign policy ideology.

Foreign Policy Analysis

The interdisciplinary approach of this book sits within the IR subfield of Foreign Policy Analysis (FPA), which is so designated because it is committed to the unit level of analysis; eschewing questions of what behaviours exist *between* states in favour of analysing how these behaviours are determined by what happens *within* each state.[38] Crucially,

36 See Anthea Roberts, *Is International Law International?* (Oxford University Press, 2017); Anthea Roberts et al. (eds.), *Comparative International Law* (Oxford University Press, 2018).

37 Louis Henkin, *How Nations Behave: Law and Foreign Policy* (Columbia University Press, 1979), pp. 4–5.

38 See Stephen G. Walker, 'Foreign Policy Analysis and Behavioral International Relations', in Stephen G. Walker, Akan Malici & Mark Schafer (eds.), *Rethinking Foreign Policy Analysis: States, Leaders, and the Microfoundations of Behavioral International Relations* (Routledge, 2011).

FPA is located at the level of 'human decision-makers' where ideology and legal beliefs necessarily exist.[39] This yields a further distinction in FPA's focus on '*decision-making*' rather than '*out-comes*'.[40] The advantages of arbitrating FPA into legal scholarship aligns precisely with Ku's observation that law is limited to making 'broad propositions with regard to governance', but that social science is needed to:

> test and to understand law's specific effects. We realize more and more that the functionality of a governing unit may differ dramatically in different contexts. It is therefore important to create a mode of inquiry that can explain the behaviour of actors at a fine grained level, but still maintain the ability to enhance understanding of the broader system within which these actions take place.[41]

The ideological analysis of American IL policy in this book presents such an account of legal decision-making, which is the foundation for yielding finely grained explanations of the current and future trajectory of IL policy.

Whereas 'foreign policymakers' more generally are the focus of analysis in the FPA subfield, in this interdisciplinary study the focus turns to 'legal policymakers' as a unit of analysis.[42] The concern is with the real people conferred with power to make 'authoritative' decisions about the American government's interests and strategy when engaging with IL.[43] Responsibility falls primarily to the Department of State and the Office of the Legal Adviser within,[44] but extends to the Office of Legal Counsel within the Department of Justice and legal advisers in the Department of Defense, the National Security Council and beyond. Each agency has demonstrated a distinct identity, but, even within departments, the evidence is that legal advisers hold 'a diverse array of perspectives and have differing opinions as to their role in ensuring proper adherence to

[39] Valerie M. Hudson, 'Foreign Policy Analysis: Actor-Specific Theory and the Ground of International Relations' (2005) 1 *Foreign Policy Analysis* 1, p. 2.

[40] Ibid., p. 6, original emphasis.

[41] Ku, *International Law, International Relations*, p. 14.

[42] See Valerie M. Hudson & Christopher S. Vore, 'Foreign Policy Analysis Yesterday, Today, and Tomorrow' (1995) 39 *Mershon International Studies Review* 209.

[43] On policymakers as 'authoritative decision units' see Margaret G. Hermann, 'How Decision Units Shape Foreign Policy: A Theoretical Framework' (2001) 3 *International Studies Review* 47, p. 48.

[44] David Kaye, 'The Legal Bureaucracy and the Law of War' (2006) 38 *George Washington International Law Review* 589, p. 591.

international law'.[45] Legal policymakers are tasked with authoritatively deciding US approaches toward particular international institutions and rules, and are guided in that task by foreign policy ideology.

Legal policymakers include lawyers and non-lawyers alike, but the prevalence of lawyers among senior policymakers is notable – including half of all US presidents and three-quarters of US Secretaries of State.[46] Moreover, under these senior figures sit large teams of lawyers trained to advise on international legal obligations. The significance of identifying the role of lawyers in policymaking is that these individuals are expected to adopt a distinctive approach compared to other possible stakeholders. International legal policy is not infinitely malleable and must make its terms with existing structures and methods of IL. Legal policymaking 'has points of reference in the Constitution, statutes, and court precedents' and therefore 'should be more objective and reliable'.[47] International legal policymaking is thus constrained within more pronounced structural limitations than general foreign policy. International legal policymakers are distinguished by a duty to 'ensure that, even in dangerous times, regard is given to the strategic, to the system of law by which we live – not only to the tactical, the operational, the imperative of the moment'.[48] The evidence is that US State Department legal advisers have not perceived their duty as merely implementing government directions – as they would if retained by a private client. Rather, there is recognition of 'a special or higher professional responsibility to provide a disinterested assessment, because . . . advice is not normally tested in courts of law or by other outside checks'.[49] Global efforts to establish a permanent international criminal court have accordingly presented US legal policymakers with a uniquely complex set of challenges, as they seek to reconcile national foreign policy ideologies with international criminal justice under the rule of law.

45 Scharf & Williams, *Shaping Foreign Policy*, p. 1.

46 Shirley V. Scott, *International Law, US Power: The United States' Quest for Legal Security* (Cambridge University Press, 2012), p. 10.

47 Harold H. Bruff, *Bad Advice: Bush's Lawyers in the War on Terror* (University Press of Kansas, 2009), p. 1.

48 Daniel Bethlehem, 'A Transatlantic View of International Law and Lawyers: Cooperation and Conflict in Hard Times' (2009) 103 *American Society of International Law Proceedings* 455, p. 459.

49 Scharf & Williams, *Shaping Foreign Policy*, p. 206.

The International Criminal Court

International Criminal Courts through American History

US policy toward international criminal courts has a history extending to the earliest days of the republic's rise as a great power.[50] Indeed, the United States actively thwarted the creation of such a court in 1919, when the prospect was raised pursuant to a provision in the Treaty of Versailles. The proposed court had jurisdictional reach extending from the foot soldiers of Imperial Germany all the way up to Kaiser Wilhelm II, but American leaders rejected the proposal as an unacceptable incursion on state sovereignty.[51] The United States has nevertheless long championed the idea of an international court for prosecuting war crimes and other breaches of IL by individuals. The United States strongly advocated the creation of the Nuremberg and Tokyo War Crimes Tribunals, which reproduced key elements of due process upheld in American municipal courts. As military tribunals with jurisdiction over personnel only from the defeated enemies, these fell well short of the protections offered by regular civilian courts. Nevertheless, they were created in the face of considerable scepticism by British allies, who preferred more summary treatment of defendants, and contrary to Soviet enthusiasm for mere show trials.[52] More particularly, US advocacy for the tribunals flowed from a specific strategy for augmenting its rising political power by fostering an international rule of law that positioned the United States as the exemplar of that ideal.

It was in these immediate post-WWII years that the UN General Assembly (UNGA) commissioned and acted on a report by the International Law Commission (ILC) that recommended creating a permanent court.[53] A founding statute was drafted along with a code of offences, but the project ultimately stalled with the onset of the Cold War. Despite the long history of American and ILC interest in an international criminal court, it was not until 1989, in the waning years of the Cold War, that a resolution was passed in the UNGA calling once again

[50] For a history going back millennia see M. Cherif Bassiouni, *The Legislative History of the International Criminal Court: Introduction, Analysis, and Integrated Text of the Statute, Elements of Crimes and Rules of Procedure and Evidence* (Transnational Publishers, 2005), pp. 3–40.

[51] Eric K. Leonard, *The Onset of Global Governance: International Relations Theory and the International Criminal Court* (Ashgate, 2005), p. 22.

[52] Ibid., p. 24.

[53] International Law Commission, *Report of the International Law Commission on the Work of Its Forty-Second Session (1 May–20 July 1990)*, UN Doc A/45/10, (1990), p. 20.

on the ILC to consider and report on the creation of a court – mindful of the Charter obligation of 'encouraging the progressive development of international law and its codification'.[54] A seeming precedent was set by US leadership creating the International Criminal Tribunal for the Former Yugoslavia (ICTY) in 1993, as the first such tribunal addressing individual criminal responsibility since Nuremberg, and later the International Criminal Tribunal for Rwanda (ICTR).[55] The ICC project was realised within the decade, at the 1998 *United Nations Conference of Plenipotentiaries on the Establishment of an International Criminal Court* (Rome Conference), where 160 states convened along with 33 international governmental coalitions and more than 200 non-governmental organisations (NGOs) for negotiations that lasted five weeks through June to July. The *Rome Statute of the International Criminal Court* (Rome Statute) established a court with jurisdiction that ultimately covered four crimes: genocide, crimes against humanity, war crimes, and the crime of aggression. On 17 July 1998, 120 states voted to adopt the Rome Statute, 21 states abstained and 7 voted against – including the United States.

The 'Canary in the Coalmine'

The history of US ICC policy stands out as perhaps the most intriguing demonstration of competing conceptions of the international rule of law as they influence global legal order. The court has been described as 'the most important institutional innovation since the founding of the United Nations'[56] and as 'the central player in a contemporary battle over the place of justice in international politics'.[57] For rule of law advocates, it is seen to herald 'a new world order based on the rule of international law'[58] and, 'more so than almost any other international organisation, [it]

[54] GA Res 44/39, *Individual Criminal Responsibility of Individuals and Entities Engaged in Illicit Trafficking in Narcotic Drugs across National Frontiers and Other Transnational Criminal Activities: Establishment of an International Criminal Court with Jurisdiction over Such Crimes*, 72nd Sess. UN GAOR, Supp. 47, UN Doc A/44/39, (1989).

[55] ICTY, UN Doc S/Res/827 (1993); ICTR, UN Doc S/Res/955 (1994).

[56] Robert C. Johansen (1997), cited in William Schabas, *An Introduction to the International Criminal Court* (Cambridge University Press, 2011), p. x.

[57] David Kaye & Kal Raustiala, 'The Council and the Court: Law and Politics in the Rise of the International Criminal Court' (2016) 94 *Texas Law Review* 713, p. 714.

[58] Antonio Cassese, 'On the Current Trends towards Criminal Prosecution and Punishment of Breaches of International Humanitarian Law' (1998) 9 *European Journal of International Law* 2, p. 8.

stands for the primacy of the rule of law over injustice'.[59] Yet, the ICC now enters a critical period as a series of major signatories seek to withdraw from the project, or have already done so, including Russia, the Philippines and a cluster of African Union members. More specifically, the United States responded to a protracted ICC prosecutorial request relating to the armed conflict in Afghanistan since 2003 ("Afghanistan Situation"), which then seemed likely to result in the investigation of US military and official personnel, by reaffirming its 2002 act of 'unsigning' the Rome Statute.[60] In the weeks immediately following President Trump's inauguration, former State Department Legal Adviser John Bellinger noted that the ICC remained a topic both 'perennially controversial and divisive' yet sharply defined for the purposes of scholarly analysis. Any policy change toward the ICC therefore promised to serve as a 'canary in the mine' for the Trump administration's IL policy generally.[61]

The ICC emerges as the most prominent focal point for claims of contradiction and hypocrisy in post-Cold War American IL policy, with inconsistent approaches creating 'perhaps the classic example of an interpretive challenge to observers of international law'.[62] Schabas depicts US policy as a 'muddle of arguments',[63] while van der Vyver sees it as 'confusing' and beset by 'schizophrenia'.[64] Cohen observes incomprehension in other states at the United States refusing to participate in the ICC 'despite its seeming reification of American

[59] Heiko Maas, 'Speech by Foreign Minister Heiko Maas at the Nuremberg Forum 2018 Marking the 20th Anniversary of the Rome Statute', 19 October 2018, www.auswaertiges-amt.de/en/newsroom/news/maas-nuremberg-rome-statute/2151548.

[60] International Criminal Court, *Situation in Afghanistan: Summary of the Prosecutor's Request for Authorisation of an Investigation Pursuant to Article 15* (The Office of the Prosecutor, 20 November 2017). See John R. Bolton, 'Protecting American Constitutionalism and Sovereignty from International Threats', The Federalist Society, Washington, DC, 10 September 2018, www.lawfareblog.com/national-security-adviser-john-bolton-remarks-federalist-society. The request to investigate was ultimately rejected by the ICC Pre-Trial Chamber, although subject to further appeal.

[61] John Bellinger & Rosa Brooks, 'Will International Law Matter to the Trump Administration? International Law in the Trump Era: Expectations, Hopes, and Fears', Georgetown University Law Center, Washington, DC, 23 January 2017, www.youtube.com/watch?v=NHo9GeBr8pI, [1:04:06].

[62] Scott, *International Law, US Power*, p. 1.

[63] Schabas, *An Introduction to the ICC*, p. 25.

[64] Johan D. van der Vyver, 'American Exceptionalism: Human Rights, International Criminal Justice, and National Self-Righteousness' (2001) 50 *Emory Law Journal* 775, p. 776.

values'.[65] Du Plessis describes US policy as 'ironic' where 'an important element of the United States' conception of its own national interest has been the development and maintenance of an international rule of law',[66] while Paulus notes that a record of leading establishment of the World Trade Organization dispute settlement system yet opposing the ICC reveals 'contradictory attitudes towards international adjudication'.[67] The frustration is evident in Cherif Bassiouni's statement, after negotiations establishing the court, that 'the interests of the United States in having an ICC far outweigh the marginal and far-fetched concerns that have been articulated by political opponents'.[68] Finally, Ambassador David Scheffer, as one of the most forceful advocates among US legal policymakers, has noted the contradiction of the United States creating and associating itself with the principles of the post-WWII tribunals, yet appearing 'awkwardly conflicted' by the more robust regime of the ICC. In consequence, the project 'has proven to be an enigma for Americans from its beginning to the present day'.[69]

What is not documented adequately in extensive writings on the issue is the extent to which contradictions stem from contestation over the very concept of the international rule of law – between key parties and the United States, and among American legal policymakers themselves. Opponents of US policy specifically characterise a failure to 'uphold the rule of international law'[70] and 'a profound rejection of what makes America great: our deep and abiding commitment to the rule of law'.[71] British Queens Counsel Cherie Blair and US legal policymakers Chayes and Slaughter have all described US policy as 'a high-

[65] Harlan G. Cohen, 'The American Challenge to International Law: A Tentative Framework for Debate' (2003) 28 *Yale Journal of International Law* 551, p. 572.

[66] Max du Plessis, 'Seeking an International International Criminal Court: Some Reflections on the United States Opposition to the ICC' (2002) 15 *South African Journal of Criminal Justice* 301, p. 305.

[67] Andreas L. Paulus, 'From Neglect to Defiance? The United States and International Adjudication' (2004) 15 *European Journal of International Law* 783, pp. 783 & 785.

[68] M. Cherif Bassiouni et al., 'War Crimes Tribunals: The Record and the Prospects: Conference Convocation' (1998) 13 *American University International Law Review* 1383, p. 1403.

[69] David J. Scheffer, *All the Missing Souls: A Personal History of the War Crimes Tribunals* (Princeton University Press, 2012), p. 164.

[70] van der Vyver, 'American Exceptionalism', p. 832.

[71] Leila Nadya Sadat, 'Summer in Rome, Spring in the Hague, Winter in Washington: US Policy towards the International Criminal Court' (2003) 21 *Wisconsin International Law Journal* 557, p. 596.

profile rejection of a major initiative for the rule of law in international affairs'.[72] Yet the historical record is equally clear that American attitudes to the ICC have always exhibited a continuity consistent with ideological beliefs about the nature of IL, which are systematically defended as good faith commitment to the 'international rule of law'. This book presents the case that if international legal scholarship continues to quarantine IL from the insights of foreign policy ideology, it will ultimately weaken the foundations not only of the ICC but also of IL itself.

Book Structure

Part I of the book explores the role of foreign policy ideology in meeting the interpretive challenge of contradictory American IL policy. Chapter 1 assesses the extent to which IL scholars and analysts provide compelling explanations for distinctive American IL policy. An increasing number of analyses have drawn on the pedigree of a long-established literature on 'American exceptionalism'. This chapter unpacks these accounts by focusing on three common explanations for idiosyncratic policy: the expected rational behaviour of a state with uniquely preponderant global power; distinctive American jurisprudence; and unique political culture forged in the nation's historical experiences. Reviewing this literature demonstrates the merit in each approach, but also that a fresh account is needed that maps the relationship between distinct yet clearly correlated explanations.

Chapter 2 draws insights from FPA to explain the relationships among power, beliefs and interests as causes of distinctive American IL policy. The focus is on 'foreign policy ideology' as the ideational concept best capturing the transformation of power into ideas capable of shaping global interests. A generation of empirical survey research, combined with a rich history of diplomatic thought, has shown American foreign policy ideology to be structured along two dimensions that form an influential four-part typology. A *governance* dimension measures whether American power is exercised primarily through international institutions dominated by elites, or, conversely, whether US foreign policy interests are advanced through domestic law and institutions

[72] Ewen MacAskill, 'Cherie Booth Hits Out at US Over International Court', *The Guardian*, 13 June 2002, www.theguardian.com/uk/2002/jun/13/cherieblair.politics; Abram Chayes & Anne-Marie Slaughter, 'The ICC and the Future of the Global Legal System', in Sarah B. Sewell & Carl Kaysen (eds.), *The United States and the International Criminal Court: National Security and International Law* (Rowman & Littlefield Publishers, 2000), p. 238.

under popular control. A second *values* dimension measures whether US policy is constructed to promote universal liberal values through law, or whether it is used primarily to promote illiberal national security or non-universal cultural and identity values. Accordingly, IL policy can be located between *internationalist–nationalist* positions on the governance dimension and between *liberal–illiberal* positions on the cross-cutting values dimension, which together form four ideal policy types: *liberal internationalism, Illiberal internationalism, liberal nationalism* and *illiberal nationalism*.

Chapter 3 revisits explanations for contradictory US policy via the ideological typology to develop a model of competing conceptions of the international rule of law. Opposition to US legal policy has converged on forms of 'legalism', as a set of beliefs that law consists of non-instrumental rules and that the international legal system should be developed by analogy with municipal law. The four ideal types, as well as legalism, are applied to reinterpret the classic Anglo-American institutional conception of the rule of law comprising three elements that, when translated to the global level, are concerned with: how to develop non-arbitrary global governance; how to define equality under IL; and how to determine the integrity of international judicial power. Each element of the rule of law has been interpreted in a distinctive form by the competing ideologies, thus establishing a structured contest over principles for designing and developing global legal institutions. The meaning of 'coherence' becomes that a legal policymaker's interpretation of any one of the three elements is a reliable indicator of positions taken on remaining elements.

Part II of the book applies this model to reconsider the history of American ICC policy in its full ideological context. Each of the post-Cold War presidencies, up to that of President Obama, is analysed in terms of ideology's impact on the three identified rule of law elements. Chapter 4 considers the Clinton administration (1992–2000), where US policy was characterised as contradictory for traversing from prominently advocating the project in the early years to conspicuously voting against the final treaty establishing the court, then signing it, but warning against Senate ratification. The dominant conception of the international rule of law is shown to be liberal internationalism, combined with competing illiberal internationalist beliefs. Despite similar policy outcomes, this represented a shift from the primarily illiberal internationalist policy of the George H. W. Bush (Bush 41) administration. The design put foward by global advocates remained structured by legalist principles not recognised by US policymakers, such that US policy appeared contradictory for following internally coherent ideological conceptions of IL.

Chapter 5 considers the first term of the George W. Bush (Bush 43) administration (2000–4) when the United States 'unsigned' the founding ICC statute and used a combination of domestic legislation and bilateral agreements to obstruct its further development. This period demonstrates a clear rejection of both legalist and liberal internationalist conceptions of the court. The dominant rule of law conception was instead that of illiberal nationalism combined with elements of illiberal internationalism, leading to widespread global criticism that US policy was contrary to the international rule of law. US policymakers nevertheless continued to defend US compliance with legal obligations and international criminal justice, while opposing a court advancing the principles recognised by legalist advocates.

Chapter 6 turns to the second term of the Bush 43 administration (2004–8) which was characterised by more pragmatic engagement and even tacit endorsement of the court, yet also by continued insistence on legal privileges through the United Nations Security Council (UNSC). Here, the United States is shown to express illiberal internationalist conceptions that appeared more complementary with legalism, but remained distinct from it. Significantly, the negation of exceptionalist ideological beliefs by the Abu Ghraib prisoner abuse scandal led to acceptance of limited equal rights under the UNSC consistent with legalism. This episode corroborates the claim for ideology's controlling role in interpreting legal principle, but also the power of contesting American IL policy at the level of ideological beliefs.

Chapter 7 concludes analysis of the ICC with the Obama administration (2008–16), in which there was a conspicuous 'reset' of ICC policy to positive engagement. The United States attended annual meetings for the first time and contributed substantively to negotiations establishing the crime of aggression. There was no formal 'resigning' of the ICC treaty, however, the aggression definition agreed by other states was rejected and the United States continued to deny any prospect of becoming a member of the court. Here, US policy is shown to reflect an amalgam of ideologies, but predominantly that of liberalism in both its internationalist and nationalist forms. The consequence was that US re-engagement was always distinct from the legalist position, and thus it highlighted incompatible legal ideals even as all parties pledged fidelity to the international rule of law.

The Conclusion considers the implications of these findings in the Trump era and beyond, which so far exhibits clear continuity with the ideological structure of its predecessors. The case of the ICC provides compelling evidence that foreign policy ideology structures distinct conceptions of the international rule of law among American legal policymakers and that these received principles set hard limits to reaching a universal understanding of the proper design and development of international legal order. Defining the international rule of law remains a dialectical process in which ideological visions of global order contest power through the shared space of the international legal system. Continued commitment to this contest is evidence nevertheless of the consequence of IL as a framework for sustaining discourse about global power and transcendent values.

PART I

Ideology in American International Law Policy

1

America's 'Exceptional' International Law Policy

In 2013 'American Exceptionalism' became a focal point in US–Russian wrangling over the alleged use of chemical weapons in the Syrian Civil War. President Barack Obama advocated a military intervention over the top of strict legal prohibitions against the use of force outside UNSC authorisation. To make the case, he turned to American 'ideals and principles' as the more fundamental source of legitimacy. For the end of 'enforcing' international agreements, Obama argued: 'I believe we should act. That's what makes America different. That's what makes us exceptional.'[1] These assertions and the attempt to 'bypass the United Nations' were rejected by Russian President Vladimir Putin in *The New York Times*:

> It is extremely dangerous to encourage people to see themselves as exceptional, whatever the motivation. There are big countries and small countries, rich and poor, those with long democratic traditions and those still finding their way to democracy. Their policies differ, too. We are all different, but when we ask for the Lord's blessings, we must not forget that God created us equal.[2]

The high-level conversation on exceptionalism concluded that month when Obama responded in the UNGA: 'Some may disagree, but I believe America is exceptional – in part because we have shown a willingness through the sacrifice of blood and treasure to stand up not only for our own narrow self-interests, but for the interests of all.'[3]

[1] Barack H. Obama, 'Remarks by the President in Address to the Nation on Syria', 10 September 2013, www.whitehouse.gov/the-press-office/2013/09/10/remarks-president-address-nation-syria.

[2] Vladimir Putin, 'A Plea for Caution from Russia: What Putin Has to Say to Americans about Syria', *The New York Times*, 11 September 2013, www.nytimes.com/2013/09/12/opinion/putin-plea-for-caution-from-russia-on-syria.html.

[3] Barack H. Obama, 'Remarks by President Obama in Address to the United Nations General Assembly', 24 September 2013, www.whitehouse.gov/the-press-office/2013/09/24/remarks-president-obama-address-united-nations-general-assembly.

Part I of this book makes the case for bringing 'foreign policy ideology' into legal scholarship, as the missing puzzle piece to explain the meaning and causes of 'exceptional' American international law (IL) policy. As a term of art in political science, American exceptionalism refers to the idea that history and values set the country qualitatively apart from other nations, which is the meaning followed in this book as the most historically grounded and analytically useful. In contrast, its increasing use in legal scholarship has more often narrowed the concept to pejorative shorthand for the American practice of seeking 'exceptions' to global legal rules, and therefore as uniformly detracting from the international rule of law. This meaning has not therefore drawn a strong distinction between policymakers' beliefs that the United States is normatively 'exceptional' and observations that the United States is an outlier in IL policy outcomes, instead classifying both under the exceptionalism umbrella. Isolating the causal effect of exceptionalist beliefs is necessary, however, when seeking to understand the rationale and thereby the apparent hypocrisy behind divergent US legal policy in specific cases. By tracing the influence of exceptionalist beliefs, while distinguishing from the influence of other variables, the 'exceptionalism' label can be saved from reduction to a tautological restatement of the primary observation that US policy is different.

This chapter disaggregates and unpacks three prevalent explanations for policy distinctiveness embedded in exceptionalist legal accounts. The first is relative political power and the consequences of its unequal distribution in the international system. The second is distinctive American jurisprudence, which redefines IL less as formalised rules and more as a policy process embedded in broader political and social contexts. The final explanation is cultural, where the contours of American IL policy are structured by a unique political culture forged across the nation's history. This comes closest to the insights of exceptionalist literature by identifying the importance of belief in American difference as a cause of divergent legal policies. Read together, these three explanations exhibit striking correlation, indicating the need for a fresh account that maps deep-seated connections between the ideas and interests shaping IL policy.

The Turn towards 'American Exceptionalism'

References to 'American exceptionalism' have become ubiquitous in discussions of US foreign policy, with its use increasing exponentially over time.[4] In this process, the term has sometimes swollen into a catch-all explanation for every idiosyncrasy in American politics, in accordance with the ordinary dictionary definition of 'the condition of being different from the norm'.[5] More usefully defined, American exceptionalism is 'the notion that the United States was born in, and continues to embody, qualitative differences from other nations. Understanding other nations will not help in understanding it; understanding it will only mislead in understanding them.'[6] Seymour Lipset's leading work claimed that, properly used, the concept does not mean that 'America is better than other countries or has a superior culture', only that it is 'qualitatively different, that it is an outlier'.[7] Yet the idea has always been accompanied by a notion that the distinctive values of American political culture do offer a superior alternative to those of global counterparts.

The term resonates by virtue of the long history of exceptionalist analysis, often traced back to the nineteenth-century writings of Alexis de Tocqueville. A defining formulation was in John Winthrop's 1630 invocation that the American people 'shall be as a city upon a hill, the eyes of all people are upon us'.[8] The core of this strand of exceptionalism was a conviction that the founding of the American polity marked a break from the values and practices of the Old World. Politics in the European continent continued to be marked by relentless wars and the dominance of mercenary political interests over moral purpose. For Anatol Lieven, 'the most important root' of exceptionalist ideas was thus geographic and cultural separation from the destructive experiences of European war and

[4] McCoy found the term in national publications only 457 times for the twenty years up to 2000; 2,558 times during the next ten years; and approximately 4,172 times when he published these findings: Terrence McCoy, 'How Joseph Stalin Invented "American Exceptionalism"', *The Atlantic*, 15 March 2012, www.theatlantic.com/politics/archive/2012/03/how-joseph-stalin-invented-american-exceptionalism/254534/.

[5] Merriam-Webster, *Merriam-Webster Online Dictionary and Thesaurus*, www.merriam-webster.com/dictionary/exceptionalism. Notably, since this chapter was first drafted, the Merriam-Webster definition has been expanded to include a second meaning: '*also*: a theory expounding the exceptionalism especially of a nation or region'.

[6] Byron E. Shafer, 'American Exceptionalism' (1999) 2 *Annual Review of Political Science* 445, p. 446.

[7] Seymour M. Lipset, *American Exceptionalism: A Double-Edged Sword* (W. W. Norton & Co., 1996), p. 18. Lipset's well-known 'American creed' sets out the exceptional elements of political culture as 'liberty, egalitarianism, individualism, populism, and laissez-faire': p. 19.

[8] Cited in John F. Kennedy, '"City upon a Hill" Speech', 9 January 1961, www.jfklibrary.org/learn/about-jfk/historic-speeches/the-city-upon-a-hill-speech.

revolution.[9] The colonists of New England embraced a confluence of religious puritan values and secular enlightenment ideals of human progress, forging a worldview that America had a uniquely reforming role in its global relations and thereby an exceptional place in history. In his 1776 rallying cry for the American Revolution, Thomas Paine expressed the conviction that 'we have it in our power to begin the world over again'.[10]

Because this book focuses on the influence of foreign policy ideology over policymaking, the truth or otherwise of appeals to normative superiority is not relevant.[11] What matters is that there has been 'throughout American history a strong belief that the United States is an exceptional nation, not only unique but also superior among nations'.[12] As long as policymakers genuinely hold such beliefs, and employ them in formulating and garnering support for policy, then 'exceptionalism is a genuine and confirmedly empirical phenomenon'.[13] Former Secretary of State Madeleine Albright explicitly affirmed her belief in American exceptionalism and used it to underpin her frequent portrayal of the United States as 'the indispensable nation'.[14] Irrespective of the veracity of the concept, she remained equally aware of the term's political power. Acknowledging global allies' negative associations with the idea of 'American exceptionalism', she defended her invocation for its power 'to stir a sense of pride and responsibility among Americans, so that we would be less reluctant to take on problems'.[15] In other words, whatever the empirical basis for the claim, it is a concept with real political influence in directing political actions. Starkly divergent formulations have been propounded under the exceptionalist rubric, but the core belief that America is exceptional persists and shapes discourse at the highest levels.

[9] Anatol Lieven, *America Right or Wrong: An Anatomy of American Nationalism* (Oxford University Press, 2005), p. 30.

[10] Cited in Ronald W. Reagan, 'Ronald Reagan's Announcement for Presidential Candidacy', 13 November 1979, www.reaganlibrary.gov/11-13-79.

[11] For empirical research sceptical of the truth of exceptionalist claims see Joseph Lepgold & Timothy McKeown, 'Is American Foreign Policy Exceptional? An Empirical Analysis' (1995) 110 *Political Science Quarterly* 369.

[12] Trevor B. McCrisken, *American Exceptionalism and the Legacy of Vietnam: US Foreign Policy since 1974* (Palgrave Macmillan, 2003), p. 4.

[13] Shafer, 'American Exceptionalism', p. 446.

[14] Albright attributes the phrase to President Clinton from the period when she served as UN Ambassador: Madeleine K. Albright, *Madam Secretary: A Memoir* (Macmillan, 2003), p. 506.

[15] Ibid., p. 506.

Exceptionalist Analysis in Legal Scholarship

Legal scholarship has seized upon the concept with particular vigour, with critical assessments of American IL policy as beset by 'exceptionalism' becoming an article of faith. These accounts harness the pedigree and familiarity of the ideas in politics to shed light on the American practice of seeking 'exceptions' in the legal sphere – a case of 'international law for others and not for itself'.[16] However, treatments vary significantly in whether they find it necessary to analytically distinguish between the exceptionalist beliefs influencing decision-making processes and the outcomes said to comprise exceptions. An illustrative definition from a scholar and practitioner is in the memoirs of former US Ambassador-at-Large for War Crimes David Scheffer, which in part explore his difficulties in securing US support for establishment of the ICC. For Scheffer, 'the siren of exceptionalism enveloped the entire enterprise of the International Criminal Court on my watch'. His definition demonstrates how this single label encompasses multiple competing influences on policy:

> By 'exceptionalism' in the realm of international law, I mean that the United States has a tradition of leading other nations in global treaty-making endeavors to create a more law-abiding international community, only to seek exceptions to the new rules for the United States because of its constitutional heritage of defending individual rights, its military responsibilities worldwide requiring freedom to act in times of war, its superior economy demanding free trade one day and labor protection and environmental concessions the next, or just stark nativist insularity. We sometimes want the rest of the world to 'right itself' but to leave the United States alone because of its 'exceptional' character.[17]

It is clear that divergent IL policy shaped by 'constitutional heritage' fits squarely within a conventional exceptionalist explanation. On the other hand, legal exceptions designed to protect a 'superior economy' are not necessarily a product of beliefs in 'American exceptionalism' but, rather, the outcome of preponderant US power. Since this book is concerned with decision-making processes, it remains essential to isolate the effect of different exceptionalist beliefs from other causes of unique policy. Doing so has the potential to shed light on a spectrum of US IL policies that are more complex than binary support for or opposition to the international rule of law.

16 James Crawford, 'International Law and the Rule of Law' (2003) 24 *Adelaide Law Review* 3, p. 8.

17 David J. Scheffer, *All the Missing Souls: A Personal History of the War Crimes Tribunals* (Princeton University Press, 2012), p. 165.

John Murphy's exceptionalist account sets out to address the apparent contradiction that, despite being the key proponent of the major twentieth-century international institutions, the United States has itself found it 'increasingly difficult to adhere to the rule of law in international affairs'.[18] He argues that US legal policy is shaped by attitudes of 'triumphalism, exceptionalism, and provincialism' that 'stand in the way of US support of the rule of law in international affairs'. This troika of concepts encompasses but is not limited to exceptionalist thinking, with 'exceptionalism' itself defined as the idea that 'the United States bears special burdens and is entitled to special privileges because of its status as the sole surviving superpower'.[19] Slaughter observes, however, that, despite the clear relevance of these related attitudes, Murphy's formulation has 'shed no light on the microfoundations of U.S. decisions to take specific positions in individual cases'.[20]

Hilary Charlesworth focuses more directly on beliefs, by defining exceptionalism to mean that 'while other states should comply with international legal norms, it is not appropriate to subject the United States to the same regime'. Charlesworth lists relevant beliefs to include that 'the United States is already an exemplary international citizen and its domestic legal system can be relied on to provide appropriate accountability and/or the expectation that international law will inevitably be used in a politicised way to discriminate against the United States'. For Charlesworth, such exceptionalism, whatever its constitutive beliefs, is antithetical to the rule of law.[21] Similarly, Natsu Saito defines exceptionalism in relation to 'uniquely American' IL policy as the belief that 'America is special, or exceptional, because it claims certain incontestable values; the possibility that its hegemony was consolidated and continues to be exercised at the expense of those values can be ignored in the name of a greater good.'[22] Only by overcoming the 'tremendous power of the

[18] John F. Murphy, *The United States and the Rule of Law in International Affairs* (Cambridge University Press, 2004), pp. 4 & 349.

[19] Ibid., p. 7. More detailed definitions are found in: John F. Murphy, 'The Quivering Gulliver: US Views on a Permanent International Criminal Court' (2000) 34 *International Lawyer* 45, p. 46.

[20] Anne-Marie Slaughter, 'Book Reviews: The United States and the Rule of Law in International Affairs' (2005) 99 *American Journal of International Law* 2, p. 516.

[21] Hilary Charlesworth, *No Country Is an Island: Australia and International Law* (University of New South Wales Press, 2006), p. 147.

[22] Natsu T. Saito, *Meeting the Enemy: American Exceptionalism and International Law* (New York University Press, 2010), p. 4.

narrative of American exceptionalism' can the United States contribute to strengthening the rule of law.[23]

More systematic analyses are sought in Michael Ignatieff's edited volume *American Exceptionalism and Human Rights*[24] and Harold Koh's article 'On American Exceptionalism',[25] each of which provides a definition and typology that have shaped broader legal scholarship. For Ignatieff, American exceptionalism is the uniquely contradictory 'combination of leadership and resistance' to IL that has produced the 'paradox of being simultaneously a leader and an outlier'.[26] Ignatieff identifies three types of policy outcome that he labels exceptionalism: *exemptionalism*, *double standards* and *legal isolationism*.[27] These are said to constitute an exceptional and harmful IL policy in that no other democracy engages in these practices to the same extent as the United States, or does so while simultaneously claiming to lead the global human rights movement.[28] In all three forms, Ignatieff groups together causal beliefs and policy outcomes under the single 'exceptionalism' banner.

Koh finds Ignatieff's typology 'both under- and over inclusive' in that it conflates some forms of exceptionalism and omits others.[29] Koh's own piece acknowledges the indeterminacy of exceptionalist ideas by calling on the United States to 'preserve its capacity for positive exceptionalism by avoiding the most negative features of American exceptionalism'.[30] Here, Koh adopts a four-part typology, listed 'in order of ascending opprobrium': *distinctive rights culture*, *different labels*, *the 'flying buttress' mentality*, and *double standards*.[31] The advantage of this formulation is in its distinguishing between unique IL practices according to whether underlying beliefs strengthen or weaken the rule of law. Invoking Gothic architectural imagery, the 'flying buttress' mentality, for instance, describes the idea that the United States frequently provides support for

23 Ibid., p. 229.

24 Michael Ignatieff, 'Introduction: American Exceptionalism and Human Rights', in Michael Ignatieff (ed.), *American Exceptionalism and Human Rights* (Princeton University Press, 2005).

25 Harold H. Koh, 'On American Exceptionalism' (2003) 55 *Stanford Law Review* 1479.

26 Ignatieff, 'Introduction', p. 1. Ignatieff writes about US human rights legal policy, but makes clear that his conclusions are relevant to US IL policy generally: p. 2.

27 Ibid., pp. 3–11. Ignatieff cross-references Koh's piece for the concept and meaning of 'double standards': p. 7.

28 Ibid., p. 4.

29 Koh, 'On American Exceptionalism', p. 1483.

30 Ibid., p. 1503.

31 Ibid., p. 1483.

treaty regimes from outside the institution, while refusing to stand as a pillar within.[32] For Koh, this represents a threat to America's own interests far more than to the system of IL generally. It is only in the final form of policy that Koh identifies a challenge to IL, where the United States 'uses its exceptional power and wealth to promote a *double standard*'.[33]

The key question for present purposes remains: What specific factors cause America to exhibit contradictory IL policy behaviours, including the disjunct between expressions of commitment to the rule of law and policy outcomes? In particular, are these outcomes explained by exceptionalist beliefs properly so-called, thereby justifying adoption of the terminology? As with other legal accounts, the typologies of Ignatieff and Koh mask a range of competing and perhaps interrelated causes of distinctive behaviour such that the exceptionalism label sometimes does more to obscure than to clarify. Ignatieff identifies four possible explanations for distinctive US policy:

> a realist one, based in America's exceptional power; a cultural one, related to an American sense of Providential destiny; an institutional one, based in America's specific institutional organization; and finally a political one, related to the supposedly distinctive conservatism and individualism of American political culture.[34]

Of these, only the 'cultural' explanation directly encapsulates the influence of exceptionalism as the term is used here. The distinct elements are not mutually exclusive, however, such that exceptionalist beliefs indirectly shape each of the alternative explanations for policy uniqueness. Ignatieff recognises these linkages to the degree that American IL policy goes further than realism strictly requires in 'defending a mission, an identity, and a distinctive destiny as a free people'.[35] Cultural attachment to messianism is thereby a key explanation for the 'power dynamics and the distinctive ideology' underpinning different forms of 'exceptional' IL policy.[36]

[32] The analogy is Henkin's: 'In the cathedral of human rights the United States is more like a flying buttress than a pillar – choosing to stand outside the international structure supporting the international human rights system, but without being willing to subject its own conduct to the scrutiny of that system.' Louis Henkin, *How Nations Behave: Law and Foreign Policy* (Columbia University Press, 1979), p. 183.

[33] Koh, 'On American Exceptionalism', pp. 1486–7, original emphasis.

[34] Ignatieff, 'Introduction', p. 11.

[35] Ibid., pp. 13–14.

[36] Ibid., p. 16.

Institutional explanations likewise reveal much about unique IL outcomes, but ultimately depend on exceptionalist and ideological factors to explain policy contradictions. The power to develop and execute IL policy resides primarily with the US executive, but it is institutionally divided between the branches of federal government and subject to the prerogatives of the various states. The '*invitation to struggle* for the privilege of directing American foreign policy'[37] means that IL policy is determined not merely by a competitive market of ideas across government, but through amplification or suppression of certain ideas via 'decentralized and fragmented political institutions'.[38] Citing institutional factors, however, merely begs the question: *What* divergent beliefs distinguish policymakers competing for influence across divided government? Within Ignatieff's volume, Andrew Moravcsik identifies the roots of US failure to ratify key human rights treaties in 'senatorial suspicion of liberal multilateralism' among a minority of senators 'disproportionately representative of the conservative southern and rural Midwestern or western states'.[39] Although institutional veto points such as 'supermajoritarian treaty ratification rules in the Senate' shape legal policy outcomes,[40] this book addresses the more fundamental content of ideology itself. In this sense, exceptionalist beliefs of legal policymakers remain prior to institutional explanations for unique policy preferences.

To his typology, Koh adds a fifth positive element of *exceptional global leadership*, which comes closer to capturing the variable influence of exceptionalist ideas on American IL policy.[41] He concludes by posing a choice between an American exceptionalism that is 'power-based' and disregards IL and 'good exceptionalism'[42] that is 'norm-based', showing deference to 'universal values of democracy, human rights, and the rule of law'.[43] Understanding the variable influence of exceptionalism confirms that any useful typology must be built not upon policy outcomes but, rather, on the content of competing exceptionalist beliefs guiding policymakers' decisions and the ways these interact with power. Returning to the questions posed by this book, these illustrative legal

[37] Edward S. Corwin, *The President: Office and Powers 1787–1957* (New York University Press, 1957), p. 171, emphasis added.
[38] Andrew Moravcsik, 'The Paradox of US Human Rights Policy', in Michael Ignatieff (ed.), *American Exceptionalism and Human Rights* (Princeton University Press, 2005), p. 150.
[39] Ibid., p. 187.
[40] Ibid., p. 150.
[41] Koh, 'On American Exceptionalism', p. 1487.
[42] Ibid., p. 1501.
[43] Ibid., pp. 1526–7.

accounts emphasise the need to identify more sharply underlying exceptionalist beliefs and their interaction with other causes of distinctive IL policy.

Sources of Unique American International Law Policy

Three leading explanations for the outlier status of American IL policy will be subjected to closer interrogation in order to refine exceptionalist legal treatments. The first is that hegemonic US power creates capabilities and incentives to reshape or evade IL. This is not a product of exceptionalist beliefs but, rather, a manifestation of general principles of great power behaviour. The second is that distinct institutionalised jurisprudence influences the American approach to IL. Specifically, ingrained in the academy and practitioners are conceptualisations of IL as a purposive process of policymaking, rather than formalised rules. Finally are cultural explanations that directly identify the role of exceptionalist ideas in shaping American engagement with IL. The possible effect of these ideas is to alter American commitment to legal rules in ways directly influenced by national political culture. In analysing these common explanations, the focus is on both isolating the independent influence of each variable and mapping how they relate to one another as complementary causes of distinctive legal policy.

Power-Based Explanations: Hegemonic International Law

In the year prior to the 2003 Iraq War, Robert Kagan surveyed divided transatlantic approaches to IL to conclude that 'Americans are from Mars and Europeans are from Venus'.[44] Kagan's thesis proved especially significant during the Bush 43 administration, where it was widely circulated and read in 2002. Then senior administration lawyer Jack Goldsmith wrote that the 'essay gave structure to intuitions that top administration officials already possessed'.[45] For Kagan, Europeans evinced a preference for 'a world where strength doesn't matter, where

44 Robert Kagan, 'Power and Weakness' (2002) June–July *Policy Review* 3, p. 3. For a fuller treatment see also Robert Kagan, *Of Paradise and Power* (Vintage Books, 2004).

45 Jack Goldsmith, *The Terror Presidency: Law and Judgment Inside the Bush Administration* (W. W. Norton & Co., 2007), pp. 126–7. Kagan is also cited approvingly by the former Deputy Assistant U.S. Attorney General in the Office of Legal Counsel, Department of Justice during the Bush 43 administration: John C. Yoo, *War by Other Means: An Insider's Account of the War on Terror* (Atlantic Monthly Press, 2006), p. 47.

international law and international institutions predominate, where unilateral action by powerful nations is forbidden, where all nations regardless of their strength have equal rights and are equally protected by commonly agreed-upon international rules of behaviour'.[46] The success of the European Union (EU) in ending centuries of interstate conflict encouraged faith in this formula as the answer to a more peaceful world. The United States, in contrast, continued to perceive a 'Hobbesian world where international laws and rules are unreliable and where true security and the defence and promotion of a liberal order still depend on the possession and use of military might'.[47] For Kagan, 'these differences in strategic culture do not spring naturally from the national characters of Americans and Europeans'; rather, they emerge from underlying power differentials.[48] Tracing shifts in global power over 200 years:

> When the United States was weak, it practiced the strategies of indirection, the strategies of weakness; now that the United States is powerful, it behaves as powerful nations do. When the European great powers were strong, they believed in strength and martial glory. Now, they see the world through the eyes of weaker powers.[49]

The disparity of transatlantic power has accordingly lain behind 'a broad ideological gap' in which 'material and ideological differences reinforce one another' to crystallise in irreconcilable conceptions of IL.[50]

The decisive role of preponderant global power provides the first explanation for distinctive American IL policy. Lassa Oppenheim argued over a century ago that, without a functioning balance of power at the global level, 'an overpowerful State will naturally try to act according to discretion and disobey the law', thereby becoming 'omnipotent'.[51] Hedley Bull likewise recognised a mutual relationship between the efficacy of the balance of power and that of IL.[52] For Hans Morgenthau, the condition of international anarchy[53] meant that enforcement of IL was

[46] Kagan, 'Power and Weakness', pp. 10 & 15.
[47] Ibid., p. 3.
[48] Ibid., p. 5.
[49] Ibid., p. 6.
[50] Ibid., p. 6.
[51] Lassa Oppenheim, 1912, cited in Hans Joachim Morgenthau, *Politics Among Nations: The Struggle for Power and Peace* (Knopf, 1973), p. 274.
[52] Hedley Bull, *The Anarchical Society* (Macmillan Press, 1995), pp. 125–6.
[53] In the IR sense of an absence of global government rather than a world in chaos.

ultimately left to 'the vicissitudes of the distribution of power between the violator of the law and the victim of the violation'.[54] Morgenthau thus recognised that applying a legal 'positivist' account 'cannot but draw a completely distorted picture of those rules which belong in the category of *political* international law'.[55] In consequence, 'the rights and duties established by them appear to be clearly determined, whereas they are subject actually to the most contradictory interpretations'.[56] This expresses political realism's basic view of institutions as 'epiphenomenal': a mere expression of power distribution between states and of their self-interested behaviour. IL has an instrumental value when serving state interests, but any general commitment to its terms is anomalous.[57] The bulk of IL may even command voluntary compliance by virtue of its useful administrative functions, but in cases where IL has a direct bearing on relative power between states, especially in matters of national security, power and not law determines compliance.

The most influential modern account in these terms is Jack Goldsmith and Eric Posner's *The Limits of International Law*.[58] The authors' aim is 'to explain how international law works by integrating the study of international law with the realities of international politics'. Specifically, they theorise 'that international law emerges from states acting rationally to maximise their interests, given their perceptions of the interests of other states and the distribution of state power'.[59] Thus, 'the best explanation for when and why states comply with international law is not that states have internalized international law, or have a habit of complying with it, or are drawn by its moral pull, but simply that states act out of self-interest'.[60] In this view, the expectation that the United States will act in the same way as every other state is implausible for expecting US policymakers to acquiesce to the legal fiction of sovereign equality. In earlier writing defending an American 'double standard', Goldsmith noted: 'The explanation is not subtle. The United

54 Morgenthau, *Politics Among Nations*, p. 290.
55 Hans Joachim Morgenthau, 'Positivism, Functionalism, and International Law' (1940) 34 *American Journal of International Law* 260, p. 279, emphasis added.
56 Ibid., p. 279.
57 John J. Mearsheimer, 'The False Promise of International Institutions' (1994) 19 *International Security* 5, p. 13.
58 Jack Goldsmith & Eric A. Posner, *The Limits of International Law* (Oxford University Press, 2005).
59 Ibid., p. 3.
60 Ibid., p. 225.

States declines to embrace international human rights law because it can.'[61]

Anu Bradford and Posner apply this perspective to the exceptionalist literature and conclude that, since all powerful states claim the mantle of exceptionalism, such beliefs cannot be treated as the cause of distinctive policies: 'great powers typically support a view of international law that embodies their own normative commitments but is presented as a universal set of commitments'.[62] Exceptionalism thus defined is 'the view that the values of one particular country should be reflected in the norms of international law' by virtue of being 'a model or leader in international relations because of its unique attributes'.[63] Where the United States, Europe and China have each translated great power in this way, the 'criticism of exceptionalism, then, is just a criticism of power, or the use of power to achieve ends of which the critic disapproves'.[64] Exceptionalist beliefs, of American, European and Chinese IL policy, are in the end considered epiphenomenal.

Accounts of power being systematically transformed into the norms of the legal system can be refined yet further by specifying how *hegemonic* power specifically shapes distinctive IL policy. Ian Brownlie defined the 'hegemonial approach' to lawmaking as 'an approach to the sources which facilitates the translation of the difference in power between States into specific advantages for the more powerful actor'. Doing so maximises the hegemonic state's ability to gain 'legal approval', while minimising occasions when approval is 'conspicuously withheld'.[65] The power to fashion unique privileges out of general rules creates incentives for a hegemon to blunt their *constraining* effect upon itself while enhancing their value as *enabling* instruments that facilitate strategic objectives. Doing so challenges any assumption that binding a hegemon to legal rules protects the international order against imperialism. Rather, in the words of ICJ Judge Charles De Visscher, 'the great powers after imprinting a definite

[61] Jack Goldsmith, 'International Human Rights Law & the United States Double Standard' (1998) 1 *Green Bag* 365, p. 371.

[62] Anu Bradford & Eric A. Posner, 'Universal Exceptionalism in International Law' (2011) 52 *Harvard International Law Journal* 1, p. 12.

[63] Ibid., p. 7.

[64] Ibid., p. 53.

[65] Ian Brownlie, *The Rule of Law in International Affairs: International Law at the Fiftieth Anniversary of the United Nations* (Martinus Nijhoff Publishers, 1998), p. 33.

direction upon a usage make themselves its guarantors and defenders'.[66]

Wilhelm Grewe speculated in the immediate post–Cold War period whether 'we have entered a new age of United States hegemony' in which the United States would play a distinctive role shaping the global legal order.[67] The weight of evidence strongly suggests as much, with broad and frequent system-wide tasks providing unique opportunities to legally entrench American interests. American hegemony has thereby manifested not as control over every legal development but, rather, as the United States becoming 'the one against whose ideas regarding the system of international law all others debate'.[68] At times hegemonic impulses have translated into explicit US privileges under the law, as most conspicuously achieved in its designation as one of the five permanent members of the UNSC (P5). However, the most contentious debates over American IL policy relate to its de facto exceptional legal status rather than the limited cases where it is accorded *de jure* privileges. Michael Byers notes two strategies through which the United States has achieved hegemonial lawmaking within the existing framework of IL. Firstly, laws may sanction behaviour that is only practically available to a limited number of states. Preponderant military power over any other state or alliance means that broad legal rights may in practice become '*de facto* exceptionalism' exercisable only by the United States.[69] A second form of hegemonial lawmaking is where rules remain deliberately indeterminate, 'enabling power and influence to determine where and when' actions are legal, thus deflecting criticism under the guise of legality.[70] Precise 'rules' enable *ex ante* decisions about acceptable conduct, whereas creating vague 'standards' enables *ex post* definitions of legality.[71]

66 Cited in Oscar Schachter, 'New Custom: Power, Opinio Juris and Contrary Practice', in Jerzy Makarczyk (ed.), *Theory of International Law at the Threshold of the 21st Century: Essays in Honour of Krzysztof Skubiszewski* (Kluwar Law International, 1996), p. 531.

67 Wilhelm G. Grewe, *The Epochs of International Law: Translated and Revised by Michael Byers* (Walter de Gruyter, 2000), p. 703.

68 Shirley V. Scott, 'The Impact on International Law of US Non-Compliance', in Michael Byers and Georg Nolte (eds.), *United States Hegemony and the Foundations of International Law* (Cambridge University Press, 2003), pp. 450–1.

69 Michael Byers, 'Preemptive Self-Defense: Hegemony, Equality and Strategies of Legal Change' (2003) 11 *The Journal of Political Philosophy* 171, p. 184.

70 Ibid., p. 180.

71 Kenneth W. Abbott, Robert O. Keohane, Andrew Moravcsik, Anne-Marie Slaughter & Duncan Snidal, 'The Concept of Legalization' (2000) 54 *International Organization* 401, p. 413.

The logic of hegemonial lawmaking cuts both ways, shaping the interests of states forced to adapt to conditions of international hegemony. Those opposing preponderant American influence have a vested interest in an international legal system that diminishes political advantages. An overriding incentive thus exists to structure international legal rules and institutions in accordance with 'counter-hegemonic' interests.[72] In this vein, Martti Koskenniemi persuasively argues that the shape of the international legal system represents a form of 'hegemonic contestation' in which participants aim to 'make their partial view of . . . [legal doctrines] appear as the total view, their preference seem like the *universal preference*'.[73] As such, the 'fight for an international Rule of Law is a fight against politics'.[74] Here, the rule of law will be achieved through the levelling of international power via rules that are nominally universal and therefore place constraints on states that increase in a magnitude commensurate with geopolitical power. Counter-hegemonic dynamics effectively corroborate the arguments of those US scholars who perceive 'universal' legal rules as a challenge to American political power. The validity of Kagan's insight into the nexus between law and power is therefore highly persuasive even for those critical of his normative conclusions.[75]

Nevertheless, returning to the puzzle of contradictory US IL policy, Kagan's argument equally illustrates the explanatory limits of a purely power-based explanation for US IL policy. Kagan relies on the problematic assumption that divergent US and EU legal policies correspond to a binary opposition between American political interests and the ideal of the rule of IL. Kagan, for example, characterises European policy as being 'all about subjecting inter-state relations to the rule of law', whereas the United States chooses to operate outside of the rule of law.[76] It is the

[72] In contrast to the more established literature on 'hegemonic international law'. For use of the term in relation to the ICC see José Manuel, 'Defensive and Oppositional Counter-Hegemonic Uses of International Law: From the International Criminal Court to the Common Heritage of Mankind', in Boaventura de Sousa Santos & César A. Rodríguez-Garavito (eds.), *Law and Globalization from Below: Towards a Cosmopolitan Legality* (Cambridge University Press, 2005).

[73] Martti Koskenniemi, 'International Law and Hegemony: A Reconfiguration' (2004) 17 *Cambridge Review of International Affairs* 197, p. 199, original emphasis.

[74] Martti Koskenniemi, 'The Politics of International Law' (1990) 1 *European Journal of International Law* 4, p. 5.

[75] Kalypso Nicolaidis, 'The Power of the Superpowerless', in Tod Lindberg (ed.), *Beyond Paradise and Power: Europeans, Americans and the Future of a Troubled Partnership* (Routledge, 2005), p. 94.

[76] Kagan, 'Power and Weakness', p. 17, quoting Steven Everts (2001).

claim of this book, however, that the evidence instead points to legal policymakers on both sides interpreting legal principles through political interests, such that the concept of law itself is contested. There are clearly intimate connections between preponderant power and the 'exceptional' outcomes of American IL policy, which are influenced by incentives to follow certain patterns of behaviour. But at the level of analysing processes of IL policy decision-making, power is indeterminate as an explanation for the positions taken in domestic debates between opposing legal policymakers, each claiming to advance American national interests. Explanation at the level of political realism 'discounts the influence of particular normative values, history, and culture, all of which shape the attitudes of a country's leaders toward international law and foreign affairs'.[77] Power alone cannot explain observed contradictions in policy in circumstances where US legal policymakers express fidelity to the rule of law even while giving contradictory accounts of how this advances political interests.

Institutional Explanations: Policy-Oriented Jurisprudence

A second common explanation for distinctive American IL policy is institutionalised jurisprudence in the US academy and practice, which has a causal effect distinct from either relative power or cultural beliefs. The most distinguishing feature of American IL jurisprudence is a greater scepticism toward conceptions of IL isolated from social and political context.[78] American international legal jurisprudence is instead strongly influenced by various 'policy-oriented' approaches, which originated in response to perceived limitations in legal positivism and have grown into the dominant IL jurisprudence in American scholarship and practice. The most well-known is the distinctive New Haven School, but elaborate variants abound and continue to be fiercely debated.[79] The precise formulation is less important than the general

[77] John E. Noyes, 'American Hegemony, U.S. Political Leaders, and General International Law' (2004) 19 *Connecticut Journal of International Law* 293, pp. 294 & 297.

[78] On historical stages of American IL jurisprudence see David Kennedy, 'The Twentieth-Century Discipline of International Law in the United States', in Austin Sarat, Bryant Garth & Robert A. Kagan (eds.), *Looking Back at Law's Century* (Cornell University Press, 2002).

[79] See Harold H. Koh, 'Is There a "New" New Haven School of International Law?' (2007) 32 *Yale Journal of International Law* 559.

observation that 'policy-oriented law is, by now, an accepted orthodoxy in the United States'.[80]

The chief innovation is to approach IL as a form of policymaking, while rejecting the plausibility of treating IL as a body of value neutral rules. Rules represent 'merely the accumulated trends of past decisions' stripped of the context of their creation and their connection to contemporary circumstances.[81] Koskenniemi's account of this jurisprudence identifies the 'one theme' connecting different approaches as a 'deformalized concept of law'. By this is meant that IL has not been seen as

> merely formal diplomacy or cases from the International Court of Justice but that . . . it had to be conceived in terms of broader political processes or techniques that aimed towards policy "objectives." A relevant law would be enmeshed in the social context and studied through the best techniques of neighboring disciplines.[82]

David Kennedy documents the rise of this approach across the twentieth century, where it was the proponents of IL themselves who

> slowly abandoned the doctrinal purity and institutional isolation characteristic of the pre-war generation . . . They imported into public international law precisely the realist attack on doctrinal formalism which the pre-war generation had resisted. They rejoiced as the discipline lost its coherence – renaming it 'transnational' law. These men were also successors to the progressive faith in international administration – and they brought to the United Nations their faith in New Deal federal reform.[83]

The conception built upon the work of American legal realism, which had aimed to penetrate the legal formalist myth that law was a self-contained body of rules by which judges could produce determinate outcomes.[84] Most significant, for present purposes, is recognition of the relationship between decision-makers and law: 'legal history could not simply chronicle the emergence and development of legal doctrines, nor treat them largely as intellectual insights divorced from the actual world

[80] Rosalyn Higgins, *Themes and Theories: Selected Essays, Speeches, and Writings in International Law* (Oxford University Press, 2009), p. 20.

[81] Ibid., p. 101.

[82] Martti Koskenniemi, *The Gentle Civilizer of Nations 1870–1960* (Cambridge University Press, 2001), pp. 478–9.

[83] David Kennedy, 'A New Stream of International Law Scholarship' (1988) 7 *Wisconsin International Law Journal* 1, p. 4.

[84] See Oliver Wendell Holmes, Jr, *The Common Law* (Little, Brown and Company, 1881), p. 1.

in which they occurred'.[85] Here the compatibility with hegemonial dynamics becomes clear in the inherent 'tension between the [legal] realist understanding of law as an instrument of policy and the legalist view of law as a constraint on policy'.[86]

The New Haven School of Myres McDougal and Harold Lasswell aimed to move legal realism beyond mere critique toward a methodology that made these insights '*operational in a systematic way*'.[87] 'Law' is recast as a *process* in which legality is conditional upon attaining social, moral and political goals through 'authoritative and effective decision-making'. Policy decisions are 'authoritative' in cases that advance 'world public order' and 'human dignity',[88] while they are 'effective' when backed by enforcement mechanisms and therefore 'controlling'.[89] In each case, the interests and values shaping foreign policy decisions more generally are imbued with a legal function, of providing predetermined criteria that permit legal subjects to organise their actions with known consequences. With the twin criteria of authority and control, the policy-oriented approach aims to overcome a misperception in International Relations (IR) and IL scholarship that 'law is concerned with authority (but not power) and that international relations is concerned with power (but not authority)'.[90] Decisions that lack one or both of the elements of authority and efficacy are distinguished from law and remain merely political acts.

Siegfried Wiessner and Andrew Willard advocate the merits of policy jurisprudence by drawing a contrast with a perceived 'counterimage' of legal positivists, who 'gain no help from their theory when asked what the law "should" be. Indeed, their theory eschews any creative or prescriptive

[85] Stephen Diamond, 'Legal Realism and Historical Method: J. Willard Hurst and American Legal History' (1979) 77 *Michigan Law Review* 784, p. 785.

[86] Simon Chesterman, 'An International Rule of Law?' (2008) 56 *American Journal of Comparative Law* 331, p. 358, n. 150.

[87] Richard A. Falk, 'Book Reviews: *Studies in World Public Order* by M. S. McDougal, New Haven: Yale University Press, 1960, pp. xx, 1058' (1961) 10 *American Journal of Comparative Law* 297, p. 299, original emphasis.

[88] Myres S. McDougal & Michael W. Reisman, 'International Law In Policy-Oriented Perspective', in Ronald St J. MacDonald & Douglas M. Johnston (eds.), *The Structure and Process of International Law: Essays in Legal Philosophy, Doctrine, and Theory* (Martinus Nijhoff Publishers, 1983), pp. 112–14.

[89] Harold D. Lasswell & Myres S. McDougal, *Jurisprudence for a Free Society: Studies in Law, Science, and Policy* (Martinus Nijhoff Publishers, 1992), p. 190.

[90] Higgins, *Themes and Theories*, p. 106.

function.'[91] This is an influential retort among American legal policy-makers who have portrayed positivist rules as no less politicised than the US policy decisions they seek to constrain. John Bellinger here draws a distinction between the Anglo-American common law tradition and the civil law tradition of continental Europe. On the one hand, American jurisprudence is inclined toward 'pragmatism and scepticism':

> we probe the purpose and function of law, examine it through the lenses of other disciplines such as economics and sociology, weigh its costs against its benefits, test its flexibility against the facts at hand, judge its value by its effectiveness, and seek, where we can, an equitable solution.[92]

Law must therefore be devised to reflect 'the virtues that have been drummed into us'. On the other hand, Bellinger acknowledges that such claims give rise to suspicion from Continental jurisprudence that American IL policy is 'opportunistic or, worse, self-serving'. Nevertheless, to American lawyers, the European conception is marked by 'excessive formalism, a doctrinal inflexibility, and an unwillingness to acknowledge that different paths may lead to the same end'.[93] Although Bellinger depicts worldviews uniting the common law tradition, the divergence is one more specific to American legal culture. Former ICJ President Rosalyn Higgins' observation that conflicts between 'American' and 'British' views 'now permeate the entire fabric of international law' precisely mirrors Bellinger's comparison with Continental Europe.[94]

A concrete example of a practitioner's defence in these terms comes from Abraham Sofaer, who served as Legal Adviser to the Department of State under Presidents Reagan and Bush 41. Sofaer wrote: 'Many, if not most international lawyers, have reacted to the need to use force in self-defense and in the defense of humanitarian rights by seeking to preserve what they consider the purity of international law.' Sofaer was responding to an article by Professor Tom Franck entitled 'Break It, Don't Fake It', which argued that the United States should have explicitly breached IL when it failed to obtain UN authorisation for the 1999 Kosovo

91 Siegfried Wiessner & Andrew R. Willard, 'Policy-Oriented Jurisprudence and Human Rights Abuses in Internal Conflict: Toward a World Public Order of Human Dignity' (1999) 93 *American Journal of International Law* 316, p. 320.

92 John B. Bellinger III, 'Reflections on Transatlantic Approaches to International Law' (2007) 17 *Duke Journal of Comparative and International Law* 513, p. 518.

93 Ibid., p. 519.

94 Higgins, *Themes and Theories*, pp. 17 & 21.

intervention, rather than trying to fit it into existing doctrine.[95] Franck's rationale was that, by so doing, the purity and therefore the integrity of IL would be preserved. To this, Sofaer responded:

> It would be like people in the 1930s dealing with Constitutional issues in the U.S. saying 'Don't make up new constitutional law, it's going to mess up our Constitution. Just break the Constitution, violate the Constitution, with no explanation, and that way we will keep the purity of this rigid Constitution that the pre-New Deal Supreme Court was insisting on applying. Everything will be fine someday when we all return to the purity of the intended words.'[96]

Policy jurisprudence sees such expunging of policy from law as chimerical, and instead aims to make law conform to the *right* sort of policy. The proper distinction for the policy-oriented approach is that 'the terms "political dispute" and "legal dispute" refer to the decision-making process which is to be employed in respect of them, and not to the nature of the dispute itself'.[97]

Cases of divergent international legal decision-making reinforce the significance of this institutionalised jurisprudence as an explanation for contradictions in IL policy. Yet, it is also clear that the jurisprudence remains profoundly intertwined with explanations from both power and culture, in ways not always fully acknowledged. IR realism and American legal realism assume in common that law is a '"means to social ends and not . . . an end in itself"; a "distrust" of "traditional legal rules and concepts," as a description of what the system actually does; and an "insistence on evaluation of any part of the law in terms of its effects."'[98] Shared assumptions buttress the undeniable compatibility between hegemonial lawmaking and policy jurisprudence, such that it is problematic to view either in isolation as a causal explanation for unique policy outcomes. Specific policy-oriented theories developed across the twentieth century inevitably reflected prevailing national interests and, in particular, the long fixation of US foreign policy on Cold War politics. In this process, American lawyers 'increasingly conceived international law from the perspective of a world power, whose leaders have "options" and routinely choose among alternative

95 Thomas M. Franck, 'Break It, Don't Fake It' (1999) 78 *Foreign Affairs* 116.

96 Abraham D. Sofaer, 'The International Court of Justice and Armed Conflict' (2003) 1 *Northwestern Journal of International Human Rights* i, p. vii.

97 Higgins, *Themes and Theories*, p. 34.

98 Karl N. Llewellyn, cited in Jonathan D. Greenberg, 'Does Power Trump Law?' (2003) 55 *Stanford Law Review* 1789, p. 1805.

"strategies" in an ultimately hostile world'.[99] For some accounts of the New Haven jurisprudence, 'world public order' was effectively defined to coincide exactly with the interests of the Western Bloc.[100] More generally, a well-founded criticism is that powerful states are able to use this jurisprudence to self-judge their parochial interests as 'law'. The clear prescriptions of legal rules and the decisions of international courts are liable to be set aside for inconsistency with claimed 'fundamental goals of the international community'.[101]

Hedley Bull thus rejected the imprecision of the policy-oriented approach as liable to render law unintelligible.[102] Likewise, the former president of the ICTY declared the tribunal 'bound only by international law' to the exclusion of 'meta-legal analyses'. Accordingly, 'a policy-oriented approach in the area of criminal law runs contrary to the fundamental customary principle *nullum crimen sine lege*'.[103] Professor Oscar Schachter levelled a particularly strident critique while sitting on a conference panel with McDougal, warning that the approach produced a 'unilateralist version of policy jurisprudence in which law plays a secondary role and policy is determined by the [American] perception of self-interest'.[104] On the same panel, Professor Richard Falk wryly described the 'miraculous' capacity of McDougal's jurisprudence to coincide with US foreign policy interests.[105] Even Higgins, as a strong advocate of the jurisprudence, accepts that there is 'a very fine line between insisting that decisions be taken in accordance with the policy objectives of a liberal, democratic world community and asserting that *any* action taken by a liberal democracy against a totalitarian nation is lawful'.[106] Modern exponents have applied policy-oriented analysis to support the legality of the most prominent examples of American IL policy diverging from orthodox interpretations of IL. These include

[99] Koskenniemi, *The Gentle Civilizer*, p. 475.

[100] See Richard A. Falk, *Legal Order in a Violent World* (Princeton University Press, 1968), pp. 86–7.

[101] Michael W. Reisman, *Nullity and Revision: The Review and Enforcement of International Judgements and Awards* (Yale University Press, 1971), p. 562.

[102] Bull, *The Anarchical Society*, pp. 123–4 & 153–4.

[103] 'No crime without law.' *Prosecutor* v. *Drazen Erdemovic (Appeal Judgment), Separate and Dissenting Opinion of Judge Cassese* (1997) IT-96–22-A, par. [11].

[104] Oscar Schachter, 'McDougal's Jurisprudence: Utility, Influence, Controversy: Remarks' (1985) 79 *American Society of International Law Proceedings* 266, p. 273.

[105] Richard A. Falk, 'McDougal's Jurisprudence: Utility, Influence, Controversy: Remarks' (1985) 79 *American Society of International Law Proceedings* 266, p. 281.

[106] Higgins, *Themes and Theories*, p. 52.

arguments for the legality of the 2003 Iraq War[107] and using policy analysis to challenge the legal definition of torture.[108] In all such cases, jurisprudence is both distinct from and yet correlates with American hegemonic power, as presumptive causes of unique IL policy.

Cultural Explanations: Exceptionalist Beliefs

The final causal explanation embedded in 'exceptionalist' accounts is the role of culturally specific beliefs about America's unique role in the international legal system. These explanations come closest to capturing the exceptionalist concept, in the sense of distinctive practices drawn not from hegemonic power or institutionalised jurisprudence but from beliefs and identity. John Murphy's characterisation of 'exceptional' American legal practice is sceptical of Kagan's conclusion that distinct approaches to IL are fundamentally rooted in transatlantic differences in power and weakness. Rather, sovereignty limitations created by the EU 'are simply inconceivable' to most Americans, who possess 'an historical distrust of power, especially centralized power'.[109] Here, culturally based beliefs remain a principle explanation for distinctive IL policy.

One of the most enlightening interventions from this perspective is an argument by Jed Rubenfeld that a primary source of exceptional IL policy is America's distinctive constitutional democracy and the divergent transatlantic lessons of WWII.[110] For Continental Europe, WWII represented the perverse outcome of unrestrained popular will and confirmed for European leaders that national politics must be answerable to the explicitly antinationalist and antidemocratic higher authority of IL. In contrast, the lesson for America was confirmation that its nationalism, in the form of popular sovereignty, was the surest guardian of individual liberty. Far from seeking to curb American popular will, the post-war

107 For a contrary argument from a policy-oriented approach see Michael W. Reisman & Andrea Armstrong, 'The Past and Future of the Claim of Preemptive Self-Defense' (2006) 100 *American Journal of International Law* 525.

108 Tai-Heng Cheng, *When International Law Works* (Oxford University Press, 2012), pp. 227–48.

109 Murphy, *The US and the Rule of Law*, p. 354.

110 Jed Rubenfeld, 'Commentary: Unilateralism and Constitutionalism' (2004) 79 *New York University Law Review* 1971; Jed Rubenfeld, 'The Two World Orders', in Georg Nolte (ed.), *European and US Constitutionalism* (Cambridge University Press, 2005). Koh describes Rubenfeld's views as 'a powerful statement' of a 'deeply rooted American culture of unilateralism and parochialism': see 'On American Exceptionalism', p. 1495, n. 52.

years saw a US strategy to extend its democratic values outward and 'Americanise' the rest of the world.[111] The contradiction entailed in that lesson, however, was that legal regimes moderating the politics of other states had no legitimate claim over the United States itself. Henceforth, the United States became both the principal architect of IL and its most conspicuously reluctant subject.

Rubenfeld traces these formative experiences into two distinct understandings of how constitutionalism guards liberty. For European states, 'international constitutionalism' perceives supranational legal institutions transcending state sovereignty as the ultimate guardians of liberty. Power is deliberately transferred from the control of popular sovereignty to 'international experts – bureaucrats, technocrats, diplomats, and judges – at a considerable remove from popular politics and popular will'.[112] In contrast, American 'democratic constitutionalism' identifies the legitimacy of constitutional law in its foundations as a special act of popular lawmaking. These beliefs reinforce distinctive American jurisprudence and its scepticism toward the possibility of a higher law divorced from democratic political foundations.[113] Henry Nau concurs that, from 'the European point of view, law must be inclusive of all cultures and check democratic as well as non-democratic states'. In contrast, for Americans, 'democratic politics legitimates law'. For Nau, this explains much of the divergence in beliefs about the binding authority of the UN in the 2003 Iraq invasion relative to the democratic legitimacy of US policy.[114] Intentionally undemocratic foundations of IL are therefore illegitimate fetters on American constitutional government.

Rubenfeld's argument is especially significant for understanding the meaning of hypocrisy in US IL policy, as considered in this book. He suggests that, because European international constitutionalism dominates global conceptions of IL, the United States is relegated to being an outlier consistent with its exceptionalist beliefs. In this, Rubenfeld agrees with Kagan's conclusion that, although US actions are exceptional, they are not thereby hypocritical in the proper sense of that word. In Paul Kahn's terms, the price of US resistance to legal constraints is that: 'To the rest of the world, this is bound to look hypocritical. In the

[111] Rubenfeld, 'Commentary', p. 1986.
[112] Ibid., p. 1987.
[113] Ibid., p. 1997.
[114] Henry Nau, *Perspectives on International Relations: Power, Institutions, and Ideas* (CQ Press, 2014), p. 266.

United States, it will look like an insistence on democratic self-government.'[115] The argument does not deny the clear correlation between exceptional conceptions of IL and their facilitation of exceptional American power since WWII. However, self-interest is not determined objectively but is received through a nation's 'history, culture, values, and worldviews'.[116] Two forces have thus guided American IL policy: a 'high-minded' messianic impulse to spread American constitutional rights and a 'geopolitical' motive to construct an order augmenting American economic and political power. Both motives are united in the objective of establishing a new global order replicating American values.[117] The convergence of two distinct causal explanations thus resolves potential hypocrisy in the decision-making of US IL policymakers.

Rubenfeld's argument raises questions about whether exceptionalist explanations provide insights beyond the influence of power. Robert Delahunty accepts that the explanatory value of Rubenfeld's argument is 'incontestable', particularly in relation to the depth of commitment of opposing sides to their worldview.[118] Nevertheless, he concludes that more orthodox explanations, such as that propounded by Kagan, retain equivalent or greater explanatory power, while eschewing complex historical narratives.[119] The value of the richer analysis lies in a different analytical purpose, however, of identifying the contested meanings of 'the international rule of law', as understood by American policymakers and as they shape decision-making processes. Delahunty's conclusions confirm an abstract theory of the fundamental dynamics of states' IL policies, making it unnecessary to unpack the concept of 'national interests'. However, when the objective is to develop a framework for understanding the IL policy of a named state in specific policy contexts, then an abstract concept of national interest is simply inadequate. The national interest is a dependent concept, requiring specification of both perceived objectives and a state's strategy for advancing them through IL. Upholding *America's* national interest, as defined by Rubenfeld, entails

[115] Paul W. Kahn, 'American Exceptionalism, Popular Sovereignty, and the Rule of Law', in Michael Ignatieff (ed.), *American Exceptionalism and Human Rights* (Princeton University Press, 2005), p. 221.

[116] Rubenfeld, 'Commentary', p. 1984.

[117] Ibid., pp. 1987–8.

[118] Robert J. Delahunty, 'The Battle of Mars and Venus: Why Do American and European Attitudes toward International Law Differ?' (2006) 4 *Loyola University Chicago International Law Review* 11, pp. 36–7.

[119] Ibid., p. 38.

constructing a system of IL that reproduces distinct American constitutional values, while using those same values to shield American domestic law against the world. Each account is equally valid and compatible. But, just as a parsimonious approach best explains abstract motivations, it is weakest in providing an ideographic account of interests as they actually guide policymakers.

Chapter Conclusion

The most striking features of flourishing 'exceptionalist' legal scholarship are the multiplicity of causal explanations embedded in the central concept and the analytical potential for mapping connections between them. Although legal applications engage with the broader literature, they have tended to categorise any unique cause and outcome of American legal policy as 'exceptional'. Questioning this use of language is no mere terminological dispute since it weakens the insights offered by exceptionalist ideas: believing that America is guided by exceptional values sustains support for IL just as often as it erodes it. Benjamin Coates identifies the fallacy whereby 'it has become conventional to think about exceptionalism and empire, on the one hand, and compliance with international law, on the other, as mutually exclusive. More international law means less empire; more exceptionalism means less international law.'[120] Exceptionalist beliefs, properly understood, are equally capable of sustaining enlarged conceptions of IL – imperial or otherwise.

Placed side by side, it is impossible to ignore the correlation and overlap between the three common causal explanations examined here. In the case of power-based explanations, even strong defenders of IL policy based on American preponderance have sought reconciliation with normative explanations of why such might is also right. Kagan acknowledges that the 'modern liberal mind is offended by the notion that a single world power may be unfettered except by its own sense of restraint ... [T]he spirit of liberal democracy recoils at the idea of hegemonic dominance, even when it is exercised benignly.'[121] Responding in these terms, he asserts that by 'nature, tradition, and ideology, the United States has generally favoured the promotion of

120 Benjamin A. Coates, *Legalist Empire: International Law and American Foreign Relations in the Early Twentieth Century* (Oxford University Press, 2016), p. 178.

121 Robert Kagan, 'America's Crisis of Legitimacy' (2004) 83 *Foreign Affairs* 65, p. 70.

liberal principles over the niceties of Westphalian democracy'.[122] Conversely, from a critical perspective, Charlesworth acknowledges that the exceptionalist ideas evident in American IL policy that she finds so problematic have 'at least some basis in US political, military and economic dominance globally'.[123]

Likewise, the substantive content of policy-oriented jurisprudence is to be found in 'exceptionalist' ideas as defined in this book. In the New Haven approach, conceptions of 'world public order' and 'human dignity' and of the American role in bringing these values about necessarily draw upon long-established conceptions of America's global mission.[124] The main contemporaneous challenge to the New Haven approach was led by Professor Falk of Columbia University, who criticised its overt parochialism. Yet, in practice, the competing approaches merged: 'one on the right, the other on the left, but alike in projecting American values on the rest of the world'.[125] In this way, the dominant American approach to jurisprudence opens the way for messianic and teleological forms of exceptionalism to be instituted as a foundational element of American IL policy. Interpretations of IL that are inconsistent with exceptionalist values can be rejected not only as politically undesirable, but also, for that very reason, as lacking *legal* authority.

So what does this observed convergence mean for our understanding of the international rule of law? One way of proceeding is to treat these explanations as located at different levels of analysis reflecting the distinction between IR and FPA.[126] The rationality of hegemonic power approaches the question of policy contradictions at the level of the international system and the incentives for a uniquely powerful state to institutionalise its position in law. Policy jurisprudence provides the framework within which these interests can be flexibly promoted while reconciling with fidelity to legal principle. Finally, exceptionalist beliefs provide the substantive content informing legal policy. These different sources of distinctiveness fall short of a complete answer for observed contradictions when considered in isolation but complement each other as nested levels of explanation.

[122] Ibid., p. 79.
[123] Charlesworth, *No Country Is an Island*, p. 147.
[124] Oscar Schachter, 'McDougal's Jurisprudence: Utility, Influence, Controversy: Remarks', p. 270.
[125] Terry Nardin, 'Theorising the International Rule of Law' (2008) 34 *Review of International Studies* 385, p. 389.
[126] See Introduction, *supra*, pp. 9–10.

The overall picture challenges suggestions that American legal policymakers perceive a simple choice between the ideal of the rule of IL and national political interests. Shirley Scott concludes that the exceptionalism term has more often been employed 'cynically' where 'key figures in US foreign policy circles apparently believe that a different rule should apply to the United States than applies to the rest of the world'.[127] Yet, by virtue of the symbiotic relationship among power, jurisprudence and culture, a legal policymaker could conceivably pledge good faith fidelity to the rule of IL while departing significantly from global expectations. For this reason, Chapter 2 turns to the role of foreign policy ideology, as a compound concept encompassing interests and ideas as they structure IL policy.

[127] Shirley V. Scott, *International Law, US Power: The United States' Quest for Legal Security* (Cambridge University Press, 2012), p. 20.

2

The Structure of American Foreign Policy Ideology

In *The American Tradition of International Law*, Mark Janis opens with the statement: 'How we think about any aspect of the law is largely an inheritance', setting the scene for a contest between ideas of 'exceptionalism' and those of 'universalism' since the earliest days of the republic.[1] By identifying the influence of exceptionalist beliefs over conceptions of IL, Janis concludes that 'some of America's fierce debates about the nature and advantages of international law have been generated by the disputants failing to acknowledge that they were actually talking about somewhat different things'.[2] Chapter 1 demonstrated how power, ideas and interests are interrelated as causes of 'exceptional' American IL policy. This chapter turns to the role of 'ideology' in IL, as the concept that best captures power transformed into beliefs that interpret interests.

Identifying America's several foreign policy ideologies yields a framework for understanding how US IL policy can be consistent with broad expectations of power-based explanations, yet also conform to particularistic commitments within American political culture. The structure of American foreign policy ideology is established via an influential four-part typology developed through empirical research on both political leaders and the mass public. The Wittkopf-Holsti-Rosenau (WHR) typology has repeatedly demonstrated an underlying structure of beliefs that has proven a powerful indicator of foreign policy preferences and the contradictions between them. Synthesising the WHR typology with evidence from diplomatic history yields four ideal ideological types, which together form the parameters of American approaches to IL. Policymakers' *governance* preferences are arrayed along an *internationalist–nationalist* dimension, while *values* shaping legal policy sit along a *liberal–illiberal* dimension. The crossing

[1] Mark W. Janis, *The American Tradition of International Law: Great Expectations 1789–1914* (Oxford University Press, 2004), p. 1.
[2] Ibid., p. 2.

of these dimensions produces four discrete ideal types of American IL policy: *liberal internationalism*, *illiberal internationalism*, *liberal nationalism* and *illiberal nationalism*. That typology provides the ideological structure applied throughout this book to analyse competing conceptions of the international rule of law.

The Power of Foreign Policy Ideology

International Relations Theory and Ideology

The key question emerging from Chapter 1 is not whether unique dynamics of American IL policy are best explained by power *or* ideas, since they are evidently interrelated; rather, the question is: how do culturally ingrained ideas about America's global role mediate between the fact of preponderant power and legal policymakers' engagement with IL? In IR terms, this becomes a question of how a state's perception of interests alters the way that it behaves within the international system and therefore the causal role of ideas. It has become almost ritualistic to begin such an enquiry by identifying the limitations of Kenneth Waltz's neorealist tenet that 'considerations of power dominate considerations of ideology'[3] and then describing the advantages of a flourishing array of alternative IR theories that reassert the power of ideas.[4]

Richard Steinberg observes that international legal scholarship tends to 'perpetuate a common misperception that realism is a monolithic approach that denies any role for law'.[5] Yet theoretical variants do recognise that ideas, including legal beliefs, can be mutually constitutive of power, and among these the 'softest realist position is that of the traditional or neoclassical realists'.[6] Gideon Rose explains that adherents of the IR school of neoclassical realism recognise, first, that 'the scope and ambition of a country's foreign policy is driven first and foremost by its place in the international system and specifically by its relative material power capabilities. This is why they are realist' but, second, that 'the

[3] Kenneth N. Waltz, 'Realist Thought and Neorealist Theory' (1990) 44 *Journal of International Affairs* 21, p. 31.

[4] The standard triumvirate includes variants of 'liberal institutionalism' and 'constructivism', each of which identifies a causal role for human agency and ideational variables. For an overview see Richard H. Steinberg & Jonathan M. Zasloff, 'Power and International Law' (2006) 100 *American Journal of International Law* 64.

[5] Richard H. Steinberg, 'Overview: Realism in International Law' (2002) 96 *Proceedings of the Annual Meeting (American Society of International Law)* 260, p. 261.

[6] Ibid., p. 261.

impact of such power capabilities on foreign policy is indirect and complex, because systemic pressures must be translated through intervening variables at the unit level. This is why they are neoclassical.'[7] Those 'intervening variables' include ideology, comprised of the foreign policy ideas 'embedded in social norms, patterns of discourse and collective identities'.[8] Ideology operates to 'filter and limit options, ruling out policies that fail to resonate with the national political culture'.[9] The mutually constitutive relationship between policymakers' beliefs and the material structure of the international system renders realism compatible with 'constructivist' theories of IR, which lawyers have conventionally seen as the ideal entry point for interdisciplinary research. IL scholarship often 'echoes the flavour and ontology of constructivist theory' in that both treat ideas and identity as the fundamental building blocks of international politics.[10] Within these approaches, IL policy can be analysed by reference to the 'competing general conceptions of what legal institutions and rules should look like', which are in turn 'shaped by the actors' conceptions of their interests and their identities'.[11]

The advantages of theoretical synthesis are evident in Rose's analysis of America's rising relative power and the concomitant assertion of its normative exceptionalism. He argues that 'instead of viewing ideas as either purely independent or purely dependent variables', there is scope for identifying 'how, in conjunction with relative power, they could play both roles simultaneously'. Specifically, Rose considers shifting interpretations of the exceptionalist belief that American 'domestic institutions should be disseminated to others'. This idea has been expressed by both the 'examplars' of the nineteenth century and the 'crusaders' of the twentieth century.[12] By adopting a neoclassical realist framework, he argues that the most important explanation for this shift remains the 'massive increase in relative power' that gave the United States the means to contemplate a strategy of shaping global politics. The role of political

[7] Gideon Rose, 'Neoclassical Realism and Theories of Foreign Policy' (1998) 51 *World Politics* 144, p. 146.

[8] Nicholas Kitchen, 'Systemic Pressures and Domestic Ideas: A Neoclassical Realist Model of Grand Strategy Formation' (2010) 36 *Review of International Studies* 117, p. 131.

[9] Ibid., p. 141.

[10] Kal Raustiala & Anne-Marie Slaughter, 'International Law, International Relations and Compliance', in Walter Carlsnaes, Thomas Risse & Beth A. Simmons (eds.), *Handbook of International Relations* (SAGE Publications, 2002), p. 544.

[11] David Wippman, 'The International Criminal Court', in Christian Reus-Smit (ed.), *The Politics of International Law* (Cambridge University Press, 2004), p. 154.

[12] Rose, 'Neoclassical Realism', p. 169.

power and the basic premise of political realism thereby remain intact. Yet analysts 'still need to know the content of American political ideology . . . in order to understand the specific policy choices officials made in either era'.[13] The causal role of ideology and law is thereby preserved, even when proceeding from an ostensibly political realist foundation.

Ideas as Beliefs

To achieve greater clarity in the meaning of 'ideology', it is useful to start with a more precise definition of 'ideas' as its basic building blocks. There is a degree of imprecision in formulations that variously label the constitutive elements of ideology as 'ideas', 'opinions', 'values', 'symbols' and 'beliefs'. For this book, Judith Goldstein and Robert Keohane's approach is instructive, as it defines ideas simply as 'beliefs held by individuals'.[14] Focusing on beliefs is persuasive, as it expresses the interconnection between abstract political ideas and the real actors who hold them – who emerge as central characters in these pages. For Goldstein and Keohane, foreign policy beliefs are of three types: worldviews defining possible modes of thought and discourse;[15] principled beliefs providing normative criteria for assessing right from wrong;[16] and causal beliefs about the cause–effect relationships that yield strategic outcomes.[17] As will be seen, all three forms of belief inhere in a single ideology.

Building on this treatment, Alexander George and Andrew Bennett argue that, rather than exerting a deterministic influence, political beliefs increase the propensity of decision-makers to reach particular 'diagnostic' and 'choice' decisions. Beliefs create in policymakers a propensity to reach a particular diagnosis about what is happening in a case, which is followed by policymakers' strategic choices about what action to then take.[18] The distinction alludes to the role of political beliefs in not merely recognising interests but in defining what they are. Blyth reminds that a useful understanding of beliefs must distinguish between the *concept* of

13 Ibid., p. 170.

14 Judith Goldstein & Robert O. Keohane, 'Ideas and Foreign Policy: An Analytical Framework', in Judith Goldstein & Robert O. Keohane (eds.), *Ideas and Foreign Policy: Beliefs, Institutions, and Political Change* (Cornell University Press, 1993), p. 3.

15 Ibid., p. 8.

16 Ibid., p. 9.

17 Ibid., p. 10.

18 Alexander L. George & Andrew Bennett, *Case Studies and Theory Development in the Social Sciences* (MIT Press, 2005), p. 193.

interests and the necessarily prior *cognates* of interest. This distinction permits interests to be 'less about *a priori* structural determination and more about the construction of wants as mediated by beliefs and desires (i.e., ideas)'.[19] Although structures such as relative global power remain important in determining interests, they 'do not come with an instruction sheet'.[20]

Defining Ideology

'Ideology' emerges as the bridge between 'interests' and 'ideas' in legal and political analysis. Michael Freeden's influential definition of political ideology is of

> a set of ideas, beliefs, opinions, and values that:
> 1 exhibit a recurring pattern;
> 2 are held by significant groups;
> 3 compete over providing and controlling plans for public policy; [and]
> 4 do so with the aim of justifying, contesting or changing the social and political arrangements and processes of a political community.[21]

Here, ideology is identified as pervasive in all political thought, being composed of the 'ideas and symbols through which political actors find their way and comprehend their social surroundings'.[22] The way beliefs are configured in a specific ideology enables the 'decontesting' of their meaning, thereby narrowing the valid policy implications for any political situation.[23] Miroslav Nincic and Jennifer Ramos approvingly adopt Freeden's definition for highlighting ideology as a form of 'structured thinking: a stable and coherent relationship among the cognitions and preferences people hold'.[24] Importantly, for present purposes, Freeden addresses the question of the correlation between material power and belief. Ideology is characterised as both a representation of an objective reality and part of the discourse that constructs it:

[19] Mark Blyth, 'Structures Do Not Come with an Instruction Sheet: Interests, Ideas, and Progress in Political Science' (2003) 1 *Perspective on Politics* 695, p. 697.
[20] Ibid., p. 698.
[21] Michael Freeden, *Ideology: A Very Short Introduction* (Oxford University Press, 2003), p. 32.
[22] Ibid., p. 123.
[23] Ibid., pp. 54–5.
[24] Miroslav Nincic & Jennifer M. Ramos, 'Ideological Structure and Foreign Policy Preferences' (2010) 15 *Journal of Political Ideologies* 119, p. 121.

> [Ideologies] interact with historical and political events and retain some representative value. But they do so while emphasizing some features of that reality and de-emphasizing others, and by adding mythical and imaginary happenings to make up for the 'reality gaps'. A constant feed-back operates between the 'soft' ideological imagination and the 'hard' constraints of the real world.[25]

Crucially, this approach recognises the dialectical nature of ideology. A nation's political ideology does not develop in a vacuum but, rather, through encounters with the constraints and opportunities afforded by power.

Jonathan Zasloff explores the meaning of ideology in a context closer to home, albeit from the reverse angle to this book's: analysing the influence of 'legal ideology' on early American foreign policy. His account of the 'notoriously treacherous' concept is on point for drawing attention to ideology's causal role in mediating between power and international legal policy.[26] Zasloff adopts David Davis's definition of ideology as 'an integrated system of beliefs, assumptions, and values, not necessarily true or false, which reflects the needs and interests of a group or class at a particular time in history'.[27] Davis's own further explanation is useful for reminding that 'there is a continuous interaction between ideology and the material forces of history'.[28] This element comports with Rose's observation that the rise in ideas about America's 'exceptional' global role has paralleled and reinforced the reality of growing preponderant global power. Zasloff's most important point for present purposes is that so defining ideology means that it cannot be approached as merely 'a cynical cover for the naked pursuit of self-interest'.[29] That conclusion is pivotal to the argument of this book: although US IL policy is often defended in idiosyncratic terms that align with politicised interests, that cannot itself be evidence of hypocrisy on the part of legal policymakers. Zasloff puts the case well:

> [I]deologies carry power precisely because they allow people to believe that they are acting properly while at the same time serving their own interests. Legitimation, then, is directed more at the producer of ideology than at the consumer. Put another way, an effective ideology enables action because it helps avoid the cognitive dissonance that arises when

25 Freeden, *Ideology*, p. 106.

26 Jonathan M. Zasloff, 'Law and the Shaping of American Foreign Policy: From the Gilded Age to the New Era' (2003) 78 *New York University Law Review* 239, pp. 247–50.

27 Ibid., p. 247. See David B. Davis, *The Problem of Slavery in the Age of Revolution, 1770–1823* (Cornell University Press, 1975), p. 14.

28 Davis, *The Problem of Slavery*, p. 14.

29 Zasloff, 'Law and the Shaping of American Foreign Policy', p. 248.

> a person advocates something she knows to be unjust or destructive simply to further her own interest.[30]

American IL policymakers thus perform an 'important ideological function' that has 'helped to reconcile imperial power with republican traditions and universal principles'.[31] The implications are significant in cases of apparent legal contradiction, since to so observe 'is not to say that people were disregarding the "true" law but rather to underline the claim that all international law, to one degree or another, relies on such ideological construction'.[32] Within this process, ideology operates to translate power into legal principle – in effect deriving an 'ought' from an 'is'[33] – which adherents can then adopt as simultaneously both a good faith commitment to IL and an affirmation of American power.

Especially pronounced consequences arise in the specific context of *foreign policy ideology*, since policymakers are faced with inherent uncertainties about the intentions of external parties owing to 'gaps in distance, culture, and understanding'. Even more so than in domestic politics, policymakers are 'forced to rely upon ideological assumptions to guide their action'.[34] Michael Hunt's leading account defines American foreign policy ideology as 'an interrelated set of convictions or assumptions that reduces the complexities of a particular slice of reality to easily comprehensible terms and suggest[s] appropriate ways of dealing with reality'.[35] For George, foreign policy ideology is 'a belief system that explains and justifies a preferred political order for society, either one that already exists or one that is proposed, and offers at least a sketchy notion of strategy … for its maintenance and attainment'.[36] Jeffrey Legro's definition identifies three characteristics of ideas specific to the domain of foreign policy ideology. These are that ideas: '(1) are collectively held; (2) involve beliefs about effective means; and (3) refer specifically to national conceptions about international society'.[37] For Legro, these ideas 'are not so much mental as symbolic and organizational; they are embedded not only in

[30] Ibid., p. 248, citations omitted.
[31] Benjamin A. Coates, *Legalist Empire: International Law and American Foreign Relations in the Early Twentieth Century* (Oxford University Press, 2016), p. 3.
[32] Ibid., p. 7.
[33] A form of David Hume's 'is-ought' fallacy.
[34] Zasloff, 'Law and the Shaping of American Foreign Policy', pp. 248–9.
[35] Michael H. Hunt, *Ideology and U.S. Foreign Policy* (Yale University Press, 1987), p .xi.
[36] Alexander L. George, 'Ideology and International Relations: A Conceptual Analysis' (1987) 9 *Jerusalem Journal of International Relations* 1, p. 1.
[37] Jeffrey W. Legro, *Rethinking the World: Great Power Strategies and International Order* (Cornell University Press, 2005), p. 4.

human brains but also in the "collective memories," government procedures, educational systems, and the rhetoric of statecraft'.[38] Moreover his definition of ideology draws attention to the inherent 'instrumentality' of foreign policy ideas, which are beliefs not just about the objectives of policy but also about the effective means for achieving them.[39] His final element is of particular interest to the present analysis, which is that a foreign policy ideology entails beliefs about the proper attitude toward the existing international order: whether to join, remain outside or revise it.[40]

From these accounts, foreign policy ideology can be defined as a shared set of interrelated beliefs that interpret global power and help define a state's international interests and strategies for achieving them. The nature of ideology as beliefs entrenched in a political community ensures that evaluations of success will be heavily biased by a conviction that an ideology is effective. It is hard, if not impossible, to conclusively falsify beliefs about foreign policy once ideologically entrenched. They do not provide an 'absolute truth' about foreign policy interests and strategies, merely beliefs that resonate as an article of faith. Any established American foreign policy ideology entails a claim to a formula for strengthening national power and interests.

The Structure of American Foreign Policy Ideology

The Wittkopf-Holsti-Rosenau Typology

Attention can now turn to the substance and structure of American foreign policy ideologies influencing conceptions of IL. The underlying rationale of the WHR typology is the same as this book's, which is that it 'is useful in understanding the frequent inconsistency of American foreign policy, for the maintenance of a coherent foreign policy is more difficult in a domestic environment characterized by the absence of consensus'.[41] Although the foundational literature does not use the term 'ideology', it is clear that the underlying concept is the same.[42] In a review of foreign policy ideology

[38] Ibid., p. 6.

[39] Ibid., p. 7.

[40] Legro typologises these positions as 'integrationist', 'separatist' and 'revisionist': ibid., p. 10.

[41] Eugene R. Wittkopf, 'On the Foreign Policy Beliefs of the American People: A Critique and Some Evidence' (1986) *International Studies Quarterly* 425, p. 443.

[42] The term 'ideology' is used in this literature to describe political placement on a left-right spectrum, which may explain reluctance to apply the term to the structure of beliefs as a whole.

literature, Michael Hunt cited the work of Ole Holsti and James Rosenau as an example of 'a new concern with ideology' that had 'infiltrated the field of diplomatic history'.[43] Those authors' own terminology of 'attitude structures',[44] 'worldviews'[45] and, in particular, 'belief systems'[46] entails the key elements of interrelated ideas about the nature of the world and political strategies for responding to it. The model is accordingly adapted here to identify and classify the constitutive beliefs and structure of American foreign policy ideology and thereby of American IL policy.

As a preliminary point, the most analytically useful typology in social science is one that moves beyond mere listing and instead maps out the structure of how different types relate to one another. David Collier et al. define an analytical typology as 'an organized system of types that breaks down an overarching concept into component dimensions and types'.[47] 'Dimensionality' is a broader concept than 'type' and refers to the 'number of variables entailed in a concept or a data set'.[48] Common variables may be evident in different types and so the goal of the analyst is to isolate each variable, then show how types are connected and differentiated through them. Where the concept under analysis exhibits multidimensionality, a clear typology will be one constructed by the intersection of orthogonal dimensions to form discrete types. An underlying strength of the WHR typology is that it goes beyond merely listing different forms of ideology, instead meeting the more rigorous standard of mapping out how different types relate to one another. A further point is that the product of this typology is four 'ideal types' of foreign policy ideology. In Max Weber's terms, 'an ideal type is formed by the one-sided accentuation of one or more points of view and by the synthesis of a great many diffuse, discrete, more or less present and occasionally absent concrete individual phenomena, which are arranged according to

[43] Michael H. Hunt, 'Ideology' (1990) 77 *The Journal of American History* 108, pp. 112–13.

[44] Ole R. Holsti & James N. Rosenau, 'The Structure of Foreign Policy Beliefs among American Opinion Leaders: After the Cold War' (1993) 22 *Millennium: Journal of International Studies* 235, p. 235.

[45] As described by Matthew A. Baum & Henry R. Nau, 'Foreign Policy Views and U.S. Standing in the World' (2009) 28 *Harvard Kennedy School Faculty Research Working Paper Series*, pp. 5–6.

[46] Ole R. Holsti, 'The Belief System and National Images: A Case Study' (1962) 6 *Journal of Conflict Resolution* 244.

[47] David Collier, Jody LaPorte & Jason Seawright, 'Putting Typologies to Work: Supplementary Material' (2012) 65 *Political Research Quarterly*, https://journals.sagepub.com/doi/suppl/10.1177/1065912912437162/suppl_file/Putting_Typologies-Supplementary_Material.pdf.

[48] Ibid.

those one-sidedly emphasized viewpoints into a unified analytical construct'.[49] These types are therefore analytical constructs that usefully capture patterns of observed behaviour, rather than an account of any particular person's belief system. Outlying cases and inconsistencies do not necessarily falsify the typology; rather, they remind that it represents a synthesised ideal.

Holsti first described a 'three-headed eagle' of foreign policy types in 1979; it comprised 'two versions of internationalism', identified previously by Michael Mandelbaum and William Schneider as 'conservative internationalism' and 'liberal internationalism', plus 'isolationism'.[50] *Conservative internationalism* emphasised elements of traditional *realpolitik*, including a zero-sum contest between the United States and its adversaries and the importance of US leadership maintaining a favourable balance of power.[51] In contrast, *liberal internationalism* rejected the wisdom of pursuing US primacy, instead emphasising global interdependence and thus the need for cooperation – particularly on economic and humanitarian issues.[52] Mandelbaum and Schneider then arranged these types in relation to a third 'noninternationalist' category[53] to conclude that foreign policy is best thought of in terms of two dimensions: 'an internationalist–isolationist dimension (*whether* the United States should play an active role in world affairs) and a cross-cutting liberal–conservative dimension (*what kind* of role it should play)'.[54]

Survey data from the Chicago Council on Foreign Relations (CCFR)[55] and the Foreign Policy Leadership Project (FPLP) corroborated a bi-dimensional ideological structure of support–oppose 'militant internationalism' (MI) and support–oppose 'cooperative internationalism' (CI), which together forms four foreign policy belief types (see Table 1).[56]

49 Max Weber, *The Methodology of the Social Sciences* (The Free Press, 1949), p. 90.

50 Ole R. Holsti, 'The Three-Headed Eagle: The United States and System Change' (1979) 23 *International Studies Quarterly* 339, p. 356; Michael Mandelbaum & William Schneider, 'The New Internationalisms' (1978) 2 *International Security* 81, p. 93.

51 Holsti, 'The Three-Headed Eagle', pp. 343–5.

52 Ibid., pp. 346–7.

53 Equivalent to Holsti's 'isolationism'.

54 Michael Mandelbaum & William Schneider, 'The New Internationalisms', in Kenneth A. Oye, Donald Rothchild & Robert J. Lieber (eds.), *Eagle Entangled: U.S. Foreign Policy in a Complex World* (Longman, 1979), p. 41, original emphasis.

55 Now The Chicago Council on Global Affairs.

56 Eugene R. Wittkopf, 'The Structure of Foreign Policy Attitudes: An Alternative View' (1981) 62 *Social Science Quarterly* 108, p. 115; Ole R. Holsti & James N. Rosenau, 'The Structure of Foreign Policy Attitudes among American Leaders' (1990) 52 *Journal of Politics* 94, p. 96.

Table 1 *Wittkopf-Holsti-Rosenau typology*

	Oppose MI	Support MI
Support CI	Accommodationists	Internationalists
Oppose CI	Isolationists	Hardliners

Accommodationists support CI and oppose MI. They adopt an internationalist focus according to a liberal worldview that emphasises non-traditional security threats such as democratisation and human rights, with a preference for working multilaterally through IL and institutions. *Internationalists* support both CI and MI. They have an internationalist focus but according to a conservative worldview that is willing to combine diplomatic cooperation with military superiority to maintain America's global position. *Isolationists* oppose both CI and MI. They resist unnecessary international involvement in order to protect liberal values at home. Finally, *hardliners* oppose CI and support MI. They adopt a nationalistic rather than international focus, but do so to uphold national security and America's global position rather than for liberal objectives.

Subsequent survey research confirmed that these dimensions structure the beliefs of both American masses and American foreign policy elites – rebutting pioneering findings by Philip Converse that elite foreign policy beliefs diverged from the beliefs of the mass public.[57] Eugene Wittkopf analysed the beliefs of 'leaders' within the CCFR survey data, taking them to be those respondents 'in leadership positions with the greatest influence upon and knowledge about foreign relations'.[58] Falling in this category are 'policymakers' in the sense used in this book, including members of Congress (in particular members of the Foreign Relations and Foreign Affairs committees) and the executive (including State Department officials and 'officials with international responsibilities from other government departments').[59] The real difference between elites and masses was in the distribution between types. Survey results demonstrated a relatively even distribution of the mass public among the

[57] See Philip E. Converse, 'The Nature of Belief Systems in Mass Publics (1964)' (2006) 18 *Critical Review* 1.

[58] Eugene R. Wittkopf & Michael A. Maggiotto, 'Elites and Masses: A Comparative Analysis of Attitudes toward America's World Role' (1983) 45 *Journal of Politics* 303, p. 308.

[59] Ibid., pp. 308–9, n. 9.

four types.[60] In contrast, leaders were more likely to support CI compared to the mass public, with a far greater distribution between the two internationalist quadrants (accommodationists and internationalists). This difference stemmed specifically from the occupancy of leadership positions itself rather than from the demographic characteristics of those leaders.

Distribution of leaders and masses among types was determined foremost by political ideology and party affiliation, with data indicating that self-identified liberals were more likely to adopt a support CI/oppose MI position. In contrast, conservatives and moderates were more likely to adopt a support MI/oppose CI position.[61] In terms of partisanship, this translated into a greater number of Democrats identifying as accommodationists, while internationalists and hardliners were more likely to be Republicans. Partisan affiliation of isolationists was less apparent but leaned toward Republican or independent.[62] Subsequent analysis of CCFR data by Joshua Busby and Jonathan Monten suggested an increase in the proportion of Republican elites categorised as hardliners, and thereby a narrowing gap between the mass public and elites in levels of support for both forms of internationalism.[63] In something of a prologue to the surge of 'populist-nationalism' in the 2016 US presidential election, the research showed forms of partisanship emerging from 2002, with growing support for CI among Democrat leaders matched by increasing support for MI among Republican leaders.[64] Busby and Monten's updated analysis nevertheless confirmed both the persistence of the WHR structure of beliefs and the continued concentration of leaders among internationalist types.

The WHR typology has been repeatedly verified through empirical data on the structure of foreign policy ideology among the American public and elites,[65] and through evidence that the types correlate with

[60] Holsti & Rosenau, 'The Structure of Foreign Policy Attitudes among American Leaders', p. 103; Eugene R. Wittkopf, 'What Americans Really Think about Foreign Policy' (1996) 19 *Washington Quarterly* 88, pp. 94–5.

[61] Eugene R. Wittkopf, 'Elites and Masses: Another Look at Attitudes toward America's World Role' (1987) 31 *International Studies Quarterly* 131, p. 134.

[62] Holsti & Rosenau, 'The Structure of Foreign Policy Beliefs among American Opinion Leaders: After the Cold War', pp. 248 & 278.

[63] Joshua W. Busby & Jonathan Monten, 'Who Are the Hardliners? Public Opinion and Republican Elite Attitudes on U.S. Foreign Policy after the Cold War', Annual Meeting of the International Studies Association, San Francisco, CA, 27–30 March 2008, pp. 17–18.

[64] Ibid., pp. 27–8.

[65] See Ole R. Holsti, *Public Opinion and American Foreign Policy* (University of Michigan Press, 2004).

domestic political beliefs.[66] The historical context of the typology was, of course, heavily influenced by Cold War thinking and US–Soviet relations. However, a 'remarkable continuity' in ideological structure followed the end of the Cold War.[67] Holsti and Rosenau traced the evidence across a period spanning the immediate post–Vietnam War to the post–Cold War era and concluded that belief structures have 'persisted through a period of historic international change'. That continuity is evident not only in 'high politics' on the causes of war and peace but also in emerging non-traditional security threats that span state boundaries.[68] As such, there is strong evidence that the WHR ideological structure is invariant over time and independent of changing distributions of international power. Critiques of the typology have been offered over the years, including that foreign policy beliefs are structured either by more[69] or by less[70] than the two MI/CI dimensions. No formulation has eclipsed the WHR scheme, however, in popularity or influence. Matthew Baum and Henry Nau more recently endorsed the typology as 'impressively reliable at predicting support or opposition to U.S. approaches toward foreign policy in general, and specific policy initiatives in particular'.[71] Alternative formulations may have merit, therefore, but the WHR has proven adequate to the task of providing an analytical typology of foreign policy ideology, while offering the advantages of parsimony and an impressive pedigree as the 'gold standard' within the literature.[72]

[66] Ole R. Holsti & James N. Rosenau, 'Liberals, Populists, Libertarians, and Conservatives: The Link between Domestic and International Affairs' (1996) 17 *International Political Science Review* 29; Brian C. Rathbun, 'Steeped in International Affairs?: The Foreign Policy Views of the Tea Party' (2012) 9 *Foreign Policy Analysis* 21.

[67] Shoon K. Murray, Jonathan A. Cowden & Bruce M. Russett, 'The Convergence of American Elites' Domestic Beliefs with Their Foreign Policy Beliefs' (1999) 25 *International Interactions* 153, p. 478.

[68] Holsti & Rosenau, 'The Structure of Foreign Policy Beliefs among American Opinion Leaders: After the Cold War', p. 252.

[69] See Brian C. Rathbun, 'Hierarchy and Community at Home and Abroad: Evidence of a Common Structure of Domestic and Foreign Policy Beliefs in American Elites' (2007) 51 *Journal of Conflict Resolution* 379 who introduces an 'isolationist dimension' independent from the MI/CI scheme. William O. Chittick, Keith R. Billingsley & Rick Travis, 'A Three-Dimensional Model of American Foreign Policy Beliefs' (1995) 39 *International Studies Quarterly* 313 introduces a 'third dimension' of 'multilateralism-unilateralism'.

[70] Murray, Cowden & Russett, in 'The Convergence of American Elites' Domestic Beliefs with Their Foreign Policy Beliefs', argue that a single ideological 'liberalism-conservatism' dimension constrains both the MI and the CI dimensions.

[71] Baum & Nau, 'Foreign Policy Views and U.S. Standing in the World', p. 3.

[72] Nincic & Ramos, 'Ideological Structure and Foreign Policy Preferences', p. 122.

Evidence from Diplomatic History

The WHR scheme is valuable for using quantitative research to map the interrelation between ideological beliefs, but it remains a parsimonious rendering of rich traditions of thought long shaping American foreign policy. Foremost, this history provides clear evidence of analogous dimensionality in attitudes to foreign policy. An early analysis by Frank Klingberg observed that the US foreign policy 'mood' has cycled between periods of 'extroversion' and 'introversion'.[73] Louis Hartz identified a similar pattern, but in the context of two distinct forms of a Lockean 'liberal tradition'.[74] The first is an 'exemplarist' strand that seeks to spread American values primarily by preserving the unique character of the nation as an example to the world.[75] This has meant promoting the superiority of the American example within the confines of the existing international order. Alternatively, American foreign policy has taken a 'messianic' form in which the United States seeks to actively spread exceptional values abroad. Here, the focus is on using American values as a blueprint for reforming the international order in line with its own values. For Hartz, the connection between these divergent outlooks is that 'absolute national morality is inspired either to withdraw from "alien" things or to transform them: it cannot live in comfort constantly by their side'. In consequence, liberalism can variously manifest in internationalist or nationalist form so that, for America, 'messianism is the polar counterpart to its isolationism'.[76] Hartz's thesis of a defining liberal tradition has not gone unchallenged, however, with scholars such as Anatol Lieven describing the importance of an 'American antithesis' grounded not in universal values but in particularistic ethnoreligious roots.[77] For William Brock, the universal and liberal view of American purpose has been 'constantly at war with the idea that Americanism belongs exclusively to the American people and must be defended against alien influences rather than shared with mankind'.[78] In these terms,

73 Frank L. Klingberg, 'The Historical Alternation of Moods in American Foreign Policy' (1952) 4 *World Politics* 239, pp. 239–40.

74 Louis Hartz, *The Liberal Tradition in America: An Interpretation of American Political Thought since the Revolution* (Harcourt Brace, 1955).

75 The term is Brands': see H. W. Brands, *What America Owes the World: The Struggle for the Soul of Foreign Policy* (Cambridge University Press, 1998), p. vii.

76 Hartz, *The Liberal Tradition in America*, p. 286.

77 Anatol Lieven, *America Right or Wrong: An Anatomy of American Nationalism* (Oxford University Press, 2005), p. 5.

78 William R. Brock, 'Americanism', in Dennis S. R. Welland (ed.), *The United States: A Companion to American Studies* (Methuen, 1974), p. 59.

a former Trump administration official warned of the contempt engendered when liberal-minded policymakers set aside parochial defence of the American nation and instead act as if it is 'immoral to prefer one's fellow citizens to strangers on the opposite side of the world'.[79]

These connections were recognised in Holsti and Rosenau's earlier work, which noted that their isolationists 'revived a theme with venerable roots in American political thought – that the ability to nurture and sustain democratic institutions at home is inversely related to the scope of the nation's commitments abroad'.[80] They cited as evidence George Kennan's contemplation: 'I think I am a semi-isolationist.'[81] Similarly, the strong connection between domestic liberalism and accomodationist beliefs is explained as the legacy of the ideas of democracy promotion, human rights and collective security in the foreign policy of Woodrow Wilson.[82] Finally, hardliners are described in terms directly attributable to what is sometimes labelled the 'Jacksonian' tradition of foreign policy, with strong Southern roots and an emphasis on military virtues.[83] In the WHR typology, hardliners are identified as predominantly Southern, typified by former chairman of the Foreign Relations Committee Senator Jesse Helms and 'strongly pro-military and right wing, but staunchly nationalist and outspokenly protectionist opponents of the New Deal'.[84]

Fleshing out the WHR model requires attention to the sets of ideas that have developed around each point of intersection across American diplomatic history. Policymakers' beliefs are not derived from the logic of the scheme itself, but are informed by culture and diplomatic history, which have rendered determinate sets of ideas about policy means and ends. Freeden notes the importance of cultural and historical influences rendering a circumscribed 'range of meanings and arguments' from

[79] Michael Anton, 'America and the Liberal International Order' (2017) 1 *American Affairs* 113.

[80] Ole R. Holsti & James N. Rosenau, 'Consensus Lost. Consensus Regained?: Foreign Policy Beliefs of American Leaders, 1976–1980' (1986) 30 *International Studies Quarterly* 375, p. 379.

[81] George Kennan, 'An Appeal for Thought' (1978) *The New York Times Magazine*, May 7, cited in Ole R. Holsti & James N. Rosenau, *American Leadership in World Affairs* (George Allen & Unwin Ltd, 1984), p. 123.

[82] Holsti & Rosenau, 'Liberals, Populists, Libertarians, and Conservatives', pp. 47–9.

[83] Walter R. Mead, *Special Providence: American Foreign Policy and How It Changed the World* (Routledge, 2002), pp. 227 & 254–5.

[84] Thomas Ferguson, 'The Right Consensus?: Holsti and Rosenau's New Foreign Policy Belief Surveys' (1986) 30 *International Studies Quarterly* 411, p. 414.

a broader ideology.[85] Similarly, for Hunt, this process permits a 'relatively coherent, emotionally charged, and conceptually interlocking sets of ideas',[86] while for Colin Dueck, 'culture' establishes a 'set of interlocking values, beliefs, and assumptions that are held collectively by a given group and passed on through socialisation'.[87] These all suggest the formation of an American foreign policy *Weltanschauung*, largely defining the universe of acceptable policy options. The two dimensions of the WHR scheme provide a skeleton for analytically ordering more diffuse sets of competing ideas that American policymakers hold about the nature of American power and its purpose in the world. Perhaps the strongest evidence of the WHR typology's external validity is that the four ideal types are corroborated by these well-established sets of foreign policy beliefs that precede the specific typology by many decades and even centuries.

The WHR schema now sits atop an identifiable body of literature that draws upon American diplomatic history to divide American foreign policy into four distinct types.[88] These formulations necessarily differ given that they are developed through a forensic reconstruction of observed patterns of conduct. Inevitable overlaps and inconsistencies exist among the types, but a review of this literature reveals sufficient correspondence to treat these as corroborating the approach. The most well-known is that of Walter Russell Mead, who argues that his classification of the Wilsonian, Hamiltonian, Jeffersonian and Jacksonian traditions of thought allows for the interpretation of 'American foreign policy as more of a unified whole and less as a sequence of unrelated episodes'.[89] Mead sees these four traditions as an organic product of the American experience, with each deeply rooted in regional, economic, social and class interests. More specifically, he speculates that the traditions may be

85 Freeden, *Ideology*, p. 50.

86 Hunt, *Ideology and U.S. Foreign Policy*, p. 12.

87 Colin Dueck, *Reluctant Crusaders: Power, Culture, and Change in American Grand Strategy* (Princeton University Press, 2006), p. 15.

88 See Mead, *Special Providence*; Dueck, *Reluctant Crusaders*; Alexander Nacht, 'U.S. Foreign Policy Strategies' (1995) 18 *Washington Quarterly* 195, p. 203; Barry R. Posen & Andrew L. Ross, 'Competing Visions for U.S. Grand Strategy' (1996/7) 21 *International Security* 5, p. 4; Henry R. Nau, *At Home Abroad: Identity and Power in American Foreign Policy* (Cornell University Press, 2002). For related but alternative four-part typologies see Henry R. Nau, *Conservative Internationalism* (Princeton University Press, 2008), p. 27; Colin Dueck, *Hard Line: The Republican Party and U.S. Foreign Policy since World War II* (Princeton University Press, 2010); John van Oudenaren, 'Transatlantic Bipolarity and the End of Multilateralism' (2005) 120 *Political Science Quarterly* 1, p. 65.

89 Mead, *Special Providence*, pp. 87–90.

traced to the four 'folkways' inherited from the regional cultures of the British Isles.[90]

Wilsonians focus on the moral dimension of US political culture and the interests in spreading these values internationally through democracy promotion and the rule of law. Mead sees the roots of this tradition lying deep in nineteenth-century American missionary activities[91] so that, despite the moniker, 'there were Wilsonians long before Woodrow Wilson was born'.[92] This tradition is more than mere idealism, emerging 'as a middle way between reactionary militarism and revolutionary internationalism'.[93] *Hamiltonians* focus on strengthening the state through an alliance between government and big business, which serves as the basis for policies directed toward protecting the nation's economic power.[94] *Jeffersonians* emphasise liberty at home as the pre-eminent American value, and thus focus on avoiding the corrupting influence of an activist foreign policy. For Mead, this is the only tradition 'that believes history is not necessarily on the side of the American experiment', producing a fear that overseas commitments erode American liberty through both neglect and centralisation of government power.[95] H. W. Brands' 'exemplarists' terminology captures the idea that America owes the world only the example of its constitutional freedoms. Going any further threatens to 'jeopardize American values at the source. In attempting to save the world, and probably failing, America would risk losing its democratic soul.'[96] Finally, *Jacksonians* represent a nationalist-populist tradition in US foreign policy, which values the security and preservation of the American 'folk community' above all else. 'American exceptionalism' is seen by Jacksonians 'not as a function of the universal appeal of American ideas, or even as a function of a unique American vocation to transform the world, but rather as rooted in the country's

[90] Ibid., p. 87, citing David H. Fischer, *Albion's Seed: Four British Folkways in America* (Oxford University Press, 1989).

[91] Mead, *Special Providence*, p. 139.

[92] Ibid., p. 88.

[93] Eileen P. Scully, 'The United States and International Affairs, 1789-1919', in Michael Grossberg & Christopher L. Tomlins (eds.), *The Cambridge History of Law in America: Volume 2: The Long Nineteenth Century (1789–1920)* (Cambridge University Press, 2008), p. 612.

[94] Hamilton has been described as 'the American Machiavelli': see John Lamberton Harper, *American Machiavelli: Alexander Hamilton and the Origins of U.S. Foreign Policy* (Cambridge University Press, 2004).

[95] Mead, *Special Providence*, pp. 183 & 217.

[96] Brands, *What America Owes the World*, pp. vii–viii, 1–2 & 4.

singular commitment to the equality and dignity of individual American citizens'.[97] Mead argues that US foreign policy is notable for the continuity of these four traditions in shaping America's worldview and the character of its international engagement.[98] The history of US foreign policy is thus seen as one of the traditions vying for political influence separately and together in shifting combinations. Each has contributed to national power and proven naturally capable of complementing one another as if led by Adam Smith's invisible hand.[99]

The parallels between the WHR and Mead typologies are obvious. Holsti states that, although never attributed as such, the four types 'bear more than a passing resemblance to the distinction between the Hamiltonian (internationalists), Wilsonian (accommodationists), Jeffersonian (isolationists), and Jacksonian (hard-liners) approaches to American foreign policy'.[100] The WHR typology has indeed been treated as synonymous with Mead's for analytical purposes, with the primary difference being its more rigorous structure.[101] Mead himself disavows any intent to 'prove' that policymakers hold these beliefs, or indeed to treat his typology as a model suited to empirical testing.[102] His work is presented as a 'classificatory typology' listing named types, rather than a 'conceptual typology' constructed on underlying dimensions.[103] Nevertheless, Mead's typology exhibits the same dimensionality as the WHR scheme, with Wilsonianism and Hamiltonianism classed together as specific types of a 'globalist' tradition, while Jeffersonianism and Jacksonianism comprise 'nationalist' traditions.[104] Moreover, Mead emphasises the liberal values at the core of both Wilsonianism and Jeffersonianism, which distinguishes them from the other two traditions. Other variants of the typology confirm the same dimensions. In Nau's examination, his 'internationalists' and 'realists' are actively engaged in

97 Walter R. Mead, 'The Jacksonian Revolt: American Populism and the Liberal Order' (2017) 96 *Foreign Affairs* 2, p. 3.

98 Mead, *Special Providence*, p. 92.

99 Ibid., pp. 95 & 311.

100 Holsti, *Public Opinion and American Foreign Policy*, p. 54. Mead emphasises that his typology was developed independently of the WHR or associated approaches: Walter R. Mead, Personal Communication with Author (4 November 2013).

101 Busby & Monten, 'Who Are the Hardliners?'.

102 Mead, *Special Providence*, p. 89.

103 See David Collier, Jody LaPorte & Jason Seawright, 'Putting Typologies to Work: Concept-Formation, Measurement, and Analytic Rigor' (2012) 65 *Political Research Quarterly* 217, p. 218.

104 Mead, *Special Providence*, pp. 175 & 268.

the international sphere, while his 'neoisolationists' and 'nationalists' resist international engagement.[105] Dueck is more explicit, setting out two dimensions of *strongly/weakly committed to liberalism* and *strongly/weakly committed to limited liability*, which functionally replicate the WHR dimensions and resulting typology.[106]

A similar distribution of elites and masses between the historical and WHR types is also evident. Mead emphasises the popular and mass appeal of Jacksonianism and Jeffersonianism, in contrast to the greater support among foreign policy elites for his two internationalist traditions.[107] Reflecting on the 2016 US presidential election, Mead observed the nationalist mood among a 'public increasingly disenchanted' with the Hamiltonian-Wilsonian internationalism long favoured by the 'foreign policy establishment'.[108] Dueck likewise emphasises that, of his two internationalist traditions, the Wilsonian equivalent has been the most influential among elites, while his Hamiltonian equivalent has consistently failed to resonate with the American public.[109] These suppositions accord with the empirical evidence that leaders and foreign policymakers are located in the internationalist quadrants in far greater proportions than the mass public.

Revisiting American Exceptionalism

A crucial implication of thinking in terms of diplomatic history is that this brings the WHR structure to bear on the divergent strands of 'exceptionalism' evident in legal analysis. American exceptionalism has itself been called an ideology that has 'deeply shaped the structure of social and political thought'.[110] However, in the context of foreign policy, Siobhán McEvoy-Levy prefers to describe American exceptionalism as '*the* "para-ideological" umbrella' encompassing the many recurrent themes of America's global engagement. By this, she means that the concept lacks the coherence of an ideology, but rather is 'a crystallization of a set of related ideas which explain the world and the US role therein'.[111] That is

[105] Nau, *At Home Abroad*, p. 43.
[106] See Dueck, *Reluctant Crusaders*, pp. 31–3.
[107] Mead, *Special Providence*, p. 267.
[108] Mead, 'The Jacksonian Revolt', p. 2.
[109] Dueck, *Reluctant Crusaders*, pp. 31–3.
[110] Dorothy Ross, *The Origins of American Social Science* (Cambridge University Press, 1992), pp. xviii & 22.
[111] Siobhán McEvoy-Levy, *American Exceptionalism and US Foreign Policy: Public Diplomacy at the End of the Cold War* (Palgrave, 2001), p. 23, original emphasis.

the conclusion preferred in this book, which does not find exceptionalist thinking to meet the features of an ideology. Rather, the interplay between America's uniquely preponderant power and the incentive to understand and explain its own normative significance has produced exceptionalist beliefs as components of broader foreign policy ideologies. Each of the four American foreign policy ideologies has settled on distinct explanations for American uniqueness that, when taken together, represent the different faces of what has become known as American exceptionalism. The term is indeterminate as a categorical label and only provides insight into American foreign policy where the particular variants of exceptionalist ideas are specified as liberal, illiberal, internationalist or nationalist.

Mead directly describes Jacksonian thinking as combining 'a firm belief in American exceptionalism and an American world mission with deep scepticism about the United States' ability to create a liberal world order'.[112] But the label applies equally to his Wilsonians' perception of an 'American duty to remake the world in its image'[113] and the Jeffersonian view that the American Revolution 'was the start of a new era in the world'.[114] Baum and Nau are more explicit in identifying each of the WHR types as entailing a particular interpretation of exceptionalist thinking, observing that 'Americans do not have a single, uniform view of American exceptionalism or foreign policy. Instead, they have several distinct ones.'[115] For all versions of the four-part typology, the outlier in terms of exceptionalist beliefs is the WHR 'internationalist' type or Mead's 'Hamiltonian' tradition. Notably Dueck as well as Baum and Nau simply label this the 'realist' tradition. For Dueck, the internationalism of this type flows not from exceptionalist beliefs but rather 'from an attempt to promote the national interest in a balanced manner'.[116] Likewise, for Baum and Nau, adherents 'do not consider America as exceptional at all but ordinary like all other powers'.[117] Exceptionalist ideas nevertheless remain a defining component within each of the alternative foreign policy ideologies.

[112] Walter R. Mead, 'The Tea Party and American Foreign Policy: What Populism Means for Globalism' (2011) 90 *Foreign Affairs* 28, p. 35.
[113] Mead, *Special Providence*, p. 147.
[114] Ibid., p. 180.
[115] Baum & Nau, 'Foreign Policy Views and U.S. Standing in the World', pp. 5–6.
[116] Dueck, *Reluctant Crusaders*, p. 33.
[117] Baum & Nau, 'Foreign Policy Views and U.S. Standing in the World', pp. 5–6 & 26.

Foreign Policy Ideology in Legal Scholarship

Legal scholarship has been unwilling to acknowledge the influence of foreign policy ideology on receptions of IL for deep-seated epistemological and disciplinary reasons. The dominant narrative in the discipline is of a unified body of rules and institutions, with content and obligations determined independently of the identity and ideological commitments of state subjects of IL.[118] For scholarship built on these foundations, 'universalist assumptions and aspirations can make comparativism seem both irrelevant and potentially dangerous'.[119] Shirley Scott seeks to address the significance of ideology in IL, without engaging the comparativist problem, by approaching the *idea* of IL itself as an ideology built on universalist assumptions.[120] The core belief of this ideology is that 'international law is ultimately distinguishable from, and superior to, politics'.[121] Here, Scott conceives ideology in IL as a form of 'legal rhetoric in inter-State correspondence'[122] rather than as part of the belief system of any state or group of policymakers, with no requirement that any 'believe the ideology to be true'.[123] Yet, the primary power of ideology lies not in providing a rhetorical argument external to those it is directed at but in its ability to constitute the beliefs and actions of its adherents. A system of rhetorical claims remains subordinate to internalised ideological beliefs of legal policymakers situated in a particular national context. The insight from the present analysis is that an array of foreign policy ideologies are each likely to be associated with a particularistic 'idea of international law',[124] which thus manifest in the act of contesting rather than confirming a singular ideology of IL.

The internalised content of political ideologies is what makes 'legal doctrine intelligible' to particular policymakers, which must therefore be substantiated as an empirical fact rather than as a theorised

[118] Scott refers to this as the 'rule-book' image of international law: see Shirley V. Scott, 'Identifying the Source and Nature of a State's Political Obligation towards International Law' (2005) 1 *Journal of International Law and International Relations* 49, p. 56.

[119] Anthea Roberts, *Is International Law International?* (Oxford University Press, 2017), p. 3.

[120] Shirley V. Scott, *International Law, US Power: The United States' Quest for Legal Security* (Cambridge University Press, 2012), pp. 211–15 & 234–5.

[121] Scott, 'Identifying the Source and Nature of a State's Political Obligation', pp. 54–5.

[122] Shirley V. Scott, 'International Law As Ideology: Theorising the Relationship between International Law and International Politics' (1994) 5 *European Journal of International Law* 313, p. 319.

[123] Scott, 'Beyond Compliance', p. 44.

[124] Scott, 'International Law As Ideology', p. 318.

ideal.[125] Phillip Trimble undertakes that task in the analogous case of foreign policy ideology shaping competing interpretations of the US Constitution. Looking at the shifting balance of powers between the executive and Congress, he finds that 'the dominance of the Presidency is intertwined with the prevailing ideology of U.S. foreign policy, which includes a notion of U.S. example and leadership in world affairs that requires executive initiative. The President's constitutional foreign affairs power must be defined in light of this background.'[126] Constitutional interpretation thereby must 'accommodate the self-image of world leadership that the American body politic has adopted and that forms the core of American foreign policy ideology'.[127] Identifying the construction of legal meaning through ideology furnishes specific beliefs, beyond simply treating law as its own ideology. This book accordingly continues down the path of the small selection of authors who have explored the ways that substantive beliefs of American foreign policy ideology structure competing conceptions of IL.

The leading analysis for present purposes remains Harlan Cohen's sophisticated 2003 article 'The American Challenge to International Law',[128] in which he poses the question: 'Can inconsistent [IL] policies be explained as mere hypocrisy, as the pragmatic application of hegemonic power?' The answer is no:[129]

> Pragmatic assessments of American self-interest undoubtedly played a role . . . But such an answer seems empty. Observers have long noticed the power of ideas in American foreign policy, and it has become commonplace to discuss how American foreign policy history reflects various *intellectual trends* – some dating to the founding of the Republic. It seems strange to discuss American perceptions of international law as somehow divorced from these intellectual trends. Ideas have long shaped American perceptions of the outside world and the United States' relation to it; it seems logical that those same ideas would play a role in defining the tools of American international relations – the possible, the useful, the dangerous.[130]

[125] J. M. Balkin, 'Ideology As Constraint' (1991) 43 *Stanford Law Review* 1133, p. 1138.

[126] Phillip R. Trimble, 'The President's Foreign Affairs Power' (1989) 83 *American Journal of International Law* 750, p. 754.

[127] Ibid., p. 757.

[128] Harlan G. Cohen, 'The American Challenge to International Law: A Tentative Framework for Debate' (2003) 28 *Yale Journal of International Law* 551.

[129] Ibid., p. 553.

[130] Ibid., pp. 553–4, emphasis added, citations omitted.

Cohen's objective is 'to re-explain the American perception of international law as an extension of intellectual trends in American foreign policy',[131] for which he specifically cites Mead's four traditions as exemplars.[132]

Cohen identifies a specific 'foundational ideology' that he terms 'liberal constitutionalism as a utopian world vision' and that manifests in two strands equivalent to the accomodationist/Wilsonian and isolationist/Jeffersonian types, respectively.[133] The ideology is composed of America's 'particular mix of democracy, free-market capitalism, and constitutional protection of human rights', presented as a model for the rest of the world.[134] In this ideology, America 'presupposes that it is the only truly legitimate state' and therefore that 'the American utopian vision is in itself the most true international law'.[135] The crucial insight offered by Cohen's ideological analysis is that apparently hypocritical policy 'may actually be informed by a coherent, specifically American conception of international law'.[136] In consequence, 'international law cannot ignore ideology' and instead must engage with existing ideational commitments for legal doctrines and practice to be accepted as legitimate and effective.[137] In subsequent writings, Cohen reiterated: 'Predicting the positions future American administrations might take on international law and institutions requires a deeper understanding of international law's place within competing foreign policy ideas and philosophies.'[138]

Cohen is not alone in adapting Mead's typology to US IL policy, with a handful of other legal scholars being equally attracted to its pithy rendering of complex ideas into digestible categories.[139] John Noyes and David Bederman each specifically set out elements of IL policy drawn from Mead's four traditions, albeit while accepting that the impact of types 'cannot

131 Ibid., pp. 554–5.

132 Ibid., p. 553, n. 13.

133 Ibid., pp. 555 & 558–9.

134 Ibid., pp. 555, n. 19 & 558.

135 Ibid., pp. 562–3.

136 Ibid., p. 556.

137 Ibid., p. 574.

138 Harlan G. Cohen, 'Historical American Perspectives on International Law' (2009) 15 *Journal of International & Comparative Law* 485, p. 489.

139 See Julian Ku, 'Explaining American Foreign Policy: Obama's Liberal Internationalism v. Bush's Neoconservativism', *Opinio Juris*, 6 April 2010, http://opiniojuris.org/2010/04/06/explaining-american-foreign-policy-obamas-liberal-internationalism-v-bushs-neoconservativism/.

always be neatly compartmentalized', with 'overlap in views' likely.[140] Noyes' approach is notable for taking seriously the implications of the foreign policy ideology approach: employing his account of Jacksonian opposition to UNCLOS in order to strategically engage Jacksonians on their own terms.[141] This targeted dialogue is precisely the type of contribution that ideology can make when engaging American IL policy. Philippe Lagassé considers the specific case of the ICC, setting out competing conceptions of IL informed by Walter McDougall's ideologies of 'exceptionalism, unilateralism and Wilsonianism'.[142] Like the foregoing authors, Lagassé argues that characterisations of hypocritical US ICC policy are misplaced to the extent that they overlook basic ideological conflicts. McDougall's exceptionalists, for example, mirror Jeffersonians in their rejection of any incursion on protections for individual liberty under US constitutional government.[143] Ratification of the Rome Statute becomes untenable for conflicting with the constitutionally guaranteed right to a trial by jury, protection against double jeopardy and the status of the US Supreme Court as the truly supreme judicial body of the US legal system.[144] Wilsonians, in contrast, do support the ICC, as a key element of an overarching desire to promote international legal structures in furtherance of the rule of law.[145] Lagassé concludes: 'Were American foreign policy consistent and unified in its aspirations, . . . [accusations of hypocrisy] might be accurate. American foreign policy, however, is not driven by a single philosophy.'[146]

The Structure of American International Law Policy

Reviewing legal scholarship on the influence of foreign policy ideology leads to two main conclusions. The first is that this is a compelling response to the gap between existing legal accounts and observed

140 John E. Noyes, 'The United States and the Law of the Sea Convention: U.S. Views on the Settlement of International Law Disputes in International Tribunals and U.S. Courts' (2009) 1 *Berkeley Journal of International Law Publicist* 27, p. 32; David J. Bederman, 'Globalization, International Law and United States Foreign Policy' (2001) 50 *Emory Law Journal* 717.

141 See generally Noyes, 'The United States and the Law of the Sea Convention', p. 627.

142 Phillippe Lagassé, 'The International Criminal Court and the Foreign Policies of the United States' (2004) 59 *International Journal* 433. See Walter A. McDougall, *Promised Land, Crusader State: The American Encounter with the World since 1776* (Houghton Mifflin, 1997).

143 McDougall, *Promised Land, Crusader State*, pp. 37–8.

144 Lagassé, 'The ICC', p. 436.

145 Ibid., p. 431; McDougall, *Promised Land, Crusader State*, p. 136.

146 Lagassé, 'The ICC', p. 442.

Table 2 *Ideological structure of American international law policy*

	Liberal	Illiberal
Internationalist	Liberal internationalists *(accommodationists)** *(Wilsonians)†*	Illiberal internationalists *(internationalists)** *(Hamiltonians)†*
Nationalist	Liberal nationalists *(isolationists)** *(Jeffersonians)†*	Illiberal nationalists *(nationalists)** *(Jacksonians)†*

* Wittkopf's terminology (1981); † Mead's terminology (2002).

contradictions within American IL policy. The second is that the literature presents opportunities for further development, including synthesising the inductive WHR typology with the deductive typologies drawn from diplomatic history to establish an analytical model of four ideal types of American IL policy. The ambition is to present complex conclusions from political science in a parsimonious framework available for legal scholars wanting to avoid specialised political science methodology. Moreover, understanding the ideas of each of the WHR types is artificially limited if disconnected from their historical underpinnings. With these objects in mind, the typologies are synthesised as the intersection of an internationalist–nationalist *governance* dimension with a liberal–illiberal *values* dimension, which forms four ideal type IL policies: *liberal internationalism*, *illiberal internationalism*, *liberal nationalism* and *illiberal nationalism* (see Table 2).

Internationalist–Nationalist Governance Dimension

Parsimonious explanations from political power predict that a powerful state will tend to 'oscillate between two poles: instrumentalization of and withdrawal from international law'.[147] In ideological terms, this 'governance' dimension measures US commitment to governing foreign policy through the international legal system. Legal policymakers have at times demonstrated a belief that American interests are enhanced by actively engaging to develop the architecture of international legal rules and

[147] Nico Krisch, 'International Law in Times of Hegemony: Unequal Power and the Shaping of the International Legal Order' (2005) 16 *European Journal of International Law* 369, p. 379.

institutions. In this view, American interests and security are dependent on the nature of the world beyond national borders, with the international legal order being a meaningful determinant of how that world looks. This also entails a commitment to elite authority in IL, since global governance is by its nature a domain properly controlled by legal and diplomatic personnel with technocratic expertise on how to advance identified interests through law. Internationalism may be expressed through a diversity of values and rationales, but there is evidence of a persistent belief in the strategic advantages of governance through a global system of law.

Alternatively, legal policymakers have identified the national interest in decreasing American enmeshment in international institutions and law. In this view, governing through law and institutions located at the national level is a superior strategy for meeting American foreign policy interests, which should therefore be shielded from increasing global entanglement. In particular, policymakers with a nationalist commitment are more concerned with how certain IL policies 'will best advance the kind of *domestic* policies and order they wish to promote'.[148] Nationalist positions are by their nature a domain centred on and more directly responsive to popular preferences of ordinary American citizens, rather than of foreign policy elites. In this sense, the concept of 'populism' in American IL policy can be best understood not as itself an ideology but as a position along the ideological governance dimension.[149] The governance dimension thus encompasses the WHR 'support CI–oppose CI' dimension, Mandelbaum and Schneider's 'internationalist–isolationist' dimension and the internationalist–nationalist dimension evident in diplomatic history.

Liberal–Illiberal Values Dimension

The second dimension concerns the 'values' informing American IL policy. At one end are American legal policymakers who identify the legitimacy of IL in its realisation of universally defined liberal values, as encapsulated in human rights and the protections of US constitutional democracy. The essence of liberalism is that, in questions of governance,

[148] Mead, *Special Providence*, p. 176, emphasis added.

[149] Common categorisation of populism as 'a thin-centered ideology' indicates the awkwardness of defining it as an ideology in its own right: see Cas Mudde & Cristóbal R. Kaltwasser, 'Populism and (Liberal) Democracy: A Framework for Analysis', in Cas Mudde & Cristóbal R. Kaltwasser (eds.), *Populism in Europe and the Americas: Threat or Corrective for Democracy?* (Cambridge University Press, 2012), p. 8.

natural persons be accorded 'equal concern and respect.'[150] IL thus has Lockean foundations in which people, rather than states or classes of people, are its fundamental sovereign subjects holding 'certain unalienable Rights'.[151] To this end, liberal conceptions have tied the legitimacy of IL to a functioning municipal rule of law, which is the necessary foundation for securing substantive democratic values and fundamental human rights as 'the core of international law'.[152] Crucially, liberalism in US IL policy means only recognising the equal *normative* status of all people but does not necessarily translate into an equal *political* status for those outside of the American polity, whose perceived rights remain dependant on governance beliefs.

Conversely, IL policy has been motivated by illiberal values – being any values that prevail over the defence of universally defined liberal rights as the foundation for IL. Specifically, these include strengthening national security, using foreign policy to maintain a particular balance of global power and upholding parochial ethnocultural values and group identity. Illiberal approaches to IL policy reject the principle of promoting cosmopolitan values that transcend the state, focusing instead on guarding what is uniquely American. As such, there is an equally strong case that the values dimension captures the 'oppose MI–support MI' dimension, Mandelbaum and Schneider's 'liberal–conservative' dimension and the liberal–illiberal dimension evident in diplomatic history.

Chapter Conclusion

Evidence from empirical data and American diplomatic history casts foreign policy ideology as all-pervasive in structuring conceptions of IL. In this respect it is a mistake to treat power-based accounts such as Goldsmith and Posner's *Limits of International Law* as 'stripping away the veil of ideology'.[153] Their largely illiberal internationalist account is shaped by a particular ideology interpreting power and interests no less than the liberal internationalist approaches they critique. The same

[150] Ronald Dworkin, *A Matter of Principle* (Harvard University Press, 1985), p. 190.

[151] See Brian Rathbun, 'Wedges and Widgets: Liberalism, Libertarianism, and the Trade Attitudes of the American Mass Public and Elites' (2016) 12 *Foreign Policy Analysis* 85, p. 90.

[152] Anne-Marie Slaughter & Jose E. Alvarez, 'A Liberal Theory of International Law' (2000) 94 *Proceedings of the Annual Meeting (American Society of International Law)* 240, p. 246.

[153] Kenneth Anderson, 'Remarks by an Idealist on the Realism of the Limits of International Law' (2005) 34 *Georgia Journal of International and Comparative Law* 253, p. 257.

proviso applies to Philippe Sands' criticism of legal advice rendered by Goldsmith to the US government; that 'ideology infects the content of the actual advice, bending it to support a particular conclusion'.[154] The IL conception advocated by Sands is itself constituted by ideology, and thus the contention is really about the normative and political merits of competing ideologies. This chapter has made these connections explicit by explaining precisely how power, jurisprudence and political culture are related through the concept of foreign policy ideology.

A passing similarity exists between the typology developed in this chapter and an earlier set of four conceptions of IL identified by Wolfgang Friedman.[155] In order respective to that presented here, they were: 'genuine belief in the supremacy of international legal order over national sovereignty'; 'use of international law as rhetorical argument'; 'limited respect for the "live and let live" rules of international law as an appropriate guide to the conduct of nations, subject to the overriding national interests of States'; and an 'attitude of open contempt for international law as incompatible with the nature of man, which is controlled by the survival of the fittest, and the destiny of nations, which is realised in constant struggle and war'.[156] Although this typology is an imperfect fit,[157] Friedman draws the same conclusion that 'much depends on the Legal Adviser's conception of the appropriate role for international legal considerations in the formulation of foreign policy'.[158] The promise of Friedman's approach, and the one developed here, is that the idiosyncrasies and contradictions in American IL policy will be revealed as the consequence of ideology structuring IL policy in ways quite predictable and internally coherent.

Importantly, the present rationale for developing a typology of four conceptions of IL is not to make a normative argument that law therefore *ought* to be constructed upon the 'parochial foundation' of

154 Philippe Sands, 'Poodles and Bulldogs: The United States, Britain, and the International Rule of Law' (2009) 84 *Indiana Law Journal* 1357, p. 1364.

155 Wolfgang Friedmann, 'The Reality of International Law: A Reappraisal' (1971) 10 *Columbia Journal of Transnational Law* 46.

156 Ibid., pp. 46–51.

157 Apart from a lack of dimensionality, his types are also historically bounded to specific examples drawn from WWII, during which he had fled Nazi Germany, and from the Cold War, during which he was writing.

158 See Tamara L. Tompkins, 'A Theory of Ethical Conduct for the Legal Advisor to the State Department: Applied for a Fresh Look at Abraham Sofaer and the ABM Treaty Reinterpretation Debacle' (1993) 7 *Georgetown Journal of Legal Ethics* 523, p. 546.

American foreign policy ideology.[159] Cohen suggests that IL may need to do so strategically in order to resonate with the American polity, albeit with the aim of locking the United States into dialectical progress toward 'self-perpetuating universal norms' over the long term.[160] This is itself a utopian argument that US policymakers are receptive to progressive change, as liberal internationalism assumes for global politics. This may indeed be one advantage of understanding ideological structures, but uncovering the interconnectedness of legal ideals and power is equally a powerful tool for unmasking and managing hegemonic interests in the present, especially where they are least visible to those articulating them. Accordingly, the remaining task in Part I of this book is to apply the theorised ideological structure to define elements of competing meanings of the 'international rule of law'. Identifying divergent logics internal to law promises a framework for understanding the observed contradictions at the heart of this book, and therefore for contesting global power.

159 Cohen, 'The American Challenge to International Law', p. 575.
160 Ibid., p. 577.

3

Competing Conceptions of the International Rule of Law

This concluding section of Part I looks through the lens of American foreign policy ideology to define the core elements of competing conceptions of IL. To make this possible, the chapter begins with an institutional definition of the 'international rule of law' drawn from classic tripartite formulations in Anglo-American jurisprudence. Translated to the global level, three questions must be answered to constitute an analytically useful meaning: how to develop non-arbitrary global governance; how to define equality under IL; and how to determine the integrity of international judicial power. A set of coherent answers to each of these questions will constitute a distinct ideologically informed meaning of the international rule of law.

The development of a working definition moves beyond any attempt to find a universal and fixed meaning of *the* international rule of law by instead identifying various 'received' conceptions of the rule of law that exist in the minds of identified legal policymakers. The first of these ideal type conceptions is the 'legalism' evident in the scholarship and practice of states, NGOs and individuals who have challenged American IL policy. The elements of this conception are that the international rule of law requires formalised development of global governance; a commitment to the sovereign equality of states; and separation of international judicial powers between state subjects of IL and international legal institutions. Opposition to US policy has converged sufficiently around legalist principles for this to constitute a meaningful ideal type, without denying that each state may hold its own idiosyncratic conception of law.

Turning to American legal policymakers, the constitutive elements of four rule of law conceptions are identified according to the underlying dimensions and ideal types of general foreign policy ideology. *Liberal internationalism* is centred on America's global mission to promote the liberty of natural persons through IL. The principles of this conception are: the transnational development of IL; the promotion of liberal over sovereign equality; and democratic checks and balances on international judicial power. *Illiberal internationalism* is focused on preserving national security by maintaining the capacity to project global power through law. This translates into principles of: pragmatic development of IL; maintaining hegemonic privilege; and consent as the basis for ordering international judicial powers. For *liberal nationalism* the core of the international rule of law is guarding liberal protections afforded by American constitutional government against external corruption. Resulting rule of law principles are: the protective development of IL as a shield; upholding the inviolability of national sovereignty; and vertical separation between international and municipal judicial powers. Finally, *illiberal nationalism* perceives IL as a threat to America's national security and distinctive cultural identity. This translates into principles of: permissively developing IL to maximise US autonomy; relativity of state sovereignty; and upholding the supremacy of municipal over international judicial powers. The meaning of 'coherence' in American IL policy becomes that a legal policymaker's stance on any one of the three international rule of law elements is a reliable indicator of positions taken on remaining elements.

The Indeterminacy of the International Rule of Law

Ambiguity in the meaning of American policymakers' commitment to 'the international rule of law' is symptomatic of a longstanding but inconclusive wider debate about the meaning of the concept.[1] References are ubiquitous by international legal scholars and practitioners both supportive and dismissive of its analytical worth, reflecting the centrality of the ideal to the Western legal tradition. The UN Secretary General has emphasised that the '"rule of law" is a concept at the very heart of the Organization's mission'.[2] This was followed by states' reaffirmation at the 2005 UN World Summit of their 'universal adherence to and implementation of the rule of law at both the national and international levels'[3] and in 2012 of their 'commitment to the rule of law and its fundamental importance for political dialogue and cooperation among all States'.[4]

[1] Heike Krieger & Georg Nolte, 'The International Rule of Law: Rise or Decline? Points of Departure' (October 2016) No. 1 *KFG Working Paper Series*, p. 9.

[2] UNSC, *The Rule of Law and Transitional Justice in Conflict and Post-Conflict Societies: Report of the Secretary-General*, S/2004/616 (23 August 2004), p. 4.

[3] UNGA, A/RES/60/1, Resolution Adopted by the General Assembly on 16 September 2005 (24 October 2005), par. [134].

[4] UNGA, A/67/L.1, Declaration of the High-level Meeting of the General Assembly on the Rule of Law at the National and International Levels (19 September 2012), p. 1.

This apparent consensus dissolves, however, when attention shifts to specifying the substantive meaning of the aspiration in the design and development of IL. Even in relation to municipal law, Joseph Raz warned that 'promiscuous use' threatened to reduce the concept to a procrustean 'slogan' justifying almost any exercise of government power.[5] Judith Shklar characterised the contemporary concept as

> meaningless thanks to ideological abuse and general over-use. It may well have become just another one of those self-congratulatory rhetorical devices that grace the public utterances of Anglo-American politicians. No intellectual effort need therefore be wasted on this bit of ruling-class chatter.[6]

The force of criticism aimed at the municipal rule of law only multiplies when aimed at any notion of the *international* rule of law, including scepticism about whether and how the concept applies to IL at all.[7] Simon Chesterman is surely correct that widespread support for the concept in global institutions owes much to the silence on precise meaning.[8]

John Murphy's prominent account in *The United States and the Rule of Law in International Affairs* declares that, although he is prepared to 'join the nearly universal support for the rule of law as an ideal', he does 'not intend to join the debate over its precise meaning'.[9] It is a telling choice that a work seeking to evaluate American adherence to the international rule of law avoids staking out a definition of what that would actually mean.[10] Murphy's elusion corroborates Brian Tamanaha's observation that, where the concept is raised, 'everyone is for it, but [all] have contrasting convictions about what it is'.[11] Goldsmith and Posner point out, in responding to a review of *The Limits of International Law*,[12] that

[5] Joseph Raz, *The Authority of Law: Essays on Law and Morality* (Oxford University Press, 1979), pp. 210–11.

[6] Judith N. Shklar, 'Political Theory and the Rule of Law', in Stanley Hoffmann (ed.), *Political Thought and Political Thinkers* (University of Chicago Press, 1998), p. 21.

[7] James Crawford, 'International Law and the Rule of Law' (2003) 24 *Adelaide Law Review* 3, p. 5.

[8] Simon Chesterman, 'An International Rule of Law?' (2008) 56 *American Journal of Comparative Law* 331, p. 332.

[9] John F. Murphy, *The United States and the Rule of Law in International Affairs* (Cambridge University Press, 2004), p. 1.

[10] See, for example, the assertion in relation to the 2003 Iraq War that 'the United States closely followed the rule of law, even though it was ultimately unsuccessful in this endeavour': ibid., p. 353.

[11] Brian Z. Tamanaha, *On the Rule of Law* (Cambridge University Press, 2004), p.3.

[12] Jack Goldsmith & Eric A. Posner, *The Limits of International Law* (Oxford University Press, 2005).

exhortations to promote the rule of law remain incoherent in the absence of a clear definition:

> [W]hat, then, is the international rule of law? Is it the idea that international law should apply to states generally and impartially? Regardless of their relative power, or domestic form of governance? Are states supposed to engage in principled deliberation in designing international institutions? Does this mean that relative power and self-interest should be off the table in international negotiations? How, in a decentralized world of necessarily quite different nation-states … are we supposed to establish this international rule of law?[13]

Goldsmith and Posner conclude: '*Limits* does not address the ideal of the international rule of law … because the ideal is inadequately defined – in … [the book review in question] and more generally.'[14] And yet, despite this criticism, the concept remains fundamental, with even Goldsmith acknowledging that the frequent invocation of 'rule-of-law rhetoric' is 'not empty and is not irrelevant to international law and politics. It often genuinely reflects the values and commitments of the nations uttering it.'[15]

A Working Definition of the International Rule of Law

Despite imprecision and overuse of the term, there remains great value in the 'rule of law' as more than a mere 'synonym for "law"'.[16] At the most elementary level, the concept encompasses the principle that arbitrary self-judging should be substituted with a 'pre-agreed, principled procedure for decision-making'.[17] However, where the concept is applied to the institutional design and development of an actual legal system, some justification is required for a necessarily subjective definition of core elements. This book accordingly looks to British Jurist A. V. Dicey, as the earliest and most frequently cited in Anglo-American jurisprudence, without denying the merit of

[13] Jack Goldsmith & Eric A. Posner, 'The New International Law Scholarship' (2006) 34 *Georgia Journal of International and Comparative Law* 463, p. 480.

[14] Ibid., p. 480.

[15] Jack Goldsmith, 'The Self-Defeating International Criminal Court' (2003) *The University of Chicago Law Review* 89, p. 104.

[16] Terry Nardin, 'Theorising the International Rule of Law' (2008) 34 *Review of International Studies* 385, p. 397.

[17] Michel Cosnard, 'Sovereign Equality: "The *Wimbledon* Sails On"', in Michael Byers and Georg Nolte (eds.), *United States Hegemony and the Foundations of International Law* (Cambridge University Press, 2003), p. 146.

classic municipal formulations.[18] Dicey emphasised: 'the supremacy of law' over arbitrary power as a defining element of the English and American constitutions;[19] 'equality before the law' for rulers and the ruled alike; and the determination of rights through judicial power.[20] This has formed the starting point for most major analyses of the concept, especially in an Anglo-American context, and therefore with well-documented strengths and weaknesses. More particularly, modern theorists including Simon Chesterman,[21] Stéphane Beaulac[22] and Rosalyn Higgins[23] have externalised Dicey's three municipal elements by analogy to the global level. Beaulac adopts Dicey's formulation on the basis that it 'is well known and largely accepted; it has also been analysed and criticised from a variety of angles, thus adding to [its] credibility'.[24] In Chesterman's report *The UN Security Council and the Rule of Law*, the common understanding is identified as the 'application of these rule of law principles to relations between States' and other legal subjects.[25]

Owing to the gap between municipal and global conditions, Chesterman characterises each of his principles and the international rule of law itself as more of a 'political ideal' than a legal reality, with closer adherence to ideals remaining a means rather than an end.[26] Higgins and Beaulac concur that evidence of the approximation of each element demonstrates, at most, an emergent international rule of law.[27]

[18] See, for example, Joseph Raz, *The Authority of Law*, pp. 214–18; Lon L. Fuller, 'The Morality of Law', in Dennis Lloyd, Baron of Hampstead & M.D.A. Freeman (eds.), *Lloyd's Introduction to Jurisprudence* (Stevens, 1985).

[19] Citing de Tocqueville: Albert V. Dicey, *Lectures Introductory to the Study of the Law of the Constitution* (Macmillan & Co., 1885), pp. 172–6.

[20] Ibid., pp. 180–4.

[21] Simon Chesterman, *The UN Security Council and the Rule of Law* (Federal Ministry for European and International Affairs, 2008).

[22] Stéphane Beaulac, 'The Rule of Law in International Law Today', in G. Palombella & N. Walker (eds.), *Relocating the Rule of Law* (Hart Publishing, 2009).

[23] Rosalyn Higgins, 'Speech by H.E. Judge Rosalyn Higgins, President of The International Court of Justice, at the United Nations University on "The ICJ And The Rule of Law"', 11 April 2007, http://archive.unu.edu/events/files/2007/20070411_Higgins_speech.pdf.

[24] Beaulac, 'The Rule of Law in International Law Today', p. 198.

[25] Chesterman, 'An International Rule of Law?', pp. 355–6.

[26] Ibid., pp. 360–1.

[27] Rosalyn Higgins, 'The ICJ, the United Nations System, and the Rule of Law', London School of Economics and Political Science, 13 November 2006, www.lse.ac.uk/collections/LSEPublicLecturesAndEvents/pdf/20061113_Higgins.pdf, p. 15; Beaulac, 'The Rule of Law in International Law Today', pp. 220–1. Crawford similarly concludes that 'we have only enclaves of the rule of law in international affairs': Crawford, 'International Law and the Rule of Law', p. 12.

For Beaulac in particular, these principles apply only *mutatis mutandis* to the extent that IL diverges from municipal law. The key differences are that 'there is no one formal norm-creating authority on the international level; states (not individuals) remain the principal legal actors and there is no enforcement mechanism'.[28] Higgins concludes that, although 'the phrase "rule of law" is today very much in vogue in international relations', the 'domestic rule of law model does not easily transpose to international relations in the world we live in'.[29]

The tripartite definition nevertheless remains sufficient for the defined purpose of directly comparing commitment to rule of law ideals across competing IL polices. The definition that emerges is an institutional and 'functionalist' one, in the sense that it is concerned with 'how and why the rule of law is *used*—as distinct from the formal understanding of what it *means*'.[30] Here, Chesterman means that the term is articulated at the global level within a political context: 'as a tool with which to protect human rights, promote development, and sustain peace'.[31] This also responds to the warning of a former State Department legal adviser not to attribute a 'talismanic meaning to the phrase "rule of law"'.[32] Dicey's formulation can be usefully adopted to analyse legal policy in a specific institutional context without refuting well-known criticisms[33] or claiming to exhaustively capture the term's meaning. Coherent answers to three questions amount to a distinct conception of the international rule of law:

1 **Developing non-arbitrary global governance:** For Chesterman, the first element of the international rule of law is that there be 'a government of *laws*'.[34] Here, the concept of 'global governance' is more apt for describing the situation where 'functions normally associated with governance are performed in world politics without the institutions of government'.[35] This is a broader concept than government 'concerned with purposive acts, not tacit arrangements. It emphasizes what is

[28] Beaulac, 'The Rule of Law in International Law Today', p. 204.
[29] Higgins, 'The ICJ, the UN System, and the Rule of Law,' p. 6.
[30] Chesterman, 'An International Rule of Law?', pp. 333 & 359, original emphasis.
[31] Ibid., pp. 358–9.
[32] Michael J. Matheson, Interview with Author (19 October 2011).
[33] Crawford, 'International Law and the Rule of Law', p. 5.
[34] Chesterman, *The UNSC and the Rule of Law*, p. 4, original emphasis.
[35] James N. Rosenau, 'Governance, Order, and Change in World Politics', in James N. Rosenau & Ernst-Otto Czempiel (eds.), *Governance without Government: Order and Change in World Politics* (Cambridge University Press, 1992), p. 7.

done rather than the constitutional basis for doing it.'[36] Applying Chesterman's formula, this is the requirement of 'non-arbitrariness in the exercise of power' through increasing codification of law, greater uniformity in its rules and eliminating the distinction between 'legality' and self-judging standards of 'legitimacy'.[37] Beaulac similarly focuses on 'the existence of principled legal normativity on the international plane'.[38] This translates into the development of IL sufficient to ensure '*certainty*, *predictability*, and *stability*' while eliminating '*arbitrary power*'.[39] Finally, Higgins identifies the first principle of the international rule of law by analogy from 'an executive reflecting popular choice, taking non-arbitrary decisions applicable to all, for the most part judicially-reviewable for constitutionality'.[40] In these formulations, the common question is how to develop 'systems of rule' through IL that establish non-arbitrary global governance.[41]

2 **Defining equality under IL:** The second element of the international rule of law is described by Chesterman as '*equality* before the law'.[42] This entails a 'more general and consistent application of international law to States and other entities', with less regard to disparities in power.[43] Beaulac describes equality as a 'primordial value of the rule of law' recognised by all key theorists.[44] His variation is a question of 'how these norms are made and are applicable equally to all legal subjects'.[45] Finally, in Higgins' analysis, Dicey's second element requires that there be 'laws known to all, applied equally to all'.[46] The principle of 'equality' is far from clear-cut in practice, however, since a key meaning of equality is not merely identical treatment but 'treating like cases alike'.[47] Indeterminacy unavoidably intrudes when distinguishing between different cases, since external criteria are

36 Lawrence S. Finkelstein, 'What Is Global Governance?' (1995) *Global Governance* 367, p. 369.
37 Chesterman, *The UNSC and the Rule of Law*, p. 4.
38 Beaulac, 'The Rule of Law in International Law Today', p. 204.
39 Ibid., p. 206, original emphasis.
40 See Higgins, 'The ICJ, the UN System, and the Rule of Law', p. 1.
41 James N. Rosenau, 'Governance in the Twenty-First Century' (1995) 1 *Global Governance* 13, p. 13.
42 Chesterman, *The UNSC and the Rule of Law*, p. 4, original emphasis.
43 Chesterman, 'An International Rule of Law?', pp. 360–1.
44 Beaulac, 'The Rule of Law in International Law Today', p. 210.
45 Ibid., p. 204.
46 See Higgins, 'The ICJ, the UN System, and the Rule of Law', p. 1.
47 Herbert L.A. Hart, 'Positivism and the Separation of Law and Morals' (1958) 71 *Harvard Law Review* 593, pp. 623–4.

required to measure what is 'alike' and what is 'unalike'.[48] As Beaulac concedes, equality 'cannot mean that all legal norms apply to every state in the same way; some of them may only apply to certain states because of their situations'. Thus, the principle 'entails similarly situated states being treated in the same way by international law, with no discriminatory treatment tolerated by the system'.[49] E. H. Carr's earlier formulation was that there be an 'absence of discrimination for reasons which are felt to be irrelevant'.[50] In applying this principle, 'equality' *simpliciter* is shown to be 'an empty vessel with no substantive moral content of its own. Without moral standards, equality remains meaningless, a formula that can have nothing to say about how we should act.'[51] Thus 'equality' as an element of the international rule of law is not a self-contained 'organising principle' for sovereign states,[52] but rather a question of the proper criteria for defining who is alike under IL and how to allocate correspondingly equal rights and duties.

3 **Determining the integrity of international judicial power:** The final element is described by Chesterman as 'the *supremacy* of the law', which 'distinguishes the rule of law from rule *by* law'.[53] The meaning of this principle in Dicey's and Chesterman's formulations is 'privileging judicial process'[54] sufficient to provide 'determinative answers to legal questions'.[55] This will be achieved through increasing acceptance of the jurisdiction of international courts and tribunals, and the deference to law by political institutions. Likewise, Beaulac looks to 'the way in which normativity is enforced through adjudication'.[56] The clear deficiencies of judicial power at the 'institutional level' present 'what is without doubt the most difficult set of formal values associated with the rule of law'.[57] Finally, Higgins notes that Dicey's third element

48 Peter Westen, 'The Empty Idea of Equality' (1982) 95 *Harvard Law Review* 537, p. 540.
49 Beaulac, 'The Rule of Law in International Law Today', p. 211.
50 Edward Hallett Carr, *The Twenty Years' Crisis, 1919–1939: An Introduction to the Study of International Relations* (Macmillan & Co., 1939), p. 163.
51 Peter Westen, 'The Empty Idea of Equality', p. 547. For a critical response see Steven J. Burton, 'Comment on "Empty Ideas": Logical Positivist Analyses of Equality and Rules' (1982) 91 *Yale Law Journal* 1136.
52 Gerry J. Simpson, *Great Powers and Outlaw States: Unequal Sovereigns in the International Legal Order* (Cambridge University Press, 2004), p. 41.
53 Chesterman, *The UNSC and the Rule of Law*, p. 4, original emphasis.
54 Chesterman, 'An International Rule of Law?', p. 336.
55 Ibid., pp. 360–1.
56 Beaulac, 'The Rule of Law in International Law Today', p. 204.
57 Ibid., pp. 212 & 221.

requires 'independent courts to resolve legal disputes and to hold accountable violations of criminal law, themselves applying the governing legal rules in a consistent manner'.[58]

It is evident from these formulations that this third rule of law element requires significant modification when externalised to the international level. Limited institutionalisation of judicial power at the global level is not equivalent to the *absence* of these powers; rather, it is the case that states (and the United States in particular) underwrite the international legal system by directly exercising powers variously resembling 'executive', 'legislative' and 'judicial' functions wherever they are not already delegated to global institutions. The consequence is a weak separation of powers, since it is the legal subjects of the system who often determine when and how legal powers are exercised, by creating, interpreting and executing legal rules. The repercussion of power being so diffused is that all three 'legal' powers are exercised concurrently by each member state alongside a range of institutions, and in many cases absent an entity wielding supreme authority. The integrity of international judicial power requires a principle for determining what international judicial functions are properly reserved to states and what functions should be separated into international courts and tribunals.

Received Conceptions of the International Rule of Law

The central theme of this book is the role of foreign policy ideology in structuring the reception of IL by legal policymakers. The quest for a universal and fixed concept of 'international law as an objective, apolitical body of rules'[59] is thus explicitly set aside as chimerical. Rather, what may appear to be commitment by diverse actors to a unified ideal of the rule of law is instead commitment to divergent interpretations informed by ideological beliefs. Martti Koskenniemi presents the international rule of law as a site for political contestation, describing the ideal as a 'reformulation of the liberal impulse to escape politics'.[60] Thus, it is 'impossible to make substantive decisions within the law which would imply no political choice . . .: in the end, legitimising or

[58] See Higgins, 'The ICJ, the UN System, and the Rule of Law', p. 1.

[59] Shirley V. Scott, *International Law, US Power: The United States' Quest for Legal Security* (Cambridge University Press, 2012), p. 235.

[60] Martti Koskenniemi, *The Politics of International Law* (Hart Publishing, 2011), p. 37.

Table 3 *Competing conceptions of the international rule of law*

	Developing non-arbitrary global governance	Defining equality under international law	Determining international judicial power
Legalism	Formalised development	Sovereign equality	Separation of powers
Liberal internationalism	Transnational development	Liberal equality	Democratic checks and balances
Illiberal internationalism	Pragmatic development	Hegemonic privilege	Consent-based division of powers
Liberal nationalism	Protective development	Inviolable sovereignty	Vertical separation of powers
Illiberal nationalism	Permissive development	Relative sovereignty	Municipal supremacy

criticising state behaviour is not a matter of applying formally neutral rules but depends on what one regards as politically right, or just'.[61] Foreign policy ideology informs this choice by setting out the values and interests constituting law for an identified political community. Accordingly, the structure of the four ideal type American conceptions of IL, plus a concept of 'legalism', is crossed with the three core rule of law questions to produce a model of competing conceptions of the international rule of law (see Table 3).

Legalism

It would be contradictory to interpret American IL policy through divergent foreign policy ideologies and yet treat all other states as holding an undifferentiated conception of law. That is certainly not the case, with comparative IL scholarship revealing the extent to which legal policy-makers in each state look through the lens of their own foreign policy ideologies.[62] The claim being made here is the narrower one that

[61] Ibid., p. 61.

[62] See Anthea Roberts, *Is International Law International?* (Oxford University Press, 2017), pp. 6–8.

opposition to US IL policy has converged around the beliefs of 'legalism', irrespective of culturally specific conceptions of the international rule of law.[63] Apart from evidence of legalism's dominance in the relevant scholarship,[64] and that certain states do indeed exhibit culturally entrenched commitments to variants of legalism,[65] there are clear incentives for America's global counterparts to receive law in forms that diminish advantages of preponderant power. Sustained advocacy for the 'international rule of law' has been attributed in part to its perceived 'utility in challenging American exceptionalism, which threatens . . . the legitimacy of the international legal order based on the principle of the legal equality of all states'.[66] Koskenniemi identifies the power lying behind 'the juxtaposition between European constitutional formalism and the "imperial" challenge to international institutions by the United States'.[67] There are compelling reasons for treating legalism as an ideological ideal type structuring opposition to US IL policy.

The legalist approach is best defined by Judith Shklar as 'the ethical attitude that holds moral conduct to be a matter of rule following, and moral relationships to consist of duties and rights determined by rules'.[68] In the context of IL specifically, Tai-Heng Cheng defines it as the '*claim* to apply prescriptions, through a process of reasoning and logic, neutrally to facts in an international problem'.[69] The rhetorical attraction of contesting American international legal power in these terms lies in the claim to a 'depoliticised' conception of law:

> Law aims at justice, while politics looks only to expediency. The former is neutral and objective, the latter the uncontrolled child of competing interests and ideologies. Justice is thus not only the policy of legalism, it is treated as a policy superior to and unlike any other.[70]

[63] See José E. Alvarez, 'Contemporary International Law: An Empire of Law or the Law of Empire' (2008) 24 *American University International Law Review* 811, pp. 817–18.

[64] Leslie Vinjamuri & Jack Snyder, 'Advocacy and Scholarship in the Study of International War Crime Tribunals and Transitional Justice' (2004) 7 *Annual Review of Political Science* 345, pp. 346–8.

[65] Martin Gelter & Kristoffel Grechenig, 'The Transatlantic Divergence in Legal Thought: American Law and Economics vs. German Doctrinalism' (2008) 31 *Hastings International and Comparative Law Review* 295.

[66] Randall P. Peerenboom, 'Human Rights and Rule of Law: What's the Relationship?' (2004) 36 *Georgetown Journal of International Law* 809, pp. 935–9.

[67] Koskenniemi, *The Politics of International Law*, p. 73.

[68] Judith N. Shklar, *Legalism* (Harvard University Press, 1964), p. 1.

[69] Tai-Heng Cheng, *When International Law Works* (Oxford University Press, 2012), p. 83, original emphasis.

[70] Shklar, *Legalism*, p. 111.

In this view, 'the appeal of a global rule of law lies in the promise of protection against the pathologies of internal domestic politics'.[71] For Nardin, the international rule of law comes to mean 'no more than that states conduct their relations within a framework of non-instrumental law'.[72]

Leading accounts describing legalism at the municipal level remain relevant here owing to the power of a 'domestic analogy' in which '[c]ustom, usage, conventions, and treaties provide a complete system of law, analogous to municipal law'.[73] Legalist beliefs thus possess the features of 'a political ideology which comes into conflict with other policies' no less than do specifically American conceptions.[74] Such 'deliberate isolation of the legal system – the treatment of law as a neutral social entity – is itself a refined political ideology, the expression of a preference'.[75] Moreover, Shklar suggests that conceptions of international (as opposed to municipal) law are 'perhaps the most striking manifestation of legalistic ideology. Its ideological character is especially discernible because the principles of international law are not supported by effective institutions.'[76]

The 'legalism' appellation has more often been employed from a critical perspective to challenge those who oppose American legal policy. Posner defines legalism as 'the view that law and legal institutions can keep order and solve policy disputes. It manifests itself in powerful courts, a dominant class of lawyers, and reliance on legalistic procedures in policymaking bodies.'[77] In the externalised form of 'global legalism', the concept is defined pejoratively as 'an excessive faith in the efficacy of international law'.[78] Nevertheless, in the present work, adoption of the legalist rubric is for comparative purposes only and disavows any strong normative implications. It is merely 'intended to express social facts about a specialized mode of interaction in the process of decision-making in international problems, without engaging in unnecessary conceptual debates about whether or not this mode of interaction is

[71] Paul W. Kahn, 'American Exceptionalism, Popular Sovereignty, and the Rule of Law', in Michael Ignatieff (ed.), *American Exceptionalism and Human Rights* (Princeton University Press, 2005), pp. 198–9.
[72] Nardin, 'Theorising the International Rule of Law', p. 399.
[73] Shklar, *Legalism*, p. 136.
[74] Ibid., p. 3.
[75] Ibid., p. 34.
[76] Ibid., p. 129.
[77] Eric A. Posner, *The Perils of Global Legalism* (University of Chicago Press, 2009), p. 21.
[78] Ibid., p. xii.

actually "law"'.[79] This use in no way excludes the possibility of advocating the normative merits of legalist conceptions. Importantly, Shklar wrote not to defeat legalism but to harness its potential to advance liberal values.[80] Her primary objective remained 'to save legalism for liberal politics by showing central liberal ideas like the rule of law to be useful ideologies'.[81] Criticism was directed only at 'those of its traditional adherents who, in their determination to preserve law from politics, fail to recognize that they too have made a choice among political values'.[82]

It is instructive to compare how legalist conceptions of IL align with the governance and values dimensions structuring American IL policy. At the risk of stating the obvious, the legalist conception is internationalist, in the sense that it advocates forms of governance through global legal architecture. In particular, legalist conceptions envision domestic decisions with transnational implications, including about war and peace, being transferred to the international level. Along the values dimension, legalism draws upon the 'cosmopolitan ethos' embedded in modern IL, which mirrors the aspiration in the wider project of modernity for more than a normatively agnostic international order. Cosmopolitanism requires that the rule of law uphold 'non-instrumental' rules that treat persons as ends and not merely means for satisfying political objectives. The effect of seeking politically neutral normative foundations is to displace the controlling role of democratic accountability so central to American understandings of liberalism. Consistently with this idea, authors variously identify the norms underpinning IL with 'universal values'[83] and an 'international value system'.[84] Believing in the genuinely cosmopolitan foundations of global legal order has the same effect as faith in American exceptionalism, which is the tendency toward a 'messianic' IL policy.[85]

[79] Cheng, *When International Law Works*, pp. 80–1.

[80] Shklar, *Legalism*, p. 5.

[81] Samuel Moyn, 'Judith Shklar versus the International Criminal Court' (2013) 4 *Humanity: An International Journal of Human Rights, Humanitarianism, and Development* 473, p. 475.

[82] Shklar, *Legalism*, p. 8.

[83] Pierre-Marie Dupuy, 'Some Reflections on Contemporary International Law and the Appeal to Universal Values: A Response to Martti Koskenniemi' (2005) 16 *European Journal of International Law* 131.

[84] Erika de Wet, 'The International Constitutional Order' (2006) 55 *International and Comparative Law Quarterly* 51.

[85] Andrea Bianchi, 'Human Rights and the Magic of Jus Cogens' (2008) 19 *European Journal of International Law* 491, p. 495.

It is important to note that included among legalist advocates are prominent American individuals and organisations, which can and have vocally advocated a range of policies in legalist terms (especially within NGOs). The theorised IL policy typology does not encompass all policies capable of being internalised by American citizens, only those influential among American legal policymakers. George Kennan identified an attachment to 'moralistic-legalistic' beliefs as an affliction of American foreign policy itself.[86] However, attachment to legal rules and solutions as described by Kennan is largely encompassed by the liberal internationalist type and remains distinct from legalism as that term is used here.[87] The adoption of legalist beliefs by Americans other than legal policymakers would not in itself falsify the typology unless such positions were accepted by and structured American IL policy.

Formalised Development of International Law

The first element of the legalist international rule of law is that the primary and secondary rules of the international legal system should be progressively formalised as binding legal obligations. Attainment of the rule of law at the municipal level is not a static condition, but a process of progressively adapting and extending the law to achieve a complete legal system.[88] The rule of law in the common law world, for example, was advanced in 1689 when the English Bill of Rights removed the monarch's prerogative to suspend the operation of the law or its application to certain categories of people. International legal scholarship has likewise maintained a strong presumption against declaring a *non liquet* in which the law remains silent on rights and duties.[89] The 'Grotian tradition' of IL, for example, envisions the 'subjection of the totality of international relations to the rule of law'.[90] The rationale behind that sometimes 'unrealistic' presumption is 'to "tame" state sovereignty and to subject states to

[86] George F. Kennan, *American Diplomacy* (University of Chicago Press, 1984), pp. 101–2.

[87] Use of the term here can also be distinguished from Abebe and Posner's 'foreign affairs legalism' on the same basis: Daniel Abebe & Eric A. Posner, 'The Flaws of Foreign Affairs Legalism' (2010) 51 *Virginia Journal of International Law* 507.

[88] Helen Duffy, *The 'War on Terror' and the Framework of International Law* (Cambridge University Press, 2005), p. 9.

[89] Literally that the law 'is not clear': see Michael W. Reisman, 'International Non-Liquet: Recrudescence and Transformation' (1968) 3 *International Lawyer* 770, p.771.

[90] Hersch Lauterpacht, 'The Grotian Tradition in International Law' (1946) 23 *British Yearbook of International Law* 1, p. 19.

the rule of law'.[91] That principle is now recognised in the UN Charter and as the central purpose of the International Law Commission (ILC) in promoting 'the progressive development of international law and its codification'.[92]

For adherents of legalism, the case for global law displacing global politics relies on the advantages of 'formalism', which for Shklar is the idea of law as 'a self-contained system of norms that is "there," identifiable without reference to the content, aim, and development of the rules that compose it'.[93] Shklar saw Hans Kelsen's formalism as a creature of his own positivist jurisprudence, in which law was 'its own creation' progressively derived from his *Grundnorm*.[94] Hans Morgenthau described the positivist claim as being to a 'logically coherent system which virtually contains, and through a mere process of logical deduction will actually produce, all rules necessary for the decision of all possible cases'.[95] The claimed advantage of this jurisprudence is to establish legal rules 'without the ideological bias or the historical and cultural myopia' entailed in non-formal approaches.[96] For legalism, policy is legitimate because it complies with formalised sources of authority and not merely because it is congruent with policy objectives. Having rules that are progressively more comprehensive, internally consistent and clear becomes the necessary presumption for the central legalist claim that 'following rules impartially is a virtue'.[97]

Sovereign Equality

US IL policy has been most forcefully challenged by the principle that all states must accede to international rules and institutions according to equal rights and duties. The principle of equality before the law was described by Dicey as the 'universal subjugation of all classes, to one law'.[98] Legalism extends that norm to the rights and duties of states as IL's

91 Prosper Weil, 'The Court Cannot Conclude Definitively . . . Non Liquet Revisited' (1998) 36 *Columbia Journal of Transnational Law* 109, p. 113.

92 *Charter of the United Nations* (1945), Art. 13(1)(a); *Statute of the International Law Commission* (1947), Art. 1(1).

93 Shklar, *Legalism*, p. 33.

94 Ibid., p. 131, citing Hans Kelsen, *General Theory of Law and State* (Harvard University Press, 1945; reprinted Russell & Russell, 1961).

95 Hans Joachim Morgenthau, 'Positivism, Functionalism, and International Law' (1940) 34 *American Journal of International Law* 260, p. 262.

96 Shklar, *Legalism*, p. 33.

97 Ibid., p. 113.

98 Dicey, *Lectures Introductory to the Study of the Law of the Constitution*, p. 178.

primary subjects, irrespective of external influence or internal character. For Gerry Simpson, this has meant 'formal equality' according to 'the principle that in *judicial settings* states have equality in the vindication and "exercise of rights"'. This conception of sovereign equality constitutes a 'basic rule of law notion'.[99]

The very purpose of the international rule of law in the legalist approach is to minimise the significance of power disparities when determining rights and duties. The structure of the international system remains an 'association of independent and diverse political communities, each devoted to its own ends and its own conception of the good'.[100] Such an arrangement necessitates common constraints for respecting one another's autonomy, with 'sovereign equality' becoming the constitutional principle on which the international legal system is constructed.[101] 'Equality' in this sense is a legal fiction, but a necessary one to establish legal rights not dependent on the reality of inequality. To derive rights from actual distributions of power would result in a world with states at the periphery lacking legal personality and a 'corresponding gradation of rights'.[102] The rule of law in these terms protects the structure of the international order without reference to the idiosyncratic beliefs and cultural commitments of particular states.

In more robust incarnations, this legalist rule of law element extends beyond mere obligation to respect equal sovereignty and encompasses positive obligations to participate equally in multilateral treaties having near universal membership. A US claim to significant treaty reservations, or exemption entirely even from multilateral instruments such as the Paris Climate Agreement, 'seems now to require some justification if it deviates from the stance of the great majority of states'. In this sense 'freedom of contract plays an ever-decreasing role when it comes to law-like treaties'.[103]

Separation of Powers

Closely related to sovereign equality is the principle that the integrity of international judicial power is determined by its separation from

[99] Simpson, *Great Powers and Outlaw States*, p. 43, original emphasis.

[100] Terry Nardin, *Law, Morality, and the Relations of States* (Princeton University Press, 1983), p. 19.

[101] See *Charter of the UN*, Art. 2(1): 'The Organization is based on the principle of the sovereign equality of all its Members.'

[102] Nico Krisch, 'More Equal Than the Rest? Hierarchy, Equality and US Predominance in International Law', in Byers & Nolte, *United States Hegemony*, p. 147.

[103] Ibid., p. 151.

competing legal powers of global governance. No domestic system implementing the rule of law would vest executive control over judicial decisions, nor would it allow citizens to determine the legality of their own actions under the state's civil or criminal jurisdiction. Likewise, the supremacy of IL restricts states' discretion to determine the scope of their own global privileges and obligations. The domestic analogy influences legalism to 'read international law in the image of our domestic legalism: multilateral treaties as legislation, international courts as an independent judiciary, the Security Council as the police'.[104] States continue to exercise the key 'legislative' and 'executive' functions of global governance and therefore cannot also be the final arbiters in international judicial matters.

Shklar notes that legalism generally supports policies 'promoting the institutionalization of the administration of justice'. The objective of resolving 'as many social conflicts by judicial means as possible' provides the rationale for separating international legal powers and institutionalising judicial power in independent courts.[105] Crucial here is the legalist presumption that judges 'lie outside politics; they resolve cases impartially by appealing to the rules'.[106] At the international level, this translates into supremacy of institutionalised judicial power as the only form of legal power independent of national politics.[107] Article 20 of the ICJ Statute expresses the ideal that its judges must solemnly declare to exercise their powers 'impartially and conscientiously'. For Roslyn Higgins, as former ICJ president, this constitutes 'a proper separation of powers'.[108] Executive power in the international system is approximated in the UNSC and so, apart from its distortion of sovereign equality, its control cannot properly extend over an international court. The principle was reflected in the separate opinion of Judge Simma in *The Armed Activities Case*[109] in reference to the role of the ICJ as the UN's 'principal *judicial* organ'. It followed that the court had a duty 'to arrive at decisions based on law and nothing but law', reflecting the 'division of labour between the Court and the political organs of the United Nations'.[110]

[104] Martti Koskenniemi, 'International Law in Europe: Between Tradition and Renewal' (2005) 16 *European Journal of International Law* 113, p. 117.

[105] Shklar, *Legalism*, p. 117.

[106] Posner, *The Perils of Global Legalism*, p. 19.

[107] Ibid., p. 25.

[108] Higgins, 'The ICJ, the UN System, and the Rule of Law', p. 3.

[109] *Armed Activities on the Territory of the Congo (Democratic Republic of Congo* v. *Uganda)* (2005) *ICJ Rep* 168.

[110] Ibid., par. [3], original emphasis.

Liberal Internationalism

Of the four ideal American policy types, liberal internationalism is the most important for understanding the beliefs of American policy-makers strongly committed to international legal order. The unparalleled commitment to developing IL has often led liberal internationalists to view alternative American conceptions as 'IL sceptics' or what Spiro memorably called 'new sovereigntists'.[111] Liberal internationalism identifies the international rule of law in externalisation of American constitutional government to establish a seamless system of law, with international and national legal systems reinforcing universal liberal values. Self-identified liberal internationalist Anne-Marie Slaughter defines the essence of the rule of law as 'ordered liberty'.[112] At the global level, however, that ideal involves a 'continual tension between the requirement under international law that we respect *nations*, meaning governments, and our own democratic value of respecting all *peoples*'.[113] Here, Slaughter invokes the belief that the reason for establishing the rule of law is identical across the municipal and international levels: to achieve 'a steady progression toward greater freedom of conscience, choice and country – first within America and then beyond our borders'.[114] This forms the foundational principle of a liberal internationalist conception of IL:

> At the most fundamental level, an image of the world as a projection of the United States means that international order, like domestic order, requires the rule of law. From this perspective multilateralism is nothing more than the internationalization of the liberal conception of the rule of law.[115]

General accounts of 'Wilsonianism', as an equivalent tradition of thought, have focused on democracy promotion as the 'first

[111] Peter J. Spiro, 'The New Sovereigntists: American Exceptionalism and Its False Prophets' (2000) *Foreign Affairs* 9. See also Jens David Ohlin, *The Assault on International Law* (Oxford University Press, 2014).

[112] Anne-Marie Slaughter, *The Idea That Is America: Keeping Faith with Our Values in a Dangerous World* (Basic Books, 2007), p. 36.

[113] Ibid., p. 190, original emphasis.

[114] Ibid., p. 36.

[115] Anne-Marie Burley, 'Regulating the World: Multilateralism, International Law, and the Projection of the New Deal Regulatory State', in John Gerard Ruggie (ed.), *Multilateralism Matters: The Theory and Praxis of an Institutional Form* (Columbia University Press, 1993), p. 144.

principle',[116] the 'most essential ingredient'[117] and the 'keystone'[118] of the tradition. Liberal internationalism identifies democracy as the conduit between the enjoyment of liberty by natural persons and an international system of law. In 1917, Elihu Root wrote: 'The world cannot be half democratic and half autocratic ... If it is democratic, international law honored and observed may well be expected as a natural development of the principles which make democratic self-government possible.'[119] Liberal internationalism is distinctive among the American ideal types for valuing democracy as constitutive of the international rule of law itself: 'the global rule of law depends on the domestic rule of law'.[120] Believing that liberal states adhere more consistently to the rule of law at both the national and the international level thus presents a utopian vision in which a world of liberal states progressively enforces mutual respect for IL.[121]

The vision of taming global politics through law is what forms the common ground with the legalist conception of IL, with both promoting a 'Kantian vision of a law-governed international society'.[122] However, liberal internationalism diverges categorically in identifying the centrality of American power and values to the project. John Ikenberry advocates the establishment of 'American "rule"' through 'the provisioning of international rules and institutions and its willingness to operate within them'. In short: 'Liberal order building is America's distinctive contribution to world politics.'[123] In this way, IL and American constitutional government share the same firm foundation in hard-won political bargains.

116 Walter R. Mead, *Special Providence: American Foreign Policy and How It Changed the World* (Routledge, 2002), p. 162.

117 Tony Smith, 'Wilsonianism after Iraq', in G. John Ikenberry, Thomas J. Knock, Anne-Marie Slaughter & Tony Smith (eds.), *The Crisis of American Foreign Policy: Wilsonianism in the Twenty-First Century* (Princeton University Press, 2009), p. 58.

118 Anne-Marie Slaughter, 'Wilsonianism in the Twenty-First Century', in G. John Ikenberry, Thomas J. Knock, Anne-Marie Slaughter & Tony Smith (eds.), *The Crisis of American Foreign Policy: Wilsonianism in the Twenty-First Century* (Princeton University Press, 2009), p. 97.

119 Elihu Root, 'The Effect of Democracy on International Law' (1917) 11 *Proceedings of the Annual Meeting (American Society of International Law)* 2, pp. 166–7.

120 Anne-Marie Slaughter, 'A Liberal Theory of International Law' (2000) 94 *Proceedings of the Annual Meeting (American Society of International Law)* 240, p. 246.

121 This is a variant of the 'democratic peace theory': see Bruce Russett, Christopher Layne, David E. Spiro & Michael W. Doyle, 'The Democratic Peace' (1995) 19 *International Security* 164.

122 Harold H. Koh, *The Trump Administration and International Law* (Oxford University Press, 2019), p. 3.

123 G. John Ikenberry, 'Liberal Order Building', in Melvyn P. Leffler & Jeffrey W. Legro (eds.), *To Lead the World: American Strategy after the Bush Doctrine* (Oxford University Press, 2008), p. 86.

Transnational Development of Global Governance

Legalism and liberal internationalism are united by a commitment to closing gaps in the law. The very notion that effective legal regimes *can* and *should* be crafted to respond to global challenges is 'shaped by a liberal conception of the rule of law'.[124] What distinguishes liberal internationalism is the function of formalised legal authority in achieving that outcome. Whereas legalism seeks the codification of all internationally relevant rights at a global level, liberal internationalism values variants of 'transnational legal processes' by which international standards are equally integrated and enforced at the level of US municipal law. For Harold Koh, legal compliance is determined through a process whereby 'public and private actors, including nation states, . . . interact in a variety of fora to interpret, enforce, and ultimately internalize rules of international law'.[125] In this view, increasing establishment of non-arbitrary global governance is achieved through formal and informal processes by which 'domestic decision-making becomes "enmeshed" with international legal norms'.[126]

By virtue of transnational processes, it may even be preferable to limit development of supranational legal authority where legal obligations are sufficiently internalised to provide effective global governance. To this end, liberal internationalism welcomes the penetration of foreign and international legal decisions into American courts, even to the extent of interpreting the US Constitution in light of universal liberal standards.[127] A defining element of liberal internationalism distinguishing it from legalism, and every other American conception, becomes the value attached to aspirational support for IL short of formal accession to legal obligations – what one US legal policymaker has termed 'dexterous multilateralism'.[128] For legalism, this degrades IL by permitting deformalised obligations, while for each of the alternative American conceptions it falsely suggests legal constraints beyond what the United States is actually willing and able to accept.[129]

[124] Burley, 'Regulating the World', p. 145.

[125] Harold H. Koh, 'Jefferson Memorial Lecture: Transnational Legal Process after September 11th' (2004) 22 *Berkeley Journal of International Law* 337, p. 339.

[126] Harold H. Koh, 'Transnational Legal Process' (1996) 75 *Nebraska Law Review* 181, p. 204.

[127] See Peter J. Spiro, 'Treaties, International Law, and Constitutional Rights' (2003) 55 *Stanford Law Review* 1999, pp. 2021–5.

[128] Eric P. Schwartz, 'The United States and the International Criminal Court: The Case for Dexterous Multilateralism' (2003) 4 *Chicago Journal of International Law* 223.

[129] For criticism along these lines see Simon Lester, 'Should the United States Use Treaties to Make the World "More Like Us"?' (2013) 54 *Virginia Journal of International Law Digest* 1, p. 8.

Liberal Equality

The second rule of law principle is that the equal access of natural persons to universal liberal freedoms trumps the formal equality of states as juridical legal persons. For liberal internationalism, the purpose of IL is to uphold basic rights of 'citizens rather than states as subjects', which is 'the hallmark of a new and distinctively liberal conception of a world under law'.[130] To realise this principle, a distinction is drawn between the sovereignty of states who uphold liberal norms through democratic processes and those who do not. The principle of sovereign equality treats states as the legal persons of IL, and in so doing is 'at least one remove, and often at two removes' from actual individuals.[131] Accordingly, states should be treated equally to the extent that their municipal law protects the liberal freedoms of their own citizens, but compromise any claim to equal sovereign integrity should they fail to do so. In its most robust iterations, the commitment to liberal equality can translate into conceptions of IL as a 'progressive sword to extend those rights to others'.[132]

In cases of conflict between liberal and sovereign equality, exceptionalist beliefs reassure that the proven resilience of American constitutional democracy and its global role promoting these values are the stable foundations for realising true equality in the international legal order. The classic demonstration is the 1999 NATO-led Kosovo intervention, spearheaded by the Clinton administration absent UNSC authorisation. The action to prevent a 'humanitarian catastrophe' revealed a willingness to displace the right of Yugoslavia (as it then was) to equally enjoy territorial sovereignty to the right of its threatened ethnic Albanian population to enjoy equality in basic human rights.[133] In the *Princeton Project*, Slaughter and Ikenberry advocated the authority of a 'supermajority' of democratic states to override the positive obligations of the UNSC where it 'prevented free nations from keeping faith' with liberal principles.[134]

[130] Burley, 'Regulating the World', p. 146.

[131] Anne-Marie Slaughter & Jose E. Alvarez, 'A Liberal Theory of International Law' (2000) 94 *Proceedings of the Annual Meeting (American Society of International Law)* 240, p. 245.

[132] Harlan G. Cohen, 'The American Challenge to International Law: A Tentative Framework for Debate' (2003) 28 *Yale Journal of International Law* 551, p. 561.

[133] See Michael P. Scharf & Paul R. Williams, *Shaping Foreign Policy in Times of Crisis: The Role of International Law and the State Department Legal Adviser* (Cambridge University Press, 2010), pp. 166–7.

[134] Anne-Marie Slaughter & G. John Ikenberry, *Forging a World of Liberty under Law: U.S. National Security in the 21st Century* (Woodrow Wilson School of Public and International Affairs, 27 September 2006), p. 26.

Slaughter later became a strong advocate for a form of humanitarian intervention in the Syrian civil war, externalising ideas from Thomas Jefferson and the US Declaration of Independence to render sovereignty contingent on the liberal equality of Syrian citizens.[135] For Koh, refusal to read a humanitarian exception into IL is flawed for exhibiting an 'absolutist, formalist, textualist, originalist quality' that cannot be squared with beliefs that 'international law should serve human purposes'.[136] That argument can appear incoherent to competing ideological perspectives, which tend not to distinguish between legalism and liberal internationalism. Goldsmith finds Koh's position 'hard to square with his commitment to transnational legal process, which at its core is about taking international legal rules seriously and absorbing them into domestic legal culture'.[137] Yet it is the crucial nuance of liberal internationalism's 'rejection of legalism' that reveals the foundations of IL in liberal equality.[138]

Democratic Checks and Balances

The keystone role of democracy means that the integrity of IL is determined by the effective separation of powers at the municipal rather than at the international level. There is no mechanism in the international legal system itself to ensure that international courts determine rights and duties solely on a judicial basis. Liberty guaranteed under American constitutional government is achieved not merely through the good faith of its participants, but also by ensuring: 'Ambition must be made to counteract ambition.'[139] The primitive structure of the international legal system is, in contrast, incapable of sustaining the integrity of an effective institutional separation of executive, legislative and judicial powers of global governance.[140] Rather, the anchoring role of the domestic rule of

[135] Anne-Marie Slaughter, 'How the World Could – and Maybe Should – Intervene in Syria', *The Atlantic*, 23 January 2012, www.theatlantic.com/international/archive/2012/01/how-the-world-could-and-maybe-should-intervene-in-syria/251776/.

[136] Koh, *The Trump Administration and International Law*, pp. 129–30.

[137] Jack Goldsmith, '*The Trump Administration and International Law*. By Harold Hongju Koh. New York, New York: Oxford University Press, 2019. Pp. viii, 221. Index' (2019) 113 *American Journal of International Law* 408, p. 413.

[138] Richard A. Falk, 'Kosovo, World Order, and the Future of International Law' (1999) 93 *American Journal of International Law* 847, pp. 852–3.

[139] James Madison (1788) *Federalist No. 51*, cited in Thomas S. Mowle, *Allies at Odds?: The United States and the European Union* (Palgrave Macmillan, 2004), p. 94.

[140] Alex Mills & Tim Stephens, 'Challenging the Role of Judges in Slaughter's Liberal Theory of International Law' (2005) 18 *Leiden Journal of International Law* 1, pp. 12–14.

law provides democratic checks and balances on international judicial institutions that counter their inherent political weaknesses.

In some formulations of a liberal legal order, domestic legislative and judicial institutions are projected onto the international plane. This was the view of Wilson's contemporaries, including Elihu Root in designing the Permanent Court of International Justice attached to the League of Nations. However, the politically influential variant of liberal internationalism does not conceive of IL as centralised in these institutions, but, rather, as existing foremost at the state level, and only secondarily in international bodies. The modern liberal internationalist emphasis on transnational process relies on rules and decisions from the international sphere being internalised and enforced by domestic courts. International institutions should therefore only fulfil this role in a 'backstopping' capacity where a state's own legal institutions are incompatible with the rule of law – by design, or owing to disruption in the case of conflict. Slaughter identifies backstopping as being effected either by 'provision of a second line of defense when national institutions fail' or through 'the ability of the international process to catalyze action at the national level'.[141] States are incentivised to comply with IL, even absent formal separation of judicial power into international courts.

Illiberal Internationalism

Illiberal internationalism actively engages with global rules and institutions to facilitate foreign policy objectives, but does so for the overriding purpose of strengthening US national security. The rule of law for illiberal internationalists means a flexible framework of legal rules and institutions that facilitates US strategic autonomy and diplomatic justifications. The absence of concern for the moral purpose of states has parallels with the *realpolitik* and balance of power politics of Continental Europe.[142] IL is thereby preserved as a diplomatic tool between states rather than a means for vindicating the legal rights of natural persons. Former US Attorney General John Ashcroft objected to the US Supreme Court holding in *Hamdan* v. *Rumsfeld* that litigants had rights exercisable

[141] Anne-Marie Slaughter & William Burke-White, 'The Future of International Law Is Domestic (or, the European Way of Law)' (2006) 47 *Harvard International Law Journal* 327, p. 341.

[142] Dueck labels adherents of his equivalent set of beliefs simply 'American realists': Colin Dueck, *Reluctant Crusaders: Power, Culture, and Change in American Grand Strategy* (Princeton University Press, 2006), p. 33.

against the US government under the Geneva Conventions.[143] Consistent with an international rule of law between sovereign states, Ashcroft responded that 'those treaties within themselves have provisions which limit the parties that can raise them and enforce them to the high contracting parties, not to the citizens of various nations'.[144] This reflects a fundamentally illiberal conception, addressing the interests of individual citizens only indirectly and in the aggregate through the principal focus on national security. Liberal internationalism addresses national security more indirectly, by externalising liberal values into an international legal environment to reinforce global security over the long term. Illiberal internationalism rejects such utopian visions, instead engaging with IL to manage rather than overcome security threats. The conception is further distinguished by a clear separation between the illiberalism of international legal policy and national political values, with no assumption of mutual reinforcement. The privileging of American security interests abroad has nevertheless translated into greater deference to executive power and therefore weaker institutional checks and balances integral to protecting liberty at home.

Pragmatic Development of International Law

Illiberal internationalism seeks a legal framework within which the United States can pragmatically determine the limits of IL. Contrary to both legalism and liberal internationalism, this approach embraces potential gaps and ambiguities in IL for enhancing discretion to exercise effective diplomatic power as a part of law itself. Michael Glennon has sought to define a 'pragmatist' method that treats the development of IL as 'a multifaceted method of problem-solving rather than a formula for finding a single, correct solution'.[145] The first distinguishing belief is that 'reliance upon formal legalist categories masks the decision-making process that actually occurs, which is situationally contingent'.[146] Applying this principle to the vexed question of whether the Geneva

143 Referring to Art. 75 of Protocol I to the *Geneva Conventions* (1949): *Hamdan* v. *Rumsfeld* (2006) 548 *U.S.* 557, pp. 70–1 per Stevens J.

144 Responding to a question posed by the author: John Ashcroft, 'The Constitution and the Common Defense: Who Ensures America's National Security?', *Preserve the Constitution*, The Heritage Foundation, Washington, DC, 11 October 2011, last accessed 27 February 2015.

145 Michael J. Glennon, *The Fog of Law: Pragmatism, Security, and International Law* (Woodrow Wilson Center Press, 2010), p. 2.

146 Ibid., p. 3.

Conventions applied to Al-Qaeda and Taliban detainees during the 2001 War in Afghanistan, Glennon considers the full range of factors, including the negative reactions of US allies and the status of US prisoners of war seeking reciprocal protections. For Glennon, '[w]hether such factors are, strictly speaking, legal or political is, to the pragmatist lawyer, beside the point: in the real world, these are, to varying degrees, the kinds of factors that international lawyers do take into account'.[147] This approach, however, does not 'open the door to a law-free zone', since it relies on the default principle that 'in the absence of a rule a State is deemed free to act'.[148] In this sense, the 'formalists are, perversely . . . right that there are no gaps in the international legal order'.[149] Kenneth Anderson characterises this as a case of the legal system 'formalizing its pragmatism'. In so doing, pragmatism 'serves to protect international law from itself', which is threatened by formalism to become 'ever more internally "pure" but ever more disconnected from the world of international politics where, ultimately, it must live'.[150] Using national security interests to clearly demarcate the sphere in which the United States accepts the development of IL, and where it does not, is seen as the only non-arbitrary basis for developing IL. The United States demonstrates fidelity to the international rule of law in the sense of complying with carefully adapted legal obligations, thereby facilitating appeals to law rather than naked power.

Pragmatic development approaches IL as a valuable tool for arranging the relations between states, but otherwise as lacking autonomous institutional force. Former Deputy Secretary of State Robert Zoellick argued that IL 'can facilitate bargaining, recognise common interests, and resolve differences cooperatively. But international law, unlike domestic law, merely codifies an already agreed-upon cooperation.'[151] A specific example of this view is endorsement of a developing UNSC practice to alter formal treaty provisions on an ad hoc basis in order to address threats to international peace and security. John Bellinger welcomes the 'significant development' of 'tailoring a specialized body of international

[147] Ibid., p. 20.

[148] Applying the 'freedom principle' from *S.S. Lotus, The (France* v. *Turkey)* (1927) No. 10 *PCIJ Ser A*, p. 44.

[149] Michael J. Glennon, 'The Road Ahead: Gaps, Leaks and Drips' (2013) 89 *International Law Studies* 362, p. 373.

[150] Kenneth Anderson, 'Readings: Michael Glennon on the "Incompleteness" of International Law Governing the Use of Force', *Lawfare*, 13 May 2013, www.lawfareblog.com/2013/05/readings-michael-glennon-on-the-incompleteness-of-international-law-governing-the-use-of-force/.

[151] Robert B. Zoellick, 'A Republican Foreign Policy' (2000) 79 *Foreign Affairs* 63, p. 69.

law to better work in a specific set of circumstances'.[152] Stefan Talmon responds critically within a legalist rubric that 'adaptation' here is merely a euphemism for 'abrogation' of formal treaty provisions pursuant to 'a culture of exceptionalism' among Council members.[153] The practice accordingly 'raises serious concerns from the point of view of the rule of law'.[154] From the illiberal internationalist perspective, however, these are examples of pragmatic development in IL, where the coherent logic of strategic and security judgements is valued over arbitrary rule obedience.

Hegemonic Privilege

The fact of American power preponderance precludes any international legal arrangement that presumes to level political power through sovereign equality. Rather, the meaning of equality is that states should be accorded privileges commensurate with their unequal role in upholding the international legal order.[155] Of the four ideal legal conceptions, exceptionalist beliefs remain weakest in this variant, and so any such privileges are grounded foremost in the prudence of acknowledging preponderant power, with a normative defence of American political culture playing a secondary role only. Prior to his tenure as Secretary of Defense in the Obama administration, Chuck Hagel argued that 'long-term security interests' are strengthened where international legal institutions are developed 'as extensions of our influence, not as constraints on our power'.[156] The rule of law will never be more than an idealistic aspiration if it requires powerful states to submit to the interests of weaker states as sovereign equals. Neither will it be effective where powerful states are incentivised to remain outside of the law. Rather, IL should seek a stable structure for global power relations, without shifting the balance of that power.

[152] John B. Bellinger III, 'Legal Adviser Address to International Institute of Humanitarian Law in San Remo', 9 September 2005, https://2009-2017.state.gov/s/l/2005/87240.htm. This power is authorised under *Charter of the United Nations*, Art. 103: see José E. Alvarez, 'Contemporary International Law: An Empire of Law or the Law of Empire', p. 821.

[153] Stefan Talmon, 'Adaptation of Treaties by the Security Council and the Rule of Law' (2009) 103 *Proceedings of the Annual Meeting (American Society of International Law)* 249, p. 249.

[154] Ibid., p. 251.

[155] This has parallels to IR 'hegemonic stability theory', which posits that 'hegemony will lead to openness and stable regimes': see Michael Mastanduno, David A. Lake & G. John Ikenberry, 'Toward a Realist Theory of State Action' (1989) *International Studies Quarterly* 457, p. 461.

[156] Chuck Hagel, 'A Republican Foreign Policy' (2004) 83 *Foreign Affairs* 64, p.68.

The thinking is evident in Jacob Cogan's concept of 'operational noncompliance', defined as noncompliance with parts of IL for the purpose of upholding the system as a whole through 'bridging the enforcement gap created by inadequate community mechanisms of control'.[157] The primitive nature of the international legal system weakens the integrity of law, mandating formally illegal actions of 'law making and law termination' to make the system work.[158] This becomes a principle for granting unequal legal privileges to the United States in answering the question of the proper relationship between sovereign states. Cogan emphasises that 'law is the congruence of policy, authority, and control, and, thus, without power there is no law'. Accordingly, 'international lawyers should acknowledge and take account of the special responsibilities of the powerful'.[159] Exceptionalist beliefs are relevant to the extent that checks against the abuse of operational noncompliance are provided by the United States itself as a state with 'acculturation' consistent with rule of law values.[160]

Consent-Based Division of Powers

The integrity of international judicial power is not determined by a general illiberal internationalist ordering principle, but, rather, by states consenting to international judicial constraints according to material interests. Resistance to any non-consensual legal authority reflects scepticism that global 'judicial power' is truly independent from real decision-makers situated in states equally motivated to protect relative power.[161] Any reliance on the separation of powers to prevent abuse of power at the global level will itself be a vulnerability for US security. The scepticism extends to municipal courts that directly exercise international judicial powers via 'universal jurisdiction', thereby eliminating the requirement of consent.[162]

157 Jacob Katz Cogan, 'Noncompliance and the International Rule of Law' (2006) 31 *Yale Journal of International Law* 189, p. 191.
158 Ibid., p. 196.
159 Ibid., p. 207.
160 Ibid., p. 194.
161 For an argument that greater independence reduces the effectiveness of international adjudication see Eric A. Posner & John C. Yoo, 'Judicial Independence in International Tribunals' (2005) 93 *California Law Review* 1.
162 This objection has been equally applied to reject the legitimacy of US courts claiming universal jurisdiction over other states under the *Alien Tort Statute* 28 U.S.C. § 1350: John B. Bellinger III, 'The U.S. Can't Be the World's Court', *Wall Street Journal,* 27 May 2009, www.wsj.com/articles/SB124338378610356591.

The emphasis on consent has manifested in significant resistance by illiberal internationalism to the penetration of IL through domestic courts. Policymakers influenced by this conception have placed a heightened emphasis on the distinction between 'self-executing' and 'non-self-executing' treaties.[163] Under this doctrine, the president's constitutional power to enter into treaties does not create rights enforceable in US courts unless the treaty is designated as 'self-executing' and thereby effective by its own force. Treaties deemed 'non-self-executing' may not be invoked in the courts unless implemented through legislation passed by the US Congress. The distinction is an elementary principle in American law, but one subject to ongoing disagreement as to the indices of a self-executing treaty and whether the supremacy clause of the US Constitution creates a presumption that treaties are self-executing.[164] The illiberal internationalist approach favours a narrow interpretation of the doctrine and even the reverse presumption that legislative consent is mandatory for treaty obligations to be enforceable in domestic courts.[165]

Resistance to judicial incorporation of IL into domestic law is evident in Henry Kissinger's characterisation of international adjudication 'being pushed to extremes which risk substituting the tyranny of judges for that of government'.[166] One expression is rejection of the hitherto settled principle that customary IL automatically forms part of the US federal common law.[167] Ashcroft disapprovingly cited reasoning in *Hamdan* that the United States is bound by a customary legal obligation contained in a treaty it has declined to ratify. For Ashcroft, it was

> strange that a justice of the United States Supreme Court basically is arguing there are only two kinds of international treaties that ought to be appropriate to shape our behaviour: the ones that we have signed and the ones we haven't signed. I think that carries the international law situation far beyond what is prudent and in the interests of the country.[168]

163 A distinction established in *Foster* v. *Neilson* (1829) 27 *U.S.* 253.

164 Curtis A. Bradley, *International Law in the U.S. Legal System* (Oxford University Press, 2015), pp. 41–4.

165 Sloss draws the relevant distinction as being between 'nationalists', who favour non-self-execution, and 'transnationalists', who favour self-execution: see David L. Sloss, 'Executing Foster *v.* Neilson: The Two-Step Approach to Analyzing Self-Executing Treaties' (2012) 53 *Harvard International Law Journal* 135, p. 137.

166 Henry Kissinger, *Does America Need a Foreign Policy?: Toward a Diplomacy for the 21st Century* (Simon and Schuster, 2002), p. 273.

167 See Curtis A. Bradley & Jack Goldsmith, 'Customary International Law As Federal Common Law: A Critique of the Modern Position' (1997) 110 *Harvard Law Review* 815.

168 Responding to a question posed by the author: John Ashcroft, 'The Constitution and the Common Defense'.

Similarly, Julian Ku and John Yoo reject judicial incorporation of IL as undemocratic and a challenge to US sovereignty. They argue that 'NGOs have used creative and effective litigation strategies to develop and enforce global governance regimes via the U.S. court system. Such litigation can result, and has resulted, in the adoption of an interpretation of international law over the opposition of the government's chief foreign policy organ: the executive branch.'[169] The penetration of IL may on rare occasions be accepted where it strategically demonstrates credible commitment to previous US consent,[170] but this remains unlikely where national security is at stake.

Liberal Nationalism

Liberal nationalist legal policy honours liberalism by engaging with IL to guard against global governance and preserve the example of American constitutional government. The ideology has a long tradition extending back to the founding fathers' belief that the United States represented a break from the European 'old order of diplomacy'.[171] Whereas liberal internationalists believe that a greater US role in international governance extends and strengthens democracy, liberal nationalists often perceive 'fundamental conflicts between democracy and international law'.[172] IL itself is said to suffer from a 'democratic deficit' such that, to the extent of any conflict, IL should be subordinated to domestic laws with democratic legitimacy.[173] The appearance of unilateralist tendencies is 'not simply out of self-interest but because the United States is committed to democratic self-government'.[174] The intervention of IL may well be legitimate for 'the many nations incapable at present of sustaining flourishing democratic politics', for whom IL 'offers the hope of

169 Julian Ku & John Yoo, *Taming Globalization: International Law, the US Constitution, and the New World Order* (Oxford University Press, 2012), pp. 3–4.

170 The Bush 43 administration's response to the ruling in *Avena and Other Mexican Nationals (Mexico* v. *United States of America)* (2004) *ICJ Rep* 12 represents a key example of illiberal internationalist IL policymaking concessions within municipal law for international institutional gains. The administration's policy was, however, ultimately struck down by the Supreme Court in *Medellín* v. *Texas* (2008) 491 *U.S.* 552.

171 Paul A. Varg, *Foreign Policies of the Founding Fathers* (Penguin Books, 1970), p. 3.

172 See Jed Rubenfeld, 'The Two World Orders', in Georg Nolte (ed.), *European and US Constitutionalism* (Cambridge University Press, 2005), p. 292.

173 Jon Kyl, Douglas J. Feith & John Fonte, 'The War of Law: How New International Law Undermines Democratic Sovereignty' (2013) 92 *Foreign Affairs* 115, p. 121.

174 Rubenfeld, 'The Two World Orders', p. 289.

economic and political reforms'.[175] But the imperative of preserving the outward example of liberalism excludes IL extending inward to America's own institutions.

Liberal internationalists are wary of any exceptional US role enmeshed in global governance, since 'American presidents may be tempted to use the role of the world's law enforcer as a justification for a new American militarism', thereby fostering broad and unaccountable executive powers.[176] These beliefs establish a preference for the US Congress to control IL policymaking, as more directly democratically accountable than presidential prerogative.[177] For these reasons, and consistent with theorised weaker support among elites, few contemporary legal policymakers advocate IL policy primarily in these terms, although it has enjoyed some resurgence, including in the policy platform of 2016 and 2020 Democratic presidential candidate Senator Bernie Sanders. The outlier status of liberal nationalism was demonstrated in the wary reception toward 2012 presidential candidate and then Congressman Ron Paul and his son Senator Rand Paul, each of whom has been categorised according to equivalent belief types.[178] Both have cast themselves as 'libertarian' candidates, and for this reason oppose US government intervention domestically and internationally as equally a threat to liberal values.[179]

This legal conception frequently aligns with the two illiberal American conceptions, with all united by a scepticism toward the utopian visions of legalism and liberal internationalism. Legal policymakers advocating quite illiberal policies have accordingly been drawn to justify municipal consequences of their positions consistently with liberal nationalism. Curtis Bradley and Jack Goldsmith have bolstered support for pragmatic US engagement with IL by arguing that the automatic incorporation of customary IL into American municipal law 'is in tension with basic notions of American representative democracy'. The danger is that law derived from the 'views and practices of the international community' is 'neither representative of the American political community nor responsive to it'.[180] Similarly, Ku and Yoo warn that the pressure to conform to international

[175] Ibid., p. 295.
[176] Ibid., pp. 295–6.
[177] See Rubenfeld's criticism of a unilateral Whitehouse decision to withdraw from treaty obligations absent congressional approval: ibid., p. 296.
[178] Walter R. Mead, 'The Tea Party and American Foreign Policy: What Populism Means for Globalism' (2011) 90 *Foreign Affairs* 28, p. 40.
[179] Ron Paul, *A Foreign Policy of Freedom* (Ludwig von Mises Institute, 2007), p. i.
[180] Bradley & Goldsmith, 'Customary International Law As Federal Common Law', p. 857.

legal obligations 'could undermine the existing balance of powers' among the three branches of US federal government.[181] In these cases, the outwardly focused illiberal internationalism is treated as complementary to rather than in competition with the inwardly focused liberal nationalism.

Protective Development of International Law

The key interest of liberal nationalism is limiting the reach of IL so that it does not encroach on the integrity of American constitutional government. IL is supported primarily as a protective framework shielding liberal states as autonomous political units. The international rule of law is therefore advanced by developing non-arbitrary legal rules necessary to uphold the stability of global relations, but without shifting the legal rights and obligations of American citizens. This creates scepticism toward institutions of global governance, which necessarily take up functions otherwise left to states themselves. The UN itself may pose a threat, for drawing the president to engage internationally, while providing authority to bypass Congress to force domestic compliance with UN standards. On this basis, Ron Paul repeatedly presented a bill to the House of Representatives to end US membership of the UN for threatening American values 'from the beginning', while his son has made similar gestures in the Senate.[182] Rubenfeld rejects suggestions that such wariness toward IL represents a 'categorical' rejection of law. Rather, the United States can legitimately submit to treaties provided 'the agreement is narrow in scope, and when it creates no third-party, supranational entities empowered to supervise U.S. policy or to make, interpret or apply U.S. law'.[183] In its strongest form, a liberal nationalist policy would isolate the United States from negotiations to establish international institutions and treaty regimes and engage only to craft laws that oppose encroachment on US autonomy.

IL may equally be developed protectively as a *constraint* against US government actions seen to erode liberty.[184] During the 2012 presidential campaign, Ron Paul made perhaps the only supportive statement about

[181] Ku & Yoo, *Taming Globalization*, p. 4.

[182] *American Sovereignty Restoration Act* 2009, H.R. 1146, introduced 24 February 2009 (2009); S.Amdt.381 to S.Con.Res.8 (2014). See Ron Paul, *A Foreign Policy of Freedom*, p. 133.

[183] Jed Rubenfeld, 'Commentary: Unilateralism and Constitutionalism' (2004) 79 *New York University Law Review* 1971, pp. 2021–4.

[184] Support among some members of the Bush 43 administration for the decision in *Hamdan* is consistent with IL being employed to correct the federal government's illiberal detainee policies: William H. Taft IV, Interview with Author (22 November 2011).

IL among Republican candidates when he called the practice of waterboarding 'torture'. This he condemned as 'illegal under international law and under our law', with it being 'really un-American to accept on principle that we will torture people that we capture'.[185] This perhaps seems contradictory given Paul's strong stance against the UN, but it is logical when read as an implication of Paul's own legal conception grounded in liberty. From the opposite side of domestic politics, Sanders has also appealed to a rule of law that constrains executive discretion. On issues of 'War and Peace', Sanders committed in 2016 to '[c]lose Guantanamo Bay, rein in the National Security Agency, abolish the use of torture, and remember what truly makes America exceptional: our values'.[186] So, arguing sharply distinguishes liberal nationalist policymakers from counterparts who invoke similar arguments to defend American sovereignty but have been among the strongest advocates of illiberal legal rights, including to engage in forms of torture.[187]

Inviolable Sovereignty

It is precisely the absence of political and normative equality between sovereign states that necessitates a framework of international legal rules maintaining inviolable sovereign equality. Here, the United States, 'suspicious of the dangerous outside world, uses international law as a shield, reifying the state system to protect its borders and its citizens'.[188] IL thus upholds reciprocal rights and duties by America and its global counterparts not to interfere in one another's affairs. Because the US system is *sui generis*, this equality does not extend to a positive obligation to participate equally in multilateral institutions. Equality is expressed only as a negative obligation to respect inviolable sovereignty – including as a constraint on the United States itself. Perennial third-party presidential candidate Ralph Nader[189] levelled strident criticism at president Obama for taking actions that 'violate international law because they infringe upon national sovereignties with deadly drones, flyovers and secret

[185] The American Presidency Project, 'Republican Candidates Debate in Spartanburg, South Carolina', 12 November 2011, www.presidency.ucsb.edu/node/297510.

[186] Bernie Sanders, 'War and Peace', Bernie Sanders for President 2016 Website, https://berniesanders.com/issues/war-and-peace/, last accessed 1 September 2016.

[187] See John C. Yoo, *War by Other Means: An Insider's Account of the War on Terror* (Atlantic Monthly Press, 2006), pp. 155–87.

[188] Cohen, 'The American Challenge to International Law', p. 564.

[189] Mead and Dueck both identify Nader with their equivalent belief type: Walter R. Mead, 'Do Jeffersonians Exist?', *The American Interest*, 8 January 2010, www.the-american-interest.com/2010/01/08/do-jeffersonians-exist/; Dueck, *Reluctant Crusaders*, p. 32.

forays by soldiers'.[190] In an analysis by Ron Paul's own think tank, Flynt and Hillary Leverett criticised the Obama administration's argument that, under the Nuclear Non-proliferation Treaty, Iran has no legal right to enrich uranium, even for civilian purposes. For the Leveretts, 'the right to indigenous technological development – including nuclear fuel-cycle capabilities, should a state choose to pursue them – is a sovereign right'.[191] No breach of IL had therefore occurred allowing the United States to intervene internationally. These arguments contradict the assumption of hegemonic IL and realist political scholarship that the United States will always seek to shape law to enhance its autonomy. For Nader, interpreting sovereignty as a constraint on US action draws back to a demand that 'the United States comply with international law and our constitution on the way to ending the American Empire's interventions worldwide'.[192] Paul's institute seeks to constrain US foreign policy by denying the Obama administration's 'main motive' of seeking 'to maximize America's freedom of unilateral military initiative and, in the Middle East, that of Israel'.[193] In both cases, states are treated as sovereign equals in law precisely to protect the integrity of the American polity against foreign entanglement.

Vertical Separation of Powers

For liberal nationalism, IL governs the relations between states while municipal law governs the relations between American citizens, which therefore should not conflict as a matter of course. The international rule of law is determined by a vertical separation between international and domestic judicial powers, rather than by a horizontal separation between international executive, legislative and judicial powers. Legalist conceptions emphasise the separation and institutionalisation of international judicial power while vertically integrating international judicial power as a check on domestic judiciaries. Liberal nationalism, in contrast, strongly resists any design purporting to fuse the judicial power of international courts to American law. The constraints of IL are ultimately set by real

190 Ralph Nader, 'Obama to Putin: Do As I Say Not As I Do', *The Nader Page*, 21 March 2014, https://blog.nader.org/2014/03/21/obama-putin-say/.

191 Flynt Leverett & Hillary M. Leverett, 'America's Lead Iran Negotiator Misrepresents U.S. Policy (and International Law) to Congress', Ron Paul Institute for Peace and Prosperity, 5 November 2013, www.ronpaulinstitute.org/archives/featured-articles/2013/november/05/america-s-lead-iran-negotiator-misrepresents-us-policy-and-international-law-to-congress/.

192 Nader, 'Obama to Putin'.

193 Leverett & Leverett, 'America's Lead Iran Negotiator Misrepresents U.S. Policy'.

policymakers who represent particularistic state interests and values foreign to the traditions defining US constitutional government. To the suggestion that the United States could democratically elect to submit to such constraints, Jed Rubenfeld provocatively warned that the 'crucial transition to beware is the moment when international cooperation shifts to international governance ... A person can sell himself into slavery voluntarily, but he will still be a slave thereafter.'[194] In this way, IL continues to operate as a framework for the basic structure of global relations without unsettling constitutionally guaranteed liberal values at the national level.

Illiberal Nationalism

Illiberal nationalism rejects the strategic value of a freestanding body of IL altogether, engaging only to defend national security and protect non-universal cultural values and identity. More than any of the other ideal types, illiberal nationalists are defined by a transactional conception of IL, being 'fundamentally dubious of the ability of law to order relations in an international community that is strikingly reminiscent of a lawless Western frontier town'.[195] In this tradition, John Bolton, former US ambassador to the UN and later a national security adviser to President Trump, sees any submission to IL as 'the first step to abandoning the United States of America. International law is not law; it is a series of political and moral arrangements that stand or fall on their own merits, and anything else is simply theology and superstition masquerading as law.'[196] The conception has a lineage in pre-enlightenment worldviews of an order founded in folk wisdom and tradition, with adherents of Mead's equivalent belief type valuing 'rule of custom' over the rule of law.[197]

Former acting US Attorney General and federal judge Robert Bork criticised IL as an expression of global anti-Americanism that targets both American moral standing and US national security.[198] For Bork, IL advocates are characterised as liberal elites who, consistent with legalism and liberal

194 Rubenfeld, 'Commentary', pp. 2022–3.
195 David J. Bederman, 'Globalization, International Law and United States Foreign Policy' (2001) 50 *Emory Law Journal* 717, p. 722.
196 John R. Bolton, 'Is There Really "Law" in International Affairs?' (2000) 10 *Transnational Law & Contemporary Problems* 1, p. 48.
197 Mead, *Special Providence*, p. 246.
198 Robert H. Bork, *Coercing Virtue: The Worldwide Rule of Judges* (AEI Press, 2003), pp. 15 & 21.

internationalism, are in search of 'transcendent principles and universalistic ideals'.[199] Elites wield these values in a 'transnational culture war' that circumvents popular democratic will.[200] Bork identified both himself and the 'great mass of citizens' with a contrary conception, centred on 'particularity – respect for difference, circumstance, tradition, history, and the irreducible complexity of human beings and human societies'.[201] These values form the populist heart of illiberal nationalism, which is incompatible with the deliberately elitist intent of internationalist legal conceptions that seek to remove popular passions from foreign policy. Daniel Bodansky clearly distinguishes Bork from Goldsmith and Posner in this respect, for viewing IL as solely a constraint rather than a tool for American foreign policy.[202]

The conception is distinct from illiberal internationalism to the extent that it interprets IL through substantive cultural values at all. Michael Ignatieff observes that Senator Jesse Helms and Southern senators generally have made the United States unique among its peers for having 'a strong domestic political constituency opposed to international human rights law on issues of family and sexual morality'.[203] Bork specifically criticised the transformation of modern IL into 'a body of rules about the rights of individuals against their own nations'[204] and the trend for courts to strike down traditional moral prohibitions by reading 'universal' values into the constitution.[205] Doing so may ensure that 'we are all more free', but it would be an improper freedom 'to act in ways that most of us had decided were unacceptable'.[206] Ultimately, there 'can be no authentic rule of law among nations until they have a common political morality or are under a common sovereignty', neither of which is at hand.[207] Illiberal nationalists thus diverge from illiberal internationalists in willingly acting against 'short-term interest' to defeat the existential threat that IL will 'constrict the United States' over time.[208]

199 Ibid., p. 3.
200 Ibid., pp. 5–6 & 11.
201 Ibid., pp. 3–4.
202 Daniel Bodansky, 'International Law in Black and White' (2006) 34 *Georgia Journal of International and Comparative Law* 285, pp. 291–2.
203 Michael Ignatieff, 'Introduction: American Exceptionalism and Human Rights', in Michael Ignatieff (ed.), *American Exceptionalism and Human Rights* (Princeton University Press, 2005), pp. 19–20.
204 Bork, *Coercing Virtue*, pp. 31 & 50.
205 Such as those relating to homosexuality, abortion rights and women's rights: see ibid., p. 5.
206 Ibid., p. 12.
207 Ibid., p. 47.
208 John R. Bolton, cited in Committee on Foreign Relations, United States Senate, *The Nomination of John R. Bolton to be U.S. Representative to the United Nations with Rank of*

Permissive Development of International Law

Where illiberal nationalists do engage with IL, they seek to interpret law permissively to eliminate any possible constraining effect on American foreign and domestic policy. Global governance is denounced as a strategy of global adversaries to constrain American sovereignty and its exceptional political culture. Any IL development that constrains US global autonomy is aggressively opposed, particularly in areas such as military policy where the United States maintains a material advantage. Here, Bork argued that it was one of the 'great deceptions practiced by proponents of international law that there is something deserving the name of "law" by which the use of armed force between nations can be controlled'.[209] Paul Wolfowitz, Deputy Secretary of Defense under President Bush 43,[210] likewise dismissed use of force rules for requiring the United States to go 'to the United Nations, or previously the League of Nations, to get a unanimous vote to do nothing, or whatever it is that those organisations do'.[211]

The critique that IL is 'infinitely flexible and indeterminate'[212] sustains a strategy of employing the rhetorical form and language of IL while rejecting accepted conventions of international legal reasoning drawn from non-American sources. The presumptively arbitrary constraints of IL are thereby neutralised through permissive interpretations that privilege national interests. This does not mean flagrant breach of treaty obligations, however, but rather that illiberal nationalists 'hesitate to ratify a treaty if they felt that at a later date the treaty would either limit American freedom of action or put the US in the position of having to break its freely given word to achieve some necessary goal'. Equally, however, adherents will 'insist on being the sole and final judge of

Ambassador and U.S. Representative to the United Nations Security Council and U.S. Representative to Sessions of the United Nations General Assembly during His Tenure of Service as U.S. Representative to the United Nations, 1st Session 109th Congress (2005), p. 53.

209 Bork, *Coercing Virtue*, p. 38.

210 Mead identifies Wolfowitz's worldview in ideas that 'resonate strongly' with the Jacksonian belief type: Walter R. Mead, 'Email from Walter Russell Mead to James Fallows', *The Atlantic*, 27 December 2001, https://www.theatlantic.com/past/docs/unbound/fallows/jf2001-12-06/mead3.htm.

211 Responding to a question posed by the author: Paul Wolfowitz, 'In Uncertain Times: American Foreign Policy after the Berlin Wall and 9/11', 13 October 2011, www.wilsoncenter.org/event/uncertain-times-american-foreign-policy-after-the-berlin-wall-and-911.

212 Bork, *Coercing Virtue*, p. 44.

whether they had kept or broken their word'.[213] President Bush 43 sought to redefine the UN's powers in entirely permissive terms in 2002 by labelling it 'irrelevant' unless it sanctioned an otherwise illegal use of force in Iraq.[214] Likewise, the notorious 'torture memos' sought to alter a well-settled definition of torture by adopting legalistic phrasing from an unrelated healthcare law.[215] That latter approach was rejected by illiberal internationalist lawyers such as Jack Goldsmith, among other senior legal policymakers, for failing to follow any accepted international conventions for interpretation.[216] Nevertheless, each of these cases remained consistent with the principle of permissively developing IL to remove any possible encumbrance on American foreign policy.

Relative Sovereignty

For illiberal nationalists, the principle of sovereign equality is foremost an attempt to constrain legitimate discrimination between states on moral and political grounds. The mischief is to create what Bork refers to as a false 'moral equivalence' that prevents the United States from distinguishing between democratic and tyrannous regimes.[217] Phyllis Schlafly colourfully denounced President Clinton's enthusiasm for international treaties by invoking Saint Paul's Second Letter to the Corinthians: 'Be ye not unequally yoked together with unbelievers, for what fellowship hath righteousness with unrighteousness?'[218] This belief is the foundation of relative sovereignty, where IL should be developed to recognise degrees of sovereignty based on the threat states pose to US national security and cultural values. Ronald Reagan's ambassador to the UN Jeane Kirkpatrick declared, in relation to the international rule of law, that 'we are as committed to that proposition today as ever in our history'.[219] Her defence of US intervention in Nicaragua was expressed in illiberal

213 Walter R. Mead, Personal Communication with Author (19 January 2015).

214 George W. Bush, 'President's Remarks at the United Nations General Assembly', 12 September 2002, https://georgewbush-whitehouse.archives.gov/news/releases/2002/09/20020912-1.html.

215 See Jay S. Bybee, 'Memorandum for Alberto R. Gonzales, Counsel to the President: Re: Standards of Conduct for Interrogation under 18 U.S.C. §§ 2340–2340A', 1 August 2002, www.justice.gov/sites/default/files/olc/legacy/2010/08/05/memo-gonzales-aug2002.pdf.

216 Jack Goldsmith, *The Terror Presidency: Law and Judgment inside the Bush Administration* (W. W. Norton & Co., 2007), pp. 165–6.

217 Bork, *Coercing Virtue*, p. 46.

218 Phyllis Schlafly (1998), cited in Anatol Lieven, *America Right or Wrong: An Anatomy of American Nationalism* (Oxford University Press, 2005), p. 16.

219 Jean J. Kirkpatrick, 'Law and Reciprocity' (1984) 78 *Proceedings of the Annual Meeting (American Society of International Law)* 59, p. 67.

nationalist terms, however, according to which the principle of 'equal application of the law' was flawed for assuming that 'all parties want the same thing, that what they really want is peace'. In circumstances where Nicaragua was seen to defy that assumption, the United States could not 'feel bound to unilateral compliance with obligations which do in fact exist under the [UN] Charter, but are renounced by others. This is not what the rule of law is all about.'[220]

The idea of states enjoying sovereignty commensurate with their moral standing has been expressed in the concept of 'rogue states'.[221] The *National Security Strategy 2002* defined the attributes of 'rogue states' to include that they 'display no regard for international law . . . and callously violate international treaties to which they are party' and that they 'reject basic human values and hate the United States and everything for which it stands'.[222] Despite being couched in terms of IL, the rogue state concept strengthened the so-called 'Bush Doctrine', of a right to 'pre-emptive' self-defence, contrary to any generally accepted legal interpretation.[223] The heart of the doctrine can be interpreted as a claim that states exhibiting proscribed attributes were 'unlike' the United States and therefore enjoyed a relative diminution in sovereignty. Eyal Benvenisti suggests that the doctrine upholds the principle of 'reciprocity' in relation to states who fail to mutually honour the foundational obligations of the international legal system.[224]

The notion of relative sovereignty has clear parallels with the theorisation of Carl Schmitt, who envisioned a bifurcation of legal personality between the full rights enjoyed by 'civilised' European states and the lesser rights of states deemed otherwise.[225] William Scheuerman's review of the Bush 43 response to the 'War on Terror' goes so far as to suggest that 'anyone familiar with Schmitt's work on international law occasionally finds herself wondering whether the White House playbook for foreign policy might not have been written by Schmitt or at least by

220 Ibid., p. 67.

221 Alex Miles, *US Foreign Policy and the Rogue State Doctrine* (Routledge, 2013), p. 113.

222 The White House, *The National Security Strategy of the United States of America 2002* (The White House, 2002), p. 14.

223 Heiko Meiertöns, *The Doctrines of US Security Policy: An Evaluation under International Law* (Cambridge University Press, 2010), pp. 179–224.

224 Eyal Benvenisti, 'The US and the Use of Force: Double-Edged Hegemony and the Management of Global Emergencies' (2004) 15 *European Journal of International Law* 677, pp. 694–5.

225 See Carl Schmitt, *The Nomos of the Earth in the International Law of the Jus Publicum Europaeum* (Telos Press Publishing, 2003), pp. 94–5 & 292.

one of his followers'.[226] This is consistent with Simpson's observation that states have long been 'differentiated in law according to their moral nature, material and intellectual power, ideological disposition or cultural attributes'.[227] Powerful states have adopted a stance of 'anti-pluralism' to reduce the sovereign rights of 'outlaw states' deemed 'mad, bad or dangerous'.[228] All such determinations by illiberal nationalists become a claim to respect sovereignty under IL in proportions equal to the threat that each state poses to US national security and values.

Municipal Supremacy

The straightforward principle for determining the integrity of judicial power is municipal supremacy, to the point of denying the character of so-called judicial power at the global level. In a 2000 address to the UNSC, Senator Helms declared: 'We abide by our treaty obligations because they are the domestic law of our land, and because our domestic leaders have judged that the agreement serves our national interest. But no treaty or law can ever supersede the one document that all Americans hold sacred: the U.S. Constitution.'[229] For illiberal nationalists, the 'insidious appeal of internationalism'[230] is that IL advocates have sought to have 'liberal views adopted abroad and then imposed in the United States'.[231] The role of international courts in this process is aimed at 'the wholesale reconstruction of American society' according to views antithetical to the traditions that define the American people.[232] The proper policy approach toward institutionalised global judicial power is therefore to oppose forcefully its influence over American government and, ultimately, its relevance to questions of international politics.

The international rule of law is not advanced through attempts to differentiate and separate forms of global power and designate some as independent 'judicial' powers. There is a long history of the United States refusing to recognise or withdrawing consent to international judicial forums. In 2018, John Bolton responded to an ICJ ruling ordering the

[226] William E. Scheuerman, 'International Law As Historical Myth' (2004) 11 *Constellations* 537, p. 537.
[227] Simpson, *Great Powers and Outlaw States*, p. 6.
[228] Ibid., pp. xi–xii.
[229] Cited in Jesse Helms, *Here's Where I Stand: A Memoir* (Random House, 2005), p. 298.
[230] Bork, *Coercing Virtue*, p. 22.
[231] Ibid., p. 16.
[232] Robert Nisbet (1982), cited in ibid., p. 10.

United States to ease sanctions against Iran by saying that 'the ICJ failed to recognize that it has *no jurisdiction* to issue any order with respect to sanctions the United States imposes to protect its own essential security under the treaty'.[233] Bolton then announced a decision to withdraw from dispute resolution provisions under the 1961 *Vienna Convention on Diplomatic Relations* (VCDR) and to 'commence a review of all international agreements that may still expose the United States to *purported binding jurisdiction* dispute resolution in the International Court of Justice. The United States will not sit idly by as baseless, politicized claims are brought against us.'[234] In neither case was the jurisdiction of the ICJ in doubt from any orthodox legal interpretation, yet it remained inherently illegitimate for illiberal nationalists. The underlying legal conception was more nuanced than a simple denial of IL, with Bolton reminding that the United States remained a party to the VCDR and therefore 'we expect all other parties to abide by their international obligations under the Convention'.[235] From competing American ideologies the withdrawal appeared to be 'an overreaction, motivated more by ideological dislike of the ICJ . . . than by any real legal necessity'.[236] Yet, for Bolton, the policy was precisely an ideological necessity: rejecting the legitimacy of judicial power at the international level.

Chapter Conclusion

What unifies the four American conceptions of the international rule of law is the belief that the United States is *not* a like case in international legal matters. Each of the ideal types in some way draws upon exceptionalist or hegemonic beliefs that justify greater autonomy and unequal treatment as a principled position for the United States within the international legal system. The legalist principle of sovereign equality – that all states enjoy equal legal personality without reference to their

[233] John R. Bolton, 'Press Briefing by Press Secretary Sarah Sanders, Small Business Administrator Linda McMahon, and National Security Advisor', 3 October 2018, www.whitehouse.gov/briefings-statements/press-briefing-press-secretary-sarah-sanders-small-business-administrator-linda-mcmahon-national-security-advisor-100318/, emphasis added. See *Alleged Violations of the 1955 Treaty of Amity, Economic Relations, and Consular Rights (Iran* v. *United States), Provisional Measures* (2018) 3 October 2018.

[234] Bolton, *Press Briefing*, emphasis added.

[235] Ibid.

[236] John B. Bellinger, 'The Trump Administration's Approach to International Law and Courts: Are We Seeing a Turn for the Worse?' (2019) 51 *Case Western Reserve Journal of International Law* 7, p. 19.

international power – is itself founded on a conscious legal fiction that all states are 'like cases'. Yet, for that reason, the presumption is inconsistent with conceptions of law that incorporate policy considerations about America's role in the operation of the legal system itself. Nico Krisch concluded that 'the hierarchical superiority of the United States is either inconsistent with sovereign equality, or – if one wants to defend hierarchy – sovereign equality has to be abandoned as a principle of international law'.[237] Any recognition of the unequal normative status of the United States entails the fiction of sovereign equality falling away in order to advance the international rule of law. For US policymakers, the principle that 'like cases are treated alike' is filtered through foreign policy ideology to reconcile privileges and the principle of 'equality' within the foundations of IL.

Each of the competing conceptions entails a distinctive definition of American national interests and a strategic formulation for advancing them through law. Mary O'Connell defends her liberal internationalism by challenging the illiberal internationalism of Goldsmith and Posner, not because they err doctrinally, but because 'if the authors of this and other attacks on international law believe they are acting in the interest of the United States, or any state, they are mistaken'.[238] National interests underpinning the concept of law are informed and structured by foreign policy ideology, with each formulation set out in this chapter founded on an alternative understanding of the purpose of IL in American global engagement. The meaning of 'coherence' in American policy toward the ICC, the subject of the remainder of this book, becomes that a legal policymaker's stance on any one of the three international rule of law elements is a reliable indicator of legal positions taken on the remaining two elements.

[237] Krisch, 'More Equal Than the Rest?', p. 174.
[238] Mary Ellen O'Connell, *The Power and Purpose of International Law* (Oxford University Press, 2008), p. 14.

PART II

Contesting Global Legal Power through the ICC

4

Clinton Administration, 1992–2000

The presidency of Bill Clinton coincided with the most decisive years for the ICC as the project progressed from a preliminary ILC report in 1992[1] to the foundational treaty signed by 139 countries by the end of 2000.[2] In 1992, the project consisted merely of provisional agreements by the Bush 41 administration about the notion of the court, thereby leaving the new administration the task of negotiating the ICC's function and design. These years were also notable for persistent allegations of contradictory policy: that the United States was a prominent ICC advocate in the early years; conspicuously voted against the final treaty concluded in 1998; then ultimately signed, but while warning against Senate ratification. This is therefore fertile ground for explaining whether and how ideology illuminates these apparent contradictions in American IL policy.

International opposition to US policy was expressed in clear legalist terms by NGOs, who occupied a uniquely influential and officially sanctioned position in developing the court.[3] Since the earliest days, the peak body for these NGOs has been the Coalition for the International Criminal Court (CICC), which has dedicated itself to achieving US ratification of the Rome Statute.[4] Based in New York, the CICC has been particularly significant in the extent to which it was directly involved in challenging US policy from the negotiations at Rome through to the present day. At its founding, the CICC established core principles for a court developed in accordance with the international rule of law that included:

[1] International Law Commission, *Report of the International Law Commission on the Work of Its 44th Session*, 47th Sess. UN GAOR, Supp. 10, U.N. Doc. A/47/10 (4 May–24 July 1992).

[2] *Rome Statute of the International Criminal Court* (1998).

[3] See M. Cherif Bassiouni, *The Legislative History of the International Criminal Court: Introduction, Analysis, and Integrated Text of the Statute, Elements of Crimes and Rules of Procedure and Evidence* (Transnational Publishers, 2005), vol. 1, pp. 74–5.

[4] See Fanny Benedetti, Karine Bonneau & John Washburn, *Negotiating the International Criminal Court: New York to Rome, 1994–1998* (Martinus Nijhoff Publishers, 2013), p. 68.

1 A court that would be fair to all, not with one system for the strong (i.e. the Permanent Members of the Security Council) and another for others;
2 A court that would be effective, not hampered by the veto power set forth in Article 27, 3 of the UN Charter; and
3 Guaranteed independence from the Security Council for both the court and the prosecutor.[5]

These principles represented the core elements of a legalist conception of the ICC as it structured global challenges to the integrity of US policy.

Significant divergence, of course, existed *between* states opposing US ICC policy in this period, with positions during the Rome Conference ranging from a more legalist conception by Germany[6] to a French position reflecting many of the American preferences. Nevertheless, although P5 UNSC members maintained a loose coalition for much of the negotiations, the UK eventually broke away, and France and Russia ultimately approved the statute after obtaining last-minute concessions.[7] France, in particular, thereafter defended its altered position against US demands as 'a matter of principle'.[8] The assumption of a largely united approach opposing US policy is corroborated by the close alignment between the ICC policy of the European Union (EU), the CICC and the bloc of over 60 countries comprising the so-called 'like-minded states' (LMS). The LMS included every member of the EU (with the notable exception of France) along with middle powers such as Australia and Canada, and were always 'sympathetic' to the position taken by NGOs at the Rome Conference.[9] Moreover, the EU has cited the CICC as playing a central role coordinating policy among the three groups.[10]

[5] Cited in Claude E. Welch Jr & Ashley F. Watkins, 'Extending Enforcement: The Coalition for the International Criminal Court' (2011) 33 *Human Rights Quarterly* 927, p. 967.

[6] See Yvonne Dutton, *Rules, Politics, and the International Criminal Court: Committing to the Court* (Routledge, 2013), pp. 70–1.

[7] Specifically a seven-year 'opt-out provision' against prosecution: William K. Lietzau, 'International Criminal Law after Rome: Concerns from a US Military Perspective' (2001) 64 *Law and Contemporary Problems* 119, p. 131.

[8] Caroline Fehl, *Living with a Reluctant Hegemon: Explaining European Responses to US Unilateralism* (Oxford University Press, 2012), pp. 103 & 108.

[9] Theo van Boven, 'The European Union and the International Criminal Court' (1998) 5 *Maastricht Journal of European and Comparative Law* 325, p. 325. See Philippe Krisch QC & Darryl Robinson, 'Reaching Agreement at the Rome Conference', in Antonio Cassese, Paola Gaeta & John R. W. D. Jones (eds.), *The Rome Statute of the International Criminal Court: A Commentary* (Oxford University Press, 2002), pp. 70–1. Also termed 'the Like-Minded Group' in some accounts.

[10] General Secretariat of the Council, 'The European Union and the International Criminal Court', May 2010, https://publications.europa.eu/en/publication-detail/-/publication/c3f8f6f3-b507-4adf-8111-b8b6f2cf8bfd, p. 29.

Despite expectations among some participants that US involvement might lead to its membership, Michael Struett concluded that 'the court that was promoted by the U.S. government is not the one whose charter was adopted in Rome in 1998'.[11] This chapter analyses decision-making processes to demonstrate that US policy never accepted legalist ideals but, rather, was structured by ideologically informed American conceptions of the international rule of law. The administration's approach often aligned with that of global court advocates in the commitment to ending international criminal impunity, but it diverged on the ideal form of global governance for achieving that objective. Positions crucially diverged in US resistance to sovereign equality, instead arguing for legal recognition of exceptional global responsibilities and unique global power. The administration additionally insisted that the court's judicial and prosecutorial powers be subjected to US checks and balances. For each of these elements, US interests were crystallised in conceptions of law itself, which structured US decision-making to the exclusion of legal ideals advocated by other major participants.

Inherited ICC Policy: Bush 41 Administration

The Clinton administration did not instigate US engagement with the ICC but, rather, faced the choice of either adopting policies set in place by the Bush 41 administration or forging a new path. The Bush administration had reacted to the issue only as it arose partway through its term, and largely as a second order issue, but its response exhibited the relatively clear ideological structure evident in its IL policy more generally. Stuart Malawer described a 'Reagan corollary' to IL consisting of 'the assertion of unilateral state action and a broad right of self-defense, less reliance on international institutions such as the United Nations, and an emphasis on a state's right to pursue its national interests'. This was no mere 'careless disregard' for law; rather, it was 'an attempt to pressure the international legal system into changing in a manner beneficial to United States interests'.[12] Struett reviewed interactions with the ICJ across both the Reagan and the Bush 41 administrations to find 'an entirely strategic

[11] Michael J. Struett, *The Politics of Constructing the International Criminal Court: NGOs, Discourse, and Agency* (Palgrave Macmillan, 2008), pp. 70–1.

[12] Stuart S. Malawer, 'Reagan's Law and Foreign Policy, 1981–1987: The "Reagan Corollary" of International Law' (1988) 29 *Harvard International Law Journal* 85, p. 85.

attitude' in which each administration 'sought to use that international court as one instrument to obtain its strategic objectives'.[13]

This analysis is corroborated by the account of Michael Scharf who, as Attorney Adviser at the Office of the Legal Adviser, was tasked with implementing much of US ICC policy during the period from the 1989 UNGA recommitment to the project until the end of the Bush 41 administration.[14] Although Scharf cited his 'personal support for the concept of an ICC', he described the policy direction as one of '"cautious scepticism" about the feasibility and desirability of establishing an ICC'.[15] That translated into engaging diplomatically with ICC advocates but pragmatically opposing their agenda. The misgivings of State and Justice Department officials led the administration to consistently cite problems with UN proposals as a strategy for stalling progress. As a whole, the establishment of the ICC 'never received serious consideration by top officials'.[16]

The administration's policy revealed an illiberalism in prioritising development of the law to enhance American national security interests, over and above the court's stated purpose of addressing human rights violations. Crimes were relevant to this IL policy only to the extent to which they had a direct impact on American security, with the administration concerned primarily with the legal regime governing terrorism and international drug trafficking.[17] It is notable that the administration's strongest support was tied to the specific context of American preparation for the 1991 Persian Gulf War. Secretary of State James Baker and Under Secretary of State Robert Kimmitt both suggested they were open to the idea of an international court to prosecute Saddam Hussein when framed as part of overall military action.[18] The administration nevertheless remained resistant to the idea, causing former Nuremburg prosecutor Professor Ferencz to express incomprehension given the atrocities being committed in Iraq.[19] However, the

[13] Struett, *The Politics of Constructing the ICC*, p. 68.

[14] See Benjamin B. Ferencz, 'International Criminal Code and Court: Where They Stand and Where They're Going' (1992) 30 *Columbia Journal of Transnational Law* 375, p. 388.

[15] Michael P. Scharf, 'Getting Serious about an International Criminal Court' (1994) 6 *Pace International Law Review* 103, pp. 103–4.

[16] Ibid., p. 105.

[17] See Michael P. Scharf, 'The Jury Is Still Out on the Need for an International Criminal Court' (1991) 1 *Duke Journal of Comparative and International Law* 135, pp. 149–54.

[18] Stuart H. Deming, 'War Crimes and International Criminal Law' (1994) 28 *Akron Law Review* 421, p. 422.

[19] Ferencz, 'International Criminal Code and Court', pp. 385–6.

apparently contradictory policy cohered to an illiberal internationalist international rule of law that embraced legal architecture with a limited jurisdiction to facilitate narrowly defined security interests. This is distinct from supporting the court to vindicate breaches of human rights perpetrated by Hussein as its primary objective, as would be the case according to a legalist or liberal internationalist policy. Support for a tribunal advancing limited strategic objectives in the aftermath of a war is easily distinguished from general support for a standing judicial institution.

An internationalist outlook was also evident in the administration's concern for maintaining the existing framework governing international criminal law composed of a loose network of treaties and extradition agreements. Pursuant to the 1989 UNGA resolution, the ILC submitted a report on the scope and feasibility of establishing international criminal jurisdiction.[20] The US representative to the UN Sixth Committee John Knox responded that, in the area of criminal law, there were already 'effective national and international systems in place' and, as such, it was 'not clear to us that the court would contribute to the existing system'.[21] In essence the proposed court was seen to derogate from the international rule of law as established by existing legal relations between national courts and treaty regimes, which enabled rather than constrained pragmatic pursuit of national interests.

The intersection of illiberal and internationalist beliefs was most clearly demonstrated in the administration's responses toward policy-makers advocating competing IL policies. A key initiative of Bush's opponents, led principally by Senator Arlen Specter, was the passage of legislation through the US House of Representatives in October 1990 calling for the president, among others, to explore the establishment of an international court and report their findings back to Congress.[22] The initial bill was ultimately amended to incorporate the administration's concerns, expressed through Assistant Secretary of State for Legislative Affairs Janet G. Mullins. She wrote that 'it would be premature and unwise for the Congress to go on record' supporting the court. Reasons cited included that the proposal would potentially 'divert attention and

20 International Law Commission, *Report of the International Law Commission on the Work of Its Forty-Second Session*, UN Doc. A/CN.4/SER.A/1990 (1990).

21 Office of the Legal Adviser, Department of State, *Digest of United States Practice in International Law: 1989–1990* (International Law Institute, 2003), p. 134.

22 Ultimately passed by both houses as *Foreign Operations, Export Financing, and Related Programs Appropriations Act* 1991 Pub L 101–513, s. 599E.

resources away from more practical and readily achievable means for combating international criminal activities'. An internationalist stance was affirmed by emphasising means that included strengthening 'international organisations . . ., modernising extradition treaties, negotiating Mutual Legal Assistance Treaties' and 'devising new international agreements'.[23] At the same time, the policy toward the court was constructed upon an illiberal view of IL as a political tool employed by states to further non-universal security interests. Foremost among reasons for scepticism were risks that the court 'could develop into a politicised body, in which case we might find the court interpreting crimes in unhelpful ways'.[24] The inevitable politicisation of an international court was a concern raised repeatedly, with the State Department previously warning the House Foreign Affairs Committee of a court 'acting contrary to US interests on a whole range of issues or contrary to US notions of governing international law and fundamental fairness'.[25]

Scharf well summed up the overall Bush 41 policy when recommending, during the closing months of the administration, that the US continue advancing interests through the court while preserving its strategic autonomy. Although joining the court as a member 'might be of little utility to the United States', it was unavoidable that the court would affect US interests. American policy should therefore be to influence the 'structure, procedures, and substance' of the court, while avoiding its most ambitious claims.[26] Doing so became the illiberal internationalist IL policy inherited by the newly inaugurated Clinton administration.

Dominant Foreign Policy Ideology

The general foreign policy worldview of the Clinton administration is commonly characterised as strongly internationalist and more inclined toward liberal values.[27] Ivo Daalder and James Lindsay describe the Clinton presidency and its initial advocacy for the ICC as 'a continuation of the traditional Wilsonian approach of building a world order based on

[23] Janet G. Mullins, *Letter from Assistant Secretary Mullins to Dante B. Fascell, Chairman, Committee of Foreign Affairs, House of Representatives* (11 December 1990), p. 3.
[24] Ibid., p. 2.
[25] Department of State, *Digest of US Practice: 1989–1990*, p. 128.
[26] Scharf, 'The Jury Is Still Out on the Need for an ICC', p. 168.
[27] Walter R. Mead, *Special Providence: American Foreign Policy and How It Changed the World* (Routledge, 2002), pp. 282–96; Colin Dueck, *Reluctant Crusaders: Power, Culture, and Change in American Grand Strategy* (Princeton University Press, 2006), pp. 128–37.

the rule of law'.[28] Clinton's first Secretary of State, Warren Christopher, noted Clinton's early embrace of democracy promotion as a 'core tenet of his foreign policy'.[29] During the 1992 presidential election, Clinton had pointed to conflicts in the former Yugoslavia, Haiti and Somalia and to the 1989 Tiananmen Square protests, to argue that 'the [Bush 41] administration is turning its back on the violations of basic human rights and our democratic values'.[30] Mead saw this as flowing from Clinton's desire 'to use the window of the "democratic spring" [following the end of the Cold War] to strengthen the role of international judicial and political institutions, to usher in an era of law-based international relations'.[31] In Clinton's own words:

> [P]romoting democracy does more than advance our ideals. It reinforces our interests. Where the rule of law prevails, where governments are held accountable, where ideas and information flow freely, economic development and political stability are more likely to take hold and human rights are more likely to thrive. History teaches us that democracies are less likely to go to war, less likely to traffic in terrorism and more likely to stand against the forces of hatred and destruction, more likely to become good partners in diplomacy and trade. So promoting democracy and defending human rights is good for the world and good for America.[32]

This formulation of democracy promotion combines liberalism and internationalism to directly structure the design and development of IL and thereby promote US interests.

Liberal internationalist beliefs were recurrent themes for both of Clinton's Secretaries of State. For Warren Christopher, the United States supported democracy and human rights in Asia because 'states that respect the rule of law at home are more likely to observe the rule of international law abroad'.[33] By recognising America's values as universal, and its exceptional role in spreading them, the United States was 'not imposing an American model; we are supporting a universal impulse for freedom'. Moreover, American 'involvement is essential to regional peace, prosperity, and the promotion of freedom ... [T]he universal

[28] Ivo H. Daalder & James M. Lindsay, *America Unbound: The Bush Revolution in Foreign Policy* (Brookings Institution Press, 2003), p. 12.

[29] Warren Christopher, *In the Stream of History: Shaping Foreign Policy for a New Era* (Stanford University Press, 1998), p. 63, n. 2.

[30] Cited in Dueck, *Reluctant Crusaders*, p. 128.

[31] Mead, *Special Providence*, p. 284.

[32] William J. Clinton, 'Remarks at the University of Connecticut in Storrs', 15 October 1995, www.presidency.ucsb.edu/node/220652.

[33] Christopher, *In the Stream of History*, p. 159.

values we embody – freedom, democracy, and the rule of law – make us a beacon for all the peoples of the region.'[34]

Clinton's second Secretary of State, Madeleine Albright, turned to an exceptionalist portrayal of the United States as 'the indispensable nation'.[35] Her explanation of the phrase is revealing for both the meaning and the legal impact of her beliefs. Albright acknowledged that the claim could be seen as 'arrogant', but asserted that it referred primarily to 'the reality that most large-scale initiatives required at least some input from the United States if they were to succeed'. If this were all that Albright meant, it would demonstrate not exceptionalist thought per se, but merely an awareness of uniquely preponderant global power. Her more ideologically informed meaning is evident in the belief that America is 'an exceptional country, but that is because we have led in creating standards that work for everyone, not because we are an exception to the rules'. Here, Albright appeals to a perceived universality of US values and motivations and, thus, to the claim that US legal obligations and political interests are reconciled. In this frame, Albright declared: 'If we attempt to put ourselves above or outside of the international system, we invite everyone else to do so as well. Then moral clarity is lost, the foundation of our leadership becomes suspect, the cohesive pull of law is weakened, and those who do not share our values find openings to exploit.'[36] The United States as 'indispensable nation' is not merely a claim to the global significance of US power but, more fundamentally, that the liberal values directing US policy are indispensable to the international rule of law.

The historical record also indicates that the administration was influenced more generally by internationalist principles spanning both ends of the liberal–illiberal dimension. Albright appeared mindful of straddling competing values when saying:

> I hoped never again to hear foreign policy described as a debate between Wilsonian idealists and geopolitical realists. In our era, no President or

[34] Ibid., p. 159. Notably Christopher fails to mention the ICC in this or his subsequent memoir: Warren Christopher, *Chances of a Lifetime: A Memoir* (Simon and Schuster, 2001). Scheffer notes the same omission in Albright's memoir: David J. Scheffer, *All the Missing Souls: A Personal History of the War Crimes Tribunals* (Princeton University Press, 2012), p. 230.

[35] Albright attributes the phrase to President Clinton from the period when she served as UN Ambassador: Madeleine K. Albright, *Madam Secretary: A Memoir* (Macmillan, 2003), p. 506.

[36] Ibid., p. 506.

> Secretary of State could manage events without combining the two. Under President Clinton we were determined to do the right thing but in a tough-minded way.[37]

Albright's rendering of these traditions is something of a strawman argument in that few policymakers would advocate the pure idealism or amoral realism that she claimed to reject. Nevertheless, her characterisation does recognise the influence of beliefs underpinning the two variants of internationalism: promoting democracy internationally at the same time as working with nondemocratic states, and defending human rights but being prepared to balance them against national security issues.

The most consequential figure for US ICC policy through this period was David Scheffer, who worked under Albright as the first Ambassador-at-Large for War Crimes Issues.[38] The very creation of this role was significant in signalling US commitment to addressing war crimes as a central component of its IL policy.[39] Scheffer's memoir is a valuable account of his conception of the court and the political machinations that produced final policy outcomes. His support for the ICC aimed to make credible the Clinton administration's principled claim that it 'took the rule of law seriously'.[40] Scheffer's own beliefs are unequivocal in the American obligation to engage internationally through IL to uphold liberal values, yet his public statements make it equally clear that no single set of ideas captured the logic of US IL policy during the period. His account demonstrates especially that competing legal conceptions were not as compatible as Albright claims. Albright herself testified to the House of Representatives that any US position was subject to the restriction that, in relation to the Departments of Defense and Justice, 'the key agencies have to feel comfortable'.[41] For Scheffer, the administration's 'commitment to international justice made a significant difference' and yet, through the influence of competing beliefs, leading figures were 'sometimes weakened in their resolve'.[42] Understanding the specific legal positions taken by the United States therefore requires an account

[37] Ibid., p. 505.
[38] Described by Albright as the 'father of the war crimes tribunals': Scheffer, *All the Missing Souls*, pp. 8–9.
[39] Ibid., p. 3.
[40] Ibid., p. 172.
[41] Ibid., pp. 178–9.
[42] Ibid., p. 7.

that disaggregates competing policymaking voices to reveal underlying belief structures about the international rule of law.

Developing Non-arbitrary Global Governance

The explicit policy shift from obstruction under the Bush 41 administration to active support under Clinton was interpreted by both America's global counterparts and domestic court advocates as renewed commitment to 'greatly strengthen the rule of law'.[43] It is thus relevant to ask whether the preferred American policy of negotiating a treaty binding on all parties, including itself, was evidence that US policymakers shared a common understanding of non-arbitrary global governance. If so, the eventual refusal to endorse a court design greatly strengthening the formal structure of global governance could be interpreted as erosion of the legal ideal by interests extraneous to law. Alternatively, US policy was structured from the beginning by a particularistic conception of the international rule of law, in which formalised development of international criminal law was only one path toward non-arbitrary governance. The liberal internationalism evident in the administration's legal policy more generally would suggest formalised obligations only as a means for achieving that end, but not a necessary one. The more consequential requirement for realising the international rule of law would remain effective transnational processes to promote the integrity of law. US policy shown to be structured by ideologically informed American conceptions would provide robust evidence that legalist beliefs remained external to decision-making processes.

Legalist Policy

Global advocates for the ICC framed the project as a natural evolution to close gaps in the governance of international criminal law. At the time of its negotiation, then UN Secretary General Kofi Annan described the ICC as 'a missing link in the international legal system'.[44] From this perspective, any gap in defining and enforcing international rights and duties was necessarily filled by discretionary

[43] See Johan D. van der Vyver, *The International Criminal Court: American Responses to the Rome Conference and the Role of the European Union* (Inst. für Rechtspolitik, 2003), p. 3.

[44] Cited in James Podgers, 'Praised and Prodded: U.N. Conferees Urge Lawyers to Build on Past Efforts to Bolster Human Rights' (1998) 84 *American Bar Association Journal* 92, p. 92.

decisions of states and was thereby *ipso facto* inconsistent with the rule of law. The task of developing non-arbitrary forms of global governance translated into broad ICC jurisdiction, to eliminate as far as possible the extra-legal discretion of states when responding to international criminal matters. That principle was demonstrated most clearly in opposition to granting amnesties from international prosecutions as part of negotiated peace settlements. Gerhard Hafner et al. argued that it was imperative for the ICC to exclude recognition of amnesties 'irrespective of the political implications of the situation'. To do otherwise ran 'counter to the basic objectives of the United Nations'.[45] Here, legalist advocates applied a doctrinal analysis to the formal 'legal effect' of the Rome Statute crimes, which were held to establish an *erga omnes* duty to prosecute. The case for removing prosecutorial discretion from states turned on a view that '[u]nlike the horizontal relations in extradition and judicial assistance, the relation between the ICC and states parties is a vertical one'.[46] Realising the international rule of law thus required both universal accession to the court's founding statute and substitution of the court's formal authority for political discretion in global governance.

Beliefs of American Legal Policymakers

The Exceptionalist Foundation of Liberal Internationalist Support

Scharf, who continued in his role as Attorney Adviser during the transition to the Clinton administration, cited a 'major policy reversal' taking place from October 1993.[47] State Department Legal Adviser Conrad Harper announced that the new administration had 'decided to take a fresh look' at supporting the court, accepting that the project was 'a serious and important effort which should be continued, and we intend to be actively and constructively involved'.[48] According to Scheffer, on as many as six occasions prior to the Rome Conference, the president himself expressed his personal belief that 'before this decade and this century end, we should establish a permanent international court to

45 Gerhard Hafner, Kristen Boon, Anne Rübesame & Jonathan Huston, 'A Response to the American View as Presented by Ruth Wedgwood' (1999) 10 *European Journal of International Law* 108, pp. 109 & 111.

46 Ibid., p. 112.

47 Scharf, 'Getting Serious about an ICC', p. 103.

48 Cited in ibid., p. 109.

prosecute crimes against humanity'.[49] The US Senate fortified this stance by stating that the ICC 'would greatly strengthen the international rule of law' and thereby 'serve the interests of the United States and the world community'.[50] Yet careful examination reveals that, despite a common desire to end impunity under the law, the administration's renewed support always remained distinct from that of global partners.

The commitment to developing global governance through IL was evident in the 1993 Senate confirmation hearings of Warren Christopher. Chairman Claiborne Pell opened by framing the immediate post–Cold War world in internationalist terms as one where 'we face the task of devising or revising mechanisms to deal with new circumstances. In particular, we have an opportunity to reclaim the dream of the U.N. as an effective agent for world peace.' The Chairman concluded his remarks by reminding the nominee that 'you will take office at a time when you can truly reshape the world'.[51] The specific issue of the ICC was raised by Senator Christopher Dodd, who lamented that IL policy under the Reagan and Bush 41 administrations 'robbed us of the moral authority to be the standard bearer of the rule of law internationally'.[52] Dodd's own father had been Deputy Prosecutor at the Nuremberg trials,[53] with the vision of both father and son cited by Clinton as contributing to his ultimate support for the permanent court.[54] In the nomination hearing, Dodd recognised a 'tremendous opportunity for this country to help rewrite the rules of international law' and specifically to 'strengthen international institutions that can then act as impartial guardians of this new world order'. In this context, Dodd continued:

> [D]espite opposition in the past by the Bush Administration, I am firmly convinced that the time is particularly auspicious for the United States to call for the establishment of a permanent international crimes tribunal . . .

[49] David J. Scheffer, 'The United States and the International Criminal Court' (1999) 93 *American Journal of International Law* 12, p. 13. See William J. Clinton, 'Remarks in New York City Commemorating the 50th Anniversary of the Universal Declaration of Human Rights', 9 December 1997, www.presidency.ucsb.edu/node/223909.

[50] *Foreign Relations Authorization Act, Fiscal Year 1994 and 1995,* 1994 Pub L 103–236.

[51] Committee on Foreign Relations, United States Senate, *Nomination of Warren M. Christopher To Be Secretary of State: Hearing before the Committee on Foreign Relations United States Senate,* 1st Session 103rd Congress (1993), pp. 1–2.

[52] Ibid., p. 13.

[53] See Christopher Dodd, *Letters from Nuremberg: My Father's Narrative of a Quest for Justice* (Random House Digital, Inc., 2008).

[54] William J. Clinton, *My Life* (Hutchinson, 2004), p. 674.

> Recent events suggest that a crimes tribunal is a critical element to restoring and maintaining the international rule of law.[55]

Even from this point, the project was signalling a special US role and, moreover, one likely to challenge a formalised design excluding policy discretion. Dodd emphasised that the ICC would 'never happen, in my view, unless the United States takes the leadership role in this issue'.[56] Warren Christopher concurred in rejecting the Bush 41 policy as 'fairly abysmal', while framing the court as realising rather than superseding American exceptionalism:

> In the International Court of Justice, our refusing to cede or grant jurisdiction and our retaining the right of unilateral withdrawal is one of the things that sets back the entire enterprise. If the leading nation in the world feels that when it does not want to risk a bad outcome it simply picks up its marbles and goes home, that is a very unsatisfactory result . . . I think the United States, as the leading power in the world now, has special responsibilities that we ought to undertake to carry out.[57]

The distinction from legalism matters, since this exchange presupposes an exceptional US role making IL work, and one advocated throughout the Clinton administration as more decisive to the international rule of law than the substance of any ICC agreement.

The significance of this more policy-oriented understanding of the ICC is evident in the words of Christopher's successor Madeleine Albright, who contextualised the court within broader liberal internationalist commitment to 'building a more integrated, stable, and democratic world, with increased security for all who respect the interests and rights of others'.[58] That understanding again emphasised transnational connections between international criminal law and democracy as central to promoting non-arbitrary governance. US commitment to underwriting any process that strengthened these liberal values mattered, and more so than any specific court design formalised in a binding treaty, or of securing its universal membership.

Pragmatic Development of the ICC

Although liberal internationalist beliefs dominated in this period, they competed throughout with alternative ideologically informed conceptions of IL.

[55] United States Senate, *Nomination of Warren M. Christopher*, p. 13.
[56] Ibid., p. 72.
[57] Ibid., pp. 72–3.
[58] Albright, *Madam Secretary*, pp. 504–5.

In particular, legal policymakers from the Department of Defense strongly emphasised a more pragmatic approach, and one moreover that Scheffer believed 'undercut my negotiating posture with other governments'.[59] Immediately before the Rome Conference, the Pentagon issued a cable to military representatives from over 100 states expressing concerns that advocates were expanding crimes within the court's statute beyond their customary limits. The cable warned that the ICC 'must not be used to push the envelope of international law'.[60] The most detailed account of these military views is found in the jurisprudence of Major William Lietzau, who joined the US delegation to Rome in his capacity as Deputy Legal Counsel to the Office of the Chairman of the Joint Chiefs of Staff. Following the Conference, he went on to prepare the draft elements of crimes relied on at the Preparatory Commission for the Establishment of an ICC between 1999 and 2002.[61] Scheffer described Lietzau as 'instrumental' in persuading participants at Rome and the Preparatory Commission to explicitly define elements of crimes falling under the court's jurisdiction rather than leaving them to judicial discretion.[62]

Lietzau's jurisprudence was firmly internationalist in advocating global institution building and in opposing the Rome Statute for threatening American international engagement.[63] Along the values dimension, his position primarily emphasised illiberal concerns to maximise American strategic autonomy for national security purposes. He did acknowledge the broader liberal context of the court as a means for addressing atrocities, but this concern was addressed by advocating greater US strategic autonomy rather than through the formalised authority of a court. Broadly, he advocated an IL policy balancing liberal concerns of attaining justice on the one hand with 'preservation of state sovereignty and current practices that promote international peace and security' on the other.[64]

[59] Ibid., p. 190. See Karl K. Schonberg, 'The General's Diplomacy: US Military Influence in the Treaty Process, 1992–2000' (2002) 3 *Seton Hall Journal of Diplomacy and International Relations* 68, pp. 78–9.

[60] Dated 31 March 1998 and reproduced as 'Appendix C' in Ellen Grigorian, *The International Criminal Court Treaty: Description, Policy Issues, and Congressional Concerns* (Congressional Research Service, 6 January 1999), p. 32.

[61] See UN, 'Preparatory Commission for the International Criminal Court', Rome Statute of the International Criminal Court, 1999–2002, http://legal.un.org/icc/prepcomm/prepfra.htm.

[62] Scheffer, *All the Missing Souls*, pp. 231–2.

[63] See Lietzau, 'International Criminal Law after Rome', p. 126.

[64] Ibid., p. 139.

What is notable about Lietzau's recollections of and proposals for the court is his framing that 'the rule of law must itself be preeminent'.[65] This became a touchstone in Lietzau's criticism of the ICC design and informed his argument against US accession. He expressed apprehension at the 'paradigm' guiding court proponents 'that international humanitarian law progresses in a linear fashion, with progress equalling more law.'[66] The process of establishing the municipal rule of law necessitates the taming of political power by closing gaps in the legal framework regulating citizens' rights and duties. Lietzau rejected the projection of a domestic analogy to the international level, however, as not only misguided but also a threat to the realisation of the international rule of law itself. Rather than seeing law controlling politics in the court, he identified the court itself as threatening to constrain American foreign policy through 'politically-motivated charges'.[67] This view was no less focused on the idea of the international rule of law than the dominant approach within the administration, but it eschewed the central focus on liberal values, which were promoted only indirectly through pragmatic considerations of national security.

Pragmatism was also evident in the preferences among some US legal policymakers to exclude the role of IL altogether, where strictures of international criminal law were seen to impede peace agreements. This initiative was led in part by then national security adviser Sandy Berger, with specific reference to the 1994 amnesty given to coup leaders in Haiti to facilitate the return of ousted president Jean-Bertrand Aristide.[68] Here, Scheffer acknowledged that the very idea of limiting jurisdiction by political amnesties 'seemingly flew in the face of the entire purpose' of the ICC.[69] John Czarnetzky and Ronald Rychlak observed that the ICC jurisdictional regime was 'intended to make clear that a *purely* juridical model is the only appropriate method for dealing with human rights violations'.[70] However, in illiberal internationalist

65 Ibid., p. 139.

66 William K. Lietzau, 'Checks and Balances and Elements of Proof: Structural Pillars for the International Criminal Court' (1999) 32 *Cornell International Law Journal* 477, p. 487.

67 William K. Lietzau, 'Comments to the Panel on the International Criminal Court: Contemporary Perspectives and Prospects for Ratification' (2000) 16 *New York Law School Journal of Human Rights* 512, p. 516.

68 Michael P. Scharf, 'Justice versus Peace', in Sarah B. Sewell & Carl Kaysen (eds.), *The United States and the International Criminal Court: National Security and International Law* (Rowman & Littlefield Publishers, 2000), p. 180.

69 Scheffer, *All the Missing Souls*, p. 183.

70 John M. Czarnetzky & Ronald J. Rychlak, 'An Empire of Law: Legalism and the International Criminal Court' (2003) 79 *Notre Dame Law Review* 55, p. 94, original emphasis.

terms, pragmatically defining exceptions to law's proper reach remained entirely consistent with eliminating arbitrariness within a stable global legal system.

Nationalist Objections

From the very first discussions in 1994, competing internationalist conceptions were met with forceful nationalist opposition to the very concept of the court and any enlargement of the international legal system. At a 1998 US Senate hearing on the Rome Conference, the chairman, Senator Rod Grams, expressed liberal nationalist concerns that the court's jurisdiction came at the expense of US constitutional protections and that judges might be selected from undemocratic countries lacking the rule of law at home. He concluded with the plea that the court 'shares the same fate as the League of Nations and collapses without U.S. support ... [T]his court truly I believe is the monster and it is the monster that we need to slay.'[71] The voice of illiberal nationalist opposition was led by Senator Jesse Helms, who served as Chairman of the Senate Committee on Foreign Relations from 1995 to 2001. In an open letter to Secretary Albright he declared himself 'unalterably opposed to the creation of a permanent U.N. criminal court' that would be 'dead-on-arrival' in the Senate unless 'a clear U.S. veto' was provided for.[72] Scheffer took the 'veto' demand to mean total UNSC control, which equated the legitimacy of the court with its development as a permissive institution enabling but never constraining US power. In the absence of this unlikely design, Scheffer concluded that Helms' singular intention became 'to kill the court and any American role in it'.[73] For these reasons, Scheffer described feeling only 'soiled' when Helms later congratulated him for ultimately rejecting the Rome Statute.[74] In these examples, nationalist US legal policymakers contested not only legalism but also internationalist American policymakers, with agreement only on the outcome of all opposing the final agreement at Rome.

[71] Committee on Foreign Relations, United States Senate, *Is a U.N. International Criminal Court in the U.S. National Interest?: Hearing before the Subcommittee on International Operations of the Committee on Foreign Relations United States Senate,* 2nd Session 105th Congress (1998), pp. 2–4.

[72] Jesse Helms, 'Helms Vows to Make War on U.N. Court', *The New York Times,* 27 March 1998, www.nytimes.com/1998/03/27/world/helms-vows-to-make-war-on-un-court.html.

[73] Scheffer, *All the Missing Souls,* p. 188.

[74] Ibid., p. 231.

Conclusion

US policy toward developing global governance has been perceived as the high-water mark of contradictions in its ICC policy. The United States situated itself as a champion of the ICC, rejected the court's founding treaty at Rome, signed it more than two years later on the last day possible after significant internal lobbying, but did so while advising against future US membership of the court. At the point of signing, President Clinton declared:

> I believe that a properly constituted and structured International Criminal Court would make a profound contribution in deterring egregious human rights abuses worldwide, and that signature increases the chances for productive discussions with other governments to advance these goals in the months and years ahead.[75]

Clinton later recalled of this statement: 'I had been among the first world leaders to call for an International War Crimes Tribunal, and I thought the United States should support it.'[76] The outcome is incoherent from a legalist perspective, combining commitment to the rule of law with an explicit refusal to submit to the formal obligations of the Rome Statute.

Yet the policy of securing an exceptional US role while standing outside formal treaty obligations hews closely to the legal ideals evident within the administration. Clinton's Acting State Department Legal Adviser Michael Matheson later argued that the 'critical question' was not whether the United States ratified the Rome Statute but, rather, whether the United States sought to 'be helpful, to facilitate, to cooperate, to pursue common aims ... [T]hat's much more important than the technical question of whether the US is a party.'[77] Scheffer was well aware that the distance between American policy and the legalist position created an impression of the United States being 'opposed to the whole concept' of the ICC. That view was, however, 'simply false, as I had the task of trying to build the court on an alternative foundation'.[78] This claim is consistent with the evidence of a genuine commitment by key US legal policymakers to design and develop the ICC but subject to pre-existing ideological commitments. The 'alternative foundation' identified

[75] BBC, 'Clinton's Statement on War Crimes Court', *BBC News*, 31 December 2000, http://news.bbc.co.uk/2/hi/1095580.stm.

[76] Clinton, *My Life*, pp. 942–3.

[77] Michael J. Matheson, Interview with Author (19 October 2011).

[78] Scheffer, *All the Missing Souls*, p. 217.

by Scheffer was formed by the competition between a dominant liberal internationalist commitment to transnational legal processes and countervailing beliefs structured by illiberal and nationalist American foreign policy ideologies.

Defining Equality under International Law

During the period of designing and establishing the ICC, the principle articulated as indispensable by global advocates was sovereign equality. From the view of legalism, a court that did not accord equal rights and duties to all states parties would, for that very reason, be inconsistent with the international rule of law. The policy outcome for the Clinton administration was, in contrast, insistence on a design that acknowledged and facilitated the unequal role of the United States in undertaking global military operations. The US position translated into insistence that the ICC be structured around the UNSC and the unequal veto power of the P5. Scheffer, who advocated this policy, conceded that the proposal amounted to a 'means of carving out an exceptionalist enclave for the United States'.[79] The beliefs of US legal policymakers about the connection between sovereign equality and the international rule of law are, therefore, central to the question of whether, and how, distinct legal conceptions informed the divergent US position.

Legalist Policy

Michael Scharf noted that a key factor in moving from UNSC created ad hoc criminal tribunals to a permanent court was the desire by a majority of UN members to eliminate unjustified P5 privileges.[80] Whereas a shared feature of both the Yugoslav and the Rwanda tribunals was being creatures of the UNSC, replicating this design would yield an ICC that had 'lost its political independence and compromised its impartiality and equal application of the law to all concerned'.[81] Van der Vyver compared explicit commitments to the rule of law by President Clinton and the US Senate to argue that US policy outcomes amounted to 'insistence on an international legal regime deprived of the rule of law

[79] Ibid., p. 233.

[80] Michael P. Scharf, *Balkan Justice: The Story Behind the First International War Crimes Trial since Nuremberg* (Carolina Academic Press, 1997), p. 228.

[81] Bassiouni, *The Legislative History of the ICC*, vol. 1, p. 156.

and equal justice for all'.[82] This is replicated in Caroline Fehl's observation that delegates at Rome saw US demands as 'conflicting with the principles of state equality and judicial fairness, and thus detrimental to the court's legitimacy'.[83] Unsurprisingly, the push to separate the ICC design from the UNSC was supported most forcefully by larger states, including Germany and countries of the Non-Aligned Movement such as India, for whom UNSC powers were a distortion of the post-Cold War distribution of international power.[84] For these states, establishing sovereign equality was always a key element of an ICC design consistent with the international rule of law. The case for a design based on state party rather than on UNSC referral gained traction in the years leading up to the Conference and, through a 'palace revolution',[85] largely prevailed in the Rome Statute.

Beliefs of American Legal Policymakers

Achieving Liberal Equality

At the level of general legal principles, Scheffer affirmed 'two basic building blocks' necessary for the rule of law, being 'reciprocity' in the rights and duties exercised between states and 'equality of nations' under international treaties. Prima facie, these principles meant that 'no nation and no people have superior rights or exceptional privileges in the realm of international law'. Applied to the specific case of the ICC crimes, however, this meant that 'no perpetrator of atrocity crimes should be able to avoid justice'.[86] Contradictory commitments to the rule of law are concealed by the simplicity of Scheffer's formulation but become visible in the many scenarios in which upholding sovereign equality is a practical barrier to prosecuting perpetrators of international crimes.

Scheffer's own conception expresses the internationalist belief that has been the main source of hypocrisy accusations: that the United States faced 'the paradox of being a leader for international justice but at the

[82] Johan D. van der Vyver, 'American Exceptionalism: Human Rights, International Criminal Justice, and National Self-Righteousness' (2001) 50 *Emory Law Journal* 775, p. 777.

[83] Fehl, *Living with a Reluctant Hegemon*, p. 102.

[84] M. Cherif Bassiouni, *The Legislative History of the International Criminal Court: Summary Records of the 1998 Diplomatic Conference* (Transnational Publishers, 2005), vol. 3, p. 179.

[85] Ruth Wedgwood, 'The International Criminal Court: An American View' (1999) 10 *European Journal of International Law* 93, p. 97.

[86] Scheffer, *All the Missing Souls*, pp. 165–6.

same time a leader for international peace and security'.[87] Justice under the ICC depended on the equal application of the law, but, as with any effective system of justice, the court also presumed a framework of effective enforcement mechanisms. For liberal internationalists, the ICC must not 'handcuff governments that take risks to promote peace and security and undertake humanitarian missions'. This was more explicitly pursuant to a belief that the 'US military, in particular, is called upon to carry out mandates of the Security Council' in combination with other further responsibilities that advance liberal equality.[88] Scheffer's paradox was that, to achieve equal justice, it may sometimes be necessary to recognise inequality in American responsibilities before the law.

Murphy's explanation for contradictory policies toward the ICC was a belief that 'global responsibilities for maintaining the peace' should exempt US military personnel and civilians from appearing before the court.[89] A design that reduced the status of the United States to a single voice among many thereby risks undermining real commitment to the international rule of law. It is notable that Scheffer's reflections on the Rome Conference attributed significant blame not to the United States' insistence that its disproportionate military role be recognised through unequal legal protections but to its failure to properly explain its unique legal responsibilities. This represented a 'disconnect between our military commanders and those of other nations because they were not confronting atrocity crimes with the same understandings'.[90] The 'disconnect' is evident in Richard Goldstone's retort: 'What the US is saying is, "In order to be peacekeepers ... we have to commit war crimes." That's what the policy boils down to.'[91] The suggestion of hypocrisy recedes only when the US position is seen as drawn from beliefs in America's messianic global role in promoting liberty.

In the context of the existing post–Cold War legal architecture, the clearest way to recognise this status was to graft the ICC onto the

[87] Thomas W. Lippman, 'War Crimes Court Approval Gives U.S. a Dilemma', *The Washington Post*, 23 July 1998, www.washingtonpost.com/archive/politics/1998/07/23/war-crimes-court-approval-gives-us-a-dilemma/a9fb27cf-8640-4a29-a253-14eb26c1c146/.

[88] See Scheffer's 1997 statement: Office of the Legal Adviser, Department of State, *Digest of United States Practice in International Law: 1991–1999* (International Law Institute, 2005), p. 626.

[89] John F. Murphy, *The United States and the Rule of Law in International Affairs* (Cambridge University Press, 2004), p. 7.

[90] Scheffer, *All the Missing Souls*, p. 228.

[91] Farhan Haq, 'Goldstone: US Stance Contradictory', 3 *Terra Viva*, 17 June 1998, www.legal-tools.org/doc/f83fcc/pdf/, p. 7.

structure of the UNSC and the oversight of US veto power. It is significant that Warren Christopher's guarded support for the ICC at his Senate confirmation hearing was at all times framed as an extension of the 'U.N. system' to be achieved through 'leadership at the U.N.'.[92] Read in the context of the United States' beliefs about its role promoting liberal equality, insistence on UNSC privileges remained consistent with a liberal internationalist conception of IL.

Institutionalising Hegemonic Privilege

Liberal internationalist policy converged neatly with illiberal internationalist preferences for an institutional design preserving hegemonic privilege. The Pentagon made it clear from the beginning that the UNSC must retain sole power of referral over ICC crimes, reflecting beliefs in effective international legal power, as already institutionalised in P5 membership. Scheffer was informed by a Pentagon representative that the sheer global responsibilities of the United States, including 200,000 troops deployed in 40 countries, 'had to mean something in the negotiations'.[93] Lietzau was sceptical about the fixation on sovereign equality and any suggestion to treat the court as an apolitical judicial body. His conception took account of the 'unique and vital national security responsibilities' of the United States in maintaining international peace and security.[94] By way of example, it was noted that the design of the UN itself integrated power relations that did not reflect sovereign equality – '"fairness" has never been the talisman of international peace and security'.[95] The evidence from decision-making processes does not therefore point toward Defense Department lawyers disregarding legal principles for political expediency. Rather, policy was structured by beliefs that principles of sovereign equality actually sat in opposition to the international rule of law, as established by existing legal processes spanning municipal and international jurisdiction.

It is important not to conflate the two variants of internationalist thinking, which conflicted significantly at Rome. Despite Scheffer's insistence on a central UNSC role, he believed that the Defense approach 'made little sense', since it insisted on immunity for US forces while denying it to others.[96] That contradiction can again be understood in the

92 United States Senate, *Nomination of Warren M. Christopher*, pp. 71–2.
93 Scheffer, *All the Missing Souls*, p. 184.
94 Lietzau, 'International Criminal Law after Rome', pp. 126 & 138–9.
95 Ibid., p. 135.
96 Scheffer, *All the Missing Souls*, p. 184.

light of competing views on the proper legal relationship to be established between states. From a liberal perspective, the special US status in the UNSC allowed for the extension of constitutional values into the international arena, which could be applied in principle to US forces who fell short of them globally. From the illiberal perspective, the fact of US global preponderance required recognition within the law of absolute privileges for US forces. Pentagon demands for a right to withhold consent to prosecutions were integral to an institutional design recognising power realities, albeit structured by predetermined legal principles. The internal US compromise was ultimately to propose a design requiring consent only for *non*-parties to the Statute as a middle ground between liberal internationalist resistance to a design establishing sovereignty as a shield against criminal liability and the illiberal internationalist demand that the law take account of America's hegemonic status. Both positions were rejected outright by other negotiating parties for enshrining sovereign inequality in the law.[97]

Conclusion

Scheffer's characterisation of a 'paradox' in the US position cannot be understood apart from the context of exceptionalist beliefs about a US mission to vindicate liberal rights. The question of the proper relationship between sovereign states was framed in terms of the principle of liberal equality and the need to facilitate US power to vindicate the rights of natural persons. For both variants of internationalism, the privileged UNSC role was seen as consistent with the international rule of law, either because of the exceptional US role in promoting human rights globally, or because the rule of law could not be divorced from the realities of US global military power. Through these positions, US policy directly contradicted the central legalist tenet of sovereign equality before the law. The director of Human Rights Watch's ICC campaign, Richard Dicker, rejected the compatibility of these conceptions with the rule of law: 'The Defense Department insisted on a 100 percent foolproof mechanism [against prosecution]. To get that, they essentially needed to cut the heart out of equal application of the law to all who came before it.'[98]

To the extent that there was legal incoherence in US policy toward the principle of equality, this reflected the compromise between competing

[97] See the position of UK legal adviser Frank Berman: ibid., pp. 211–12.
[98] Lippman, 'U.S. Caught in Bind on War Crimes'.

American conceptions, rather than a tactical compromise with legalist principles. Van der Vyver recognised the importance of the belief among US policymakers that their nation responds to 'almost all international 911 calls' as 'the major or only peace-keeping force of our times'. He concluded, however, that, owing to competing internal positions on the ICC, American policy was 'not a matter of principle or of self-interest but [one of] internal political expedience'.[99] This distinction, and his critique of the campaign led by Senator Helms, merely beg the question, however, since they do not explain what principles guided the individuals and constituencies internally opposing the ICC. The most persuasive explanation remains that the meaning of equality in US ICC policy was defined by competing legal principles, each of which expressed a coherent logic when viewed in ideological terms.

Determining International Judicial Power

Throughout the Rome negotiations, legalist advocates insisted on a design achieving effective separation between the ICC's judicial and prosecutorial powers on the one hand, and parallel legal powers exercised by states parties and established international institutions on the other. This reflected a view that formally separating powers determined their integrity in the ICC as much as in municipal legal systems. These proposals entailed a deeper claim that it was both desirable and possible to institutionalise judicial power in an independent global court. In contrast, from an early stage, the Clinton administration settled on an institutional design that strictly circumscribed the court's exercise of jurisdiction and located primary referral power within the UNSC. These principles were incorporated in a 1994 draft statute supported by the United States, which introduced the novel principle of 'complementarity', privileging national over international enforcement of Rome Statute crimes, and which required state consent or a UNSC referral for the ICC to exercise jurisdiction. That modest design avoided any claims to true universal jurisdiction, or the necessity of separating and institutionalising independent judicial power. Thus the question arises of whether US preferences to dilute judicial independence represented a tactical compromise on the international rule of law, or whether ideals of law itself were being contested.

99 van der Vyver, 'American Exceptionalism', pp. 796–804.

Legalist Policy

Max du Plessis identified among ICC proponents 'a growing conceptual awareness that because individuals live under the international legal system, they must necessarily have rights and obligations flowing from it'.[100] The institutional ideal entailed in such claims is for global judicial power that operates separately from national governments and courts implementing criminal law. Du Plessis cited the precedent of the post-WWII war crimes tribunals as a model with 'defining characteristics that draw their inspiration from the rule of law' including 'independent prosecutors and judges'.[101] For advocates, the independence of the court became a necessary element of the 'adequate safeguards built into the ICC system of criminal justice to protect nationals of all states against frivolous investigations and prosecutions'.[102]

The legalist position was set forth in 1999 by Executive Director of Human Rights Watch Kenneth Roth, as a key member of the CICC. At a point where the United States had rejected the integrity of judicial powers in the Rome Statute, Roth demanded that the United States sign 'to reaffirm America's commitment to justice and the rule of law'.[103] Responding to US scepticism about the plausibility of a depoliticised international court, Roth argued that it was 'not a political body, such as the United Nations, or even a tribunal to resolve political disputes between states, such as the International Court of Justice'. Rather, the ICC 'will have the fact-specific task of determining whether evidence exists to investigate or prosecute a particular suspect for a specific crime'.[104] In other words, the international rule of law was determined by a clear separation of ICC judicial power from other powers of international governance. This was reinforced by a design that ensured that the court's primary and secondary rules were separately determined by a '"legislature" – the governments that join the court'.[105]

Faith in the capacity of the court to transcend political interests was anchored in a variety of sources. Bassiouni argued that it was 'international

[100] Max du Plessis, 'Seeking an International International Criminal Court: Some Reflections on the United States Opposition to the ICC' (2002) 15 *South African Journal of Criminal Justice* 301, p. 304.

[101] Ibid., p. 303.

[102] van der Vyver, 'American Exceptionalism', p. 825.

[103] Kenneth Roth, 'Speech One: Endorse the International Criminal Court', in Alton Frye (ed.), *Toward an International Criminal Court?: Three Options Presented As Presidential Speeches* (Council on Foreign Relations, 1999), p. 19.

[104] Ibid., p. 28.

[105] Ibid., p. 29.

civil society' that had 'finally reached the limits of its tolerance for impunity and now demands some modicum of justice'.[106] For the LMS, it was found in their own absence of great power aspirations, leading to a self-perception of being

> depoliticized in an important sense: they lacked strong political interests and strategic entanglements in many parts of the world. Because they were not global powers, they thought of themselves as more able to construct international architecture that would be perceived as fair and legitimate by the rest of the world.[107]

French jurist Robert Badinter eloquently summarised the source of judicial independence in his vision of a court 'composed of judges independent from their home States':

> In practice, these judges will derive their whole authority from the Treaty, and thus will only be responsible for their decisions before their own conscience and before humanity, that entity so abstract and yet so present in these times. Rarely has a higher mission or a heavier responsibility been placed on judges. How may States, so proud of their sovereignty and their leaders, so caught up in the difficulties and complexity of their tasks, be brought not only to recognize this new judicial power, but also to aid it in its mission, without which the court will not be able fully to play its role?[108]

Badinter's answer, which was the final statement in a lengthy and influential ICC commentary, is that depoliticisation will be upheld by 'NGOs dedicated to humanitarian action' and 'public opinion'.[109] Through these related formulations, legalist advocates resisted any design sharing the ICC's judicial powers with states and international bodies as contrary to the international rule of law.

Beliefs of American Legal Policymakers

Democratic Foundations of International Judicial Power

It is telling that Bassiouni defended the possibility of ICC independence by drawing an analogy between its seemingly idealistic judicial aspirations and the initially ineffective separation of powers in the

[106] Bassiouni, *The Legislative History of the ICC*, vol. 1, p. 44.

[107] David Bosco, *Rough Justice: The International Criminal Court's Battle to Fix the World, One Prosecution at a Time* (Oxford University Press, 2014), p. 39.

[108] Robert Badinter, 'International Criminal Justice: From Darkness to Light', in Antonio Cassese, Paola Gaeta & John R. W. D. Jones (eds.), *The Rome Statute of the International Criminal Court: A Commentary* (Oxford University Press, 2002), p. 1934.

[109] Ibid., p. 1934.

United States. He referred to the supposed 1831 retort of President Andrew Jackson dismissing the Chief Justice of the Supreme Court: 'John Marshall has made his decision, now let him enforce it.'[110] With the authority of US judicial power only realised over time, Bassiouni suggested that likewise with the ICC, 'its moral authority will be established, and great expectations will be realized'.[111] What this claim overlooked, however, is the central role of democratic legitimacy in liberal internationalism. 'Moral authority' in US municipal law is sustained by the continuous operation of democratic checks and balances on judicial power. It did not follow therefore that the same legitimacy would attach to the ICC simply by the fact of its existence and operation. Bassiouni's claim assumed the possibility of independent judicial power in the ICC but founded instead on cosmopolitan values.

Lietzau's jurisprudence expressed liberal commitment to the rule of law founded on American constitutional government. He argued that, even though the ICC was likely to be governed by a judiciary adhering to the highest standards of competence and integrity, this was inherently inferior to American safeguards. In his view, 'Americans, for good reason, are not culturally disposed toward such "trust" of an institution'. Confidence was, however, provided by the separation of powers enshrined in the US Constitution that were simply 'not as evident in other democratic governments'.[112] 'American legal culture' was accordingly defined by a belief that judicial power must ultimately be tied to citizens' democratic control.[113] On this basis, the 'changes sought by the United States should be implemented not just because U.S. participation is key to an effective, functioning court, but because enacting them promotes the rule of law and is therefore the right thing to do'.[114] Likewise, Scheffer argued that the United States 'could not negotiate as if certain risks could be easily dismissed or certain procedures of the permanent court would be infallible'.[115] These legal ideals remained central to US challenges to ICC judicial and prosecutorial independence.

[110] Responding to the decision in *Worcester* v. *Georgia* (1832) 31 *U.S. (6 Pet.)* 515.

[111] Bassiouni, *The Legislative History of the ICC*, vol. 1, p. xx.

[112] Lietzau, 'International Criminal Law after Rome', p. 136.

[113] Lietzau, 'Comments to the Panel on the ICC', pp. 548–9.

[114] Lietzau, 'International Criminal Law after Rome', p. 136.

[115] See Scheffer's 1999 statement: Department of State, *Digest of US Practice: 1991–1999*, p. 637.

Complementarity as a Check on ICC Independence

The legalist principle for determining international judicial power was to establish ICC 'primacy' over domestic law, following the precedent of the ICTY and the ICTR.[116] The United States challenged that design from an early stage, proposing a court based on the novel principle of 'complementarity'. Primary prosecutorial obligations would be reserved to states, with ICC jurisdiction enlivened only when the state was deemed 'unwilling or unable genuinely to carry out the investigation or prosecution'.[117] The principle pressured states to 'prosecute nationally, or risk international prosecution', forming the quintessential example of IL playing a backstopping role in establishing a true transnational legal order.[118] Complementarity appeared to offer a genuine reconciliation between liberal internationalist and legalist preferences by preserving both municipal legal processes and the overarching authority of IL, with separate jurisdictions assumed to be 'guided by the same objectives'.[119] However, the record demonstrates that parties remained divided on whether the principle strengthened or derogated from the rule of law. Although states largely accepted complementarity, many held concerns that fracturing international judicial power would allow states to shield perpetrators through sham investigations. Indeed, the principle was accepted by many as a compromise to accommodate political interests and therefore it was considered to be incapable of ensuring ICC integrity in its own right.[120] For these policymakers, complementarity necessitated a counterbalance, by giving the court 'its own discretionary power to determine its jurisdiction'.[121] Advocates accordingly insisted on granting the ICC prosecutor *proprio motu* powers: the independent power to initiate an investigation and

116 Bartram S. Brown, 'Primacy or Complementarity: Reconciling the Jurisdiction of National Courts and International Criminal Tribunals' (1998) 23 *Yale Journal of International Law* 383, p. 385.

117 *Rome Statute*, Art. 17(1)(a).

118 David J. Scheffer, 'Challenges Confronting International Justice' (1998) 9 *Department of State Dispatch* 19, p. 22.

119 Adriaan Bos, 'From the International Law Commission to the Rome Conference (1994–1998)', in Antonio Cassese, Paola Gaeta & John R. W. D. Jones (eds.), *The Rome Statute of the International Criminal Court: A Commentary* (Oxford University Press, 2002), p. 44.

120 James Crawford, 'The Work of the International Law Commission', in Antonio Cassese, Paola Gaeta & John R. W. D. Jones (eds.), *The Rome Statute of the International Criminal Court: A Commentary* (Oxford University Press, 2002), p. 25.

121 Bos, 'From the International Law Commission to the Rome Conference', pp. 44–5.

bring a case before the court.[122] Germany reasoned that such power had the attraction of 'depoliticizing the process of initiating investigations'.[123] The Office of the Prosecutor (OTP) was thus created as an independent organ of the court, intended to promote the international rule of law by checking complementarity.[124]

The response from US policymakers made clear that this solution was even more objectionable than the original perceived mischief. Jamison Borek, Deputy Legal Adviser to the State Department, argued that 'bona fide national investigations and prosecutions will always be preferable' to those of the ICC. Reversing the onus would entail the fraught judgement that 'a functioning national system is not bona fide'.[125] The US preference was thus for a narrow conception of complementarity consistent with the 1996 Preparatory Committee Report:

> [I]t is not a question of the court having primary or even concurrent jurisdiction. Rather, its jurisdiction should be understood as having an *exceptional* character ... [A]s long as the relevant national system was investigating or prosecuting a case in good faith, according to this view, the court's jurisdiction should not come into operation.[126]

To ensure that outcome, US negotiators insisted on various measures to favour domestic processes, including requiring a supermajority of judges before domestic investigations could be overridden and that states be notified of potential ICC jurisdiction in any case where a state or the prosecutor intended to refer a matter to the court.[127]

In this context, the United States rejected an independent prosecutor as 'utopian', thereby risking 'rejection of the Draft by States'.[128] For the United States, the nature of prosecutorial power has been somewhat contentious even at the level of municipal law, and was acutely so around the 1998 impeachment of President Clinton. It is nominally an extension of executive functions, yet the task of prosecution requires a degree of independence from executive direction. Executive control nevertheless

122 See *Rome Statute*, Arts. 13(c), 15 & 53(1).
123 Bassiouni, *The Legislative History of the ICC*, vol. 3, pp. 175–6.
124 See *Rome Statute*, Arts. 34 & 42.
125 Jamison S. Borek, 'Agenda Item 142: Establishment of an International Criminal Court', 1 November 1995, https://2009-2017.state.gov/documents/organization/65827.pdf, p. 3.
126 UN, *Report of the Preparatory Committee on the Establishment of an International Criminal Court*, UN Doc A/51/22 (1996), par. [154], emphasis added.
127 See *Rome Statute*, Art. 18.
128 Crawford, 'The Work of the ILC', pp. 33–4.

remains crucial to ensure democratic accountability against 'frivolous or vindictive prosecutions'.[129] For American legal policymakers of all stripes, this principle did not recede merely because prosecutorial power was being exercised at the level of global governance. The legalist view of an independent prosecutor guaranteeing ICC independence directly contradicted the beliefs of American policymakers, who saw the prosecutor 'making difficult public policy decisions' and therefore eroding both the appearance and the reality of prosecutorial impartiality.[130]

Former chief prosecutor of the Yugoslav and Rwandan Tribunals Justice Louise Arbour responded to US opposition by arguing:

> [T]here is more to fear from an impotent than from an overreaching Prosecutor . . . [A]n institution should not be constructed on the assumption that it will be run by incompetent people, acting in bad faith for improper purposes . . . [T]he powers of the Prosecutor, and of the court itself, should be designed in a manner consistent with the effective enforcement of the statute.[131]

However, the division over prosecutorial independence demonstrated that, even on the apparent consensus over complementarity, divergence in ideology crystallised in incompatible proposals for the court. Parties adopted contradictory positions whereby complementarity was seen either as a democratic check on the court's independence, or as a compromise that itself required checking by an independent prosecutor.

Contesting Delegated Jurisdiction

The mechanism by which the ICC sought to establish its jurisdiction opened up a clear division between legalist and US advocates over the lawfulness of 'delegating' jurisdiction.[132] Earlier stages of negotiation had seen calls from key states and voices within the LMS and CICC for a form

[129] Katy J. Harriger, 'The Law: Executive Power and Prosecution: Lessons from the Libby Trial and the US Attorney Firings' (2008) 38 *Presidential Studies Quarterly* 491, p. 493.

[130] Bassiouni, *The Legislative History of the ICC*, vol. 3, pp. 172–3.

[131] Louise Arbour, 'The Prosecutor of the International Tribunals for the Former Yugoslavia and for Rwanda [Urges] that the International Permanent Court "Be Strong and Well Equipped to Operate As an Authoritative Mechanism"', 8 December 1997, www.icty.org/sid/7434.

[132] Alternatively 'ceded jurisdiction': Gennady M. Danilenko, 'ICC Statute and Third States', in Antonio Cassese, Paola Gaeta & John R. W. D. Jones (eds.), *The Rome Statute of the International Criminal Court: A Commentary* (Oxford University Press, 2002), p. 1881.

of universal jurisdiction.[133] Those expansive claims were rejected by the United States for being 'in conflict with certain fundamental principles of international law'.[134] The final outcome under Article 12 of the Rome Statute was instead a regime based nominally on consent to jurisdiction by states parties, but with the extension of jurisdiction to all crimes committed in the territory of member states – irrespective of whether an accused was a national of a member state.[135] In consequence, territorial jurisdiction came to divide US policymakers from their global counterparts as the 'single most problematic part of the Rome Treaty'.[136]

What was not disputed was that states had a 'fundamental' right to exercise jurisdiction over crimes committed in their own territory, as confirmed in the landmark *Lotus Case*.[137] Furthermore, that right may extend to transferring jurisdiction to a third state that met relevant criteria for extradition. However, prominent voices went on to assert a right 'to transfer jurisdiction to another state that has jurisdiction over an accused, *or to an international adjudicating body*'.[138] The ICC regime was argued to constitute an analogous 'delegation' to an international court, which did not turn on state consent any more than did the direct exercise of territorial jurisdiction.[139] In so arguing, states invoked the *Lotus* principle: 'Restrictions upon the independence of States cannot therefore be presumed.'[140] Absent a specific contrary rule, delegated jurisdiction remained presumptively legal.

The United States contested the legality of delegated jurisdiction from the beginning, and did so from a position defended as 'grounded in law'.[141] For David Scheffer, the legalist position depended on a customary IL

[133] See, for example, the German and Korean proposals: M. Cherif Bassiouni, *The Legislative History of the ICC*, vol. 3, pp. 144–6.

[134] Borek, 'Agenda Item 142', p. 4. The US did, however, support a form of universal jurisdiction over the crime of genocide.

[135] *Rome Statute*, Art. 12(2)(a).

[136] David J. Scheffer, 'The International Criminal Court: The Challenge of Jurisdiction' (1999) 93 *Proceedings of the Annual Meeting (American Society of International Law)* 68, p. 69.

[137] See *S.S. Lotus, The (France* v. *Turkey)* (1927) No. 10 *PCIJ Ser A*, p. 20.

[138] Bassiouni, *The Legislative History of the ICC*, vol. 1, p. 136, emphasis added.

[139] Antonio Cassese, Paola Gaeta & John R. W. D. Jones, 'The Rome Statute: A Tentative Assessment', in Antonio Cassese, Paola Gaeta & John R. W. D. Jones (eds.), *The Rome Statute of the International Criminal Court: A Commentary* (Oxford University Press, 2002), p. 1911.

[140] See *Lotus*, p. 18; Hafner et al., 'A Response to the American View', p. 117.

[141] See Scheffer's 1999 statement: Department of State, *Digest of US Practice: 1991–1999*, pp. 635 & 638.

assumption to the effect that states have a right to delegate territorial (or universal) jurisdiction to an international court. He 'lit a firestorm among international law scholars' by responding that, although it was 'indisputable' that municipal courts could exercise territorial jurisdiction, customary IL did not yet recognise the equal status of an international court.[142] Moreover, a state exercising territorial jurisdiction over a US national has 'no legal right to extradite' to a third state 'which has no connection to the crime or the suspect . . . for the sake of political expediency'. Therefore, neither did that right exist in relation to the ICC absent 'the consent of the non-party state'.[143] The difference thus came down to a question of whether and how the ICC was distinguished from national courts for delegation purposes.

The jurisprudence of the US legal position was developed from the academic work of Professor Madeline Morris, whose critique of the delegation analogy was picked up and endorsed by Scheffer.[144] Up to that point, the US government had relied chiefly on arguments under the VCLT that, as a 'third State', the United States could not be bound by treaty obligations it had not consented to.[145] In Scheffer's words, 'the establishment of, and a state's participation in, an international criminal court are not derived from custom but, rather, from the requirements of treaty law'.[146] The legal objections were more fundamental for Morris, however, and went to the limits of institutionalised global judicial power. Whereas the 'jurisdictional structure of the ICC is based on a view of the ICC as a criminal court, *tout court*', which adjudicates over individuals, the nature of ICC cases would necessarily also adjudicate official acts of states. In these cases, 'the ICC's role as an adjudicator of interstate disputes is not adequately accounted for in the Court's jurisdictional design'.[147] Existing customary law rights could not therefore be delegated to an international court, which would carry 'an authoritative weight and resulting political impact of a categorically different nature' to those of municipal courts. Moreover, the ICC held 'the power to create

[142] Ibid., pp. 635 & 638.
[143] Scheffer, *All the Missing Souls*, p. 234.
[144] Madeline Morris, Personal Communication with Author (16 March 2018); Scheffer, *All the Missing Souls*, p. 478, n. 13.
[145] *Vienna Convention on the Law of Treaties* (1969), Art. 34.
[146] Scheffer's 1999 statement, pp. 635 & 638.
[147] Madeline Morris, 'High Crimes and Misconceptions: The ICC and Non-Party States' (2001) 64 *Law and Contemporary Problems* 13, pp. 14–16.

international law in a manner disproportionate to that of any state', which was not easily amended through domestic legislative processes.[148]

These are intriguing arguments, since the precise factors cited by Morris are those that legalist advocates cite as evidence of the ICC *upholding* the rule of law. From an alternative perspective, the listed concerns have been interpreted as evidence of superior political and legal authority derived from an effective separation of international and domestic judicial powers, and the integrity of third-party adjudication untainted by parochial politics.[149] The US position has been criticised as politically compromised, with Georg Nolte arguing that 'it can be comparatively easily refuted'[150] and Cassese claiming that, as 'a legal objection, this is easily dismissed'.[151] Sands more forcefully rejected the 'absurd notion that it is contrary to international law for the ICC to exercise jurisdiction over Americans who commit international crimes on the territory of countries that have joined the ICC'.[152] The dispute persists nearly twenty years later, with American legal policymakers acknowledging the obstacles that disagreement has created, but with no clear resolution.[153] Such divergence, on what should be a matter of jurisprudential interpretation, presents a striking case for identifying the reception and contestation of IL through competing ideologies.

It matters that US interpretations originated in the intervention of Professor Morris speaking as an independent scholar bound by legal convention, and not as a government advocate.[154] Crucially, Morris argued that US concerns could not be dismissed as irrelevant to law, since the legality of customary obligations is itself constituted by

148 Equally applicable in cases of delegated universal and delegated territorial jurisdiction: ibid., pp. 30–33 & 45.

149 See Dapo Akande, 'The Jurisdiction of the International Criminal Court over Nationals of Non-Parties: Legal Basis and Limits' (2003) 1 *Journal of International Criminal Justice* 618, pp. 625–34.

150 Georg Nolte, 'The United States and the International Criminal Court', in David Malone & Yuen Foong Khong (eds.), *Unilateralism and US Foreign Policy: International Perspectives* (Lynne Rienner Publishers, 2003), p. 76.

151 Cassese, 'The Rome Statute', p. 1911.

152 Philippe Sands, *Lawless World: Making and Breaking Global Rules* (Viking, 2006), p. 244.

153 See Stephen Pomper, 'The US and Int'l Criminal Court May Still Steer Past Each Other–Why and How', *Just Security*, 5 April 2018, www.justsecurity.org/54543/intl-criminal-court-steer-other-why/. For a careful reconsideration of the issue see Michael A. Newton, 'How the International Criminal Court Threatens Treaty Norms' (2016) 49 *Vanderbilt Journal of Transnational Law* 371.

154 Morris, Personal Communication. Morris has served as a legal adviser and counsel to the US government, but not at the time of her intervention, or on this particular issue.

consistent state practice. Thus, these are 'not "mere policy concerns" but are, in fact, of fundamental *legal* significance'.[155] The division opened by US policy represented 'a genuine dilemma – not excuses or pretexts, but legitimate concerns on each side'.[156] Foreign policy ideology provides a compelling explanation for such divergent yet firmly held legal interpretations: that legalist and US policy determined the integrity of international judicial power through competing conceptions of IL and that they have remained coherent in these terms. David Wippman recognises that, as between the United States and its opponents, 'the dispute was framed as a disagreement over competing legal values'. These were respectively 'accountability' and 'independence and impartiality', upon which '[e]ach side claimed the legal high ground'.[157] That Morris's interpretation resonated so readily with US legal policymakers, including in the National Security Council, speaks to the power of shared ideological IL attitudes, which now manifested in sophisticated jurisprudential terms.

Consent-Based Division of Powers

Legalist advocates opposed US demands for a UNSC-centred court not only for contravening sovereign equality, but also for eroding the separation of powers at the global level. Bassiouni warned that such a design 'cannot be reconciled with the principles of judicial independence and judicial impartiality'.[158] Fears of the UNSC 'unduly tainting the independence of a judicial body' were duly noted by Borek for the State Department. She responded that, under legalist proposals, 'the initiation of cases would be subject to whatever political agenda a particular State may have, rather than a collective decision by the Council that in fact would be less likely to reflect a political bias than that of an individual State'.[159] Rather, the UNSC role 'can be defined so that it in no way undermines the judicial independence of the court, its judges and its prosecutor, but rather strengthens the court in addressing the important cases that would be part of its mandate'.[160] Proposed measures included limiting the UNSC to only referring 'over-all situations' to the prosecutor,

155 Madeline Morris, 'The Jurisdiction of the International Criminal Court over Nationals of Non-Party States' (2000) 6 *ILSA Journal of International & Comparative Law* 363, p. 366, original emphasis.

156 Ibid., p. 369.

157 David Wippman, 'The International Criminal Court', in Christian Reus-Smit (ed.), *The Politics of International Law* (Cambridge University Press, 2004), p. 173.

158 Bassiouni, *The Legislative History of the ICC*, vol. 1, p. 156.

159 Borek, 'Agenda Item 142', p. 3.

160 Ibid., p. 5.

with the prosecutor then retaining sole power to determine which individuals to indict.[161] This was a rejection not merely of the specific draft design, therefore, but also of the very compatibility of legalist principles with preserving the integrity of international judicial power. Implicit was that UNSC members, and the United States in particular, would in contrast remain faithful to rule of law principles in exercising global powers.

Liberal internationalist policymakers were prepared to endorse the formal capacity of the ICC to prosecute US nationals via complementarity, should the United States ever become a state party and fail to prosecute. In this, Scheffer expressed faith that the operation of exceptionalist constitutional values would ensure that accountability remained in US municipal courts: 'Either we are the United States of America committed to the rule of law, or we have transformed into another kind of nation.'[162] That faith was not shared by the Departments of Justice and Defense, however, who, although diverging on preferred institutional design, each turned to illiberal internationalist insistence on strict US consent. Justice insisted on UNSC control as the sole method for referring cases – despite that design being considered 'toxic' in the eyes of 'almost the entire world'.[163]

Even so, UNSC control alone remained inadequate protection for Pentagon officials, who argued, consistently with maintaining hegemonic privileges, that additional immunity for US military personnel was essential to upholding international policing duties. To that end, Defense insisted that consent of the state of nationality also be required – a position endorsed by Clinton.[164] *The Washington Post* reported on the extent to which Pentagon pressure, in conjunction with congressional support, had significantly shaped the US position going into Rome. Defense officials were said to

> vividly remember when foes of U.S. policy in Vietnam during the 1960s and 1970s and Central America in the 1980s called for prosecution of American officials and servicemen as war criminals. They now fear that without very stringent and specific safeguards, an international court could be used by present-day adversaries such as Iraq or Libya to make similar charges.[165]

Scheffer admonished the Pentagon for failing to recognise 'how impractical their insistence on the alleged war criminal's government consenting

[161] See Scheffer's 1997 statement: Department of State, *Digest of US Practice: 1991–1999*, p. 616.

[162] Scheffer, *All the Missing Souls*, p. 201.

[163] Ibid., p. 181.

[164] Ibid., pp. 197 & 201–2.

[165] John M. Goshko, 'U.S. Proposes Limit on Global Court: Critics Fear Curb Would Paralyze Prosecution of War Crimes', *The Washington Post* (26 March 1998), p. A29.

to his prosecution sounded to the rest of the world'.[166] In any case, broader international support for a UNSC-centred court had already waned in the years leading up to the Rome Conference, with all such US proposals ultimately rejected by other delegations as incompatible with rule of law beliefs.[167]

Conclusion

By the end of this period, US ICC policy had rejected any design granting unencumbered judicial or prosecutorial independence to the court. Certainly, some compromise was achieved between delegates at Rome, including that the UNSC had the right to suspend ICC investigations but not to control the referral process.[168] The United States also constrained the judicial independence of the court by exercising its 'legislative' function in defining the elements of crimes rather than leaving it to the court's discretion.[169] However, US policy was fundamentally rejected on the issues of an independent prosecutor as a check on complementarity, the legality of delegated jurisdiction, and the controlling role of the UNSC. Krisch and Robinson applauded the success of finalising a founding statute that was 'much stronger' than the initial ILC draft, thereby demonstrating the success of NGOs and the LMS in altering 'perceptions of the international community as to what was achievable and, indeed, necessary'. Yet they conceded that, in light of this success, 'it is particularly regrettable that the United States could not support the Rome Statute'.[170] Such was improbable when US policy revealed the controlling influence of an internationalist ideological stance, expressed across both ends of the liberal–illiberal dimension. At no point did American policymakers recognise the legalist principle of separating international judicial powers, with legal conceptions remaining unmoved.

Chapter Conclusion

Throughout the Clinton administration there were characterisations, even among US officials, of a contest 'between the ideal of an

166 Scheffer, *All the Missing Souls*, p. 181.
167 Bassiouni, *The Legislative History of the ICC*, vol. 1, pp. 89 & 90, n. 199.
168 Pursuant to a final negotiating position approved by Clinton: Scheffer, *All the Missing Souls*, p. 209.
169 Bos, 'From the ILC to the Rome Conference', pp. 42–3.
170 Krisch & Robinson, 'Reaching Agreement at the Rome Conference', p. 89.

international criminal court and the reality of the world today'.[171] Such statements are consistent with interpretations that contradiction flowed from a contest between a universal concept of the rule of law and US political interests. Reviewing the extensive evidence from this period leads to a more compelling account, however, in which the very definition of national interests was embedded in ideological conceptions of IL. Borek warned in 1995 that the entire enterprise would be futile if states 'approach the court from an academically pure perspective, without regard for political realities and what States are willing to participate in and fund'.[172] The implication is that legalist insistence on formalised development, sovereign equality and independent judicial power was inherently limited as a basis for reaching common agreement on ideals for ICC design and development. The dominance of liberal internationalism, combined with competing illiberal internationalist pressures, led to US insistence on a flexible role to develop international criminal law, including the preservation of amnesties as a limitation on formal legal obligations. American ICC support was always premised on a form of UNSC control, which was framed both as principled commitment to liberal values and as necessary recognition of relative global responsibilities. Finally, US policymakers rejected the compatibility of ICC independence with the rule of law, disagreeing in particular about the legitimacy of delegating core state functions to an international court.

Bassiouni noted the frustration of the LMS who felt that they 'had bent over backwards to accommodate the US'. The perception was that the United States was being held back by 'completely unrelated domestic political reasons'.[173] Yet this characterisation begs the question as to how the persons and agencies applying domestic interests conceived US legal obligations and formulated competing positions. US rejection of the Rome Statute on the basis that it met every key element of the legalist international rule of law was indeed destined to rouse claims of hypocrisy and contradiction. Yet, at every major decision point between 1992 and 2000, US policy hewed closely to competing and internally coherent sets of ideological beliefs about the meaning of the international rule of law.

[171] Jim Lobel, 'Go for Real, Not Ideal, Court', 3 *Terra Viva*, 17 June 1998, www.legal-tools.org/doc/f83fcc/pdf/, p. 3.

[172] Borek, 'Agenda Item 142', p. 5.

[173] Bassiouni, *The Legislative History of the ICC*, vol. 1, p. 88.

5

Bush 43 Administration, 2000–2004

The incoming administration of President George W. Bush was presented with an ICC design that had been largely settled during the Clinton years and that was on the cusp of exercising far-reaching powers as the Rome Statute came into force mid-2002.[1] Bush's 2000 inauguration signalled a major shift to counteract these developments, with a track record among the president's senior legal policymakers of opposing ICC policy throughout the previous eight years. Most prominent among these was John Bolton, who served both as Under Secretary of State for Arms Control and International Security and then as UN Ambassador. Bolton had sat alongside Ambassador Scheffer in the US Senate's post-mortem of the Rome Conference to strongly condemn both ICC policy and the broader IL policy of the Clinton administration.[2] Contested views foreshadowed the hostile opposition to the ICC that would become the hallmark of the first term of the Bush 43 administration.

From a legalist perspective, the achievement of a largely settled design left the primary focus for ICC supporters on consolidating the formal and universal status of the ICC as an institution of global governance. Of particular significance was the objective of ensuring that the increasingly prominent relationship between the ICC and the UNSC did not institutionalise legal inequality, which had been fought against so hard during the 1998 negotiation phase. In contrast, the United States implemented a series of policies designed to impede the realisation of the ICC project. First, the administration 'unsigned' the Rome Statute to demonstrate that it did not intend to be bound by the regime in any form. Second, through the UNSC, the United States sought and obtained immunity from ICC prosecution for all US military personnel involved in peacekeeping operations. Third, the administration sought and obtained bilateral

[1] On 1 July when the number of states acceding to the statute reached the requisite number of 60: *Rome Statute of the International Criminal Court* (1998), Art. 126.

[2] See Chapter 4, *supra*.

agreements with its allies that overrode the jurisdiction of the court in relation to US nationals. Finally, the president signed domestic legislation authorising the recovery of US nationals should they nevertheless end up in the court's custody. Each of these policies contradicted legalist principles, which painted a picture of a US worldview opposed to the international rule of law. This chapter seeks to refine otherwise persuasive observations of the Bush 43 administration seeking a diminished role for IL by demonstrating that, in doing so, US legal policymakers adhered to well-established illiberal legal conceptions. The theorised role of foreign policy ideology thus illuminates the contradiction of legal policymakers seeking to dismantle the ICC, yet continuing to defend US actions in terms of fidelity to the rule of law.

Dominant Foreign Policy Ideology

In his memoirs, President Clinton reflected that Bush 43 and Vice President Dick Cheney 'saw the world very differently from the way I did', and in particular offered a more unilateral IL policy that opposed key international institutions.[3] Curtis Bradley, Bush 43 State Department Counsellor on International Law, sceptically described the 'standard view' of the Bush era IL policy as being that:

> The Administration did not take international law seriously and routinely disregarded it whenever it was thought to conflict with the national interests of the country. In doing so, the Administration substantially undermined the rule of law and the United States' standing in the international community.[4]

The evidence is that the administration's policies distinctly diverged from its predecessor's in the perceived value of advancing foreign policy interests through law. Although the administration maintained engagement with key international institutions, those institutions were valued primarily to the extent that 'they served immediate, concrete American interests'.[5] The 2002 Kagan thesis said to resonate so strongly with senior Bush 43 policymakers claimed that, in contrast to European conceptions of IL, Americans continued to perceive a 'Hobbesian world where

[3] William J. Clinton, *My Life* (Hutchinson, 2004), p. 951.

[4] Curtis A. Bradley, 'The Bush Administration and International Law: Too Much Lawyering and Too Little Diplomacy' (2009) 4 *Duke Journal of Constitutional Law & Public Policy* 57, p. 57.

[5] Ivo H. Daalder & James M. Lindsay, *America Unbound: The Bush Revolution in Foreign Policy* (Brookings Institution Press, 2003), p. 44.

international laws and rules are unreliable and where true security and the defence and promotion of a liberal order still depend on the possession and use of military might'.[6]

In rejecting the strategic desirability of formalised or transnational development of IL, the administration was particularly influenced by a characterisation of such developments as a form of 'lawfare'. The term was popularised in a 2001 essay by Major General Charles Dunlap, as Deputy Judge Advocate General, and later defined to mean 'the strategy of using – or misusing – law as a substitute for traditional military means to achieve an operational objective', including through exploiting US commitment to rule of law values.[7] Specifically, Dunlap observed 'disturbing evidence that the rule of law is being hijacked into just another way of fighting (lawfare), to the detriment of humanitarian values as well as the law itself'.[8] The concept became popular among the administration's legal policymakers,[9] with Secretary of Defense Donald Rumsfeld defining the concept as 'a new kind of asymmetric war' that 'uses international and domestic legal claims, regardless of their factual basis, to win public support to harass American officials – military and civilian – and to score ideological victories'.[10] Like Dunlap, Rumsfeld identified the source of power in the strategy as 'America's laudable reverence for the law', which rendered the nation especially vulnerable to accusations of illegality.[11] The lawfare moniker encapsulated the claim that legalist conceptions of IL had the capacity to contradict the very principles that underpinned true fidelity to the international rule of law.

Evidence regarding Bush's personal beliefs about the international rule of law points to the transactional conception entailed in illiberal nationalism.[12] Bush demonstrated this ideology in his more general foreign policy, through a more confrontational stance against American enemies and his preference

[6] Robert Kagan, 'Power and Weakness' (2002) June–July *Policy Review* 3, p. 3.

[7] Charles J. Dunlap Jr, 'Lawfare Today: A Perspective' (2008) 3 *Yale Journal of International Affairs* 146, p. 146.

[8] Charles J. Dunlap Jr, 'Law and Military Interventions: Preserving Humanitarian Values in 21st Century Conflicts', Conference on Humanitarian Challenges in Military Intervention, Carr Center for Human Rights Policy, Kennedy School of Government, Harvard University, Washington, DC, 29 November 2001, p. 6.

[9] Some of whom now contribute to a blog with the same title: Benjamin Wittes et al., 'About Lawfare: A Brief History of the Term and the Site', *Lawfare: Hard National Security Choices,* 2010, www.lawfareblog.com/about-lawfare-brief-history-term-and-site.

[10] Donald Rumsfeld, *Known and Unknown: A Memoir* (Penguin, 2011), p. 594.

[11] Ibid., p. 596.

[12] See Condoleezza Rice, *No Higher Honor: A Memoir of My Years in Washington* (Random House LLC, 2011), pp. 158–9.

for military over diplomatic pressure to promote US interests.[13] Dueck identified that, following the 11 September 2001 terrorist attacks, 'liberal humanitarian concerns would henceforth take a back seat to considerations of US self-interest'.[14] In legal terms, Bush's overriding belief was that the United States should aim to consolidate hegemonic power 'into a more durable system', but that, unlike his predecessors, his forms of governance would not be exercised through strengthened institutions of IL.[15] The administration thus challenged the internationalist consensus of the Bush 41–Clinton years, shifting along the governance dimension to a nationalist stance that emphasised sufficiency of municipal legal power to promote American interests.

One recurrent characterisation of the administration is that its general foreign policy was structured by a hawkish strand of liberal internationalism – on the basis that it remained globally committed to spreading American democratic values.[16] An example of the type of statement supporting this conclusion is Secretary of State Colin Powell identifying a 'guiding principle' of Bush's foreign policy as being that 'there is no country on earth that is not touched by America, for we have become the motive force for freedom and democracy in the world'.[17] Subsequent military action seeking democratisation in Afghanistan and Iraq does indeed appear to exemplify a form of 'Wilsonianism with boots'.[18] The characterisation does not hold up for the Bush 43 IL policy, however, since the diplomatic history of liberal internationalist thought is inextricably intertwined with multilateralism and a robust role for IL.[19] There is no evidence that the Bush administration ever adopted a strategy to

[13] See George W. Bush & Michael Herskowitz, *A Charge to Keep* (Morrow, 1999), p. 239.

[14] Colin Dueck, *Reluctant Crusaders: Power, Culture, and Change in American Grand Strategy* (Princeton University Press, 2006), p. 150.

[15] See Walter R. Mead, *Special Providence: American Foreign Policy and How It Changed the World* (Routledge, 2002), p. 307.

[16] See Tony Smith, 'Wilsonianism after Iraq', in G. John Ikenberry, Thomas J. Knock, Anne-Marie Slaughter & Tony Smith (eds.), *The Crisis of American Foreign Policy: Wilsonianism in the Twenty-First Century* (Princeton University Press, 2009). Hoff draws a distinction between 'good' and 'bad' Wilsonianism, with the Bush 43 administration falling into the second category: Joan Hoff, *A Faustian Foreign Policy: From Woodrow Wilson to George W. Bush* (Cambridge University Press, 2008), pp. 9–12.

[17] Committee on Foreign Relations, United States Senate, *Senate Committee on Foreign Relations, Nomination of Colin L. Powell To Be Secretary of State*, 1st Session 107th Congress (2001), p. 17.

[18] Pierre Hassner & Nicole Gnesotto, 'The United States: The Empire of Force or the Force of Empire' (2002) 54 *Chaillot Papers* 5, p. 43.

[19] See Anne-Marie Slaughter, 'Wilsonianism in the Twenty-First Century', in G. John Ikenberry, Thomas J. Knock, Anne-Marie Slaughter & Tony Smith (eds.), *The*

strengthen democracy as a constitutive element of the international rule of law, or a belief that IL would in turn strengthen democratic norms. Thus, although the administration repeatedly expressed its faith in the strategic advantages of global democratisation, this did not structure key legal policymakers' conceptions of IL. Even Mead's characterisation of an attempted illiberal nationalist–liberal internationalist ideological fusion acknowledges that the former shaped policy in decisions such as the 2003 Iraq War, and it was only after the fact that justifications were made in terms of the latter.[20] Absent these beliefs, the Bush policy is distinguished from core elements of liberal internationalist IL policy: 'Clinton, not Bush, therefore was the true Wilsonian of our time.'[21]

The most well-known expression of the administration's IL policy was the 2002 *National Security Strategy* (NSS 2002), with two lone references to IL. The first was to 'rogue states', who 'display no regard for international law', thus justifying the principle of relative sovereignty that facilitated much of the administration's military policy in Afghanistan and Iraq.[22] The second reference was in the context of developing the so-called 'Bush Doctrine', which the president himself described as a new US strategic policy to 'confront the worst threats before they emerge'.[23] The NSS 2002 argued the lawfulness of the doctrine by reference to the modern threat of weapons of mass destruction, which required that the United States 'adapt the concept of imminent threat to the capabilities and objectives of today's adversaries'.[24] By removing any of the conventional constraints on self-defence requiring 'imminence',[25] the administration sought to develop law permissively, as an enabling framework rather than one capable of constraining US policy.

IL beliefs within the administration were not monolithic, however, with alternative conceptions competing for influence throughout the

Crisis of American Foreign Policy: Wilsonianism in the Twenty-First Century (Princeton University Press, 2009).

20 Walter R. Mead, 'The Carter Syndrome', *Foreign Policy*, 4 January 2010, https://foreignpolicy.com/2010/01/04/the-carter-syndrome/.

21 Anatol Lieven, *America Right or Wrong: An Anatomy of American Nationalism* (Oxford University Press, 2005), p. 12.

22 The White House, *The National Security Strategy of the United States of America 2002* (2002), p. 14.

23 George W. Bush, 'Graduation Speech at West Point', 1 June 2002, https://georgewbush-whitehouse.archives.gov/news/releases/2002/06/20020601-3.html; The White House, *The National Security Strategy of the United States of America 2002*, p. ii.

24 The White House, *NSS 2002*, p. 15.

25 See James Crawford, *Brownlie's Principles of Public International Law* (Oxford University Press, 2012), pp. 750–2.

first term. Mead characterises Colin Powell as the leading proponent of liberal nationalism, which he expressed through rejecting the Clinton administration's liberal 'overreaching' and a preference for conserving the status quo of US global exposure.[26] Contrarily, Dueck classifies Powell's beliefs as more in line with illiberal internationalism – accepting the desirability of multilateralism but according to a pragmatic worldview consistent with that of Bush 41.[27] Powell's beliefs about IL arguably straddled both these ideologies, in seeking to balance both advantages and dangers in global engagement. Powell accepted the strategic desirability of working through international institutions to advance US national security, including convincing the cabinet in 2002 of the diplomatic advantages of disarming Saddam Hussein through UN processes rather than proceeding immediately to overthrow him militarily.[28] At the same time, he expressed wariness that closer engagement with IL could erode liberal values at home, including rights guaranteed by the American constitution. That combination of beliefs provided a basis for Powell to support the principle of the international rule of law, but within constrained bounds. Powell explicitly distinguished his cautious approach from Senator Helms' opposition to even basic principles of international legal doctrine, including the status of customary IL as law. In the course of Powell's confirmation hearings, Helms posed the question:

> Clinton administration legal scholars have cultivated the notion at home and abroad that murky 'obligations' divined from so-called customary international 'law' and the unratified Vienna Convention on treaties effectively supersede Article II of our Constitution ... Will your State Department continue to perpetuate this unconstitutional myth?[29]

In response, Powell fully accepted that the VCLT codified the US obligation to 'refrain from acts which would defeat the object and purpose of a treaty'.[30] For Powell, this 'logical' position had been accepted as declaratory of customary IL by every administration from President Johnson onward and was therefore binding on the United States.[31]

Powell's beliefs were reinforced by his Legal Adviser William Taft IV, who has cited his attraction to Powell's 'commitment to the rule of

[26] In the form of his equivalent 'Jeffersonian' tradition: Mead, *Special Providence*, pp. 307–8.
[27] In the form of his equivalent 'realist' tradition: Dueck, *Reluctant Crusaders*, pp. 150 & 152.
[28] Bob Woodward, *Bush at War* (Simon & Schuster, 2003), pp. 332–6.
[29] United States Senate, *Nomination of Colin L. Powell*, p. 104.
[30] See *Vienna Convention on the Law of Treaties* (1969), Art. 18.
[31] United States Senate, *Nomination of Colin L. Powell*, p. 104.

law'.[32] Taft explicitly identified American interests in a strategy 'to promote and strengthen international law and international institutions'. Motives included that this represented 'a morally attractive position and that the rule of law in international as well as national affairs is a desirable thing ... A stable world where international obligations are undertaken and relied upon is in the interest of the United States as a matter of its own security and prosperity.'[33] At the same time, Taft emphasised that IL remains primarily a consent-based order so that 'a state is not subject to international law unless it agrees to be, and even then it can withdraw its consent as a rule and go back to other remedies for dealing with whatever problems it confronts'.[34]

The figure representing the most dominant approach to US ICC policy during the first term was, however, then Under Secretary of State John Bolton, who wielded an influence beyond his designated office.[35] Taft explains his own more limited role in ICC policy as the consequence of Bolton's decisive opposition, such that 'there was little point in discussing the subject in the abstract'.[36] Then National Security Adviser Condoleezza Rice described a deep ideological 'schism' in the State Department, with Powell representing a more conciliatory approach to international engagement and Bolton representing the 'neocons' and a hawkish uncompromising global stance.[37] In academic writings predating his appointment, Bolton attacked not only the ICC but also the '"agenda" of constraining the US through international law'.[38] Evaluating the previous administration, Bolton charged that Clinton 'forgot that the UN was an instrument to be used to advance

32 Michael P. Scharf & Paul R. Williams, *Shaping Foreign Policy in Times of Crisis: The Role of International Law and the State Department Legal Adviser* (Cambridge University Press, 2010), p. 32.

33 William H. Taft IV, Interview with Author (22 November 2011).

34 Ibid. For a report on US ICC policy that Taft cites as closely expressing his own views, see William H. Taft IV & Patricia M. Wald, *U.S. Policy toward the International Criminal Court: Furthering Positive Engagement* (The American Society of International Law, 2009).

35 John P. Cerone, 'Dynamic Equilibrium: The Evolution of US Attitudes toward International Criminal Courts and Tribunals' (2007) 18 *European Journal of International Law* 277, p. 293.

36 Taft, Interview with Author.

37 Rice, *No Higher Honor*, p. 158. Bolton plays down this distinction but agrees that he and Powell held different 'philosophies': John R. Bolton, *Surrender Is Not an Option: Defending America at the United Nations* (Simon & Schuster, 2007), p. 47.

38 John R. Bolton, 'Is There Really "Law" in International Affairs?' (2000) 10 *Transnational Law & Contemporary Problems* 1, p. 48.

America's foreign policy interests, not to engage in international social work and ivory-tower chattering'.[39] Bolton often adopted legal positions consistent with illiberal internationalism, but his views consistently gravitated back towards the same illiberal nationalist beliefs as Senator Helms. Helms himself described Bolton as 'the kind of man with whom I would want to stand at Armageddon, or what the Bible describes as the final battle between good and evil'.[40] Significantly, Bolton's legal conception ultimately prevailed in key ICC decisions central to establishing the international rule of law.

Developing Non-arbitrary Global Governance

Following the 1998 Rome Conference, states and NGOs who advocated a legalist ICC design continued to emphasise the necessity of formalised global governance for the rule of law. Tensions inevitably followed as US policy conspicuously reversed from the Clinton years, by opposing further ICC development and any obligations created by its founding statute. At his Senate confirmation, Colin Powell bluntly stated that, as far as Bush's own views on the ICC went: 'The new administration will be opposed.'[41] Most notoriously, Bolton unsigned the Rome Statute in May 2002, describing it as 'the happiest moment of my government service'.[42] No legal policymakers within the Bush administration demonstrated any commitment to the liberal internationalist belief that American interests were advanced through strengthening transnational international criminal law processes. With this being the closest of the American conceptions to legalism, a perception emerged that the rule of law itself had been rejected. Yet, through this period, American legal policymakers continued to emphasise US compliance with international legal obligations, thereby stoking accusations of hypocrisy. The immediate question that arises is thus whether US legal policymakers really recognised the international rule of law in the terms articulated by global counterparts.

[39] John R. Bolton, 'The Creation, Fall, Rise, and Fall of the United Nations', in Ted Galen Carpenter (ed.), *Delusions of Grandeur: The United Nations and Global Intervention* (Cato Institute, 1997), p. 51.

[40] Cited in Sidney Blumenthal, *How Bush Rules: Chronicles of a Radical Regime* (Princeton University Press, 2006), p. 151.

[41] United States Senate, *Nomination of Colin L. Powell*, p. 89.

[42] Bolton, *Surrender Is Not an Option*, p. 85.

Legalist Policy

The ideal of formalising the governance of international criminal law was expressed in a 2003 EU common position and a subsequent 2005 cooperation treaty with the ICC, each confirming the goal of 'consolidation of the rule of law and respect for human rights'.[43] To this end, the EU reaffirmed that 'principles of the Rome Statute of the International Criminal Court, as well as those governing its functioning, are fully in line with the principles and objectives of the Union'. Among the principles for realising the rule of law were that 'universal accession to the Rome Statute is essential for the full effectiveness of the International Criminal Court'.[44] Article 2(1) of the common position sets out the obligation on EU states 'to further this process by raising the issue of the widest possible ratification, acceptance, approval or accession to the Statute and the implementation of the Statute in negotiations or political dialogues with third States, groups of States or relevant regional organisations, whenever appropriate'.[45] This conception of an international rule of law, focused on institutionalised and universal obligations, provides the context for understanding the significance of EU 'disappointment and regret' at the US unsigning decision.[46] The action was characterised as having 'undesirable consequences on multilateral treaty-making and generally on the rule of law in international relations'.[47] Of particular note were perceptions of contradiction, where US policy inflicted a 'potentially negative effect' on a cause to 'which the United States shows itself strongly committed'.[48] The statements revealed a principled commitment to progressively extending global governance, which narrowed states' rights to take discretionary actions in lieu of formalised rules and authority.

[43] EU Commission, 'Council Common Position 2003/444/CFSP of 16 June 2003 on the International Criminal Court' (2003) 5 *Official Journal of the European Union* 67, p. 67; Council of the European Union, *Agreement between the International Criminal Court and the European Union on Cooperation and Assistance* (6 December 2005), see preamble.

[44] EU Commission, 'Council Common Position', p. 67.

[45] Ibid., p. 68.

[46] EU, *Statement of the European Union on the Position of the United States towards the International Criminal Court*, P 64/02 Brussels 8864/02 (Presse 141), (14 May 2002), p. 1.

[47] Ibid., p. 2.

[48] Ibid., p. 4.

Beliefs of American Legal Policymakers

Shift from Internationalism

A 2002 report for the US Congress identified the 'main issue' for policymakers as 'the level of cooperation to allow between the United States and the ICC'. Options presented were: 'to withhold all cooperation from the ICC and its member nations in order to prevent the ICC from becoming effective, to continue contributing to the development of the ICC in order to improve it, or to adopt a pragmatic approach based solely on U.S. interests'.[49] These effectively encompassed the competing policies drawn from foreign policy ideology: nationalist opposition to the court, a continuation of liberal internationalist support without acceding to the Rome Statute, and pragmatic illiberal internationalist development of the ICC relationship. Legalist policies, however, remained outside the range of options.

The illiberal nationalist preference of the Bush 43 administration highlighted a growing distinction from the illiberal *internationalism* that had characterised the Bush 41 ICC policy.[50] In Michael Scharf's *Recommendation for the Bush Administration*, the primary architect of the former policy posed a choice between being an 'influential insider or [a] hostile outsider'. Figures such as Senator Helms epitomised the 'hostile outsider' strategy, which would 'transform American exceptionalism into unilateralism and/or isolationism'. So doing threatened to 'erode the moral legitimacy' of the United States, which otherwise facilitated concrete military and economic interests.[51] Because the ICC was already a confirmed reality of the international system, Scharf concluded that the United States could only really sustain illiberal nationalist opposition through hostility toward the international order itself. That possibility sharply divided internationalist and nationalist forms of illiberalism, with Scharf framing his intervention as a 'detached' analysis 'based on *realpolitik* considerations'.[52] Despite apparently similar policy scepticism across the two Bush presidencies, decision-making processes were structured by categorically distinct ideologies.

49 Jennifer Elsea, *U.S. Policy Regarding the International Criminal Court* (Congressional Research Service, 9 July 2002), p. 3.

50 See Chapter 4, pp. 125–8, *supra*.

51 Michael P. Scharf, 'The United States and the International Criminal Court: A Recommendation for the Bush Administration' (2000) 7 *ILSA Journal of International & Comparative Law* 385, pp. 386–7.

52 Ibid., p. 388.

Hostility toward liberal internationalism was already evident in the weeks leading up to Clinton's decision to sign the Rome Statute, with Helms objecting that 'the President has effectively given his approval to this unprecedented assault on American sovereignty'.[53] During his 1998 appearance alongside David Scheffer before the US Senate Committee on Foreign Relations, John Bolton expressed his view that IL was mere 'sentimentality' and the ICC motivated by an 'unstated agenda of creating ever more comprehensive international structures to bind nation states in general and one nation state in particular'.[54] Rather than interpreting IL in terms of universal values recognised by liberalism, Bolton adopted the prism of particularistic American cultural values, dismissing overwhelming support of European allies by saying 'that is a major reason why they are Europeans and we are not'.[55] The attitude was shared by Bolton's former professor and colleague Robert Bork,[56] for whom the ICC illustrated the 'futility and danger of pretending that there is law' when there remained 'pervasive anti-Americanism in much of the world'. Allowing the ICC to stand would have costs for American soldiers and officials through 'propaganda defeats that may carry weight in both international and domestic politics'.[57] These statements signalled the trend away from the internationalist worldview prevailing since the end of the Cold War toward beliefs that only permissive development of IL could secure American foreign policy interests.

Once appointed as under secretary, Bolton redoubled his opposition, describing the ICC as 'an organization that runs contrary to fundamental American precepts and basic Constitutional principles of popular sovereignty, checks and balances, and national independence'.[58] Consistent with the administration's 'lawfare' concerns, Bolton identified the threat in a strategy of external forces using IL to constrain US power. The EU

53 Jesse Helms, 'Helms Opposes Clinton's Approval of the ICC Treaty', *Washington File*, 1 February 2001, https://wfile.ait.org.tw/wf-archive/2001/010102/epf206.htm.

54 Committee on Foreign Relations, United States Senate, *Is a U.N. International Criminal Court in the U.S. National Interest?: Hearing before the Subcommittee on International Operations of the Committee on Foreign Relations United States Senate*, 2nd Session 105th Congress (1998), p. 28.

55 Ibid., p. 31.

56 John R. Bolton, 'In Memoriam: Robert H. Bork', American Enterprise Institute, 19 December 2012, www.aei.org/research-products/report/in-memoriam-robert-h-bork/.

57 Robert H. Bork, *Coercing Virtue: The Worldwide Rule of Judges* (AEI Press, 2003), pp. 20–1.

58 John R. Bolton, 'American Justice and the International Criminal Court', Remarks at the American Enterprise Institute, Washington, DC, 3 November 2003, https://2001-2009.state.gov/t/us/rm/25818.htm.

was singled out to make the case that increasing secularism in the continent had contributed to a new 'theology' centred on 'the pursuit of global governance, and in particular the International Criminal Court'. More particularly, this objective was 'repeatedly and cynically designed to put the United States in an impossible position, with only unpleasant and inconsistent alternatives, in the hope and expectation that we would acquiesce in progress for the ICC in order not to frustrate other important American objectives'.[59] Where the United States was compelled to formulate policy responses to the subject matter of international criminal law, Bolton expressed a preference for transferring cases to domestic courts 'grounded in sovereign consent'.[60] This went beyond mere criticism of the ICC's particular design, instead opposing the very principle of developing global governance to address international crimes. Bork again concurred, attributing 'great credit' to Bush for withdrawing from the treaty regime. He fortified his claim of a court interwoven with anti-American sentiment by recounting the 'cheers and rhythmic stomping' that accompanied US defeat in the final vote of the Rome Conference.[61]

Compatibility of US Policy with the International Rule of Law

Rejection of ICC constraints on US foreign policy did not, however, constitute a denial of IL as an institutional structure with which the United States must engage. Despite campaigning against the ICC, Bolton carefully emphasised US compliance with existing legal obligations. The legal ambiguity of the Bush administration removing any possibility of ICC support, yet leaving its signature on the founding treaty, left Bolton 'determined to establish the precedent, and to remove any vestigial argument that America's signature had any continuing effect',[62] In liberal internationalist terms, signing and creating an obligation 'not to defeat the object and purpose of a treaty' progressed transnational development of IL, even in the absence of ratification.[63] However, as Daalder and Lindsay argue, the Bush administration rejected the idea popular in the Clinton years that 'committing good words to paper would create international norms capable of shaping state behaviour'. Rather, for the Bush administration, 'the benefits of flexibility far outweigh the diplomatic costs of declining to participate in international agreements

59 Bolton, *Surrender Is Not an Option*, p. 349.
60 Bolton, 'Remarks at the AEI'.
61 Bork, *Coercing Virtue*, p. 35.
62 Bolton, *Surrender Is Not an Option*, p. 85.
63 See *Vienna Convention on the Law of Treaties*, Art. 18.

that are popular with friends and allies'.[64] In illiberal nationalist terms, IL should be developed solely as a permissive framework, rejecting treaty commitments entailing any constraints.

The unsigning of the Rome Statute was achieved against the wishes of the State Department, but with the urging of the secretary of defense[65] and the support of the president.[66] At his confirmation hearings, Powell noted that the effect of Ambassador Scheffer's signature was that 'in legal terms you sort of bind yourself not to defeat the purpose and objectives of the treaty. But we have no plans to ask for ratification of this treaty.' Helms responded not by denying the obligation, but, rather, by quipping: 'We are going to send somebody down there to strike the signature of that ambassador.'[67] By May 2002, Bolton had relevantly communicated to the UN Secretary General that the United States had no intention to become a party to the treaty and therefore had 'no legal obligations arising from its signature'.[68] This act renounced the legal obligation not to engage in actions inconsistent with the Rome Statute, which had arisen from Clinton's 2000 signature, 'until it shall have made its intention clear not to become a party to the treaty'.[69] In following this procedure, Bolton emphasised US compliance with 'legitimate mechanisms provided for in the *Rome Statute* itself'.[70]

On the day of the unsigning, Under Secretary of State for Political Affairs Marc Grossman articulated the beliefs structuring the Bush ICC policy, beginning with a commitment to 'justice and the rule of law'. Equally identified, however, were beliefs that 'states, not international institutions' upheld this principle, with the ICC itself lacking the 'checks and balances' present in US domestic law. The United States was thus compelled to unsign the statute precisely to uphold its 'leadership role in the promotion of international justice and the rule of law'.[71] Here, Grossman's reasoning followed elements of liberal nationalist beliefs – about the sufficiency of municipal law for upholding democratic rights

64 Daalder & Lindsay, *America Unbound*, p. 45.

65 Rumsfeld, *Known and Unknown*, p. 598.

66 Bolton, *Surrender Is Not an Option*, p. 95.

67 United States Senate, *Nomination of Colin L. Powell*, p. 61.

68 John R. Bolton, 'International Criminal Court: Letter to UN Secretary General Kofi Annan', 6 May 2002, https://2001-2009.state.gov/r/pa/prs/ps/2002/9968.htm.

69 *Vienna Convention on the Law of Treaties*, Art. 18.

70 Bolton, 'Remarks at the AEI'. The correctness of this legal claim is generally agreed: see Edward T. Swaine, 'Unsigning' (2003) 55 *Stanford Law Review* 2061.

71 Marc Grossman, 'American Foreign Policy and the International Criminal Court', Remarks to the Center for Strategic and International Studies, 6 May 2002, https://2001-2009.state.gov/p/us/rm/9949.htm.

and the corrosive effect of IL on these rights. Such a position does not amount to 'isolationism' per se, which would entail structuring IL to achieve a complete separation between the United States and global affairs. It does nevertheless reflect elements of what has often been labelled isolationism, in interpreting the United States' legal interests by reference to its self-sufficient character. Grossman defined US commitment to 'promotion of the rule of law' as protecting independent states that accept 'the challenges and responsibilities associated with enforcing the rule of law'. Grossman's argument shared the liberal preference for 'self-governing democracies' to facilitate the rule of law, but remained distinct from liberal internationalism through primary emphasis on the protective development of IL rather than its role in *strengthening* transnational connections.[72]

Curtis Bradley retrospectively defended compatibility of the policy with the rule of law, which never amounted to 'repudiations of international law'.[73] In relation to Article 18 of the VCLT, the administration 'did not contravene or disregard international law; rather it carefully followed international law governing "unsigning"'.[74] However, this line of argument is effective only to confirm US fidelity to Bradley's own conception of the international rule of law. His commitment is to pragmatically develop IL based on consent as the normative foundation for global governance, while challenging worldviews 'that having more, and more expansive, international rules is always better for the world'.[75] For the actual legalist critics cited by Bradley, these commitments fall short of demonstrating any affinity for the international rule of law. The act of unsigning directly repudiated the formal development of global governance – not just the particular design of the ICC.

Bradley's argument is less persuasive in claiming that the administration 'was not antagonistic to international criminal law, but simply had particular concerns about the structure of the International Criminal Court, concerns that also had been expressed by the Clinton Administration'.[76] This conclusion flows from analysis at the level of IL policy outcomes – according to which there were broad similarities between successive administrations. But disaggregating the beliefs of legal policymakers reveals a crucial distinction between the previous

72 Ibid.
73 Bradley, 'The Bush Administration and International Law', p. 59.
74 Ibid., p. 62.
75 Ibid., p. 72.
76 Ibid., p. 62.

liberal–illiberal internationalist contest and the shift to a contest between forms of nationalism–illiberal internationalism. Bradley readily conceded that Bolton was 'openly hostile' toward the UN, but without identifying the degree to which that ideological hostility was constitutive of IL.

Conclusion

The meaning of non-arbitrary global governance remained deeply contested throughout this period. Legalist policy reaffirmed a commitment to the formalised development of ICC obligations, through progressive institutionalisation of the court's judicial supremacy and universal acceptance of its authority. In contrast, US policy sought to curtail the aspirations of the court so far as they placed constraints on US autonomy considered arbitrary. Sands observed critically that the general approach of the administration was inconsistent with the rule of law for insisting that IL 'be enforceable only selectively, and not across the board'.[77] Such selective development did indeed reflect the view of key US legal policymakers, but this does not support the further conclusion that the international rule of law was being consciously rejected. US policymakers maintained the methods and framework of IL while actively opposing the displacement of municipal governance. In this approach, American policymakers maintained fidelity to long-established nationalist conceptions of IL as necessary to uphold not merely US interests but legal principle, too.

Defining Equality under International Law

Fundamental elements of the relationship between states parties and the ICC were largely settled in the Rome Statute itself, finalised prior to the Bush administration entering office. What did receive parties' ongoing attention was the increasingly prominent, but largely undefined, relationship between the ICC and the UNSC and the legal privileges of the P5 therein. From the outset, the legalist position insisted on equality before the law in the form of equal rights and duties of all signatories to the Rome Statute. In particular, limits were established on the power of the P5 to approve ICC investigations and prosecutions. The United States resisted these arguments from the time of the Clinton administration

[77] Philippe Sands, *Lawless World: Making and Breaking Global Rules* (Viking, 2006), p. 60.

onward, consistently pushing for forms of UNSC control over the court. During the Bush 43 administration, this translated into demands that all US military personnel involved in peacekeeping operations be granted formal immunity from prosecution. That was achieved through the passing of UNSC Resolution 1422 of 2002, renewed as Resolution 1487 in 2003.[78] As such, the issue arises of whether and how US legal policy-makers squared legal privileges with equality as a core rule of law principle.

Legalist Policy

For legalist advocates, the guiding principle remained that of upholding equality in the rights and duties of all sovereign states before the court. On the eve of resolution 1422 being passed, EU representative Javier Solana argued that, although the United States was 'quite right to point to its special global responsibilities', equally, 'European nations also have peace-keeping responsibilities, but see no threat to these from the Court'. Solana appealed for the United States to honour the fact that it had 'probably done more than any other country to strengthen the rule of international law in the post-war era . . . So I hope that the United States will think again and let the Court prove its worth.'[79] Bassiouni described the eventual capitulation to US demands for absolute immunity as 'shocking':

> Only those governments who have a disregard for the international rule of law coupled with the arrogance of power, and more particularly for international humanitarian law, could have led these governments to impose these two resolutions.[80]

Similarly, Sands described preclusion of ICC jurisdiction through the UNSC as a question of: 'When can brute political power override the rule of law and legal processes?'[81] Although the resolutions did not single out named states, the intent and effect were clearly to establish distinctive legal rights for the United States. The critiques make clear that the

[78] SC Res 1422, UN Doc S/RES/1422 (12 July 2002); SC Res 1487, UN Doc S/RES/1487 (12 June 2003).

[79] Javier Solana, 'The Intertwining of Security and Economics in Transatlantic Politics', Speech at the Bertelsmann Foundation Transatlantic Strategy Group, Berlin, 11 July 2002, www.cap.lmu.de/download/2002/2002_tsg_solana.pdf.

[80] M. Cherif Bassiouni, *The Legislative History of the International Criminal Court: Introduction, Analysis, and Integrated Text of the Statute, Elements of Crimes and Rules of Procedure and Evidence* (Transnational Publishers, 2005), p. 144.

[81] Sands, *Lawless World*, p. 58.

primary charge against the United States was of pitting political interest against legal principle, with the triumph of the former.

Beliefs of American Legal Policymakers

Hegemonic Privileges through UNSC Control

Exemptions from ICC prosecution for US peacekeepers made tangible American beliefs 'that it is the exceptional, indeed "indispensable," nation entitled to the benefit of special rules'.[82] In this period the meaning of 'equality' under IL took on the particularistic meanings correlated with prevailing influences of illiberal internationalism and nationalist ideologies. The only meaningful support for the court among these ideological approaches came from illiberal internationalist policymakers, with the exemplar being Jack Goldsmith as Legal Adviser in the Department of Defense and later head of the Office of Legal Counsel in the Department of Justice. His contemporaneous and subsequent writings demonstrate the process by which the administration sought to carve out forms of hegemonic privilege, contrary to the principle of sovereign equality, and yet in furtherance of a coherent conception of the international rule of law.

Goldsmith perceived a conflict at the heart of ICC disagreement between demands for sovereign equality and a countervailing belief in hegemonic privilege as the necessary guarantor for the rule of law. Noting that the outcome of the Rome Conference was 'dominated by weak and middle powers' as well as NGOs,[83] he adopted Kagan's 2002 reasoning that transatlantic divisions in ICC policy reflected 'a broader pattern of middle power (and especially European) efforts to use international law to limit the power of militarily superior nations'.[84] Although this statement was made critically, it would likely be agreed to by the states in question, who did indeed view formal equality as a proper legal constraint on military might. Goldsmith acknowledged that states taking a principled stand was one plausible explanation for opposition to US policy, with legalist 'commitment to the equality of all nations before

[82] John F. Murphy, *The United States and the Rule of Law in International Affairs* (Cambridge University Press, 2004), p. 191.

[83] Jack Goldsmith, 'The Self-Defeating International Criminal Court' (2003) 70 *The University of Chicago Law Review* 89, p. 90.

[84] Ibid., p. 101, n. 50. Citing Kagan, 'Power and Weakness', p. 11.

international criminal law' viewed by other states as necessary for the 'rule of law'.[85]

To this claim, Goldsmith responded that a court designed in such terms was 'unrealistic', above all else, because its design as of 2002 'is, and will remain, unacceptable to the United States'. By way of explanation:

> [T]he ICC depends on U.S. political, military, and economic support for its success. An ICC without U.S. support – and indeed, with probable U.S. opposition – will not only fail to live up to its expectations. It may well do actual harm by discouraging the United States from engaging in various human rights–protecting activities. And this, in turn, may increase rather than decrease the impunity of those who violate human rights.[86]

These observations fitted within a broader conception of IL requiring a foundation not in high-minded aspirations, but in effective political power. To illustrate, the appearance of former Serbian and Yugoslavian president Slobodan Milošević before the ICTY was not achieved through the 'gravitational pull' of properly constituted judicial power, but, rather, through 'U.S. military, diplomatic, and financial might'.[87] This is equally a rebuttal to liberal internationalist arguments that transnational processes create a sense of legal obligation capable of imbuing a 'compliance pull' in IL, independent from enforcement mechanisms.[88] For Goldsmith, there was a 'perversity' in the ICC design in its potential 'chilling effect' on America's 'unique international policing responsibilities' to uphold human rights.[89] In circumstances where the United States was uniquely exposed while fulfilling this global role, the court 'appears to expose the only nation practically able to intervene to protect human rights to the greatest potential liability for human rights violations'.[90] Contrastingly, states that breached international criminal law but were not globally engaged escaped the reach of the court.

In jurisprudential terms, this is a case for institutionalising American hegemonic privilege as a core element of the international rule of law. The unstated belief squaring the account with equality under IL was that rights are defined equal to the *unequal* duties performed by each state in

[85] Goldsmith, 'The Self-Defeating ICC', p. 99.
[86] Ibid., p. 89.
[87] Ibid., p. 93.
[88] See Harold H. Koh, 'Why Do Nations Obey International Law?' (1997) 106 *Yale Law Journal* 2599, p. 2634.
[89] Goldsmith, 'The Self-Defeating ICC', p. 95.
[90] Ibid., pp. 98–9.

upholding the global system. Goldsmith certainly did not characterise his position in this way, and in fact framed his argument as 'benign hypocrisy that appears to reconcile rule-of-law values with the enforcement asymmetries of international politics'.[91] In other words, he stated his position in terms of the null hypothesis of this book: that the international rule of law had a unified meaning, but that US policy erodes the ideal according to political necessity. The power of ideology as defined here, however, is in structuring the worldview of adherents without any necessary consciousness of shared sets of interrelated beliefs. The structure of Goldsmith's beliefs remains congruent with ideas about IL long established by illiberal internationalist ideology. The argument thus corroborates legal conceptions in which sovereign equality was problematic not merely because it diminished American political influence but also because it diminished the international rule of law itself.

Exceptionalist beliefs were realised in the substantive content of resolutions 1422 and 1487. The resolutions noted that states had different legal obligations depending on whether they were parties to the Rome Statute while emphasising that 'it is in the interests of international peace and security to facilitate Member States' ability to contribute to operations established or authorized by the United Nations Security Council'.[92] That understanding became the basis for tailoring special immunity rights within the law to facilitate the policy objective of ongoing US contributions to international peace and security. The influence of these legal beliefs was further evident in the way the resolutions determined international judicial powers in relation to the ICC. The resolutions made a clear distinction between the obligations of states parties who 'have chosen to accept' ICC jurisdiction and those who have not. The latter were explicitly excluded from the reach of the Rome Statute, but nevertheless undertook to 'continue to fulfil their responsibilities in their national jurisdictions in relation to international crimes'.[93] The influence of illiberal internationalism remained coherent in dividing international legal powers according foremost to state consent.

The internationalist policies advocated by Goldsmith and others frequently melded with more nationalist legal conceptions in this period, but they remained distinct from them through a commitment to

91 Ibid., p. 104.
92 SC Res 1422.
93 Ibid.

maintaining America's global legal presence. From an illiberal nationalist perspective, states should possess a relative sovereignty equal to their alignment with American values and national security. Jesse Helms warned of 'a court run amok', which should be resisted for being controlled equally by states that included 'dictatorships'. That problem was acute where the ICC remained 'immune to a U.S. veto' through the UNSC.[94]

Conclusion

Defining the relationship between states under the ICC regime proved one of the most difficult issues for the first term of the Bush 43 administration. The position of legalist advocates articulated an absolute commitment to sovereign equality as a necessary requirement for upholding the international rule of law. A later UNSC debate about the ICC and the rule of law described resolutions 1422 and 1487 as 'the most controversial and questionable resolutions to come out of the Council ... [and] contrary to both the Charter of the United Nations and the Rome Statute'.[95] In contrast, the strength of illiberal internationalist conceptions within the administration translated into institutional recognition of American hegemonic privilege as a necessary element of an effective international rule of law. Goldsmith unapologetically asserted:

> The price for a more plausible enforcement mechanism in the ICC context is to make the United States functionally immune, at least in the ICC (as opposed to domestic and other fora), from the enforcement of international criminal law.[96]

In these circumstances, ideology set hard limits to reaching a common position on the definition of 'equality' as an element otherwise agreed as foundational to the rule of law.

Determining International Judicial Power

Through the early years of the court's operation, advocates of a legalist design continued to determine the integrity of ICC judicial power by its separation from executive and legislative powers of

[94] Jesse Helms, *Congressional Record, 107th Congress* (2 October 2001), p. S10042.
[95] UN, *6849th Meeting (Resumption 1)*, United Nations Security Council (17 October 2012), p. 2 per the Liechtenstein delegate.
[96] Goldsmith, 'The Self-Defeating ICC', p. 103.

states. That policy assumed the feasibility of ICC independence, and therefore legitimacy, through supremacy of its judicial power. In contrast, the Bush administration supported domestic legislation intended to reverse that institutional design and subordinate the court's powers to US municipal legal authority. The *American Service-Members' Protection Act* (2002) (ASPA) – colloquially known as the 'Hague Invasion Act' – represented a clear shift from the Clinton administration that had opposed the bill in 2000.[97] The effect of the ASPA was to penalise countries that declined to sign bilateral 'Article 98 agreements' granting ICC immunity for American citizens, while also authorising the recovery of US nationals 'by all means necessary and appropriate' should they nevertheless end up in the court's custody.[98] Through these actions, the ICC's judicial power would be divided and reserved to the US government insofar as it purported to apply to US citizens. The administration went so far as to write to EU governments expressing 'dismay' at what it saw as a campaign 'actively undermining' US initiatives to establish immunities for its peacekeeping forces.[99] These policies contradicted legalist principles of a separation of powers, which therefore cast US policy as contradicting the international rule of law itself.

Legalist Policy

Donald Rumsfeld had rejected the ICC because the court, among other things, lacked adequate checks and balances on its power; diluted the authority of the UNSC; and opened the door to politicised prosecutions of American nationals.[100] Sands responded that what Rumsfeld really objected to was 'that the rules will not allow the United States or other countries to use political power to control the proceedings'.[101] Underlying this argument was an opposition between a legalist conception of law and the contaminating influence of other forms of control over the court's judicial power. Sands reasoned by analogy with

97 William Schabas, *An Introduction to the International Criminal Court* (Cambridge University Press, 2011), p. 31.

98 *American Service Members' Protection Act* 2002 Pub L 107–206, 116 Stat 82, sec.2008(a).

99 Gary Younge & Ian Black, 'War Crime Vote Fuels US Anger at Europe', *The Guardian*, 11 June 2003, www.theguardian.com/world/2003/jun/11/usa.eu.

100 Rumsfeld, *Known and Unknown*, p. 599.

101 Sands, *Lawless World*, p. 48.

municipal law that, in relation to the court's prosecutorial powers, they 'have to be independent if there is to be any semblance of a rule of law'.[102]

Following the passage of the ASPA, the European Parliament declared that the Act 'goes well beyond the exercise of the United States' sovereign right not to participate in the Court, since it contains provisions which could obstruct and undermine the Court and threatens to penalise countries which have chosen to support the Court'.[103] In legalist terms, this was a criticism of US intent to reclaim elements of the court's judicial power that purported to exclude US municipal legal authority. In a July 2002 European Parliament debate, Europe Minister Bertel Haarder noted the contradictory nature of the ASPA when both the United States and the EU 'uphold freedom, democracy, human rights and the principles of the rule of law'.[104] Then German Foreign Minister Joschka Fischer corresponded personally with Secretary Powell to warn against the 'rift' that the ASPA would cause with the EU. Fischer's primary argument was that, in the joint fight against global terrorism, US obstruction would deny 'an opportunity to fight with judicial means'.[105] This is ultimately the core of the legalist case for demanding separation of powers in the ICC: that a multilateral global institution exercising judicial power independently of political interests is both feasible and desirable.

The Council of the EU responded to the Article 98 campaign with a set of guiding principles stipulating that only persons sent by the US government in an official capacity were to be covered. The effect of the guideline was to accept the exemption of military personnel and diplomatic officials from ICC jurisdiction but to entirely exclude US citizens acting in a non-governmental capacity.[106] That compromise, spearheaded by British diplomats, was criticised by Amnesty International for allowing

[102] Ibid., p. 61.

[103] European Parliament, 'Consequences for Transatlantic Relations of Law on the Protection of US Personnel; European Parliament Resolution on the Draft American Servicemembers' Protection Act', 4 July 2002, www.amicc.org/antiicclegislation.

[104] Bertel Haarder, 'Consequences for Transatlantic Relations of the Law on the Protection of US Personnel: Debate in European Parliament', 3 July 2002, www.amicc.org/antiicclegislation.

[105] Joschka Fischer, 'Text of Letter from German Foreign Minister to Secretary of State Colin Powell Dated October 24, 2001, Delivered on October 31', 24 October 2001, www.amicc.org/antiicclegislation.

[106] The guidelines maintain that the agreements as then drafted remained 'inconsistent with ICC States Parties' obligations with regard to the ICC statute': see Council of the European Union, 'Council Conclusions on the International Criminal Court', 30 September 2002, https://europa.eu/rapid/press-release_PRES-02-279_en.htm.

'the US to shift the terms of the debate from legal principle to political opportunism'.[107] Nevertheless, the Council continued to defend supremacy of the court's judicial power in relation to US nationals not acting as government representatives. The EU's offer was ultimately that it would continue to work with the United States where the objective was 'developing effective and *impartial* international criminal justice'.[108] Underlying commitment to a separation of powers and an independent court remained unchanged as a defining element of the international rule of law.

Beliefs of American Legal Policymakers

The Threat of an Independent Court

The US position on the ICC's legal powers was set out in the NSS 2002, which sought to 'reaffirm the essential role of American military strength. We must build and maintain our defenses beyond challenge.'[109] The relevant section continued:

> We will take the actions necessary to ensure that our efforts to meet our global security commitments and protect Americans are not impaired by the potential for investigations, inquiry, or prosecution by the International Criminal Court (ICC), whose jurisdiction does not extend to Americans and which we do not accept.[110]

These sentiments replicated statements that the president delivered earlier that year where he gave an assurance that no member of the American military would appear before an 'unaccountable' ICC or any such 'international courts and committees with agendas of their own'.[111] These jurisdictional interpretations directly addressed proper institutional arrangements for determining the integrity of global judicial powers, which came to be defined by opposition both to legalist arguments for a fully independent court and to liberal internationalist policy that supported a court with independent powers subject to democratic checks and balances.

[107] Ian Black, 'Britain Accused of Sacrificing New Court', *The Guardian*, 1 October 2002, www.theguardian.com/world/2002/oct/01/usa.ianblack.

[108] EU, *Statement of the EU on the Position of the US towards the ICC*, p. 6, emphasis added.

[109] The White House, *NSS 2002*, p. 29.

[110] Ibid., p. 31.

[111] George W. Bush, 'President Salutes Troops of the 10th Mountain Division', Fort Drum, New York, 19 July 2002, https://georgewbush-whitehouse.archives.gov/news/releases/2002/07/20020719.html.

The underlying contention with the ICC's structure of legal power was the implausibility of separating purely judicial power, with the court seen to exercise a form of political power by definition. Bolton characterised the ICC as 'an unaccountable prosecutor, possibly politically motivated, posing grave risks for the United States and its political and military leaders'.[112] For Rumsfeld, the ICC constituted 'a potential lawfare weapon against the United States'.[113] Guided by the principle of protecting 'America's sovereignty', Rumsfeld rejected any legal arrangement that granted legal powers to courts not held accountable by the consent of Americans themselves. He concluded that such 'growing international judicial encroachments on our sovereignty' will erode 'America's willingness to use our military as a force for good around the world'.[114]

During this period, John Yoo wrote to Alberto Gonzales, then legal counsel to the president, to argue that ICC independence could threaten the administration's use of decidedly illiberal 'enhanced interrogation' techniques.[115] Yoo argued that these possible acts of torture 'cannot fall within the jurisdiction of the ICC, although it would be impossible to control the actions of a rogue prosecutor or judge'.[116] The chief mischief lay in the fact that 'the ICC is not checked by any other international body, not to mention any democratically-elected or accountable one'. Citing various scenarios, including that of the rogue prosecutor, Yoo concluded that the Office of Legal Counsel 'can only provide the best reading of international law on the merits. We cannot predict the political actions of international institutions.'[117] Yoo later maintained with Posner that the ICC would 'not be an effective tribunal' for reasons that could be 'traced directly to the independence of the court'.[118] Sands described these as 'extreme views on the ICC' and Yoo's memorandum of advice as 'error-ridden'.[119] Yet the arguments from both Rumsfeld and

112 Bolton, *Surrender Is Not an Option*, p. 85.

113 Rumsfeld, *Known and Unknown*, p. 598.

114 Ibid., pp. 599–600.

115 Widely agreed to constitute torture: see M. Katherine B. Darmer, 'Waterboarding and the Legacy of the Bybeeyoo Torture and Power Memorandum: Reflections from a Temporary Yoo Colleague and Erstwhile Bush Administration Apologist' (2008) 12 *Chapman Law Review* 639.

116 John C. Yoo, 'Letter from the Office of the Deputy Assistant Attorney General to Alberto R. Gonzales, Counsel to the President', 1 August 2002, www.justice.gov/sites/default/files/olc/legacy/2010/08/05/memo-gonzales-aug1.pdf, p. 1.

117 Ibid., p. 6.

118 Eric A. Posner & John C. Yoo, 'Judicial Independence in International Tribunals' (2005) 93 *California Law Review* 1, p. 69.

119 Sands, *Lawless World*, p. 248.

Yoo were consistent with standard illiberal interpretations of IL drawn from the administration's foreign policy ideology, which rejected the necessity or even compatibility of independent judicial powers with the international rule of law.

The administration's preferred policy was not to consign the subject matter of international criminal law to a legal black hole, but to assert the merits of the supremacy of municipal legal powers. In 2001 David Scheffer was succeeded as Ambassador-at-Large for War Crimes Issues by Pierre-Richard Prosper, who proceeded to advocate hybrid courts constituted at the municipal level as an alternative to the ICC.[120] Prosper testified that the administration remained a committed leader in 'efforts to end impunity by holding perpetrators of war crimes accountable'. He rejected a central ICC role, however, in favour of 'lasting initiatives, especially securing the rule of law'. The United States would not abdicate its responsibilities to this task as part of the 'international community', but nor 'should that responsibility be taken away' from states by international courts.[121] Elsewhere Prosper elaborated that a strengthened ICC would 'undermine the legitimate efforts of member states to achieve national reconciliation and domestic accountability by democratic means'. This returned to previous calls for limiting the reach of formal international rules in order to resolve conflicts through non-binding measures, such as truth and reconciliation commissions. Such were ultimately more likely to create 'a lasting benefit to the rule of law'.[122] It is notable that in a subsequent public address on the topic 'War Crimes in the 21st Century', Prosper failed to even acknowledge the existence of the ICC, let alone US objections, even as he reiterated commitment to accountability for atrocities in Sudan and the rule of law more generally.[123]

Reordering International Judicial Power through the ASPA

The legislative intent of the ASPA can be conceived as a bridge between the Rome Statute and prevailing US ideological preferences. The

[120] See David Bosco, *Rough Justice: The International Criminal Court's Battle to Fix the World, One Prosecution at a Time* (Oxford University Press, 2014), p. 111.

[121] Pierre-Richard Prosper, 'Confronting, Ending, and Preventing War Crimes in Africa', Testimony before the House International Relations Committee, Subcommittee on Africa, 24 June 2004, https://2001-2009.state.gov/s/wci/us_releases/rm/33934.htm.

[122] Office of the Legal Adviser, Department of State, *Digest of United States Practice in International Law: 2004* (International Law Institute, 2006), pp. 180–1.

[123] Pierre-Richard Prosper, 'War Crimes in the 21st Century', Remarks at Pepperdine University, 26 October 2004, https://2001-2009.state.gov/s/wci/us_releases/rm/38309.htm.

preamble warned against exposing American citizens to international judicial power in terms consistent with liberal nationalism and the vertical separation of powers. This included 'procedural protections to which all Americans are entitled under the Bill of Rights to the United States Constitution, such as the right to trial by jury'.[124] The preamble also drew upon illiberal conceptions of law in structuring the ICC regime to ensure that American armed forces and senior government officials remain unimpeded in protecting the 'vital national interests' and 'national security decisions' of the United States.[125] The legislation warned in these terms that the ICC itself threatened to breach IL – either by usurping the role of the UNSC through defining the crime of aggression or by purporting to override US consent as a non-treaty member.[126]

Liberal–illiberal nationalist legal conceptions converged in many respects, with distinct sets of beliefs equally supporting domestic legislation to constrain ICC jurisdiction. Illiberal nationalist conceptions remained dominant in shaping policy, especially as they opposed legalist and liberal internationalist policy. Introducing the ASPA, and its prohibition against US authorities cooperating with the court, was one of Helms' final victories over the ICC.[127] The senator presented the ASPA as a corrective for US failures to secure UNSC control and thus an 'insurance policy for our troops and our officials – such as Secretary of State Powell – to protect them from a U.N. Kangaroo Court where the United States has no veto'.[128] Such illiberal nationalist responses were recognised not as a call for the impunity of American citizens but as a measure to reassert the supremacy of American judicial power.

The influence of liberal nationalist beliefs remained important nonetheless, evident in Powell's support for legislation preventing the external prosecution of American military personnel. Although accepting the principle of an international court, he remained cognisant of threats to constitutional liberties:

> [I]t seems to me to be a very difficult thing to say to an American family, oh, by the way, that youngster may not have the constitutional rights that were given to him at birth or her at birth. So I have always been troubled by that aspect of the court. I could not quite square it with my

124 *ASPA*, sec. 2002(7).
125 Ibid., sec. 2002(8)–(9).
126 Ibid., sec. 2002(10)–(11).
127 See ibid., sec. 2004.
128 Jesse Helms, *Congressional Record, 107th Congress*, p. S10042.

> understanding of the obligations we had to those youngsters and to their families.[129]

This returned to the principle of a vertical separation of powers whereby an international court could legitimately exercise judicial power, but only where clearly separated from judicial protection of liberal values under the US Constitution. A more hardline liberal nationalist approach was espoused by then Congressman Ron Paul, who argued that the ICC was 'inherently incompatible with national sovereignty'. Specifically, the potential for competing judicial authority presented a 'conflict between adhering to the rule of law and obeying globalist planners' so that 'America must either remain a constitutional republic or submit to international law, because it cannot do both'.[130] Paul presented a resolution to Congress in February 2001 calling on the president to 'declare to all nations that the United States does not intend to assent to or ratify the treaty and the signature of former President Clinton to the treaty should not be construed otherwise'.[131] The resolution focused centrally on the impermissibility of 'a supranational court that would exercise the judicial power constitutionally reserved only to the United States'. This offended the liberal nationalist principle that international and municipal law should govern separate spheres, with the ICC encroaching on 'the legislative and judicial authority of the United States'. The resolution never engaged in bare denials of international legal authority, however, emphasising consent requirements under the VCLT to argue the illegality of the court.[132] For sponsors of the congressional resolution, the international rule of law meant upholding the thin framework of rules facilitating coexistence between domestic jurisdictions, while protecting municipal judicial powers over the subject matter of international criminal law.

The contours of these illiberal and nationalist approaches become clearest when contrasted with the persistence of liberal internationalist beliefs as a minority position during the Bush 43 administration. Senator Dodd remained a leading champion of the ICC cause, arguing that, since the time of the Founding Fathers, the 'long-term security needs of the

129 United States Senate, *Nomination of Colin L. Powell*, p. 88.

130 Ron Paul, 'A Court of No Authority', *Texas Straight Talk*, 8 April 2002, http://ronpaulquotes.com/Texas_Straight_Talk/tst040802.htm.

131 Ron Paul et al., *Expressing the Sense of the Congress that President George W. Bush Should Declare to all Nations that the United States Does Not Intend to Assent to or Ratify the International Criminal Court*, H.CON.RES.23 (8 February 2001).

132 Ibid.

Nation' were strengthened by globally extending 'inalienable rights' established by the US Constitution. That principle, when combined with unrivalled power, created leadership responsibilities in the United States to establish a system of international criminal justice. Dodd recognised the inconsistency of his worldview with nationalist attempts to 'become a gated community and retreat from international agreements'.[133] With the establishment of the ICC appearing to be politically inevitable, the ASPA would have the effect only of placing US military personnel 'in greater jeopardy than they would be if we were to participate in trying to develop the structures of this court to minimize problems'. Dodd thus advocated sustained US commitment to stay 'at the table to try to work it out so that it becomes a viable product which we can support and gather behind'. The policy of minimising IL in the immediate aftermath of the September 11 terrorist attacks was 'stunning', with the United States traversing from once leading the creation of the UN system to now 'shirking its international duty'.[134] More acutely, in Dodd's worldview it was contradictory for the United States to call for greater international solidarity against terrorism yet, at the same time, signal an intention to act unilaterally through the ASPA.[135] Liberal internationalist preferences were ultimately legislated in the 'Dodd Amendment', which made an exception to prohibitions against US ICC cooperation in cases where the United States could provide 'Assistance to International Efforts' advancing criminal justice.[136]

Swings between competing definitions of US interests certainly confirm a form of political incoherence in US policy outcomes. However, the shifts as identified by Dodd also reveal that each distinct policy was coherent within the terms of an identifiable ideological structure. The complexity of Dodd's own position emphasises the value of ideological context since, as the Rome Statute stood in 2001, he 'would vote against it because it is a flawed agreement'.[137] That appears equally contradictory from a legalist standpoint, which his sentiments otherwise coincide with, but is consistent with his scepticism about the judicial integrity of a court lacking democratic checks and balances. Even this most forceful

[133] Christopher Dodd, *Congressional Record, 107th Congress* (26 September 2001), pp. S9861-2.

[134] Ibid., p. S9860.

[135] Ibid., p. S9861.

[136] *ASPA*, sec. 2015.

[137] Dodd, *Congressional Record*, p. S9860.

American advocate contradicted legalist rule of law principles through remaining faithful to ideological beliefs.

Article 98 Agreements and the Supremacy of American Judicial Power

From the time of the Rome negotiations, Scheffer recalled that the Joint Chiefs of Staff made clear their preparedness to give, in principle, support for the ICC – provided that it was designed as 'subordinate' to and 'strictly an adjunct to national prosecutions'.[138] This was significant evidence that defence officials were prepared to support some form of the court and were not categorically opposed. A specific stipulation was that the ICC could not eclipse a Status of Force Agreement (SOFA) with any country on whose territory US soldiers were based. These agreements upheld the 'sacrosanct' principle that the criminal investigation and prosecution of US military personnel would remain the sole province of US military or federal courts.[139] The Department of Justice joined the calls for a design allowing municipal legal processes to prevail over those of an international court, with relevant legal advisers in both cases expressing commitment to IL, yet in terms of rejecting the separation and privileging of the ICC's international judicial power. Through US insistence, the principle of a consent-based division of powers was ultimately enshrined in Article 98(2) of the Rome Statute, which prevented the ICC from requesting surrender of an accused person if the state having custody had pre-existing obligations not to do so – such as those established under a SOFA.

The United States concluded over 100 Article 98 agreements with global allies pledging to honour this form of ICC immunity. The strategy was fortified by congressional support through the ASPA and its provisions for cutting off military assistance to states who failed to sign agreements. Scheffer considered these agreements inconsistent with interpretative principles under IL, since the original intent of the provision had been to cover US military personnel and diplomatic staff from ICC jurisdiction but not individuals acting in a private capacity.[140] This avoided the appearance of asking for blanket immunity for all Americans, while still addressing internationalist concerns to preserve

[138] Scheffer, *All the Missing Souls*, p. 169.
[139] Ibid., pp. 171 & 175.
[140] David J. Scheffer, 'Article 98(2) of the Rome Statute: America's Original Intent' (2005) 3 *Journal of International Criminal Justice* 333, pp. 334 & 338–9; see *Vienna Convention on the Law of Treaties*, Arts. 31 & 32.

a US role enforcing international criminal law. Such a rationale did not therefore extend to non-government representatives who, although US nationals, were not performing legally relevant functions.

Scheffer's critique of Article 98 immunities clearly diverged from illiberal nationalist initiatives as spearheaded by John Bolton. Bolton sought immunity for every American: 'private citizens such as missionaries, journalists, NGO members, businesspeople, even tourists, who could be swept up in a conflict and used as scapegoats simply because they were Americans'.[141] During this period, Lincoln Bloomfield, as Assistant Secretary of State for Political-Military Affairs (and head of the bureau within which Bolton worked), further elaborated on the rationale for the broad immunity, arguing: 'One does not have to hold a view of American exceptionalism to acknowledge the profile and symbolic resonance of the American identity in the world.'[142] The bureau was ultimately animated by the perception of an existential threat to all Americans, thereby justifying structuring IL to enshrine the supremacy of US courts over all Americans in order to uphold the rule of law.

Conclusion

Czarnetzky and Rychlak have described the absence of 'a meaningful political check' on ICC power during its formative years as its most serious deficiency. The objective of removing political judgement was problematic where '[p]olitical negotiations are essential to building a nation where the rule of law can be established and human rights can be respected'.[143] All American legal conceptions shaping the Bush 43 policy challenged the ICC for relying merely on good faith exercise of judicial power.[144] By the end of the period, US policy toward determining the integrity of ICC judicial powers was most consistent with ideological variants of nationalism. The process of developing and promoting the ASPA as a response to the ICC design was supported most forcefully by

141 Bolton, *Surrender Is Not an Option*, p. 86.

142 Lincoln P. Bloomfield Jr, 'The U.S. Government and the International Criminal Court', Remarks to the Parliamentarians for Global Action, Consultative Assembly of Parliamentarians for the International Criminal Court and the Rule of Law, 12 September 2003, https://2001-2009.state.gov/t/pm/rls/rm/24137.htm.

143 John M. Czarnetzky & Ronald J. Rychlak, 'An Empire of Law: Legalism and the International Criminal Court' (2003) 79 *Notre Dame Law Review* 55, p. 116.

144 Bolton has said in this context, 'I don't take anything this serious on faith': cited in Erna Paris, *The Sun Climbs Slow: The International Criminal Court and the Struggle for Justice* (Seven Stories Press, 2009), p. 85.

an illiberal nationalist commitment to the supremacy of municipal legal power. The Article 98 agreements had 'almost nil' practical effect on ICC operations,[145] emphasising the degree to which they represented ideological commitments of administration officials. Judicial arrangements located at the municipal level were accordingly held out by American legal policymakers as effective and enforceable against the world. Likewise, the ASPA was underpinned by liberal nationalist preferences to develop a vertical separation between the judicial power of the court and municipal judicial power. Rejecting the separation of powers and ICC independence may have contradicted rule of law expectations of global counterparts, but underlying decision-making processes remained coherent with well-defined legal conceptions drawn from American foreign policy ideology.

Chapter Conclusion

The first term of the Bush 43 administration was marked by clear rejection of legalist prescriptions for realising the international rule of law in the ICC, but equally a rejection of the previous administration's liberal internationalism. The legalist position continued to focus on: a court that progressively developed non-arbitrary global governance through universal acceptance of formalised rules; sovereign equality that prevailed over UNSC privileges; and an independent court separating the ICC's international judicial powers from competing legal and political institutions. American policy responses were never the product of a single conception of the international rule of law and yet, among the ideologies that did compete for influence, the legalist formulation never held any serious sway. The evidence does not support the claim that American policy outcomes represented tactical political calculations compromising commonly held legal ideals. Even in the dramatic act of unsigning the Rome Statute, US policymakers showed deference to the conventions of IL and the legality of opposing the court for perceived failures in advancing non-arbitrary global governance. When arguing for privileges through the UNSC, policymakers defined equality in relation to America's unique global role and exceptional character. Finally, policymakers variously justified the ASPA by reference to the principle of determining the court's judicial power through US consent, of

[145] Caroline Fehl, *Living with a Reluctant Hegemon: Explaining European Responses to US Unilateralism* (Oxford University Press, 2012), p. 98.

maintaining a vertical separation from municipal law, or simply of upholding the supremacy of municipal law.

Sands argued that the only way to explain the virulence of Bush 43 administration opposition was that the court had become 'a useful stalking horse for a broader attack on international law and the constraints which it may place on hegemonic power'.[146] The evidence from this chapter refines that conclusion to argue that the ICC policy was indeed couched in a broader strategy, not of defeating IL per se but of forcefully rejecting the constraining aspirations of legalism and liberal internationalism. The Bush administration's aggressive ICC opposition represented not merely a clash in politics but also the hardening of ideological divisions in the concept of the international rule of law itself. Any realistic prospect of a further policy shift could therefore come only from within American foreign policy ideology, which remained at the ready with alternative, coherent and resonant conceptions of law and American interests.

[146] Sands, *Lawless World*, p. 60.

6

Bush 43 Administration, 2004–2008

The sense of ICC policy shifting between the first and second terms of the Bush 43 administration was pronounced enough for the *Wall Street Journal* to report: 'US Warms to Hague Tribunal'. The first term preference 'that countries apply their own versions of international law in their own courts' was observed to shift toward more pragmatic engagement and even tacit endorsement of the court.[1] Perceptions had grown within the administration that US diplomatic influence was being eroded, with incoming Secretary of State Condoleezza Rice describing Ambassador Bolton's antagonistic ICC policy as 'shooting ourselves in the foot'.[2] The evolving policy fuelled optimism among global court advocates that the United States might become more receptive to legalist principles. These remained unchanged, emphasising the progressive formalisation of global governance through the court, the principle of sovereign equality – especially in opposing immunities for non-states parties in UNSC referrals, and the greatest possible separation of the court's judicial power from parallel international legal powers. Softening attitudes to the ICC were indeed more complementary with elements of legalism in accepting a role for the ICC in global governance. However, more tempered rhetoric notwithstanding, the United States ultimately settled on an arm's-length relationship with the court that never included any intention to submit to its jurisdiction.

From the US perspective, the key issue to be settled in the second term was rebalancing toward an internationalist conception of IL. Despite the administration's previous unsigning of the Rome Statute, allowing it as

[1] Jess Bravin, 'U.S. Warms to Hague Tribunal', *The Wall Street Journal*, 14 June 2006, http://online.wsj.com/articles/SB115024503087679549. This piece was reportedly read and discussed by Condoleezza Rice and John Bellinger: David Bosco, *Rough Justice: The International Criminal Court's Battle to Fix the World, One Prosecution at a Time* (Oxford University Press, 2014), p. 123.

[2] Condoleezza Rice, 'Trip Briefing', En Route to San Juan, Puerto Rico, 10 March, 2006, https://2001-2009.state.gov/secretary/rm/2006/63001.htm.

a matter of law to act contrary to the objects and purposes of the treaty, the administration moved to support the treaty both directly and indirectly. Demands ceased for further renewal of UNSC immunity as a precondition to military support for peacekeeping operations. The ASPA was amended to allow for greater cooperation with US allies, and the Article 98 campaign was wound down and eventually halted. The United States thus dropped its insistence on the sole legitimacy of domestic legal processes and recommitted itself to the ICC as a real source of influence in the international legal system. Yet, despite these various acts of re-engagement, the United States continued to make clear its intention not to join the ICC as a state party and to actively oppose the positions of court advocates at every stage. In circumstances where US policymakers continued to express fidelity to the rule of law, there is again a prima facie case of contestation at the level of competing ideologically informed conceptions of the international rule of law.

Dominant Foreign Policy Ideology

Substantial continuity in IL beliefs persisted across both terms of the Bush administration. During his 2004 re-election campaign, Bush continued to dismiss the very concept of the ICC as 'a body based in The Hague where unaccountable judges and prosecutors can pull our troops or diplomats up for trial ... [I]t's the right move not to join a foreign court ... where our people could be prosecuted.'[3] There was, however, a turnover in key legal policymakers dealing with the ICC, which 'allowed room for the pragmatists to assume a greater role' in shifting policy toward a more internationalist and therefore accommodating stance.[4] Sands noted that the reality of having to work within a rules-based order was 'belatedly' recognised by this period, although he remained sceptical that this amounted to a meaningful shift in IL policy.[5]

The leading personnel change was the replacement of Colin Powell with Condoleezza Rice as Secretary of State. Statements on IL made across Rice's career reveal a strong adherence to illiberal internationalist

[3] George W. Bush, 'Transcript: What Is Kerry's Position on Pre-Emptive War?', *CNN Politics*, 1 October 2004, http://edition.cnn.com/2004/ALLPOLITICS/10/01/debate.transcript.13/index.html?iref=mpstoryview.

[4] John P. Cerone, 'U.S. Attitudes toward International Criminal Courts and Tribunals', in Cesare P.R. Romano (ed.), *The Sword and the Scales: The United States and International Courts and Tribunals* (Cambridge University Press, 2009), p. 304.

[5] Philippe Sands, *Lawless World: Making and Breaking Global Rules* (Viking, 2006), p. xix.

legal conceptions. In an influential 2000 *Foreign Affairs* article, she drew a sharp distinction between her conception of IL and the 'Wilsonian thought' of the Clinton administration.[6] Her criticism of 'at best, illusory "norms" of international behavior' appeared to replicate Bolton's antagonism toward IL, but remained distinct in a commitment to internationalism. Her objection was toward legal policy structured by liberal values of 'humanitarian interests' or a notion of an 'international community'. Rather, she supported 'multilateral agreements and institutions', provided that they were 'well-crafted' to advance narrowly defined national interests and not merely as 'ends in themselves'.[7] In her first town hall meeting as Secretary of State, Rice affirmed that IL 'is critical to the proper function of international diplomacy . . . We depend on a world in which there is some international legal order.' In this, Rice committed to IL developed as a tool for advancing American national security interests. Where 'there are so many countries in the world that don't have our own domestic . . . legal order, we depend on norms of behavior in international politics'. On that basis, Rice declared that the administration would be 'a strong voice for international legal norms, for living up to our treaty obligations, to recognizing that America's moral authority in international politics also rests on our ability to defend international laws and international treaties'.[8] Notably, these statements were taken by outsiders as evidence of the United States' 'commitment to the international rule of law'.[9]

Rice's stated beliefs also revealed the compatibility of her internationalist outlook with elements of illiberal nationalist ideology influencing the administration. In an illuminating exchange during her confirmation hearings, Senator Chris Dodd set his liberal internationalist conception of IL, expressed since the Clinton administration, against Rice's role in developing detainee policy during the first term. Rice described a personal understanding of her legal policymaking role as National Security Adviser, which was not to directly advise the president on law, but rather to consider independent legal advice 'in a policy context'.[10]

[6] Condoleezza Rice, 'Promoting the National Interest' (2000) 79 *Foreign Affairs* 45, p. 47.

[7] Ibid., pp. 47–8.

[8] Condoleezza Rice, 'Remarks at Town Hall Meeting', Dean Acheson Auditorium, Washington, DC, 31 January 2005, https://2001-2009.state.gov/secretary/rm/2005/41414.htm.

[9] Sands, *Lawless World*, p. 240.

[10] Committee on Foreign Relations, United States Senate, *Senate Committee on Foreign Relations, Nomination of Dr. Condoleezza Rice To Be Secretary of State*, 1st Session 109th Congress (2005), p. 117.

Rice maintained that the decision not to apply the Geneva Conventions to certain classes of detainees and the approval of waterboarding as an interrogation technique had been cleared by the Justice Department as 'consistent with our international obligations and American law'.[11]

To this, Dodd responded that fidelity to the international rule of law is not about 'what the law says, not dotting the I's and crossing the T's [sic], but speaking more fundamentally as to who we are as a people'. In discussing the establishment of international criminal justice specifically, the senator argued that what matters is not 'legalisms' but, rather, an IL policy expressing the principle that America is 'very, very different not just in terms of our economic plans and political plans, but how we viewed mankind'.[12] For Dodd, the legitimacy of IL was founded in the extension outward of liberal values at the heart of American constitutional democracy.

Rice responded readily accepting that Americans 'are and have been different' in their liberal values, but did not accept the further proposition that these values must prevail in IL policy. For Rice, there were 'tensions between trying to live with the laws and the norms that we have become accustomed to and the new kind of war that we are in'.[13] Resisting Dodd's argument that Americans and non-Americans alike must be granted liberal equality,[14] the nominee responded obliquely that the administration intended to 'look at what other kinds of international standards might be needed to deal with this very special war because we are a country of laws'.[15] So arguing is consistent with nationalist strands of illiberalism in addition to Rice's internationalist outlook. As Mead argues in relation to his equivalent ideal type, illiberal nationalist duties are owed based on respect for 'an honour code in international life'; those who violate it, 'who commit terrorist acts against innocent civilians', for example, 'forfeit its protection'.[16] The limits of IL in cases involving 'enemy combatants' was defended by Rice on the basis that the persons in question were not themselves 'living up to the laws of war'. Rice

[11] Ibid., p. 118; Condoleezza Rice, *No Higher Honor: A Memoir of My Years in Washington* (Random House LLC, 2011), pp. 117, 121 & 497.

[12] United States Senate, *Nomination of Dr. Condoleezza Rice*, p. 146.

[13] Ibid., p. 118; Rice, *No Higher Honor*, pp. 117, 121 & 497.

[14] See Dodd's argument for the application of the Geneva conventions without discrimination as to nationality: United States Senate, *Nomination of Dr. Condoleezza Rice*, pp. 118–19.

[15] Ibid., p. 147.

[16] Walter R. Mead, *Special Providence: American Foreign Policy and How It Changed the World* (Routledge, 2002), p. 246.

defended the president for an IL policy that 'was consistent with both living up to our international obligations and allowed us to recognize that the Geneva Conventions should not apply to a particular category of people'.[17] This contradicts both legalist and liberal internationalist conceptions of law, which resist sanctioning gaps in the legal framework determining basic rights. In contrast, the idea that the United States could designate gradations of legal rights based on the character of adversaries is entirely in line with illiberal nationalist conceptions of law. Consistent with illiberal ideological perspectives, Rice viewed strained transatlantic relations as 'the mistaken perception that the United States' detention and interrogation policies operated outside the bounds of international law'.[18] Certainly, despite certain misgivings about Bolton's clashes with Powell, Rice had some sympathy for his hardline views against IL.[19] She supported his nomination as UN Ambassador on the basis that 'his skepticism about the organization was an asset with conservatives and, from my point of view, a corrective to the excessive multilateralism of our diplomats in New York'.[20]

At this time, William Taft was also succeeded as Legal Adviser to the State Department by National Security Council Legal Adviser John Bellinger who, above all others, drove the second term shift in ICC policy.[21] Yoo observed that Bellinger 'often shared Taft's accommodating attitude toward international law', thereby resisting illiberal nationalist impulses within the government.[22] Rice had a longstanding close working relationship with Bellinger, characterising his worldview as being that of 'neither a skeptic nor an unthinking proponent of the international community's supposed code of conduct'.[23] Bellinger was sceptical about elements of liberal internationalism, denying that there was 'an incredibly tight connection between promoting the rule of law in individual countries and promoting international law'.[24] He appeared to accept

17 United States Senate, *Nomination of Dr. Condoleezza Rice*, p. 117.

18 Rice, *No Higher Honor*, p. 497.

19 Erna Paris, *The Sun Climbs Slow: The International Criminal Court and the Struggle for Justice* (Seven Stories Press, 2009), p. 60.

20 Rice, *No Higher Honor*, p. 306.

21 Michael P. Scharf & Paul R. Williams, *Shaping Foreign Policy in Times of Crisis: The Role of International Law and the State Department Legal Adviser* (Cambridge University Press, 2010), p. 137.

22 John C. Yoo, *War by Other Means: An Insider's Account of the War on Terror* (Atlantic Monthly Press, 2006), pp. 41–2.

23 Rice, *No Higher Honor*, p. 303.

24 John B. Bellinger III, Interview with Author (12 January 2012).

Robert Kagan's 2002 thesis, arguing that 'in some European countries, largely as a result of United States' efforts after World War Two, there has been a tendency to "apotheosise" international law . . . as an incredibly holy body. One merely needs to say the words "international law" and many Europeans will sort of worship the concept.' Yet, as head of the Office of the Legal Adviser, he remained committed 'to observe international law because we see that it is in our interests to do so and to always ensure that US actions, to the extent possible, are consistent with international law'.[25]

Bellinger's views were significant in particular because of his greater influence in shaping State Department ICC policy compared to his predecessor. Bellinger attributed the increased role of the Legal Adviser to recognition that marginalising State Department lawyers had eroded national interests.[26] Under Bellinger, there was renewed commitment to 'international legal diplomacy' as a guiding principle for IL policy, consistent with illiberal internationalist commitments.[27] Interwoven through these beliefs were exceptionalist influences, evident in responses to charges of US 'hypocrisy'. This Bellinger defined as the charge of wanting 'justice for others but not for the US'. He contended: 'The problem is that the US really *is* differently situated and . . . we are uniquely called upon to be the policeman around the world.'[28] The United States has thereby demanded that IL encompass its 'unique role and interests' flowing from global power, as well as its 'historically rooted suspicions of institutions with unchecked powers'.[29] These sets of rule of law beliefs became pivotal to the internationalist policies that came to define the second term.

Developing Non-arbitrary Global Governance

The ongoing vision of legalist advocates remained consolidation of the ICC as a core component of global governance architecture. That entailed measures to formally integrate the ICC into established governance frameworks

[25] Ibid.

[26] Scharf & Williams, *Shaping Foreign Policy in Times of Crisis*, p. 136.

[27] Ibid., p. 137.

[28] John B. Bellinger III, 'Interview with John Bellinger', International Bar Association, 9 November 2010, www.ibanet.org/Article/Detail.aspx?ArticleUid=37f4f087-bc3a-4c21-a108-92f15391785c, emphasis added.

[29] John B. Bellinger III, 'The United States and the International Criminal Court: Where We've Been and Where We're Going', Remarks to the DePaul University College of Law, 25 April 2008, https://2001-2009.state.gov/s/l/rls/104053.htm.

to ensure uniformity in the application of international criminal law. For its part, the United States continued to strongly express support for the principle of international criminal accountability, including a shift to publicly acknowledge the ICC as a legitimate feature of the international system. However, the Bush administration also continued to argue for the equal legitimacy of alternative forms of accountability that had the effect of limiting the reach of global governance. The seeming legal inconsistency in the US position again raised questions about the role of ideological rule of law beliefs in explaining such divergent outcomes.

Legalist Policy

During this period, the ICC concluded agreements with the UN and the EU to consolidate its formal role in existing networks of global governance. The preamble to the 2004 UN agreement affirmed that 'the International Criminal Court is established as an independent permanent institution in relationship with the United Nations system'. Under Article 2(1), the UN 'recognizes the Court as an independent permanent judicial institution' possessing 'international legal personality'. The preamble to the 2006 EU agreement confirmed 'the fundamental importance and the priority that must be given to the consolidation of the rule of law and respect for human rights and humanitarian law'.[30] In recognising the ICC's role in global governance, the EU further reaffirmed commitment to advancing 'universal support for it by promoting the widest possible participation in the Rome Statute'. Both agreements identified an objective of 'facilitating the effective discharge of their respective responsibilities' (of the ICC, the UN and the EU) toward developing global governance. These intentions to entrench ICC authority did not go unnoticed by America's UN Ambassador John Danforth. In classified communications, he warned that language that 'treats the ICC as an integral part of the international landscape' now regularly appeared in UN resolutions.[31]

Legalist advocates clearly set themselves against any design derogating from formalised global governance. In 2004 the UNSC commissioned the *International Commission of Inquiry on Darfur* to investigate alleged

[30] *Negotiated Relationship Agreement between the International Criminal Court and the United Nations* (2004), Art. 3; *Agreement between the International Criminal Court and the European Union on Cooperation and Assistance* (2006), Art. 4.

[31] John C. Danforth, 'Peace and Accountability: A Way Forward', 7 January 2005, https://nsarchive2.gwu.edu/NSAEBB/NSAEBB335/Document4.PDF.

crimes in the Darfur region of Sudan (Darfur situation) and recommend appropriate accountability measures.[32] The commission was chaired by leading ICC advocate Antonio Cassese, and concluded that the ICC was 'the only credible way of bringing alleged perpetrators to justice'.[33] In so concluding, the commission referenced the legal flaws in permitting domains of international affairs to remain the province of non-uniform or diplomatic solutions. To the US preference for a hybrid court, the commission noted that 'many of the Sudanese laws are grossly incompatible with international norms'. Contrastingly, the implementation of IL through a formalised institution at the global level would ensure uniformity in legal rights and duties: '[T]he ICC constitutes a self-contained regime, with a set of detailed rules on both substantive and procedural law that are fully attuned to respect for . . . fundamental human rights.'[34] Formalised and universal legal rules were not merely a matter of practical justice; they went to the heart of the meaning of the international rule of law.

Beliefs of American Legal Policymakers

Defining Pragmatic Limits to ICC Authority

The re-emergence of illiberal internationalism was succinctly contained in John Bellinger's statement that the administration's 'general approach to international courts and tribunals is pragmatic'. International courts were foremost 'potential tools to advance shared international interests in developing and promoting the rule of law, ensuring justice and accountability, and solving legal disputes'.[35] That framing pointedly does not endorse the role for the court proposed in the UN and EU ICC agreements. There, the court held a privileged status for embodying progressive development of global governance in the domain of criminal law. The conception advocated by Bellinger instead maintained that US accession to the Rome Statute would not in itself demonstrate 'deeper commitment to the rule of law and [prove] . . . us to be better

[32] Pursuant to SC Res 1564, UN Doc S/RES/1564 (18 September 2004).

[33] Antonio Cassese et al., *Report of the International Commission on Darfur to the United Nations Secretary-General*, Pursuant to Security Council Resolution 1564 of 18 September 2004 (25 January 2005), p. 146; SC Res 1593, UN Doc S/RES/1593 (31 March 2005).

[34] Cassese et al., *Report of the International Commission on Darfur*, p. 147.

[35] John B. Bellinger III, 'International Courts and Tribunals and the Rule of Law', in Cesare P.R. Romano (ed.), *The Sword and the Scales: The United States and International Courts and Tribunals* (Cambridge University Press, 2009), p. 2.

international citizens'. To the contrary, US scepticism was said to show 'how seriously we take international law. Embracing the Rome Statute in spite of our serious concerns could only reflect a cavalier attitude towards the Court and international law more generally.'[36] This foremost rebuffed legalist demands for the progressive formalisation of legal obligations, but also contradicted liberal internationalist beliefs in the value of symbolically aligning US policy with legal principles. Rather, for Bellinger, global governance was assigned to the ICC only to the extent that it directly complemented American national security interests, with the United States otherwise demarcating the pragmatic limits of the legal regime.

Although Bellinger acknowledged that the ICC 'has a role to play in the overall system of international justice',[37] he did so seeking to 'agree to disagree' – favouring the term *modus vivendi* to describe the new position.[38] The underlying principle was that the shared ends of 'promoting international criminal justice' remained 'far more important than the means by which we seek them'.[39] In practical terms, this was an argument for circumscribing the role of the ICC, not in opposition to international criminal justice but in the belief that it would enhance its practical realisation. The goal in the EU-ICC agreement of securing universal membership was characterised as 'counterproductive' by Bellinger for impeding a practical working relationship with the United States. Rather, 'ICC supporters will ultimately have to decide which they value more: hewing to an idealistic commitment to universality or pursing practical efforts to build an effective court'.[40] Provided the United States then complied with these predetermined obligations, the conception offered an ideal of non-arbitrary global governance.

Providing analysis at the level of legal beliefs takes on a special importance where policymakers themselves have drawn attention to outcomes rather than decision-making, to make the case for continuity. Bellinger has consistently argued, both during his time in office and subsequently, that US ICC policy has been basically unchanged – across and within US administrations. In his view presidents and congresses have differed according to 'the tone and means' by which they express concerns, but

[36] John B. Bellinger III, 'Reflections on Transatlantic Approaches to International Law' (2007) 17 *Duke Journal of Comparative and International Law* 513, p. 520.
[37] Bravin, 'U.S. Warms to Hague Tribunal'.
[38] Bellinger, Interview with Author.
[39] Bellinger, 'The US and the ICC'.
[40] Ibid.

there is otherwise a 'relatively straight line' running through US ICC opposition.[41] Focusing at the level of competing ideologies, however, provides the true measure of policy discontinuity, even between the first and second Bush 43 terms. Bellinger argued that 'people misread the Bolton letter' (notifying the 2002 unsigning decision) as evidence of a deeply conflicted US attitude toward the ICC. While the letter has been interpreted as expressing 'in aggressive or confrontational terms U.S. rejection of the ICC', Bellinger instead saw it as an attempt to clarify the nature of US obligations in conformity with treaty law.[42] Nevertheless, Bellinger's own stance on the ICC's role in global governance reveals a real shift toward pragmatic development, whereby the United States readily supports global institutions so far as they advance national security interests, while clearly distinguishing the domain of diplomatic or non-legal forms of resolution. Bellinger suggested that the 'warming' of relations reported in the 2006 *Wall Street Journal* article 'overstates the case', but that it did accurately reflect the strong desire to reach a practical understanding with the court.[43] This IL policy constituted a categorical shift away from ideological beliefs that structured decision-making in the first term.

At the level of analysing legal conceptions, Bolton's illiberal nationalist interpretation of ICC obligations *was* precisely intended to be 'aggressive or confrontational'. Bolton was nominated as UN Ambassador at a time when the United States had shifted from unyielding ICC opposition, to agreeing not to block the UNSC referring an investigation into the Darfur situation. In Bellinger's words, where there were 'no other ways to achieve accountability for the genocide in Sudan, then we don't have any problem abstaining'.[44] Bolton strongly rejected any such investigation at the level of international legal governance, dismissing EU advocates as frivolously 'getting out their wig boxes and preparing to go to court'. US acquiescence amounted merely to 'a gesture to the EUroids, which they cynically pocketed, knowing they had a precedent they could and would use against us later'. Instead the United States 'should have voted "no," insisting on actually doing something', such as establishing an ad hoc international tribunal following the model of the Extraordinary Chambers in the Courts of Cambodia.[45] Beliefs that IL should develop

[41] Ibid.
[42] Ibid.
[43] Ibid.
[44] Cited in Bosco, *Rough Justice*, pp. 111–12.
[45] John R. Bolton, *Surrender Is Not an Option: Defending America at the United Nations* (Simon & Schuster, 2007), pp. 360–1.

permissively, solely to enable US autonomy, remained distinct from the pragmatic development advocated by Bellinger.

The predominant strategic conclusion by this period was that uncompromising opposition to the ICC had harmed American interests. Ambassador Danforth warned against cases such as the Darfur situation, in which the United States was forced to abstain or even vote against UN resolutions mentioning the court, even where they advanced national interests. He recommended that the United States instead pass an 'agreement to disagree' resolution permitting greater flexibility in US voting. Such a resolution would affirm that states were governed by separate jurisdictional regimes, depending on whether they were parties to the Rome Statute, but that each approach equally represented a legal commitment 'in accordance with international standards of justice, fairness and due process of law'.[46] Permissive development had previously been followed, whereby officials avoided any acknowledgement of the court lest it embolden pretensions to constrain US policy. Policy now shifted to a pragmatic development of global governance as most consistent with an effective international legal system.

The new attitude was clear in US responses to the 2004 ICC-UN negotiated agreement and its objective of consolidating the place of the ICC in global governance. Deputy Legal Adviser to the US Mission to the UN Eric Rosand reiterated to the UNGA that the ICC 'is not part of the UN Charter System' and as such should not be treated as having an equivalent status.[47] Most significantly, Rosand reaffirmed 'U.S. commitment to accountability for war crimes, genocide, and crimes against humanity', but in a form contrary to the development of global governance advocated by ICC supporters. Rather, this commitment was demonstrated in a US record 'second to none in holding its own officials and citizens accountable for such crimes, as well as for supporting properly constituted international war crimes tribunals'. Rosand concluded: 'Properly understood, therefore, our decision not to support the ICC reflects our commitment to the rule of law, not our opposition to it.'[48] This reasoning is a repudiation of rule of law ideals embedded in the ICC-UN agreement, which seeks to invoke UN Charter commitments to the progressive development of IL. Viewed within the structure of ideologically informed American conceptions, however, the reasoning assumes a coherence it otherwise lacks.

46 Danforth, 'Peace and Accountability'.
47 Cited in Sally J. Cummins (ed.), *Digest of United States Practice in International Law: 2004* (International Law Institute, 2006), p. 177.
48 Ibid., p. 178.

Resistance to accepting the ICC as a core institution of global governance remained strong to the end of the administration. US Deputy Representative at the UN Ambassador Alejandro Wolff rejected a 2007 UNGA resolution that confirmed 'the role of the International Criminal Court in a multilateral system that aims to end impunity, establish the rule of law, promote and encourage respect for human rights and achieve sustainable peace'.[49] Wolff responded that the resolution failed to acknowledge that US rights remained outside the regime, thereby demonstrating that its sponsors and members of the LMS

> view such a basic expression of respect as inconsistent with their aspiration of universal membership of the ICC, as if it is, in fact, somehow illegitimate for a state to choose not to become party to the Rome Statute. By their actions, they have made clear that the pragmatic *modus vivendi* that we have been seeking to promote is simply not working.[50]

The frustration arose directly from the fault line between the legalist conception that *did* view US obstruction to the development of global governance as illegitimate, and the belief by US legal policymakers that pragmatic development remained a legitimate strategy for advancing the international rule of law.

Too Legalistic or Too Political?

The prevalent alternative explanation for outcomes in this period is that US legal policymakers sought to mitigate global criticism by engaging in tactical compromises between a unified rule of law ideal and US political interests. In this vein, a specific claim made by some US policymakers is of a shift from *excessive* attention to law in the first term to more politically informed decision-making in the second. Philip Zelikow served as Counselor of the US Department of State through the second term, having previously drafted the NSS 2002 that introduced the legal argument for 'pre-emptive' self-defence in the War on Terror.[51] For Zelikow, there was an unwarranted reliance on lawyers in the first term, who thought in terms of 'a binary division between the world of policy judgment and the world of

[49] GA Res 62/12, UN Doc A/RES/62/12 (26 November 2007).

[50] Cited in Sally J. Cummins (ed.), *Digest of United States Practice in International Law: 2007* (International Law Institute, 2008), p. 181.

[51] James Mann, *Rise of the Vulcans: The History of Bush's War Cabinet* (Viking, 2004), pp. 316–17 & 331. Zelikow attributes authorship of the doctrine to Bellinger: Philip D. Zelikow, 'In Uncertain Times: American Foreign Policy after the Berlin Wall and 9/11', 13 October 2011, www.wilsoncenter.org/event/uncertain-times-american-foreign-policy-after-the-berlin-wall-and-911. That claim is expressly refuted by Bellinger: Bellinger, Interview with Author.

legal analysis'.[52] The consequence was an approach to national security questions 'less as a detailed analysis of what *should* be done, and more as a problem of what *could* be done'.[53] Bradley concurs that the administration demonstrated 'an almost obsessive attention to international legal process'. The lesson learnt was that, although the 'rule of law promotes important values, framing questions in legal terms can sometimes produce undesirable outcomes'.[54] Zelikow and Bradley both commended the 'pragmatic' return to reasserting diplomatic interests over legal doctrine.[55] Rice offers some corroboration, in recalling that President Bush's first question when faced with proposed 'enhanced interrogation' techniques was whether they were legal, and then holding off interrogations until assurance was received. Rice remained faithful to Justice Department guidance, since she 'would never have engaged in – or encouraged the President to undertake – activities that I thought to be illegal'.[56]

The account of too much legality contrasts dramatically with the interpretation of Sands and others, for whom the first term was dominated by political interests and only belatedly began to acknowledge IL obligations.[57] The contradiction cannot be resolved merely by analysing US policy in terms of the opposition between law and politics, as each side has sought to do. Rather, the most coherent explanation is that of competing underlying conceptions of law, which were themselves constituted by politics. First term IL policy did rely on legalistic justifications, but it would be implausible to characterise these as strategically neutral for that reason.[58] Rather, commitments were consistently structured by an illiberal nationalist conception of IL as a permissive legal framework enabling almost unconstrained discretion to implement substantive foreign policy decisions. Zelikow's analysis chiefly considered legal justifications for detainee treatment in the War on Terror, but is equally relevant to interpreting ICC policy. In these cases, administration lawyers defined IL as malleable almost

52 Philip Zelikow, 'Codes of Conduct for a Twilight War' (2012) 49 *Houston Law Review* 1, p. 5.
53 Philip Zelikow, 'Legal Policy for a Twilight War' (2007) 30 *Houston Journal of International Law* 89, p. 94.
54 Curtis A. Bradley, 'The Bush Administration and International Law: Too Much Lawyering and Too Little Diplomacy' (2009) 4 *Duke Journal of Constitutional Law & Public Policy* 57, p. 74.
55 Ibid., p. 58; Zelikow, 'Codes of Conduct for a Twilight War', pp. 107–9.
56 Rice, *No Higher Honor*, pp. 117–20.
57 See Sands, *Lawless World*, p. xix.
58 For a response to Zelikow see David Cole, 'The Taint of Torture: The Roles of Law and Policy in Our Descent to the Dark Side' (2012) 49 *Houston Law Review* 53.

without limit in order to accommodate ideologically informed national security and cultural values.

Conclusion

Throughout the second term of the Bush administration, the ICC sought to consolidate its status as the principal institution of global governance in international criminal law. This was reflected in agreements with the UN and the EU, each confirming that formalised role. As for the United States, there was a meaningful shift in IL policy along the governance dimension – from the more nationalist conception of the first term treating municipal law as sufficient to advance American interests, to an internationalist stance seeking to advance those interests through IL. In Bellinger's terms, the shift was to 'a very pragmatic approach to the ICC in the second term that was really substantially different from the first term'.[59] Such softening of objections to the ICC may be read as signalling a US position moving closer to legalist ideals for the court. Yet the consistency of the underlying beliefs of policymakers with illiberal internationalist legal conceptions reiterates that US policy continued to be structured by fundamentally different ideological understandings of the international rule of law itself. On the evidence, at no point in this period did legalist conceptions form a meaningful element of American IL policy.

Defining Equality under International Law

US demands to carve out unequal legal privileges through UNSC resolutions were strongly opposed by other states from the earliest years of negotiating the Rome Statute. By the second term of the Bush administration, legalist policymakers focused efforts on opposing US demands for further renewal of Article 16 UNSC immunity, as a precondition to supporting peacekeeping operations.[60] It was during this period that the UNSC decided to refer the Darfur situation to the ICC, as a possible genocide case. That became a test for the United States to demonstrate how committed it was to opposing a court based on the principle of sovereign equality. Bush's IL policy notably relented, dropping demands for renewal of ICC immunity through the UNSC and acquiescing to the

[59] Bellinger, Interview with Author.

[60] See *Rome Statute*, Art. 16 'Deferral of investigation or prosecution'; SC Res 1422, UN Doc S/RES/1422 (12 July 2002); SC Res 1487, UN Doc S/RES/1487 (12 June 2003).

Darfur referral. In both cases, the outcome for US policy was to move toward a position more consistent with legalist preferences for the court. The outcome raises an intriguing challenge for the argument that foreign policy ideology creates hard limits to reaching a common conception of the international rule of law. An examination of beliefs structuring decision-making is necessary to determine whether the case supports or falsifies this book's central claim for the controlling role of ideology.

Legalist Policy

UNSC exemptions granted to US peacekeepers were always considered contrary to sovereign equality, as a core rule of law principle. In June 2004, when the United States insisted on its third annual renewal, UN Secretary General Kofi Annan responded that, in light of a developing prisoner abuse scandal in Iraq, it would be improper both for the United States to request an exemption and for the UNSC to grant it: 'It would discredit the Council and the United Nations that stands for rule of law and the primacy of rule of law.'[61] Entailed in this admonition was an insistence that rules of IL within the court's jurisdiction be applied equally to all states without allowances for any claimed special character, rights, or duties. NGO groups similarly referenced legalist principles defining the proper relationship between sovereign states. The CICC commended eventual US withdrawal of the renewal request, which 'reflected the growing international support for the ICC and the diminishing capacity of the US to stand above international law'.[62] Similarly, Amnesty International found the immunity resolutions problematic not merely for undermining the ICC and IL more generally, but because they were for that reason 'unlawful'. Amnesty head Irene Khan described the failure of the United States to gain the renewal as 'a victory for international justice and the rule of law'.[63]

At this time the UNSC also moved to refer the Darfur situation to the ICC, pursuant to Chapter VII of the UN Charter.[64] This followed the

[61] Colum Lynch, 'Annan Opposes Exempting U.S. from Court', *The Washington Post*, 18 June 2004, www.washingtonpost.com/wp-dyn/articles/A50531-2004Jun17.html.

[62] Cited in CICC, 'Chronology of the Adoption of Security Council Resolutions 1422/1487 and Withdrawal of the Proposed Renewal in 2004', Factsheet, 2004, www.iccnow.org/documents/FS-1422and1487Chronology_26March2008.pdf last accessed 27 February 2015.

[63] Amnesty International, 'US Withdrawal: Determination of International Community Is "Victory for International Justice and the Rule of Law," says AI', Amnesty International Press Release, 24 June 2004, www.amnesty.org/download/Documents/96000/ior300162004en.pdf.

[64] *Rome Statute*, Art. 13(b); SC Res 1593.

recommendation of the *International Commission of Inquiry on Darfur* in circumstances where a UNSC referral under Article 13(b) of the Rome Statute was the only way to exercise jurisdiction over Sudan, as a non-state party.[65] The existence of that power contradicted legalist insistence on sovereign equality, but it had been a concession at the Rome negotiations. In these circumstances, statements of support for the referral sought to frame the power as one being exercised on behalf of all states equally, rather than by the P5 in their own right. The *International Commission* report, for example, supported the appropriateness of the referral as a statement on behalf of 'the whole world community through its most important political organ'.[66] Similarly, in an open letter to Condoleezza Rice, the Executive Director of Human Rights Watch challenged the legitimacy of the US veto powers when exercised as parochial privilege.[67] Rather, the P5 powers were construed as legitimate when voicing the equal interest of all states in the ICC.

US insistence on a form of immunity in Resolution 1593 led Brazil, which then held the rotating UNSC presidency, to abstain from the vote. Despite confirming its support for the referral, Brazil's representative protested that the 'maintenance of international peace and the fight against impunity cannot be viewed as conflicting objectives'.[68] Brazil 'rejected initiatives aimed at extending exemptions of certain categories of individuals from ICC jurisdiction' as contrary to international criminal justice. Divergence between the assumption of sovereign equality and the competing principles structuring American IL policy fortified claims that the United States was contradicting its claimed commitment to the international rule of law.

Beliefs of American Legal Policymakers

Contradiction of Exceptionalist Beliefs in US Prisoner Abuse Scandals

In 2005, then Senator Hillary Clinton continued to defend American IL policy in broadly internationalist terms, emphasising principles of both liberal equality and hegemonic privilege. Clinton reminded European critics:

[65] Sudan signed on 8 September 2000 but failed to ratify the treaty.
[66] Cassese et al., *Report of the International Commission*, p. 149.
[67] Kenneth Roth, 'U.S.: ICC Best Chance for Justice in Darfur', Letter to Condoleezza Rice, 22 January 2005, www.hrw.org/news/2005/01/21/us-icc-best-chance-justice-darfur.
[68] Representative Ronaldo M. Sardenberg for Brazil: UN, *Record of the 5158th Meeting of the United Nations Security Council, Sudan*, UN Doc S/PV.5158 (31 March 2005), p. 11.

> [T]he United States has global responsibilities that create unique circumstances. For example, we are more vulnerable to the misuse of an international criminal court because of the international role we play and the resentments that flow from that ubiquitous presence around the world.[69]

Clinton thus framed the 'lawfare' threat as the direct cost of exceptionalist American duties: of legalist judicial institutions being used to constrain the United States and thereby eroding not merely its global power but also the international legal system it underwrote. Where Clinton sought to speak for 'all of those people looking at us and yearning to be part of what we are',[70] her determination of the proper relationship between sovereign states reflected the ideological commitment to principles of liberal equality.

The significance of exceptionalist beliefs to American legal conceptions became strongly apparent in the second Bush 43 term, but in the unique circumstances of their *elimination* from policymaking processes. Schabas documented the first sign of a shift in ICC policy from 2004, when the United States backed down on requested renewal of UNSC resolutions granting peacekeepers ICC immunity.[71] The turning point was revelations about the abuses in Abu Ghraib Prison in the aftermath of the 2003 Iraq War: '[s]hamed and humbled by the tales of abuse', the United States withdrew its deferral resolution.[72] The significance of prisoner abuse scandals in Afghanistan, Guantanamo, but especially Abu Ghraib, was that they provided compelling evidence *against* US political culture being a sufficient check against international illegality. In terms of the theoretical framework adopted here, any piercing of the exceptionalist veil would be expected to undermine US commitment to legal conceptions drawn from associated ideologies. If foreign policy ideology does play a meaningful role in structuring IL policy, then the

[69] Hillary Rodham Clinton, 'Excerpts from Remarks of Senator Hillary Rodham Clinton German Media Prize Dinner', 13 February 2005, https://web.archive.org/web/20050315191146/http://clinton.senate.gov/~clinton/speeches/2005217C29.html. When asked if this statement demonstrated a belief that it was necessary to exempt the US from ICC jurisdiction to uphold the international rule of law, Taft responded, 'I don't think she really believed that . . . It's more of a political judgement.' William H. Taft IV, Interview with Author (22 November 2011).

[70] Clinton, 'German Media Prize Dinner'.

[71] William Schabas, *An Introduction to the International Criminal Court* (Cambridge University Press, 2011), p. 31.

[72] Ibid., p.32. On the prisoner abuse scandal, generally, see Diane M. Amann, 'Abu Ghraib' (2005) 153 *University of Pennsylvania Law Review* 2085.

United States would become more likely to accede to legalist demands for sovereign equality – even as political interests were held constant.

Rice accepted that the images from Abu Ghraib diminished global perceptions of 'America as something different'.[73] She later lamented the lasting damage caused when 'the image of the U.S. soldier around the world became associated with the depravity of Abu Ghraib'.[74] Translation of this recognition into IL policy was evident in Ambassador Danforth's classified communications, which advised that failure to renew UNSC Resolution 1487 was 'principally because it came up at the same time as the Abu Ghraib abuses came to light'.[75] Bassiouni explained that the examples 'evidenced to the international community the need for accountability', and most especially for the United States, who had claimed that 'its system of criminal justice is better than that of most other countries and that its system of military justice can be relied upon to perform its mission without international monitoring'.[76] To the contrary, Amnesty International argued that the scandal demonstrated 'blatant disregard being shown for the rule of law, and the Bush Administration should be doing everything in its power to support the principles embodied in the ICC'.[77]

That these circumstances led to the withdrawal of US demands for hegemonic privilege, or even for deference to the interests of liberal equality, is compelling evidence of the extent to which foreign policy ideology was structuring conceptions of IL. Once the foundation of exceptionalist beliefs was fractured, the entire edifice of distinctive interpretations of the rule of law collapsed. The only coherent legal policy remaining that did not depend on exceptionalist beliefs was that of legalism. Following the lapsing of Resolution 1487, US policy accepted a legal status in UN peacekeeping missions that, formally at least, was as a sovereign equal. The policy outcome in this narrowly defined area therefore provided an insight into US legal policy stripped of its exceptionalist foundations – which, through its absence, confirmed the power of foreign policy ideology.

73 United States Senate, *Nomination of Dr. Condoleezza Rice*, p. 147.

74 Rice, *No Higher Honor*, p. 274.

75 Danforth, 'Peace and Accountability'.

76 M. Cherif Bassiouni, *The Legislative History of the International Criminal Court: Introduction, Analysis, and Integrated Text of the Statute, Elements of Crimes and Rules of Procedure and Evidence* (Transnational Publishers, 2005), pp. 143–4.

77 Amnesty, 'US Withdrawal'.

Reframing UNSC Referral of the Darfur Situation

The shift in US policy culminated in tacit support for a UNSC referral of the Darfur situation in March 2005, described by David Bosco as a 'major breakthrough'.[78] The congruence of the shift with the model of legal conceptions is evident in a prescient statement five years earlier by Michael Scharf, which had advocated the illiberal internationalism that made such a comeback in Bush's second term. In reference to evidence of rising illiberal nationalist hostility in the first term, Scharf warned that IL must be preserved as a diplomatic tool since 'when the next Rwanda-like situation comes along, the Bush administration will find value in having the option of Security Council Referral to the ICC in its arsenal of foreign policy responses'.[79] That was precisely the realisation reached in coming to see the ICC as the best forum for fulfilling US interests in the case of a humanitarian crisis not directly involving American security interests.

Goldsmith provided the most explicit defence of the Darfur referral in illiberal internationalist terms. In *The Washington Post* he reminded the administration that a successful UNSC referral reinforced the wisdom of the original US demands for an international court under UNSC control. Goldsmith readily acknowledged the inconsistency of UNSC control with sovereign equality, which critics would likely reject as 'a double standard for Security Council members, who can protect themselves by vetoing a referral'. Yet, rather than defending the US position as consistent with sovereign equality, he instead observed that

> this double standard is woven into the fabric of international politics and is the relatively small price the international system pays for the political accountability and support that only the big powers, acting through the Security Council, can provide.[80]

This is an assertion of hegemonic privilege as an element of the international rule of law: that IL must be harnessed to the realities of political power if it is to be a meaningful force in ameliorating raw political ambition. Bosco characterised Goldsmith as effectively calling for the United States 'to informally merge the court into the system of major-

[78] Bosco, *Rough Justice*, p. 108.

[79] Michael P. Scharf, 'The United States and the International Criminal Court: A Recommendation for the Bush Administration' (2000) 7 *ILSA Journal of International & Comparative Law* 385, p. 389.

[80] Jack Goldsmith, 'Support War Crimes Trials for Darfur', *The Washington Post*, 24 January 2005, www.washingtonpost.com/wp-dyn/articles/A31594-2005Jan23.html.

power privilege'.[81] Likewise, Corrina Heyder repeated the legalist critique that US acquiescence to the Darfur referral was contradictory in jurisprudential terms and coherent only when understood as tactical manipulations of the law to 'maintain hegemonic power over international criminal justice'. The referral thus 'must be interpreted as an attempt to safeguard American exceptionalism and enable the United States to more easily advance its particular interest'.[82] These statements are undoubtedly accurate accounts of the political dynamics underpinning policy outcomes. But, where inquiry is located at the more fine-grained level of decision-making processes, the crucial interplay between law and ideology becomes necessary to explain the underlying logic. Identifying Goldsmith's argument in illiberal internationalism reveals the ideological reconciliation of political interests with expressed commitment to IL.

The power of exceptionalist beliefs was laid bare in US explanations for why citizens of Sudan, as a non-party to the Rome Statute, should be subject to ICC jurisdiction even as the United States denied that jurisdiction over itself. For Rice, it was 'important to uphold the principle that non-parties to a treaty are indeed non-parties to a treaty', but that 'Sudan is an extraordinary circumstance'. The United States reasoned that the referring UNSC resolution itself created a general exemption to non-parties to the treaty, but this was hardly an answer given it was the United States who demanded those protections in the first place. Rice's further explanation was that, as a practical matter, Sudan represented 'a humanitarian crisis, . . . a moral crisis, and . . . a crisis that is extraordinary in its scope and in its potential for even greater damage to those populations. So I think this is a different situation, frankly.'[83] Sands described this explanation as 'flummoxed'.[84] From these statements, the most consistent principle that emerges is that, precisely because of the perceived unequal position occupied by the United States, the meaning of equality under IL properly encompassed a commensurate counterbalance in legal rights and duties. Certainly, Rice appeared satisfied that US policy was consistent with the international rule of law when she addressed the

[81] Bosco, *Rough Justice*, p. 111.

[82] Corrina Heyder, 'The UN Security Council's Referral of the Crimes in Darfur to the International Criminal Court in Light of US Opposition to the Court: Implications for the International Criminal Court's Functions and Status' (2006) 24 *Berkeley Journal of International Law* 650, pp. 666–7.

[83] Condoleezza Rice, 'Remarks with Hungarian Foreign Minister Ferenc Somogyi after Meeting', Treaty Room, Washington, DC, 1 April 2005, https://2001-2009.state.gov/secretary/rm/2005/44104.htm.

[84] Sands, *Lawless World*, p. 248.

American Society of International Law within the same day as her initial statements:

> America is a country of laws . . . [W]hen we respect our international legal obligations and support an international system based on the rule of law, we do the work of making the world a better place, but also a safer and more secure place for America.[85]

Beyond objections to the principle of UNSC control, Bosco noted that Resolution 1593 created an important precedent whereby P5 members were effectively able to circumscribe the rights and privileges enjoyed by specific states before the ICC. This appeared to go beyond the UNSC's proper power to simply refer situations to the court, but not to set the terms for prosecution.[86] Robert Cryer cited this as a key reason for raising 'serious questions' about the resolution's 'compliance with basic principles of the rule of law'.[87] He noted previous statements by Scheffer appearing to interpret Article 13(b) of the Rome Statute as permitting the United States to specifically 'define the parameters' of ICC jurisdiction over states who play a special enforcement role in the international legal system.[88] In the quest for fidelity to the international rule of law, Cryer rejected the legitimacy of elevating 'exceptionalist claims' over sovereign equality.[89]

Cryer's argument demonstrates the limitations of compartmentalising law and politics when explaining US ICC policy, and the fertile ground for ideology to bridge the gap between them. Cryer noted that, on the one hand, the possibility of selective justice resulting from exceptionalist beliefs was 'a sobering reminder that the international legal order is not one in which the rule of law is easy to realize'. Yet he also conceded that 'prosecutions for extremely serious crimes are likely now to occur, when they were unlikely to have done so if the Security Council had no role in referring cases to the ICC'. In that light, Cryer was wary of 'being too precious about principle' where practical justice was at stake.[90] This is

85 Condoleezza Rice, 'Remarks at Annual Meeting of the American Society of International Law', Lowes L'Enfant Plaza Hotel, Washington, DC, 1 April 2005, https://2001-2009.state.gov/secretary/rm/2005/44159.htm.

86 Bosco, *Rough Justice*, p. 112.

87 Robert Cryer, 'Sudan, Resolution 1593, and International Criminal Justice' (2006) 19 *Leiden Journal of International Law* 195, p. 205.

88 Ibid., p. 212, citing David J. Scheffer, 'Staying the Course with the International Criminal Court' (2001) 35 *Cornell International Law Journal* 47, p. 90.

89 Cryer, 'Sudan, Resolution 1593', p. 215.

90 Ibid., pp. 216–17.

precisely the kind of dissonance that drives evolution of ideological beliefs to reconcile law and politics in the distinct configurations now structuring American IL policy. For US legal policymakers, the perceived nexus between exceptionalism and the operation of IL is not unique to the Darfur referral but is constitutive more generally of the international legal system. In short, a system defined by reference to unyielding sovereign equality is not merely a poor description of the rule of law: it is an account incompatible with the realisation of the ideal. The quality of ideology evolving to accommodate the 'needs and interests of a group or class at a particular time in history'[91] is thus well demonstrated in this case.

Prior to the Darfur referral, Heyder opined that it was 'difficult to understand' why the United States would not support such a resolution on at least an ad hoc basis when a commitment to international criminal justice 'is a deeply rooted part of U.S. foreign policy'.[92] Yet, so long as the court was defined by the principle of sovereign equality, any vote for the referral was tantamount to endorsing an ideal unrecognised by US policymakers. Instead, US hegemonic privilege was consolidated by 2008 when, having pocketed its own immunity, the United States supported the ICC in blocking African Union requests that then Sudanese president Omar al-Bashir be granted immunity in light of the Darfur referral. Scheffer observed that by this period 'the Bush administration had finally rid itself of Bolton', thereby allowing the policy shift toward a United States–specific vision for a functioning court.[93]

Conclusion

Complex adjustments in US policy regarding the proper relationship between sovereign states demonstrated the significant influence of exceptionalist beliefs on competing conceptions of IL. During the first term of the Bush 43 administration, the United States had assertively sought and obtained unequal immunities from ICC jurisdiction through the UNSC. From a political perspective, this could be explained broadly as predictable behaviour of a powerful state manipulating international legal rules. However, in legal terms, the foundation of

91 David B. Davis, *The Problem of Slavery in the Age of Revolution, 1770–1823* (Cornell University Press, 1975), p. 14; see Chapter 2, p. 55, *supra*.

92 Heyder, 'The UNSC's Referral of the Crimes in Darfur', p. 661.

93 David J. Scheffer, *All the Missing Souls: A Personal History of the War Crimes Tribunals* (Princeton University Press, 2012), p. 416.

the US position was a conception of IL drawn from exceptionalist beliefs justifying either an exceptional US role as the guarantor of liberal equality or a form of hegemonic privilege. Revelations of prisoner abuse in the War on Terror fundamentally undermined beliefs that US democratic norms were a protection against such breaches, or that concessions to hegemonic privilege strengthened the international legal system as a whole. Only with the piercing of the exceptionalist veil did US IL policy acquiesce to legalist denial of UNSC immunity for being contrary to the rule of law.

Nevertheless, the US decision to abstain from any vote without positively endorsing the Darfur referral affirmed the limitations set by foreign policy ideology. For critics, the 'selective enforcement of international criminal law' in the referral reminded that the international legal system 'has a long way to go before it represents a system that truly reflects rule of law principles'.[94] Rather, US IL policy looked to an ideal of equality in law defined by illiberal internationalism, which recognised the opportunity to reassert the ICC as a diplomatic tool promoting US national security interests.

Determining International Judicial Power

The contest to determine the structure of international judicial power was focused on the ASPA by the second term, with its claim to alter the hierarchy of judicial and prosecutorial powers between the court and sovereign states. For legalist advocates, this was a clear contradiction of the separation of judicial powers necessary to sustain the international rule of law. The United States' legal policymakers increasingly accepted that insisting on the supremacy of its own legal powers was eroding cooperation with key partners, who now refused to formalise the revised ordering of powers in bilateral agreements. The problem had been flagged as early as Rice's confirmation hearings when Senator Dodd referenced disruptions to vital military relationships owing to the United States' 'fixation with the international criminal court, as codified by the American Servicemen's Protection Act'.[95] The United States relented and modified application of the ASPA to allow for greater cooperation with allies and for a more conciliatory policy permitting exceptions for US assistance to the ICC. Rice announced the changes by

94 Cryer, 'Sudan, Resolution 1593', p. 222.
95 United States Senate, *Nomination of Dr. Condoleezza Rice*, p. 43.

noting the negative impact upon counterterrorism, drug operations and military cooperation in Iraq and Afghanistan. The ASPA thus yielded to the preservation of 'relationships that are really important to us from the point of view of . . . improving the security environment'.[96] However, even as US policy sanctioned the legitimacy of ICC judicial power, it continued to deny that its integrity was determined by ICC independence, thus reserving judicial authority over its own nationals. Policy outcomes thereby achieved greater compatibility with the ICC's judicial power, but stopped well short of relinquishing parallel judicial powers exercised at the US municipal level. The consequence was once again a perception of contradictory US legal practice and a causal role for ideology structuring legal decision-making processes.

Legalist Policy

Legalist advocates in this period maintained beliefs that the ICC was capable of counterbalancing political interests through independent judicial power. The developing UNSC–ICC relationship contained in the *International Commission of Inquiry on Darfur* was defended for upholding the UNSC as 'the highest body of the international community responsible for maintaining peace and security' and the ICC as 'the highest criminal judicial institution of the world community'.[97] That view was equally reflected in the position of NGOs, who continued to advocate institutionalisation of ICC powers above the exercise of parallel powers by states. Amnesty International's Irene Khan expressed hope that apparent softening of US policy 'will prompt the US to review its opposition to the ICC and join the world community in reaffirming the primacy of international law'.[98] Advocates continued invoking an ideal of the international rule of law in which judicial power was determined by its separation and exercise in designated global courts.

The inadequacy of any legal policy falling short of a separation of powers was evident in the frustrations of states engaging with the United States. For France's permanent representative to the UN, Jean-Marc de La Sablière, the immunity requested by the United States in resolution 1593 was acceded to only as a compromise position, with an expectation

[96] Rice, 'En Route to San Juan'.

[97] Cassese et al., *Report of the International Commission on Darfur*, p. 149.

[98] Amnesty, 'US Withdrawal'.

that such clauses cease in future referrals.[99] Brazil was less forbearing and abstained to protest the precedent of reserving judicial power to the United States at the expense of ICC authority. This was despite acknowledging the desirability of the resolution and the practical effect it would have in the particular circumstances. Rather, Brazil affirmed the need to protect the ICC as 'an independent judicial body' that already 'provides all the necessary checks and balances to prevent possible abuses and politically motivated misuse of its jurisdiction'. The Brazilian representative accepted neither a reference to Article 98 agreements in the preamble nor operative clause 6 'through which the Council recognizes the existence of exclusive jurisdiction, a legal exception that is inconsistent in international law'. Together, these measures were likely to 'have the effect of dismantling the achievements reached in the field of international criminal justice'.[100] Likewise, the Algerian representative abstained for reasons including that, in the endeavour to achieve practical justice, the terms of the referral improperly established a form of 'two-track justice'.[101] States were seeking not merely practical US support in the immediate case but an ICC regime consistent with perceived ideals of the international rule of law, too.

Beliefs of American Legal Policymakers

ICC Judicial Power Limited by US Consent

US approaches to the Darfur referral uniformly insisted on terms contrary to a court design determined by an effective separation of international legal powers. Legal disputes among American policymakers were thus not about how to accommodate the supremacy of the ICC's judicial power; rather, they were about how to reconcile ordering principles drawn from entirely separate ideological commitments. Bellinger emphasised that, in the second term, the administration resisted only the ICC's 'method for *achieving* accountability [original emphasis]', not its aspiration to do so. This was an argument about the proper determination of international judicial power according to a 'deeply held American belief that power needs to be checked and public actors need

[99] UN, 'Security Council Refers Situation in Darfur, Sudan, to Prosecutor of International Criminal Court', Press Release SC/8351, 31 March 2005, www.un.org/press/en/2005/sc8351.doc.htm.

[100] Representative Ronaldo M. Sardenberg for Brazil: UN, *Record of the 5158th Meeting of the United Nations Security Council, Sudan*, p. 11.

[101] Representative Abdallah Baali for Algeria: ibid., pp. 4–5.

to be held accountable'.[102] The first term of the Bush administration was marked by insistence that judicial determination of international criminal matters be the sole province of municipal law – of American courts or tribunals in the case of US nationals and of locally constituted courts in the case of international prosecutions. The shift in the second term was to recognise that, in the latter case, there were strategic advantages to employing the ICC in lieu of locally constituted courts, provided the United States withheld consent for matters within its national jurisdiction. The shift along the governance dimension, from an illiberal nationalist to an illiberal internationalist conception of IL, bolstered functional cooperation but not agreement on rule of law ideals.

The United States initially continued to resist the UNSC Darfur referral according to its long-held insistence that matters of criminal justice be reserved to municipal legal processes. The United States had been among the first and most prominent states to declare that the Darfur situation met the legal definition of genocide.[103] Accordingly, policymakers were at great pains to defend US commitment to international criminal justice. Rice asserted that US resistance was instead towards the unaccountability of the ICC prosecutor to an identifiable government: 'an issue of sovereignty and a step that looked a bit too much like "world government"'.[104] Acting UN Ambassador Anne Patterson reiterated that the US preference remained for domestic-based resolutions, such as a hybrid tribunal in Africa.[105] The choice perceived by the United States was thus between blocking the referral in preference of a hybrid court using the infrastructure of the ICTR, or to 'carve out US exemption' within a referral it could support.[106] The State Department went to great lengths to achieve the former option, and it was only after failing to do so that it switched to the latter, as initially recommended by Ambassador Danforth.[107] Rice ultimately supported the referral on the basis that a change in strategy promised greater accountability under IL for Darfur perpetrators. To do otherwise would be 'just to make an ideological point about the

102 Bellinger, 'Reflections on Transatlantic Approaches to International Law', p. 520, original emphasis.

103 Rice, *No Higher Honor*, p. 387.

104 Ibid., p. 388.

105 See John R. Crook, 'United States Abstains on Security Council Resolution Authorizing Referral of Darfur Atrocities to International Criminal Court' (2005) 99 *American Journal of International Law* 691, p. 691.

106 Scott Paul, 'From Mark Goldberg on Sudan and the International Criminal Court', *The Washington Note*, 2 August 2007, https://washingtonnote.com/from_mark_goldb/.

107 Danforth, 'Peace and Accountability'.

construction of the court or the Rome Statute'.[108] This is a revealing insight into the dynamic relationship between ideology and legal accountability at the heart of shifting IL policies.

On US insistence, the terms of UNSC Resolution 1593 explicitly took note of 'agreements referred to in Article 98–2 of the Rome Statute'. The resolution directly reiterated the limits of US consent to ICC judicial authority in the sixth of its operative clauses, which stated that the UNSC:

> *Decides* that nationals, current or former officials or personnel from a contributing State outside Sudan which is not a party to the Rome Statute of the International Criminal Court shall be subject to the exclusive jurisdiction of that contributing State for all alleged acts or omissions arising out of or related to operations in Sudan established or authorized by the Council or the African Union, unless such exclusive jurisdiction has been expressly waived by that contributing State.[109]

Thus, although the resolution was designed to legitimise the ICC's exercise of international judicial power, it did so by certifying that the United States retained judicial power over international criminal matters in relation to its own nationals.

Patterson confirmed that consent to jurisdiction set the limits of US support for the Darfur referral, with any alternative arrangement striking 'at the essence of the nature of sovereignty'. On those terms the United States still wouldn't vote for the referral but ultimately

> decided not to oppose the resolution because of the need for the international community to work together in order to end the climate of impunity in Sudan, and because the resolution provides protection from investigation or prosecution for U.S. nationals and members of the armed forces of non-state parties.[110]

Far from denying the legitimacy of IL, the United States remained committed to the principle that '[v]iolators of international humanitarian law and human rights law must be held accountable'. Patterson reminded that the United States had long argued for UNSC control of referrals and that, by doing so in relation to Darfur, 'firm political oversight of the process will be exercised'. She nevertheless reiterated that US objections to the ICC remained unchanged in the absence of 'sufficient protections from the possibility of politicized prosecutions'. In this sense, politics was identified as both the guarantor of the international rule of

[108] Rice, *No Higher Honor*, p. 388.
[109] SC Res 1593. See also operative clause 2 of the resolution.
[110] Crook, 'United States Abstains on Security Council Resolution', p. 692.

law, in the UNSC, and its enemy, in the ICC. Such incoherence is resolved only by viewing the underlying conception of IL in terms of the role of foreign policy ideology and exceptionalist beliefs. Patterson concluded by asserting that the position did not equate to sanctioned impunity, since the United States itself would 'continue to discipline our own people where appropriate'.[111] The arrangement achieved in the Darfur referral thus normalised and institutionalised parallel exercises of international judicial power divided between the ICC and US courts.

Conclusion

This period saw the realisation of illiberal internationalist preferences for determining the international judicial powers of the ICC, with the court confirmed as a legitimate source of international judicial authority, but subject to clear limits of US consent. That outcome contradicted the principled objections of US global counterparts, who continued seeking an oversight role for the ICC founded on independent international judicial power. Despite some optimism about the United States' shift toward legalist policies, even advocates conceded that the dynamics likely revealed hard limits to further cooperation. Heyder's analysis is instructive in expressing the legalist belief that, by removing any exceptional US control through the UNSC, 'the ICC has the authority to act exclusively based on purely factual and judicial motives, at any time, and free from political influence'. She further accepted, however, that persisting with this design made it 'very unlikely' that US opposition would subside. Even in the best-case scenario, a properly functioning court would likely lead only to the United States providing 'possible ad hoc cooperation in the long run'.[112] Any optimism about whether the United States might revise its position faced the reality of hard structural limitations – in the form of ideologically informed conceptions of the proper determination and thus limitations of international judicial power.

Chapter Conclusion

The shift in IL policy during the second term of the Bush 43 administration followed robust agreement among administration policymakers that previous illiberal nationalist approaches to the ICC had not optimised

[111] Ibid.
[112] Heyder, 'The UNSC's Referral of the Crimes in Darfur', p. 671.

American national security interests. The so-called *modus vivendi* with the court was evident in concerted efforts toward re-engagement and qualified acceptance of ICC legitimacy within global governance. Across the entirety of the Bush 43 administration, there were repeated calls, even from American voices representing NGOs and academic perspectives, for the United States to go further and accede to the ICC in terms structured by legalism. There is no evidence, however, that any such beliefs were accepted at the level of US policymakers – even in those cases where policy appeared to align more closely to legalist preferences. Bosco's review of the period affirms that, although US ICC policy became 'more pragmatic', it remained the case that 'no influential voices on the American political spectrum advocated membership'.[113]

A powerful insight into the limits of ideology does emerge from this period, however, with potentially far-reaching implications for broader American engagement with IL. The US decision to withdraw its long-standing requests to the UNSC for peacekeeping force immunity is among the most revealing ideological contests in US–ICC relations. The policy shift followed revelations of abuses in Abu Ghraib Prison that directly challenged exceptionalist beliefs sustaining American conceptions of the international rule of law. In this narrow case, the United States ultimately relented to the legal preferences of its global counterparts, not because its conceptions of IL were shown to be contradictory when measured against the rest of the world, but because they were revealed as contradictory when measured against its own ideological commitments. That contest confirmed both the pivotal significance of foreign policy ideology in structuring conceptions of IL and, thereby, the power conferred on those who understand and directly contest American IL policy at the level of its foundational ideological beliefs.

[113] Bosco, *Rough Justice*, p. 132.

7

Obama Administration, 2008–2016

The transition from the Bush 43 administration to that of Barack Obama brought with it expectations of a new president who possessed 'a genuine concern to bring US policy into line with fundamental principles of international law, and thus represent a significant change from his predecessor'.[1] Public perceptions became tangible in the award of the Nobel Peace Prize to the president in 2009, when the Chairman of the Nobel Committee noted:

> Multilateral diplomacy has regained a central position, with emphasis on the role that the United Nations and other international institutions can play ... The USA is now paying its bills to the UN. It is joining various committees, and acceding to important conventions. International standards are again respected. Torture is forbidden; the President is doing what he can to close Guantanamo. Human rights and international law are guiding principles.[2]

Such expectation translated into high hopes for a realignment of US–ICC policy with the rest of the world up to, and including, the US 're-signing' the Rome Statute.[3] By this period, the nature of the ICC project itself had changed, from negotiation over the court design during the Clinton era to attempts to quash the project in the first term of the Bush 43 administration to accommodation of the court's first investigations in the second Bush term. By the time of Obama's election, US policymakers were developing policy toward a court actively engaged in prosecutions and further defining its powers in the process. Harold Koh, as Legal

[1] Anthony G. Dworkin, *Beyond the 'War on Terror': Towards a New Transatlantic Framework for Counterterrorism* (European Council on Foreign Relations, 2009), p. 10.

[2] Thorbjørn Jagland, 'Award Ceremony Speech,' Presentation Speech by Thorbjørn Jagland, Chairman of the Norwegian Nobel Committee, Oslo, 10 December 2009, http://nobelprize.org/nobel_prizes/peace/laureates/2009/presentation-speech.html.

[3] See Stephen Eliot Smith, 'Definitely Maybe: The Outlook for US Relations with the International Criminal Court during the Obama Administration' (2010) 22 *Florida Journal of International Law* 155, pp. 186–9.

Adviser to the State Department, described the shift in policy as having 'reset the default on the U.S. relationship with the court from hostility to positive engagement'.[4]

Advocates of a legalist US ICC policy continued to emphasise three core rule of law elements: formally developing global governance; advancing sovereign equality; and separating the court's judicial power from competing international legal powers. These efforts focused particularly on defining the crime of 'aggression', which the Nuremberg trials had declared to be 'the supreme international crime differing only from other war crimes in that it contains within itself the accumulated evil of the whole'.[5] After being set aside at the 1998 Rome Conference, the crime finally took shape at the 2010 *Review Conference of the Rome Statute*, held in Kampala, Uganda (Kampala Conference). A definition was confirmed and set to take effect after a further decision in 2017.[6] In so doing, global advocates achieved what many had considered the pinnacle of the international rule of law: subjecting decisions to use international force to judicial determination as a check not only on national governments but also on previously unfettered UNSC power.

For its part, the US began attending the annual meetings of states parties for the first time (as an observer), actively advocating and voting in favour of UNSC referrals to the ICC and contributing substantially to debates over the crime of aggression. The president broke from his predecessor in personally advocating international support for ICC investigations and prosecutions.[7] Explaining the renewed support, US policymakers declared that

> the commitment of the Obama Administration to the rule of law and the principle of accountability is firm, in line with . . . [a] historic tradition of

[4] Harold H. Koh & Stephen J. Rapp, 'U.S. Engagement with the ICC and the Outcome of the Recently Concluded Review Conference', 15 June 2010, https://2009-2017.state.gov/j/gcj/us_releases/remarks/2010/143178.htm.

[5] International Military Tribunal (Nuremberg), 'Judicial Decisions, International Military Tribunal (Nuremberg), Judgment and Sentences' (1947) 41 *American Journal of International Law* 172, p. 186, *per curium*.

[6] See *Rome Statute* (1998), Art. 8*bis* ('Crime of Aggression') & Art. 15*bis*-Art. 15*ter* ('Exercise of Jurisdiction over the Crime of Aggression'). The Assembly of States Parties adopted *Resolution ICC-ASP/16/Res.5* ('Activation of the Jurisdiction of the Court over the Crime of Aggression') on 14 December 2017, with the jurisdiction activated as of 17 July 2018.

[7] Barack H. Obama, 'Statement by President Obama on the International Criminal Court Announcement', The White House Office of the Press Secretary, 15 December 2010, www.whitehouse.gov/the-press-office/2010/12/15/statement-president-obama-international-criminal-court-announcement.

> support for international criminal justice that has been a hallmark of United States policy dating back at least to the time of Nuremberg.[8]

Yet, simultaneously, the US strongly resisted the aggression definition agreed at the Kampala Conference, reaffirmed opposition to joining the ICC and, despite previous criticism, declined to recant the 2002 unsigning notification of John Bolton. ICC policy outcomes accordingly continued to diverge from global advocates in ways correlated with the reception of IL through the lens of foreign policy ideology.

Dominant International Law Policy

The defining feature of the Obama IL policy was a rejection of the illiberal nationalist conceptions of the Bush 43 years, which proved a more readily identifiable theme than its positive guiding principles. Ideological beliefs guiding the administration's general foreign policy have proven a major interpretive challenge, with commentators variously describing them as 'liberal internationalist',[9] 'pragmatic internationalist',[10] 'progressive pragmatist',[11] 'Hobbesian optimist',[12] 'accommodationist'[13] and simply guided by '*realpolitik*'.[14] These divergent analyses capture the extent to which decision-making processes traversed the liberal–illiberal and internationalist–nationalist dimensions, albeit in unique configurations within the worldviews of administration policymakers.

Divergent ideologies notwithstanding, the dominant position of the administration remained liberal internationalist: the overarching belief

[8] Stephen J. Rapp, 'Address to Assembly of States Parties', 19 November 2009, https://2009-2017.state.gov/j/gcj/us_releases/remarks/2009/133316.htm.

[9] Walter R. Mead, 'Liberal Internationalism: The Twilight of a Dream', *The American Interest*, 1 April 2010, www.the-american-interest.com/wrm/2010/04/01/liberal-internationalism-the-twilight-of-a-dream/.

[10] Henry R. Nau, in Kim R. Holmes, Helle C. Dale & Henry R. Nau, 'The Obama Doctrine: Hindering American Foreign Policy', The Heritage Foundation, 29 November 2010, www.heritage.org/research/lecture/2010/11/the-obama-doctrine-hindering-american-foreign-policy, p. 5.

[11] Martin S. Indyk, Kenneth G. Lieberthal & Michael E. O'Hanlon, 'Scoring Obama's Foreign Policy: A Progressive Pragmatist Tries to Bend History' (2012) 91 *Foreign Affairs* 44.

[12] Jeffrey Goldberg, 'The Obama Doctrine', *The Atlantic*, April 2016, www.theatlantic.com/magazine/archive/2016/04/the-obama-doctrine/471525/.

[13] Colin Dueck, 'The Accommodator: Obama's Foreign Policy' (2011) *Policy Review* 13.

[14] Fred Kaplan, 'The Realist: Barack Obama's a Cold Warrior Indeed', *Politico Magazine*, 27 February 2014, www.politico.com/magazine/story/2014/02/barack-obama-realist-foreign-policy-103861.

that IL externalising universal values contained the promise of an international order in equilibrium with US interests. What made the administration's policy distinctive, however, was that the means for achieving those idealised ends revealed commitment to liberal nationalist and illiberal internationalist IL policies, with both ideologies setting limitations on American global liability. Obama described his own admiration for the 'postwar order that married Wilson's idealism to hardheaded realism'.[15] The president directly rejected supposed tensions between American 'realists or idealists – a tension that suggests a stark choice between the narrow pursuit of interests or an endless campaign to impose our values around the world'.[16] Obama's particular formulation nevertheless reveals beliefs that the reality of illiberalism in global politics often necessitates pragmatic and illiberal applications of law to progress a liberal vision and that IL must sometimes be employed protectively to defend liberalism at home. The president himself identified with the Christian realism of Reinhold Niebuhr in accepting inherent tensions between right belief and prudent conduct:[17]

> [T]here's serious evil in the world, and hardship and pain. And we should be humble and modest in our belief we can eliminate those things. But we shouldn't use that as an excuse for cynicism and inaction . . . [W]e have to make these efforts knowing they are hard, and not swinging from naïve idealism to bitter realism.[18]

The challenge 'of being a liberal leader in an often illiberal world'[19] thus manifested itself in fraught ideological configurations that diverged between the aspirational and the operational.

A repeated claim among politically 'conservative' critics is that, in practice, Obama was attracted to transformative liberal internationalist ideals, but lacked commitment to policies necessary to realise them.[20] Mead broadly confirms that, although Obama's general foreign policy

15 Barack H. Obama, *The Audacity of Hope: Thoughts on Reclaiming the American Dream* (Crown, 2006), p. 284.

16 Barack H. Obama, 'Nobel Lecture: A Just and Lasting Peace', Oslo, 10 December 2009, www.nobelprize.org/nobel_prizes/peace/laureates/2009/obama-lecture_en.html.

17 See R. Ward Holder & Peter B. Josephson, 'Obama's Niebuhr Problem' (2013) 82 *Church History* 678.

18 David Brooks, 'Obama, Gospel and Verse', *The New York Times*, 26 April 2007, www.nytimes.com/2007/04/26/opinion/26brooks.html.

19 Timothy J. Lynch, 'Obama, Liberalism, and US Foreign Policy', in Inderjeet Parmar, Linda B. Miller & Mark Ledwidge (eds.), *Obama and the World: New Directions in US Foreign Policy* (Routledge, 2014), p. 44.

20 Holmes, Dale & Nau, 'The Obama Doctrine,' pp. 12–13.

was influenced by aspirations of liberal internationalism,[21] substantive policy decisions remained shaped by liberal nationalism.[22] The resulting tendency to look inward thereby failed to appreciate that a 'world based more on the rule of law and less on the law of the jungle requires an engaged, forward-looking, and, alas, expensive foreign policy'.[23] For Dueck, unsuccessful attempts to reconcile internationalist and nationalist variants of liberalism meant that Obama 'allowed the term "multilateralism" to become an excuse for American inaction'.[24] Such characterisations remain incomplete, however, in that they plausibly identify the aspirations and outcomes of IL policy but not the internal logic of the administration's strategic beliefs. Closer ideological analysis demonstrates a more structured approach of subordinating high moral aspirations to recognised limitations in US power.[25]

'International Law Matters'[26]

It is useful to isolate Obama's own worldview from policy outcomes, particularly in circumstances where the president assumed greater personal control over decision-making than many of his predecessors.[27] In the widest-ranging interview of his foreign policy beliefs, Obama explicitly characterised his worldview in terms of a four-by-four matrix

[21] Mead's 'Wilsonianism': Mead, 'Liberal Internationalism: The Twilight of a Dream'. Note that Mead's approach departs from that adopted in this book by treating 'liberal internationalism' as only a specific strand of his 'Wilsonianism' tradition alongside 'neoconservatism'.

[22] Mead's 'Jeffersonianism': Walter R. Mead, 'The Carter Syndrome', *Foreign Policy*, 4 January 2010, https://foreignpolicy.com/2010/01/04/the-carter-syndrome/. For a response see Jimmy Carter & Zbigniew Brzezinski, 'Presidential Debate', *Foreign Policy*, 22 February 2010, www.foreignpolicy.com/articles/2010/02/22/presidential_debate.

[23] Walter R. Mead, 'The President's Foreign Policy Paradox', *The Wall Street Journal*, 28 March 2014, http://online.wsj.com/articles/SB10001424052702303725404579457950519734142.

[24] Colin Dueck, *The Obama Doctrine: American Grand Strategy Today* (Oxford University Press, 2015), p. 243.

[25] See Jack Goldsmith, 'The Contributions of the Obama Administration to the Practice and Theory of International Law' (2016) 57 *Harvard International Law Journal* 455, pp. 472–3.

[26] Barack H. Obama, 'Full Transcript: President Obama Gives Speech Addressing Europe, Russia on March 26', *The Washington Post*, 26 March 2014, www.washingtonpost.com/world/transcript-president-obama-gives-speech-addressing-europe-russia-on-march-26/2014/03/26/07ae80ae-b503-11e3-b899-20667de76985_story.html.

[27] See Indyk, Lieberthal & O'Hanlon, 'Scoring Obama's Foreign Policy', p. 31.

of ideal types consistent with the model set forth in this book. Geoffrey Goldberg of *The Atlantic* asked the president how he 'thought his foreign policy might be understood by historians'.[28] According to Deputy National Security Advisor Ben Rhodes, Obama appreciated the insights of academic frameworks for evaluating his broader worldviews and thus responded literate in the relevant scholarship:[29]

> He started by describing for me a four-box grid representing the main schools of American foreign-policy thought. One box he called isolationism, which he dismissed out of hand. 'The world is ever-shrinking,' he said. 'Withdrawal is untenable.' The other boxes he labeled realism, liberal interventionism, and internationalism. 'I suppose you could call me a realist in believing we can't, at any given moment, relieve all the world's misery,' he said. 'We have to choose where we can make a real impact.' He also noted that he was quite obviously an internationalist, devoted as he is to strengthening multilateral organizations and international norms.[30]

Walt observed that Obama 'believes foreign-policy making involves picking and choosing from among the [last] three', consistent with rejecting the isolationist strands of the illiberal nationalist ideology of the Bush 43 years.[31] While Obama's own self-identification with the remaining quadrants is not itself determinative, his articulation of the model is compelling corroboration of this book's analytical approach from the highest levels of US IL policymaking.

Liberalism

The most instructive account of Obama's conception of IL remains his Nobel Lecture, which was largely authored by the president and has been characterised by his closest advisers as a 'template' or 'framework'

[28] Goldberg, 'The Obama Doctrine'.

[29] Ben Rhodes, Personal Communication with Author (14 February 2019).

[30] Goldberg, 'The Obama Doctrine'. Laying Obama's four 'schools' over the ideological structure set out in this book forms the following approximate dimensions and typology:

	Liberal	Illiberal
Internationalist	'Liberal interventionism' *Liberal internationalism*	'Internationalism' *Illiberal internationalism*
Nationalist	'Realism' *Liberal nationalism*	'Isolationism' *Illiberal nationalism*

[31] Stephen M. Walt, 'Obama Was Not a Realist President', *Foreign Policy*, 7 April 2016, http://foreignpolicy.com/2016/04/07/obama-was-not-a-realist-president-jeffrey-goldberg-atlantic-obama-doctrine/.

for his foreign policy beliefs.[32] Crucially, the balance of the speech directly addressed the relationship between international power and conflicts internal to American IL policy. Obama's exceptionalist thinking is, paradoxically, revealed in his declaration that the United States cannot 'insist that others follow the rules of the road if we refuse to follow them ourselves', which would appear 'arbitrary'. A belief that the United States elevates liberal values above the ordinary geopolitical incentives to carve out legal exceptions is itself an exceptionalist claim. According to Obama, 'even as we confront a vicious adversary that abides by no rules, I believe the United States of America must remain a standard bearer in the conduct of war. That is what makes us different from those whom we fight.'[33] The anchoring of IL in liberalism was made explicit in Obama's self-identification as an 'idealist', believing that

> we should be promoting values, like democracy and human rights and norms and values, because not only do they serve our interests the more people adopt values that we share – in the same way that, economically, if people adopt rule of law and property rights and so forth, that is to our advantage – but because it makes the world a better place.[34]

These liberal values found their expression in both internationalist and nationalist approaches to global governance, with a divergence between policy means and ends.

Liberal Internationalism

The president's primary conception of liberalism was of an international rule of law in which the United States played an exceptional role upholding and promoting the system. In Obama's words: 'If you compare us to previous superpowers, we act less on the basis of naked self-interest, and have been interested in establishing norms that benefit everyone.'[35] The halting establishment of the international rule of law was attributed to an exceptional American role after each of the world wars, wherein it 'led the world in constructing an architecture to keep the peace'. This premise

[32] Ben Rhodes, *The World as It Is* (Random House, 2018), p. 80; Kaplan, 'The Realist'; Harold H. Koh in Donald F. Donovan, 'Retrospective on International Law in the First Obama Administration' (2013) 107 *Proceedings of the Annual Meeting (American Society of International Law)* 131, p. 146.

[33] Obama, 'Nobel Lecture'.

[34] Goldberg, 'The Obama Doctrine'.

[35] Ibid.

departs in key ways from legalism by asserting American values and power as constitutive of IL itself:

> [I]t was not simply international institutions – not just treaties and declarations – that brought stability to a post-World War II world. Whatever mistakes we have made, the plain fact is this: The United States of America has helped underwrite global security for more than six decades with the blood of our citizens and the strength of our arms . . . We have borne this burden not because we seek to impose our will. We have done so out of enlightened self-interest.[36]

Read in the context of a warning against 'reflexive suspicion of America, the world's sole military superpower', this was not merely a political observation but an expression of the necessary elements of an effective international legal system.

Obama's understanding of how that system enhances global peace centres on democracy as the link between the municipal and the international rule of law. The evidence was said to be that greater adherence to IL between nations, across the twentieth century, was achieved through US support for 'ideals of liberty and self-determination, equality and the rule of law'. Ultimately, Obama's liberal vision drew on a foundational belief 'that the human condition can be perfected' and in a 'fundamental faith in human progress'.[37] This animating purpose of IL remains distinct from illiberal internationalism, which promotes international engagement without accepting that IL can progressively extend shared values as a strategy for overcoming geopolitical interests.

Dominance of liberal internationalism was reinforced in Obama's preface to the 2010 *National Security Strategy* (NSS 2010),[38] which drew connections between democracy, promoting rights through transnational processes, and American national security:

> The rule of law – and our capacity to enforce it – advances our national security and strengthens our leadership . . . Around the globe, it allows us to hold actors accountable, while supporting both international security and the stability of the global economy. America's commitment to the rule of law is fundamental to our efforts to build an international order that is capable of confronting the emerging challenges of the 21st century.[39]

[36] Obama, 'Nobel Lecture'.
[37] Ibid.
[38] The White House, *The National Security Strategy of the United States of America 2010* (2010).
[39] Ibid., p. 37. See also pp. ii & 2.

The NSS 2010 importantly departed from the strategies of the Bush 43 years in commitment to 'an international order based upon rights and responsibilities' and the 'modernization of institutions, strengthening of international norms, and enforcement of international law'.[40]

Liberal Nationalism

Although Obama self-identified as also a 'realist', Walt and Dueck both rightly point out that the standard IR sense of that term is inconsistent with Obama's overriding liberal objectives.[41] Rather, what he describes is consistent with the narrow realism encompassed by liberal nationalism, that 'we can't, at any given moment, relieve all the world's misery . . . We have to choose where we can make a real impact.' This call remains in the exemplar tradition of American liberalism, being combined with recognition that

> in order to advance both our security interests and those ideals and values that we care about, we've got to be hardheaded at the same time as we're bighearted, and pick and choose our spots, and recognize that there are going to be times where the best that we can do is to shine a spotlight on something that's terrible, but not believe that we can automatically solve it.[42]

The most telling evidence of liberal nationalism was Obama's belief that dividing the burden of global leadership with other nations is desirable to protect liberalism at home, and as a guard against unchecked US global power. Obama warned that global counterparts 'who claim to respect international law cannot avert their eyes when those laws are flouted'. Rather, the responsibility for enforcing IL was a shared one: '[T]he closer we stand together, the less likely we will be faced with the choice between armed intervention and complicity in oppression.'[43] He later added: 'One of the reasons I am so focused on taking action multilaterally where our direct interests are not at stake is that multilateralism regulates hubris.'[44]

Likewise, the NSS 2010 spanned both variants of liberalism, stating that 'national security begins at home' and, accordingly, that 'moral leadership is grounded principally in the power of our example – not through an effort to impose our system on other peoples'.[45] Yet that

[40] Ibid., p. 3.
[41] Walt, 'Obama Was Not a Realist President'; Dueck, *The Obama Doctrine*, pp. 198–9.
[42] Goldberg, 'The Obama Doctrine'.
[43] Obama, 'Nobel Lecture'.
[44] Goldberg, 'The Obama Doctrine'.
[45] The White House, *NSS 2010*, pp. 9–10 & 36.

warning was tempered by beliefs that 'America has never succeeded through isolationism ... [W]e must reengage the world on a comprehensive and sustained basis.'[46] To that end, the United States 'must pursue a rules-based international system that can advance our own interests by serving mutual interests'.[47] This remained consistent with combining a restrained defence of universal American political values with the aspiration of an international environment that would ultimately reinforce them.

Illiberal Internationalism

Finally, Obama's recognition of the disjunct between liberal intentions and the reality of an illiberal world also manifested in examples of employing illiberal policies for the limited purpose of returning the global balance of power toward American values:

> I face the world as it is, and cannot stand idle in the face of threats to the American people. For make no mistake: Evil does exist in the world . . . To say that force may sometimes be necessary is not a call to cynicism – it is a recognition of history; the imperfections of man and the limits of reason.[48]

Quoting President Kennedy, Obama warned against idealistic adherence to liberal values in IL policy, favouring 'a more practical, more attainable peace, based not on a sudden revolution in human nature but on a gradual evolution in human institutions'. In this vein, he noted that, although 'engagement with repressive regimes lacks the satisfying purity of indignation', it was sometimes necessary to pragmatically advance illiberal interests in the short term, with liberal faith that 'human rights and dignity are advanced over time'.[49]

Senior Legal Policymakers

Along with the new president, a change in senior legal policymakers signalled a more robust role for IL in US foreign relations and enthusiasm for the ICC in particular. These policymakers held an array of beliefs about IL that largely complemented but at times competed with the president's conception of it. The most consequential appointment for

[46] Ibid., pp. 11 & 40.
[47] Ibid., p. 12.
[48] Obama, 'Nobel Lecture'.
[49] Ibid.

IL policy was Hillary Clinton, as Obama's first Secretary of State. Clinton was given a direct opportunity at her confirmation hearing to identify the administration's general foreign policy among variants of the four theorised ideal types, when Senator Robert P. Casey, Jr. adopted Posen and Ross's formulation:[50]

> Historically, the United States has adopted one of four grand strategies, or some combination of the four: Neoisolationism (avoidance of foreign entanglements), selective engagement (traditional balance of power realism that works to ensure peace among the major powers), cooperative security (a liberal world order of interdependence and effective international institutions), and primacy (American unilateralism and continued hegemony). Which grand strategy, or combination of strategies, do you think best describes how you would seek to promote U.S. national security today?[51]

Unsurprisingly, Clinton declined to categorise herself in these terms, arguing that 'the paradigms of the past neither adequately describe our present realities, nor provide a comprehensive guide to what we should do about them'.[52] Asking a policymaker to spontaneously categorise instinctive ideological beliefs within an imposed typology held limited probative value. By the same token, however, Clinton's dismissive response was neither a useful account of the role of foreign policy ideology nor consistent with evidence of continuity in diplomatic thought.

The indication of where to place Clinton's beliefs was in her promise of a 'new direction' that rejected the illiberal nationalism of the first Bush 43 term: 'That America is a nation of laws is one of our great strengths, and the Supreme Court has been clear that the fight against terrorism cannot occur in a "legal black hole."'[53] Clinton's distinctive conception of IL became clear in her meaning of 'a rules-based global order that could manage interactions between states, protect fundamental freedoms, and mobilize common action'.[54] For Clinton, the 'old architecture' of global governance is akin to the 'Parthenon in Greece, with clean lines and clear

[50] See Chapter 2, p. 65, *supra*: Barry R. Posen & Andrew L. Ross, 'Competing Visions for U.S. Grand Strategy' (1996/97) 21 *International Security* 5.

[51] Committee on Foreign Relations, United States Senate, *Senate Committee on Foreign Relations, Nomination of Hillary R. Clinton To Be Secretary of State,* 1st Session 111th Congress (2009), p. 212.

[52] Ibid., p. 212. See also Hillary Rodham Clinton, *Hard Choices: A Memoir* (Simon and Schuster, 2014), pp. 32–3.

[53] Clinton, *Hard Choices*, p. 184.

[54] Ibid., p. 33.

rules'. In contrast, the rules and legal institutions that Clinton sought resembled the deconstructivist architecture of Frank Gehry: 'a dynamic mix of materials, shapes, and structures'.[55] This policy-oriented and deformalised approach to IL revealed Clinton's beliefs in strongly internationalist and primarily liberal terms, without the mediating influence of liberal nationalism found in the president's worldview.

The single most influential figure shaping US ICC policy was Clinton's legal adviser Harold Koh, who was and remains an exemplar of liberal internationalist IL policy. Koh is credited with founding the school of 'transnational legal process' as a successor to the New Haven School of policy-oriented jurisprudence.[56] He forcefully contested the legality of the 2003 Iraq War, during the Bush years and at his Senate confirmation hearing.[57] Koh's conception of the international rule of law was explained to the Senate Judiciary Committee in the months prior to Obama's election in a hearing entitled *Restoring the Rule of Law*:

> [R]espect for the rule of law should not be limited to domestic constitutional law. The next President should recall the words of our founders in the Declaration of Independence to pay 'decent respect to the opinions of mankind' by supporting, not attacking, the institutions and treaties of international human rights law.[58]

Once in office, Koh declared a fundamental shift from the Bush 43 administration in the 'approach and attitude toward international law'.[59] This was captured in what Koh termed an 'emerging "Obama-Clinton Doctrine"' that comprised four elements:

1 *Principled Engagement*;
2 Diplomacy as a Critical Element of *Smart Power*;
3 *Strategic Multilateralism*; and

[55] Ibid., p. 33.

[56] See Harold H. Koh, 'Is There a "New" New Haven School of International Law?' (2007) 32 *Yale Journal of International Law* 559.

[57] Committee on Foreign Relations, United States Senate, *Senate Committee on Foreign Relations, Nomination of Harold H. Koh To Be Legal Adviser to the Department of State*, 1st Session 111th Congress (2009), pp. 25 & 29.

[58] Harold H. Koh, 'Statement of Harold Hongju Koh before the Senate Judiciary Committee, Subcommittee on the Constitution on Restoring the Rule of Law', 16 September 2008, www.fas.org/irp/congress/2008_hr/091608koh.pdf.

[59] Harold H. Koh, 'The Obama Administration and International Law', 25 March 2010, https://2009-2017.state.gov/s/l/releases/remarks/139119.htm.

4 the notion that *Living Our Values* Makes Us Stronger and Safer, by Following *Rules of Domestic and International Law; and Following Universal Standards, Not Double Standards.*[60]

The element of 'following universal standards, not double standards' emphasised the degree to which America was 'stronger and safer' by expressing fidelity to the rule of law at home while extending it outward according to common liberal values. Failure of the Bush 43 administration to do likewise had eroded the international rule of law, by converting the United States from 'the major supporter of the post-war global legal exoskeleton into the most visible outlier trying to break free of the very legal framework we created and supported for half a century'.[61] Conversely, Koh also made clear that the interpretation of IL remained subject to the policy-oriented 'smart power' concept, meaning that policy considerations and diplomatic interests shaped the interpretation of law itself. The most fundamental principle remained a 'commitment to living our values by respecting the rule of law'.[62]

Developing Non-arbitrary Global Governance

By the time Obama entered office, the ICC had evolved from an untested forum cautiously seeking state support to a fully operational international legal body engaged in investigations and prosecutions. Legalist advocates sought to harness renewed US support to consolidate the formal status of the court in global governance. For the Obama administration, the most pressing task was demonstrating that the United States had shifted to supporting IL in terms of universal liberal values rather than illiberal national security interests. The clearest demonstration of this change, and one sought by existing states parties, was to reverse the 2002 act of unsigning the Rome Statute and thereby recommit the United States to an ICC policy that, at minimum, complied with the objects and purpose of the treaty, even if not its strict terms. The United States assumed its rights as an observer state at the annual Assembly of States Parties (ASP) governing the ICC, attending and participating in sessions for the first time while actively supporting referral of matters to the court. Yet it fell short of explicitly 're-signing' the statute or of supporting its

[60] Ibid., original emphasis.
[61] Harold H. Koh, 'Jefferson Memorial Lecture: Transnational Legal Process after September 11th' (2004) 22 *Berkeley Journal of International Law* 337, pp. 350–1.
[62] Koh, 'The Obama Administration and International Law'.

eventual ratification, thereby remaining at odds with commitment to the international rule of law as understood by legalist counterparts.

Legalist Policy

The full spectrum of beliefs about the ICC and tensions with US IL policy was contained in the October 2012 UNSC agenda item: *The promotion and strengthening of the rule of law in the maintenance of international peace and security: Peace and justice, with a special focus on the role of the International Criminal Court* (UNSC rule of law meeting).[63] That meeting followed on from a declaration made the previous month committing to 'an international order based on the rule of law', for which the ICC was recognised as integral to 'a multilateral system that aims to end impunity and establish the rule of law'.[64] At the subsequent UNSC rule of law meeting, the Secretary General went further and described the ICC as 'the centre of the new system of international criminal justice'.[65]

A repeated theme at the UNSC rule of law meeting was the need to progressively formalise ICC authority. The Secretary General described a new 'age of accountability' in which the UN would no longer 'promote or condone amnesty for genocide, crimes against humanity, war crimes or gross violations of human rights' when negotiating peace agreements.[66] Similarly, the Togolese representative warned against continued reliance on 'informal mechanisms and arrangements that run the risk of bypassing transparency or control and open the way to arbitrariness'.[67] The Sri Lankan representative was more explicit in declaring that, in this area, 'codification of international law and legal obligations is an important aspect of the rule of law at the international level'.[68]

The specific expression of formalised development was in repeated calls for more states to legally join the Rome Statute. At the Kampala

63 UN, *6849th Meeting*, United Nations Security Council (17 October 2012) & UN, *6849th Meeting (Resumption 1)*, United Nations Security Council (17 October 2012).

64 The September 2012 'Declaration of the High-Level Meeting of the General Assembly on the Rule of Law at the National and International Levels' was ultimately adopted as a UNGA resolution: *GA Res 67/1, UN Doc A/RES/67/1*, 30 November 2012, www.un.org/ruleoflaw/files/37839_A-RES-67-1.pdf. See Clause 23, p. 4.

65 UN, *6849th Meeting*, p. 2.

66 Ibid., p. 2.

67 Ibid., p. 22.

68 UN, *6849th Meeting (Resumption 1)*, p. 25.

Conference, the EU representative set out its primary objective as '[p]romoting the universality and preserving the integrity of the Rome Statute'.[69] At the UNSC rule of law meeting, the UK concurred: 'Achieving the universality of the Rome Statute is the key to deepening and broadening the reach of the rule of law.'[70] Absent formal obligations, the ICC remained a mere diplomatic forum. Germany, which already believed that the ICC had 'strengthened the rule of law in international relations',[71] alluded to this distinction in accepting that although UNSC referrals to the ICC were a welcome addition, they remained merely a 'tool of last resort, as an act of political responsibility'. In contrast, the creation of legal obligation required 'ratification of the Rome Statute by the greatest possible number of States so that referrals become more and more obsolete'.[72] Similarly, Liechtenstein described UNSC referrals as a 'mixed blessing' for their advancing of criminal justice while being 'driven by [the] political convenience' of powerful ICC non-member countries.[73] Discretionary US engagement did not amount to commitment to the rule of law, even when done to alter international behaviour toward increasing legal compliance.

Beliefs of American Legal Policymakers

Maintaining Ambiguous Obligations under the Rome Statute

The Obama administration's official ICC position was set out in the NSS 2010, in terms that became something of a mantra among legal policymakers:

> Although the United States is not at present a party to the Rome Statute of the International Criminal Court (ICC), and will always protect U.S. personnel, we are engaging with State Parties to the Rome Statute on issues of concern and are supporting the ICC's prosecution of those cases that advance U.S. interests and values, consistent with the requirements of U.S. law.[74]

[69] María J. F. López-Palop, 'Declaración realizada en nombre de la Unión Europea', 31 May 2010, https://asp.icc-cpi.int/iccdocs/asp_docs/RC2010/Statements/ICC-RC-GenDeba-European%20Union-SPA-ENG-FRA.pdf.

[70] UN, *6849th Meeting*, p. 24.

[71] Markus Löning, 'Statement on Behalf of Germany, International Criminal Court Review Conference', 1 June 2010, https://asp.icc-cpi.int/iccdocs/asp_docs/RC2010/Statements/ICC-RC-gendeba-Germany-ENG.pdf.

[72] UN, *6849th Meeting*, p. 18.

[73] UN, *6849th Meeting (Resumption 1)*, p. 2.

[74] The White House, *NSS 2010*, p. 8.

The terms of renewed support were equally a confirmation of the court's subordinate status to US legal autonomy and the perceived need to shield military personnel.

The divergent path of US policy is clearest in the administration's ambiguous retraction of the 2002 unsigning statement of John Bolton, combined with emphatic assurances that a clear policy shift had occurred.[75] The act of unsigning during the first term of the Bush 43 administration was widely accepted as effective in removing minimal US obligations to not frustrate the objects of the treaty.[76] As the Bush 43 era came to a close, this remained the most conspicuous signal of the hostility flowing from illiberal nationalist conceptions of the ICC. Immediately prior to assuming the role of State Department Legal Adviser, Koh declared that,

> at the earliest opportunity, the new Secretary of State should withdraw the Bush Administration's May 2002 letter to the United Nations 'unsigning' the U.S. signature to the Rome Treaty creating the ICC, restoring the *status quo ante* that existed at the end of the Clinton Administration.[77]

Doing so was framed as a necessary step toward an IL policy 'that lives up to America's historically high standards of international responsibility and respect for the rule of international law'.[78] In Scheffer's opinion, 'a new letter could nullify the effect of Bolton's missive and resurrect the legal authority of the signature on the treaty'.[79] The call by Koh and Scheffer was therefore for the formal reacceptance of the legal obligations created by Clinton's 2000 signature, which would equally send the strongest political signal of US commitment to the international rule of law. In the years following these statements, US policy is best described as political recommitment to the substance of Rome Statute signatory obligations, but ambiguous commitment to legally binding obligations. Koh had previously characterised the Bush administration's increased ICC cooperation during its second term as '*de facto* repudiation of the political act of unsigning' that largely brought the United States back in line with its former international obligations.[80] The subsequent Obama

[75] See Chapter 5, *supra*.

[76] Under *Rome Statute*, Art. 18. See Edward T. Swaine, 'Unsigning' (2003) 55 *Stanford Law Review* 2061.

[77] Koh, 'Statement before the Senate Judiciary Committee', p. 11.

[78] Ibid., p. 12.

[79] David J. Scheffer, *All the Missing Souls: A Personal History of the War Crimes Tribunals* (Princeton University Press, 2012), p. 243.

[80] Koh, 'Jefferson Memorial Lecture', p. 351.

policy, led by Koh, suggests that this '*de facto*' shift was adopted as sufficient for the policy 'reset', without further formalised obligations.

The United States signalled its policy shift by attending the Annual Session of the ASP for the first time in November 2009. Questions soon followed about what that signified about US legal obligations in circumstances where the Bolton letter was never formally annulled. The issue was deftly avoided by US Ambassador-at-Large for War Crimes Issues Stephen Rapp, who told reporters that the United States was entitled to participate in the ASP and related conferences irrespective of the treaty signature – by virtue of signing the *Final Act* at the 1998 Rome Conference.[81] When pushed on the unsigning, he stated only that the effect of the Bolton letter was the limited one of making it 'clear that we did not, that the Bush administration did not, believe that we were bound to act as others expected a signatory to act'.[82] He pointedly did not repudiate the release from legal obligations, emphasising that US participation 'did not require an acknowledgement of our December 2000 signature to the treaty'.[83] When later asked about the same issue at the Kampala Conference, Koh agreed that the United States was legally entitled to engage as an observer nation, but was more explicit that US cooperation arose from discretionary decisions alone:

> We should make clear that there is no legal decision involved in our being here. It's not a decision about whether to change any law, to ratify any treaty, or to change any statute or change any other agreement. But it is part of a broader policy, as I said, for closer engagement with this important international institution.[84]

This is consistent with the administration's overall policy of 'principled engagement' in multilateral forums to advance American interests. Yet, in legalist terms, this remains a diplomatic stance and not a commitment to be bound by IL *stricto sensu*. That point was picked up by a questioner at the post-Kampala press conference who noted that the 'reset' in ICC

[81] The official agreement on the record of proceedings: UN, *The United Nations Diplomatic Conference of Plenipotentiaries on the Establishment of an International Criminal Court, Final Act*, UN Doc A/CONF.183/1, (17 July 1998).

[82] Stephen J. Rapp, 'Press Briefing with Stephen J. Rapp Ambassador-at-Large for War Crimes Issues', Mission of the United States Geneva, 22 January 2010, http://geneva.usmission.gov/2010/01/22/stephen-rapp/.

[83] Stephen J. Rapp, Interview with Author (15 February 2012).

[84] Harold H. Koh & Stephen J. Rapp, 'Briefing on the International Criminal Court Conference in Kampala, Uganda', 2 June 2010, https://2009-2017.state.gov/j/gcj/us_releases/remarks/2010/142585.htm.

policy had 'more of a political tinge' than a legal character. Koh's and Rapp's responses confirmed that the US reset entailed accepting the ICC as 'a tool in the international toolbox', but not as a binding regime.

Later, in 2010, some commentators perceived Koh moving closer to a de jure shift in obligations, by picking up the words of Article 18 of the VCLT to distinguish the Obama policy from that of his predecessors:

> You do not see what international lawyers might call a concerted effort to frustrate the *object and purpose* of the Rome Statute. That is explicitly not the policy of this administration. Because although the United States is not a party to the Rome Statute, we share with the States parties a deep and abiding interest in seeing the Court successfully complete the important prosecutions it has already begun.[85]

This carefully worded phrase was quoted by Koh in subsequent speeches, but without further clarification.[86] There is some uncertainty when interpreting the legal significance of these words. It is worth noting that the statement was made in the context of a quote from the NSS 2010: a document that studiously avoided any suggestion that the United States was legally bound by the ICC. At the time of Koh's statement, Beth van Schaack raised but did not answer the question of 'whether Koh has said the magic words' necessary to annul the 2002 Bolton letter. She agreed that the *policy* of obstructing the court was at an end but that no conclusive inferences could be drawn about altered legal obligations.[87] Jennifer Trahan described Koh's words as having 'orally negated' the unsigning, but conceded that the statements lacked 'the weight of a counter-note'. Rather, she reiterated her previous call, as chair of the American Branch of the International Law Association's ICC Committee, to send a legally binding note.[88] Finally, Amann drew the conclusion that 'top Obama Administration officials have made clear that the United States now acts toward the ICC treaty as any good signatory

[85] Harold H. Koh, 'The Challenges and Future of International Justice', 27 October 2010, https://2009-2017.state.gov/s/l/releases/remarks/150497.htm, emphasis added.

[86] See Harold H. Koh, 'International Criminal Justice 5.0' (2013) 38 *Yale Journal of International Law* 525, p. 537.

[87] Beth van Schaack, 'The U.S. Says It Is Not Its Goal to Undermine the ICC', *IntLawGrrls,* 12 November 2010, www.intlawgrrls.com/2010/11/us-says-it-is-not-its-goal-to-undermine.html.

[88] Jennifer Trahan, 'U.S. Affirms that It Adheres to Rome Statute Signatory Obligations: It Should Put This in Writing', *Opinio Juris,* 27 February 2013, http://opiniojuris.org/2013/02/27/u-s-affirms-that-it-adheres-to-rome-statute-signatory-obligations-it-should-put-this-in-writing/.

should'.[89] So much had already been made clear, but this goes no further than the non-binding undertakings of policymakers.

The combined force of these statements and legal opinions is that: (a) the Obama administration firmly committed to an IL policy consistent with the objects and purposes of the Rome Statute; and (b) the Obama administration conspicuously avoided accepting any formal legal obligations commensurate to its stated policy. Moreover, beyond such ambiguity, policymakers were much clearer that there was no intention to ratify the statute at any time in the foreseeable future which, by virtue of gridlocked domestic politics and the intractability of US Senate opposition, remained 'not a question of when . . . [but of] if'.[90] Those impediments are undeniable, yet there is scant evidence that the Obama administration would have moved to ratify the treaty as it then stood, even absent Congressional opposition. Attention must turn to foreign policy ideology to understand how American legal policymakers squared outcomes with simultaneous statements that the Obama ICC policy *did* represent recommitment to the international rule of law.

Transnational Development of Global Governance

The consistent position emphasised by the United States through this period was closer engagement with the court's activities and the processes through which US actions were brought in line with the entire project of international criminal justice. This exemplifies the 'transnational legal process' explanation for how IL shapes the behaviour of states. Increased US interactions with states parties and the ICC itself caused increased compliance with legal norms and, through this engagement, the United States became a part of mechanisms making the court effective. Koh had contested perceived US legal failings throughout the first term of the Bush 43 administration, arguing that 'the United States and those within it who are committed to the rule of law should now invoke transnational legal process as a way to address the continuing problems'. Indeed, Koh believed that US constitutional values were already imbued in the ICC through transnational legal processes such that 'as much as the Bush administration may wish to be free of the legal exoskeleton that the United States has helped create, already that legal framework is visibly pushing back'.[91] This

89 Diane M. Amann, 'Officials Treat United States as Once & Present Signatory of ICC's Rome Statute', 27 February 2013, http://dianemarieamann.com/2013/02/27/officials-treat-united-states-as-once-present-signatory-of-iccs-rome-statute/.

90 Rapp, 'Press Briefing with Stephen J. Rapp'.

91 Koh, 'Jefferson Memorial Lecture', p. 351.

highlights a conceptual distinction between Koh's jurisprudence and that of his predecessor John Bellinger, in circumstances where their ICC policies of re-engaging with the ICC appeared functionally alike. Bellinger expressed illiberal internationalist commitment to pragmatically develop the court by reference to clearly identified strategic interests, while limiting its reach to that extent. Koh, on the other hand, saw the shift under Bellinger less as a calculated decision and more as a consequence of the milieu of transnational forces drawing the United States back toward universal liberal values.

This is not to suggest that formally signing the Rome Statute and even creating conditions for ratification were not genuine aspirations for liberal internationalists. The Clinton administration always aimed its efforts at the ideal of a treaty drafted in such terms that the United States could formally accept its obligations. However, for these policy-makers such steps were meaningful primarily for advancing an effective regime shaping international legal behaviour. On that basis, the Obama administration placed its strongest emphasis on the degree to which it was influenced by and continued to influence the development of legal norms through the court. Secretary Clinton confirmed early in the administration that the United States intended to 'end hostility towards the ICC, and look for opportunities to encourage effective ICC action in ways that promoted US interests by bringing war criminals to justice'.[92] In the UNSC rule of law meeting, Ambassador Susan Rice characterised the ICC as 'an important tool for accountability', even as the United States repudiated formal membership. Instead:

> We will continue working with the ICC to identify practical ways to cooperate, particularly in areas such as information-sharing and witness protection on a case-by-case basis, as consistent with United States policy and law.[93]

That stance was reinforced in a major policy speech by Sarah Sewell, Under Secretary for Civilian Security, Democracy, and Human Rights, who argued that although the United States agreed that 'aggression is inimical to a rules-based international order', the real question for upholding such an order was not formalised endorsement of the crime but, rather, 'whether the Rome Statute amendments can be an effective and appropriate addition to the international community's tool-box'.[94]

[92] United States Senate, *Nomination of Hillary R. Clinton*, p. 131.
[93] UN, *6849th Meeting*, p. 8.
[94] Sarah Sewell, 'The ICC Crime of Aggression and the Changing International Security Landscape', Annual Meeting of the American Society of International Law, Washington,

Running through these arguments are strands of exceptionalist belief that reconcile a special US role with legal principle. Koh described US policy as shifting to an 'integrated approach to criminal justice', by which was meant reconciling 'incongruous' historical support for the Nuremberg, Tokyo and ad hoc tribunals with equivocation about the ICC. The objective was to 'align, integrate, and make congruent our approach towards these institutions'.[95] Koh's statements downplaying formal obligations were accompanied by reference to beliefs in a unique global mission: 'Our historic commitment to the cause of international justice remains strong.'[96] Likewise, Rapp noted that the United States had been 'a leader in international justice' in establishing the ad hoc tribunals and making them operational. In the case of the ICC, 'the opportunity to do some of those same things presents itself' with the United States again leading the initiative.[97] These are telling comparisons given that the United States was generally excluded from the jurisdiction of the ad hoc tribunals by their very subject matter,[98] whereas no such limitation would exist for a criminal court with general jurisdiction. Yet the United States sought exclusion from ICC constraints, through claims to an exceptional role fostering the institutions that made international criminal justice effective.

A reporter at the Kampala Conference observed that it was 'curious that an administration would become so engaged in shaping the kind of format of a court that it's not a signatory to'. Koh invoked exceptionalist beliefs in his response that 'international institutions and courts with which the United States is not involved tend not to be as effective', whereas the ad hoc tribunals 'have been more successful by virtue of deep U.S. engagement'. For Koh, the proper understanding of US policy was that it represented a 'process' rather than an 'end game' toward

DC, 9 April 2015, extracted in Beth van Schaack, 'U.S. Policy on the ICC Crime of Aggression Announced', *Just Security*, 21 April 2015, www.justsecurity.org/22248/u-s-policy-icc-crime-aggression/.

95 Koh, 'The Challenges and Future of International Justice'.

96 Harold H. Koh, 'Statement by Harold Hongju Koh, Legal Adviser, United States Department of State, Regarding Crime of Aggression at the Resumed Eighth Session of the Assembly of States Parties of the International Criminal Court', 23 March 2010, http://usun.state.gov/briefing/statements/2010/139000.htm.

97 Koh & Rapp, 'U.S. Engagement with the ICC'.

98 The ICTY did claim jurisdiction over US personnel involved in relevant NATO military actions, but circumstances of the tribunal's founding effectively foreclosed its exercise: See Melissa J. Epstein, 'The Customary Origins and Elements of Select Conduct of Hostilities Charges before the ICTY' (2004) 179 *Military Law Review* 68, p. 90, n. 97.

membership.[99] By necessary inference, the explanation for involvement in criminal justice without formal obligations is that the United States saw itself as enmeshed in transnational legal processes shifting behaviour in line with the international rule of law.

Conclusion

A recurring argument made by commentators is that the real break in policy was between the two terms of the Bush 43 administration, with no meaningful change leading into the Obama administration.[100] Even key figures in the Obama administration have acknowledged the possibility that 'the bigger break is between the Bush first term and the Bush second term', while accentuating a meaningful shift between administrations.[101] Here, the magnitude of any policy shift is not conclusive on the question of continuity in legal beliefs. Across both periods, the United States largely continued to work from without the system, essentially unconstrained by the regime, while supporting elements of ICC development. However, in the latter period, the beliefs structuring US policy distinctively revolved around processes creating greater compliance with universal norms of international criminal law – from the municipal through to the global level. Irrespective, US policy remained inconsistent with conceptions of the international rule of law fixed on formal and universal ICC obligations. Looking to 'U.S. legal traditions', Ferencz perceives a failure 'to advance respect for the predictable and uniform rule of law'.[102] In legalist terms: 'The words "Equal justice under law" are etched in the portico of the United States Supreme Court. If they stand for anything, they certainly stand for predictable enforcement of law', rather than the discretionary regime promoted by the United States.[103] Yet, the relationship described by US policymakers at the UNSC rule of law meeting and elsewhere followed liberal internationalist conceptions of a rule of law advanced through transnational development of global

[99] Koh & Rapp, 'U.S. Engagement with the ICC'.

[100] See especially John Bellinger who has repeatedly made this case: John B. Bellinger III, 'The United States and the International Criminal Court: Where We've Been and Where We're Going; Remarks to the DePaul University College of Law', 25 April 2008, https://2001-2009.state.gov/s/l/rls/104053.htm.

[101] Rapp, Interview with Author.

[102] Donald M. Ferencz, 'Current US Policy on the Crime of Aggression: History in the Unmaking' (2016) 48 *Case Western Reserve Journal of International Law* 189, p. 201.

[103] Ibid., p. 201, n. 42.

governance. In so doing, the United States remained fundamentally outside of the legalist vision of its global counterparts.

Defining Equality under International Law

From the earliest days of the ICC project, participating states and NGOs were motivated by a desire to 'democratise' the oligarchic configuration of the UNSC.[104] This opportunity arose in the initiative set aside at the Rome Conference to include the crime of aggression within the court's jurisdiction. The goal was ambitious and would significantly expand the subject matter of international criminal law. More fundamentally, the initiative was in large part directed at divesting the UNSC of sole legal control over this most consequential crime and subjecting it to the equal control of all ICC members. The P5 remained united in their insistence on an exclusive 'Security Council trigger' for aggression cases[105] – consistent with rational incentives for powerful states to entrench their position in law. However, that general dynamic does not explain the specific question of whether and how American legal policymakers reconciled political motives with an explicit commitment to the international rule of law. US policy adamantly held out the UNSC as the cornerstone of the international legal system, with exclusive power to delegate such matters to an international court. Moreover, the definition of the crime of aggression itself was contested on the basis that it may constrain existing US autonomy to employ force upholding IL. US policy, nominally aimed at advancing the objectives of the ICC and international criminal law, remained steadfastly opposed to sovereign equality.

Legalist Policy

Critics of the UNSC have long fixed on sovereign equality as a guiding principle for the legitimate exercise of international legal power. At the UNSC rule of law meeting, Lesotho argued that, when making referrals, 'the aspirations of the general membership of the United Nations should override the individual national interests of Council members'.[106] For Sri Lanka, the 'principle of sovereign equality . . . which is intrinsic to international rule

[104] See David Bosco, *Rough Justice: The International Criminal Court's Battle to Fix the World, One Prosecution at a Time* (Oxford University Press, 2014), p. 166.

[105] Matthew C. Weed, *International Criminal Court and the Rome Statute: 2010 Review Conference* (Congressional Research Service, 10 March 2011), p. 10.

[106] UN, *6849th Meeting (Resumption 1)*, p. 17.

of law, must be maintained, as international rules are made and implemented. It is a principle that protects all States, especially the small and the weak.'[107] These amounted to demands for constructive sovereign equality in the UNSC – requiring the P5, with formally unequal privileges, to exercise them by reference to the inferred will of the equally weighted voices of all states. The opportunity to restructure international criminal law along these lines arose at the Kampala Conference, with the agreement to establish the crime of aggression. Conference delegates saw in this agreement 'completion of the codification of the existing body of crimes under customary international law and for the closure of the last remaining important lacuna contained in the substantive part of the ICC Statute'.[108]

In terms of commitment to equality under law, advocates were specifically motivated by beliefs that the UNSC's sole authority over this subject matter remained a stumbling block to the international rule of law. Brazil refuted characterisations of aggression as an inherently political crime by arguing that 'world peace and security are by definition political in nature, but are best addressed through a legal framework that enjoys broad support and legitimacy'. By this was meant that the 'universality of the Court lies in the widely held values that it espouses. Its reach will grow as a result of fulfilling its promise and not by submitting to false pragmatism and the so-called realities of power.'[109] Likewise, Liechtenstein, then president of the ASP, conceded that, despite the UNSC's long-established authority in this area, the proposal would ensure that 'jurisdiction is not ultimately contingent upon the Council's decisions'.[110] In these statements, states reaffirmed the legalist principle of sovereign equality to circumvent the UNSC, and thereby protect the court's integrity.

Beliefs of American Legal Policymakers

The American Interpretive Gloss on the Crime of Aggression

US policymakers had long pushed for an exclusive UNSC filter over aggression – beginning as early as the 1994 draft statute. The Obama

[107] Ibid., p. 26.

[108] Niels Blokker & Claus Kreß, 'A Consensus Agreement on the Crime of Aggression: Impressions from Kampala' (2010) 23 *Leiden Journal of International Law* 889, pp. 894–5.

[109] Marcel Biato, 'Statement by Ambassador Marcel Biato on Behalf of the Brazilian Delegation to the Review Conference', 31 May 2010, https://asp.icc-cpi.int/iccdocs/asp_docs/RC2010/Statements/ICC-RC-gendeba-Brazil-ENG.pdf.

[110] UN, *6849th Meeting (Resumption 1)*, p. 3.

administration reiterated the position from its very first re-engagement with the ASP in late 2009, arguing that 'jurisdiction should follow a Security Council determination that aggression has occurred'.[111] The outcome of the Kampala negotiations was ultimately a compromise creating two routes for an aggression prosecution. The first was through an exclusive UNSC trigger in the same terms as those governing the existing Rome Statute crimes.[112] The second route was through the ICC prosecutor's own motion, where the UNSC failed to take action within a six-month period, but still subject to the existing UNSC power to halt any ICC investigation under Article 16 of the Rome Statute.[113] The primary UNSC role over cases of aggression was almost entirely maintained, with only a marginal step taken in the direction of sovereign equality.

The compromise resolution does not support any further inference that participants reached an agreed position on legal principles for guiding the court's enlarged subject matter jurisdiction. Much of the distance between the United States and other states parties and observers is reflected in what became *Annex III* to the 2010 amendments, entitled *Understandings regarding the Amendments to the Rome Statute of the International Criminal Court on the Crime of Aggression* (the Understandings). During the Kampala Conference, Koh fixed upon a suggestion from the conference chair to address concerns about the proposed amendments through written 'understandings' that placed a gloss on the meaning of draft articles, without disturbing their language. Koh stated: '[W]e believe that without agreed-upon understandings, the current draft definition remains flawed' and that 'apparent consensus on the wording of Article 8*bis* masks sharp disagreement on particular points regarding the meaning of that language'.[114] US absence from a decade of prior negotiations effectively precluded any alteration of an aggression definition 'locked in stone',[115] with the understandings becoming a backdoor means for registering concerns. As a matter of strict legal interpretation, Heller rightly points out that the understandings comprise 'nothing more than supplementary means of interpretation that the Court would have the right to ignore

111 Rapp, 'Address to Assembly of States Parties'.

112 *Amendments to the Rome Statute of the International Criminal Court on the Crime of Aggression* 2010, Art. 15*ter*.

113 Ibid., Art. 15*bis*(8).

114 Harold H. Koh, 'Statement at the Review Conference of the International Criminal Court', 4 June 2010, https://2009-2017.state.gov/s/l/releases/remarks/142665.htm.

115 Rapp, Interview with Author.

once the aggression amendments entered into force'.[116] However, they are valuable as formulations of the divergence in legal views held by American policymakers about the ideal design of the ICC.

Exceptional Humanitarian Responsibilities

Substantive US demands in the Understandings focused on bolstering exclusive UNSC control and on limiting ICC jurisdiction where authority was to be shared. Understanding 2 stated that the ICC could exercise jurisdiction pursuant to a UNSC referral 'irrespective of whether the State concerned has accepted the Court's jurisdiction in this regard'. Heller notes that this understanding is unlikely to have 'any substantive effect', as it merely mirrors the 'default position under the Rome Statute'.[117] However, it does reveal the degree of concern that American policymakers had about any erosion of existing legal privilege.

The more significant assertion of legal principles was in understandings that sought to limit ICC jurisdiction by reference to exceptionalist beliefs, and thereby to reinforce UNSC privileges. A consistent theme when defending the status quo was the exceptional role of the United States in making the system of international criminal law effective. On several occasions, Koh and Rapp framed US opposition to the aggression definition by reference to a line in Obama's Nobel Lecture: there are 'times when nations – acting individually or in concert – will find the use of force not only necessary but morally justified'.[118] The United States argued that the definition, as it then stood, could be used to entrench the principle of non-intervention as an absolute prohibition. That would be the strongest expression of sovereign equality, but, in contrast, it would conflict with any legal conception privileging the liberal equality of natural persons. Koh proposed that the Article 8*bis* definition of aggression be accompanied by written understandings explicitly protecting 'those who undertake efforts to prevent war crimes, crimes against humanity or genocide – the very crimes that the Rome Statute is designed to deter'.[119]

[116] Kevin Jon Heller, 'The Uncertain Legal Status of the Aggression Understandings' (2012) 10 *Journal of International Criminal Justice* 229, p. 231. For a response see Harold H. Koh & Todd F. Buchwald, 'The Crime of Aggression: The United States Perspective' (2015) 109 *American Journal of International Law* 257, p. 273.

[117] Heller, 'The Uncertain Legal Status of the Aggression Understandings', pp. 231–2.

[118] Koh & Rapp, 'Briefing on the ICC Conference in Kampala'.

[119] Koh, 'Statement at the Review Conference of the ICC'.

The initial draft understanding was phrased to exempt any actions 'undertaken in connection with an effort to prevent the commission of any of the crimes contained in Articles 6, 7 or 8 of the Statute'.[120] That formulation was rejected by other states, who recognised that, in practice, this amounted to creating special legal rights exercisable primarily by the United States.[121] Understanding 6 ultimately read:

> It is understood that aggression is the most serious and dangerous form of the illegal use of force; and that a determination whether an act of aggression has been committed requires consideration of all the circumstances of each particular case, including the gravity of the acts concerned and their consequences, in accordance with the Charter of the United Nations.

The intent behind 'consequences' remained exemption of claimed 'unilateral humanitarian intervention' from ICC aggression jurisdiction, as exemplified by the United States–backed 1999 NATO intervention in Kosovo. Koh pointed out: 'Regardless of how states may view the legality of such efforts, those who plan them are not committing the "crime of aggression" and should not run the risk of prosecution.'[122] Responding to a question about the meaning of the 'international rule of law', Rapp responded in part that 'where atrocities are being committed and UNSC approval is not possible, it is possible to proceed with a legitimate action to protect civilians ... The Kosovo precedent may be said to have established a new custom, applicable in truly exceptional cases.'[123] Legalistic negotiations over the scope of the aggression definition never disconnected from consciousness of the history of American global engagement and a specific understanding of how IL facilitated that role.[124]

By the end of the Kampala Conference, Koh considered that the 'final resolution took insufficient account of the Security Council's assigned role to define aggression', but that the definition had been narrowed through US efforts. He defended the privileged UNSC role sustained by

120 Articles setting out substantive crimes in the *Rome Statute*.

121 Claus Kreß, Stefan Barriga, Leena Grover & Leonie von Holtzendorff, 'Negotiating the Understandings on the Crime of Aggression', in Stefan Barriga & Claus Kreß (eds.), *The Travaux Préparatoires of the Crime of Aggression* (Cambridge University Press, 2012), p. 95.

122 Koh, 'Statement at the Review Conference of the ICC'.

123 Rapp, Interview with Author.

124 Michael J. Glennon, 'The Blank-Prose Crime of Aggression' (2010) 35 *Yale Journal of International Law* 71, p. 111.

the resolution by articulating the exceptionalist premise underpinning US policy:

> The big picture going forward ... is that as the country of Nuremberg prosecutor Justice Jackson, we are the only country that has successfully prosecuted the crime of aggression at Nuremberg and Tokyo. *Of course, we do not commit aggression* and the chances are extremely remote that a prosecution on this crime will, at some point in the distant future, affect us negatively.[125]

It is here that Koh most explicitly emphasised the substantive beliefs reconciling US legal privilege with a stated commitment to the international rule of law. UNSC privileges presupposed beliefs in both the United States' capacity to uphold liberal norms without the oversight of sovereign equals and its unique global role in advancing compliance with international criminal law.

Conclusion

Negotiations over the crime of aggression were in many ways the climax of tensions about UNSC privileges that had been simmering since the earliest days of the ICC project. Attempts to grant the court power over the crime of aggression became a tangible method for transferring the system of international criminal law onto a foundation aligned with the principle of sovereign equality. That initiative was strongly opposed by all P5 members consistent with rational state incentives to maintain legal privileges. Ferencz suggests that US resistance in Kampala, 'like its non-membership in the Court itself, may perhaps be based on perceived geo-political, rather than merely humanitarian, interest and objectives'.[126] This fairly describes political outcomes, but at the level of legal decision-making, the beliefs guiding US legal policymakers remained those drawn from the dominant legal ideologies influencing the Obama administration.

US arguments for protecting the status quo drew strongly upon the principle of liberal equality and the exceptional role of the United States as facilitated by its UNSC privileges. Scheffer sought to frame the outcome in a conciliatory light, arguing that, although the 'result is a slap at the equality of states, or at least the theory of equality', it remained the case that 'most major shifts in the international system begin that

[125] Koh & Rapp, 'U.S. Engagement with the ICC', emphasis added.
[126] Ferencz, 'Current US Policy on the Crime of Aggression', p. 211.

way'.[127] However, there is no evidence that the outcome at Kampala signalled even the embryo of converging beliefs about the proper legal relationship between sovereign states. In deGuzman's terms, the United States continued to perceive of itself as 'a supranational justice "donor" rather than as a leading member of the global justice community'.[128] Professor Jane Stromseth, deputy to the Ambassador-at-Large in the Office of Global Criminal Justice during this period and later acting head of the office, defended the US policy approach for supporting the ICC's 'work in catalyzing meaningful accountability at the national level – the primary and most important foundation for justice and the rule of law'.[129] In what might otherwise appear as a contradiction, American policymakers consistently rejected the principle of sovereign equality not as mere political expediency but as fidelity to primarily liberal internationalist legal conceptions.

Determining International Judicial Power

The final area of legal policy disagreement concerned the determination of international judicial powers in the fully operational court. The dominant approach of international advocates was to cast the ICC as ultimate guarantor of international judicial power, through independence from competing legal powers exercised by states. Many argued against the legitimacy of states parties and non-parties alike exempting themselves from ICC aggression jurisdiction. Just as sovereign equality provided a basis for opposing the creation of differential rights under UNSC referrals, so too did charges that special immunities breached the separation of international legal powers. Any design granting the United States sole authority to adjudicate ICC crimes committed by its own nationals improperly intermingled international judicial power with parallel domestic executive and legislative powers. For their part, US policymakers defended mechanisms for constraining the independence of the court, including preserving US courts' exclusive jurisdiction over US nationals, particularly in relation to the crime of aggression. The

[127] David J. Scheffer, 'The Complex Crime of Aggression under the Rome Statute' (2010) 23 *Leiden Journal of International Law* 897, p. 904.

[128] Margaret M. deGuzman, 'Inter-National Justice for Them or Global Justice for Us?: The US As a Supranational Justice Donor' (2016) 48 *Case Western Reserve Journal of International Law* 177, pp. 179 & 182.

[129] Jane Stromseth, 'Why Bolton's Assault on the ICC Is Not in U.S. Interests', *Just Security*, 14 September 2018, www.justsecurity.org/60743/boltons-assault-icc-u-s-interests/.

United States also remained largely isolated in continuing to advocate hybrid and locally constituted courts exercising international judicial power separately from the ICC. Yet, even as the legalist demand for independent judicial power was denied, US policymakers defended each of these measures as consistent with, and indeed necessary to, upholding the international rule of law.

Legalist Policy

The particular contention motivating states to resist a growing UNSC role in ICC operations was the 'double standards' in referrals granting immunities to non-states parties. These were a feature of the original Darfur referral in 2005, in order to secure US abstention, but were repeated in almost identical terms in the 2011 Libyan referral voted for by the United States.[130] This fuelled a 'growing disquiet about how power politics and international justice were mixing'.[131] In relation to both referrals, Brazil challenged distinctive US rights in order to 'promote respect for international law'. Voting for the Libyan referral, the Brazilian representative reiterated 'strong reservation' towards exempting jurisdiction over non-party states,[132] which remained inconsistent with visions of the impartial judicial power unique to an international court.[133] In the Kampala Conference general debate, Brazil further reminded delegates of the need to make legal obligations universal and that, like 'a la carte multilateralism, cherry-picking when it comes to rules is ultimately self-defeating'.[134] These principles were reiterated at the UNSC rule of law meeting, where Liechtenstein urged the UNSC to cease the practice of creating differentiated rights of immunity since they 'corroborate[d] the suspicion of selectivity in creating accountability' and were thereby 'contrary to international law'.[135] Bangladesh concluded that these exemptions were 'undermining the rule of law by infringing on the work of the ICC and ... undermining the perception of the Court as an independent legal body free of political considerations'.[136] The exclusion of entire national populations from ICC jurisdiction necessarily

[130] SC Res 1970, UN Doc S/RES/1970 (26 February 2011).
[131] Bosco, *Rough Justice*, p. 171.
[132] SC Res 1970, operative clause 6.
[133] UN, *Official Records of the Security Council*, UN Doc S/PV.6491 (26 February 2011), p. 7.
[134] Biato, 'Statement by Ambassador Marcel Biato'.
[135] UN, *6849th Meeting (Resumption 1)*, p. 3.
[136] Ibid., p. 9.

condoned the associated non-states parties to the Rome Statute exercising international judicial power parallel to, and free from, ICC oversight.

Representatives at the UNSC rule of law meeting identified a key distinction between the independent 'judicial' powers of the ICC, on the one hand, and the 'political' powers of the UNSC, on the other. The principle of separating international powers was breached wherever the UNSC exercised its powers in a way that altered the ICC's prosecutorial and judicial independence.[137] The Secretary General emphasised that the ICC was 'a judicial body, independent and impartial. Once set in motion, justice takes its own inexorable course, unswayed by politics. That is its strength, its distinctive virtue.'[138] Then ICC President Judge Sang-Hyun Song concurred on the need to separate legal powers in the ICC:

> There is an independent Prosecutor, an independent defence and an independent judiciary. The Prosecutor decides which cases to pursue, but it is the judges who have the final say on whether to issue an arrest warrant or summons to appear, or whether there is sufficient evidence for charges to proceed to a trial.[139]

Japan cautioned that the integrity of judicial power must be determined through its separation from UNSC referral powers, which were 'not for purely legal reasons'.[140] Similarly, India emphasised the 'need to strengthen the rule of law at the international level by avoiding selectivity, partiality and double standards' and freeing the ICC from 'the clutches of political considerations'.[141] At the most basic level, these states argued for 'the complete separation of the ICC's judicial process from the functions and decisions of the Security Council'.[142]

Delegations were equally opposed to setting a higher threshold for ICC jurisdiction than that required for a UNSC finding – such as requiring a 'flagrant' or 'manifest' violation.[143] The effect would be to prioritise the UNSC exercise of judicial and non-judicial powers over the ICC. The importance of the legalist ordering principle was significant enough for

137 See, for example, UN, *6849th Meeting*, p. 6 per Phakiso Mochochoko, Head of the Jurisdiction, Complementarity and Cooperation Division of the ICC (Office of the Prosecutor).

138 Ibid., p. 2.

139 Ibid., p. 4.

140 UN, *6849th Meeting (Resumption 1)*, p. 7.

141 UN, *6849th Meeting*, p. 11.

142 Weed, *ICC and the Rome Statute*, p. 11.

143 Stefan Barriga, 'Negotiating the Amendments on the Crime of Aggression', in Stefan Barriga & Claus Kreß (eds.), *The Travaux Préparatoires of the Crime of Aggression* (Cambridge University Press, 2012), p. 29.

the Togolese representative to state that 'in the name of the principle of the separation of powers, the International Criminal Court should, in principle, not have relations with the Security Council'. Granting any UNSC control over the ICC, through Articles 13(b) and 16 of the Rome Statute, was 'comparable to a regime's executive and political bodies applying laws to citizens while exempting themselves from those same laws'.[144]

Beliefs of American Legal Policymakers

Continued Role of Ad Hoc and Hybrid Tribunals

From the very first attendance at the ASP in 2009, the United States opposed any determination of international judicial powers through supranational ICC authority.[145] The 'greatest importance' was attached not to a globalised court upholding criminal justice but to 'assisting countries where the rule of law has been shattered to stand up for their own system of protection and accountability'.[146] The NSS 2010 reaffirmed that the Obama administration was foremost 'working to strengthen national justice systems and is maintaining our support for ad hoc international tribunals and hybrid courts'.[147] Only secondarily would the administration turn to 'supporting the ICC's prosecution' in a backstopping capacity.

That stance was maintained through the UNSC rule of law meeting, where US policy was distinguished by its primary emphasis on addressing international criminal justice through national justice systems and 'hybrid structures where appropriate'.[148] Even in relation to prosecuting ongoing atrocities in Syria, the United States carefully made clear that it was not 'prejudging the ultimate venue for it'.[149] Rather than seeing an independent ICC as an ideal for international criminal justice, US policymakers instead saw it embedding forms of politics into the law, and ones likely to be foreign to victims of atrocities. The operative principle for

[144] UN, *6849th Meeting*, p. 21.

[145] See Megan Fairlie, 'The United States and the International Criminal Court Post-Bush: A Beautiful Courtship but an Unlikely Marriage' (2011) 29 *Berkeley Journal of International Law* 529, pp. 529–30.

[146] Rapp, 'Address to Assembly of States Parties'.

[147] The White House, *NSS 2010*, p. 48.

[148] UN, *6849th Meeting*, p. 8.

[149] Ibid., p. 9.

determining the integrity of international judicial power remained their grounding in effective democratic checks and balances.

Dividing *In Personam* ICC Jurisdiction

US support for the court reached new levels of engagement in relation to the 2011 Libyan Civil War when, for the first time, it voted through the UNSC to refer a situation for ICC investigation.[150] Yet the resolution equally sought to divide the judicial power presumptively reserved to the court. Consistent with a rejection of formal legal obligations, the resolution was written 'recognizing that States not party to the Rome Statute have no obligation under the Statute' while still urging 'all States and concerned regional and other international organizations to cooperate fully with the Court and the Prosecutor'.[151] More particularly, the United States denied the institutional separation of international judicial power by preserving the capacity of the US legal system to exercise these powers parallel to the ICC. Substantive clause 6 of the UNSC resolution decided

> that nationals, current or former officials or personnel from a State outside the Libyan Arab Jamahiriya which is not a party to the Rome Statute of the International Criminal Court shall be subject to the exclusive jurisdiction of that State for all alleged acts or omissions arising out of or related to operations in the Libyan Arab Jamahiriya established or authorized by the Council, unless such exclusive jurisdiction has been expressly waived by the State.[152]

This replicated limitations in the Darfur referral, which upheld institutional principles other than a separation of international judicial powers. There was no suggestion that the United States was carving out the right for its military personnel to act with impunity, contrary to accusations by some states parties. Rather, the objective was always defended in terms of preserving the jurisdiction of domestic courts and military tribunals to try defendants in such matters.

In response to a question on whether there was any conceivable situation where international judges would be better placed to deal with American nationals, Ambassador Rapp reiterated that it was the United States' 'constitutional system that establishes who can be judges and generally these positions are restricted to American citizens'. The clear implication was that there was a hard limit to accepting international judicial

150 SC Res 1970.
151 Ibid., operative clause 5.
152 Ibid., operative clause 6.

power as a continuation of municipal powers. The essence of a liberal nationalist vertical separation of powers is that these remain distinct and not interchangeable in relation to the same subject matter. At the same time, Rapp gave an assurance that the administration would 'conduct ourselves in terms of our adherence to international law in such a way that we will never give cause to any legitimately motivated prosecutor to bring a case or to seek admission of a case against an American citizen in an international court'.[153] This argument from liberal internationalism is distinct from the first, in seeking to check international judicial powers through the integrity of the American system, as compared to the absolute separation of that system from international powers. By tracing ideological influences, it is clear that the administration thus charted a course rejecting the illiberal principles that shaped the Bush 43 ICC policy, of supremacy of municipal legal power and a bare right to withhold consent, yet also legalism's supremacy of international judicial power in the ICC.

The Indivisibility of Legalism and the Crime of Aggression

Although the United States maintained a constructive dialogue defining and implementing the crime of aggression, it became clear that its very inclusion in the Rome Statute ran counter to any conception of legal power held by American policymakers. Across a series of statements, Koh and Rapp emphasised that, even apart from actual politicisation of aggression prosecutions, it would be impossible to avoid the apprehension of such bias. Koh warned that any such ICC prosecution 'by its very nature, even if perfectly defined, would inevitably be seen as political'.[154] Moreover, however judicial power was determined, inevitably, '*someone* must make these political judgements'.[155] Rapp explained that aggression would take the ICC 'into the political area' dealing with 'crimes not against individual civilians, as in war crimes or crimes against humanity or genocide, but crimes against states'.[156] These were not merely criticisms about the design of the ICC but a challenge to the very principle of instituting judicial powers at the global level lacking democratic foundations. US scepticism translated into a policy of maintaining direct and indirect barriers to realising the crime in any meaningful form.[157]

153 Rapp, 'Press Briefing with Stephen J. Rapp'.
154 Koh, 'Statement Regarding Crime of Aggression'.
155 Koh & Buchwald, 'The Crime of Aggression', p. 266, original emphasis.
156 Koh & Rapp, 'U.S. Engagement with the ICC'.
157 US opposition was further expressed in Understanding 4, which sought to decouple the treaty crime from customary international law developments: see Kreß, Barriga, Grover

US policymakers raised an especial concern that inadequate consideration had been given to how complementarity could work in the case of aggression. The nature of the crime was such that political leaders would rarely be prosecuted by their own states, and thus it may fall to other states to do so.[158] US policymakers warned that this scenario would contravene basic principles of sovereign immunity by allowing 'the domestic courts of one country to sit in judgment upon the state acts of other countries in a manner highly unlikely to promote peace and security'.[159] Scenarios were envisioned of states circumventing sovereign immunity by claiming that complementarity empowered them to act as agents exercising the independent judicial powers of the ICC.[160] Since official state involvement is an element of the crime itself, there was a real risk of adversaries exploiting the crime to engage in 'lawfare'.[161] Understanding 5 was thus instituted to directly combat expansive applications of complementarity:

> It is understood that the amendments shall not be interpreted as creating the right or obligation to exercise domestic jurisdiction with respect to an act of aggression committed by another State.

The Understanding contravened legalist principles by effectively denying any exercise of universal jurisdiction by states parties.[162] Koh responded, however, that any power to prosecute aggression at the municipal level 'derives from national jurisdiction' and not from notionally impartial ICC power. The general rule that a state must consent to another state exercising jurisdiction over its leaders must hold for domestic aggression prosecutions.[163]

The eventual outcome of the Kampala negotiations was a compromise between states who opposed a UNSC monopoly on aggression cases and US insistence that it check ICC jurisdiction. The UNSC's monopoly was loosened by allowing the prosecutor to proceed where the UNSC had declined or failed to act. This minor concession came, however, at the

& Von Holtzendorff, 'Negotiating the Understandings on the Crime of Aggression', p. 93.

158 Fairlie, 'The US and the ICC Post-Bush', pp. 553–4.

159 Koh, 'Statement at the Review Conference of the ICC'.

160 Kreß, Barriga, Grover & von Holtzendorff, 'Negotiating the Understandings on the Crime of Aggression', pp. 93–4.

161 Beth van Schaack, 'Par in Parem Imperium Non Habet Complementarity and the Crime of Aggression' (2012) 10 *Journal of International Criminal Justice* 133, p. 150.

162 Weed, *ICC and the Rome Statute*, p. 13.

163 Koh, 'Statement Regarding Crime of Aggression'.

cost of granting the US immunity from all aggression prosecutions for so long as it remained a non-state party, and even as a state party through an opt out provision.[164] The agreement transformed ad hoc immunities of non-state parties set out in prior UNSC referrals and enshrined them in the Rome Statute itself. US policymakers had ensured 'total protection for our Armed Forces and other U.S. nationals going forward'.[165] The arrangement was adopted by consensus in the final resolution of the Kampala Conference.

Far from being evidence of a common understanding on the proper legal principles for determining ICC judicial powers, the outcome represented a highly contentious political trade-off. Paulus foresaw the risk of 'politicization' if the United States and other UNSC members were granted the power to control ICC judicial independence, but ultimately accepted that legal principle must give way to political expediency. The ideal of 'complete freedom' needed to be weighed against the risk that it would endanger the 'vital support of the P5 for ICC investigations in the first place, and further alienate the United States, in particular'.[166] States that had opposed US negotiators throughout the Kampala Conference viewed the agreement as an instrumental concession to political power. Minutes before the final resolution was adopted, Japan intervened to declare as its 'sad duty' that compromises within represented 'the undermining of the credibility of the Rome Statute and the whole system it represents'.[167] Throughout the conference, Japan had highlighted its 'strong belief that the activities of the ICC [contribute] . . . to the establishment of the rule of law in the international community'.[168] Faced with the final resolution, Japan condemned the exclusion of non-states parties and territories from ICC aggression jurisdiction under Article 15*bis*(5). Such a concession 'unjustifiably solidifies blanket and automatic impunity of nationals of non-States Parties: a clear departure from the basic tenet of article 12 of the Statute'. The method by which this was incorporated amounted to 'suicide of legal integrity'. With 'a heavy heart', Japan

164 See *Amendments to the Rome Statute of the International Criminal Court on the Crime of Aggression*, Art. 15*bis*(5).

165 Koh & Rapp, 'U.S. Engagement with the ICC'.

166 Andreas L. Paulus, 'Second Thoughts on the Crime of Aggression' (2009) 20 *European Journal of International Law* 1117, pp. 1125–6.

167 Cited in Stefan Barriga & Claus Kreß (eds.), *The Travaux Préparatoires of the Crime of Aggression* (Cambridge University Press, 2012), p. 810.

168 Ichiro Komatsu, 'Statement of the Government of Japan at the Review Conference of the Rome Statute of the International Criminal Court', 31 May 2010, https://asp.icc-cpi.int/iccdocs/asp_docs/RC2010/Statements/ICC-RC-gendeba-Japan-ENG.pdf.

allowed the adoption by consensus, but warned that its future cooperation depended on these concerns being addressed.[169]

Conclusion

Whereas states parties argued for separation of international judicial power into a court with supreme authority, policymakers in the Obama administration continued to argue for the merits of ad hoc and hybrid tribunals exercising those same international powers. The legalist view was necessarily anchored in the 'cosmopolitan claim of the global justice community'[170] – a set of values often convergent, yet distinct from the claims of US democratic values. Whereas states parties argued that the ICC should sit above all countries as a check over international criminal acts, US policymakers carved out exclusive rights to adjudicate those matters in relation to their own nationals. The success of the US claim for effective immunity from the crime of aggression came only at the expense of key states accepting a court design they considered to be contrary to the international rule of law.

Ultimately, the parties at the Kampala Conference could reach agreement only by deferring implementation of the crime of aggression until a further 'decision to be taken after 1 January 2017'.[171] This was a success for the US tactic of obstructing recognition of the crime in the ICC's ordinary jurisdiction. Under Obama, the United States continued to increase non-binding support for the ICC, even as it challenged the desirability or feasibility of establishing independent judicial power at the apex of the system of international criminal justice. Where 'concerns regarding the potential for politicized prosecutions are at the core of U.S. opposition', that opposition became crystallised in liberal legal principles constituting the very meaning of the rule of law for those who held them.[172]

169 Cited in Barriga & Kreß (eds.), *The Travaux Préparatoires of the Crime of Aggression*, pp. 810–12. Curiously, Koh cites these statements in support of his arguments *for* US political discretion as a check on ICC jurisdiction: Koh & Buchwald, 'The Crime of Aggression', p. 290.

170 deGuzman, 'Inter-National Justice for Them or Global Justice for Us?', p. 184.

171 *Amendments to the Rome Statute of the International Criminal Court on the Crime of Aggression*, Arts. 15*bis*(3) & 15*ter*(3).

172 Fairlie, 'The US and the ICC Post-Bush', pp. 559–60.

Chapter Conclusion

Bosco notes, perhaps cynically, that, during the Obama administration, 'US officials were becoming adept at framing efforts to guide the court as expressions of concern for its well-being'.[173] That appraisal echoes the hypothesis of US legal policymakers consciously disregarding commitment to law in favour of political interests. The evidence from this period points to a more nuanced interpretation, in which political interests were channelled through ideologically entrenched conceptions of law itself. In what reads as a veiled criticism of the legalist position, Koh intervened in the Kampala Conference to remind delegates that the ultimate objective remained 'making international criminal law for the real world'. That goal was threatened by any 'unworkable and divisive compromise that weakens the Court, diverts it from its core human rights mission, or undermines our multilateral system of peace and security'.[174] These were all charges laid by American policymakers against states and organisations insisting that the necessary elements of an ICC compliant with the international rule of law remained formalised development of global governance, sovereign equality between states and the separation of international judicial powers. Instead, across this period, US policymakers emphasised the processes of transnational development as more significant than the formal obligations of a signed treaty. The perception of an exceptional US role in upholding liberal values was maintained as a reason for opposing the equal application of legal rights. Finally, scepticism about the integrity of independent judicial power was held out as a reason for maintaining immunities from ICC jurisdiction.

Toward the end of the Obama administration, the 2015 *National Security Strategy* (NSS 2015) was released, which mentioned the ICC only once, and in terms that consolidated the preference for transnational and pragmatic development of the court. The strategy committed support to the ICC – subject to a proviso that it was 'consistent with U.S. law and our commitment to protecting our personnel'.[175] That commitment to flexible obligations under the ICC was couched within, and given meaning by, broader exceptionalist beliefs:

[173] Bosco, *Rough Justice*, p. 165.
[174] Koh, 'Statement at the Review Conference of the ICC'.
[175] The White House, *The National Security Strategy of the United States of America 2015* (2015), p. 22.

> Strong and sustained American leadership is essential to a rules-based international order that promotes global security and prosperity as well as the dignity and human rights of all peoples. The question is never whether America should lead, but how we lead.[176]

In all these ways, the Obama administration continued to receive the hegemonic impulses of US power through the lens of distinctively American conceptions of the international rule of law.

[176] Ibid., p. i.

Conclusion

Between Power and Transcendent Values

United States! the ages plead,—
Present and Past in under-song,—
Go put your creed into your deed,—
Nor speak with double tongue.

—RALPH WALDO EMERSON, 1857

Ideological Limits of the International Criminal Court

In 1964, Judith Shklar identified a motive behind the Nuremberg trials as 'a desire to do something for the future of the rule of law in international relations'.[1] Yet the extraordinary circumstances in the aftermath of WWII suggested to Shklar that the Nuremberg achievements were unlikely to be replicated in a standing international criminal court: '[N]othing effective along these lines is even imaginable at present.' To expect otherwise 'was unreasonable, an extravagance of the legalistic imagination'.[2] The twentieth anniversary of the adoption of the Rome Statute in 2018, for a court tracing its lineage to Nuremberg, seemed to vindicate the possibility of real progress toward the international rule of law.

Evidence from a quarter-century of American ICC policy does suggest that progress is possible in terms of strengthening the institutional architecture of international criminal justice. Moreover, the United States has demonstrated a practical capacity to work with other states to fight impunity and advance accountability for perpetrators of 'atrocity crimes'.[3] However, this book has found no emerging 'new transatlantic consensus on the role and scope of the international legal system',[4] or evidence of progress toward

[1] Judith N. Shklar, *Legalism* (Harvard University Press, 1964), p. 176.
[2] Ibid., p. 177.
[3] The term is Scheffer's in reference to the slate of ICC crimes: David J. Scheffer, *All the Missing Souls: A Personal History of the War Crimes Tribunals* (Princeton University Press, 2012), p. 2.
[4] William H. Taft IV & Frances G. Burwell, *Law and the Lone Superpower: Rebuilding a Transatlantic Consensus on International Law* (Policy Paper, The Atlantic Council of the United States, April 2007), p.15.

a universal conception of the 'international rule of law'. Rather, the court, as realised, uncomfortably straddles the interstices and political compromises between competing and often incompatible ideologies. Legalism and the four American ideological types each crystallise interests and beliefs in internally coherent but mutually conflicting concepts of IL. Fletcher and Ohlin reviewed the trajectory of US ICC policy to conclude:

> The more the ICC becomes like a real criminal court, operating under the rule of law, the more American politicians are likely to shelve their fears of politicized prosecution and support the ICC as an important instrument of international peace and harmony.[5]

The clear lesson from US engagement with the ICC, however, is that barriers to progress have not been a product of the special history of the court, or the idiosyncrasies of presidencies and legal policymakers, but are fundamental to the nature of the international rule of law.

The importance of interpreting American ICC policy through foreign policy ideology becomes clear in Jürgen Habermas's 2004 interpretation of US policy contradictions. Habermas agreed, consistent with this book, that Kagan's characterisation of a transatlantic divide was too crude for legal analysis.[6] For Habermas, the greatest conflicts over the conception of IL 'occurred, not between the continents, but, rather, within American policy itself':

> Kagan is suggesting a false continuity. The newly-elected Bush administration's definitive repudiation of internationalism has remained its keynote: The rejection of the (since established) International Criminal Court was no trivial delict. One must not imagine that the offensive marginalizing of the United Nations and the cavalier contempt for international law which this administration has allowed itself to be guilty of, represent the expression of some necessary constant of American foreign policy.[7]

However, Habermas departed from the insights of this book in citing policymakers such as Woodrow Wilson and Franklin D. Roosevelt as examples of a countervailing commitment to legalism in American diplomatic history. For him, the question at the end of the Cold War was whether 'the one remaining superpower would turn away from its

[5] George P. Fletcher & Jens David Ohlin, 'Reclaiming Fundamental Principles of Criminal Law in the Darfur Case' (2005) 3 *Journal of International Criminal Justice* 539, p. 561.

[6] Referring to Robert Kagan, *Of Paradise and Power* (Vintage Books, 2004). See Chapter 1, pp. 32–3, *supra*.

[7] Jürgen Habermas, 'America and the World: A Conversation with Jürgen Habermas', *Logos*, 2004, www.logosjournal.com/habermas_america.htm.

leading role in the march toward a cosmopolitan legal order, and fall back into the imperial role of a good hegemon above international law'. ICC history provides scant evidence that American policymakers were ever committed to an international rule of law founded on cosmopolitan values. As in Max Weber's analogy, policy switched between the finite number of tracks provided by American ideologies, each of which contests global legal power.

Continuity and Change in the Trump Administration

The question of ICC progress loomed large in April 2018 when, following a nearly twelve-year interlude since the first term of the Bush 43 administration, John Bolton became National Security Adviser to President Trump and thereby, during a short but eventful tenure, once again the central figure in US ICC policy. Whereas the Trump administration had barely engaged with the issue,[8] Bolton had maintained resistance throughout the intervening years, writing that the court 'constitutes a direct assault on the concept of national sovereignty, especially that of constitutional, representative governments like the United States'.[9] In his first speech for the administration, Bolton confirmed a return to the United States actively opposing the very principle of the ICC – a court pronounced 'already dead to us'. Elements of an illiberal nationalist rule of law were reprised, including the supremacy of US judicial power: 'We believe in the rule of law, and we uphold it. We don't need the ICC to tell us our duty, or second-guess our decisions.'[10] Pragmatic cooperation with the court was rejected in favour of measures up to and including denying visas to ICC judges and prosecutors seeking entry to the United States, and threatening penalties against them ranging from financial sanctions to criminal prosecutions. Institutionalised governance through IL was once again confirmed as an existential threat to US values and interests. Within

[8] Other than naming the court among a list of multilateral institutions set for 40 per cent or more reductions, despite the United States paying nothing toward the ICC: Max Fisher, 'Trump Prepares Orders Aiming at Global Funding and Treaties', *The New York Times*, 25 January 2017, www.nytimes.com/2017/01/25/us/politics/united-nations-trump-administration.html.

[9] John R. Bolton, 'The Hague Aims for U.S. Soldiers', *The Wall Street Journal*, 20 November 2017, www.wsj.com/articles/the-hague-tiptoes-toward-u-s-soldiers-1511217136.

[10] John R. Bolton, 'Protecting American Constitutionalism and Sovereignty from International Threats', The Federalist Society, Washington, DC, 10 September 2018, www.lawfareblog.com/national-security-adviser-john-bolton-remarks-federalist-society.

that same month, President Trump delivered a speech to the UNGA declaring that the ICC violated 'all principles of justice, fairness, and due process. We will never surrender America's sovereignty to an unelected, unaccountable, global bureaucracy.' Directly invoking the structured ideological contest between internationalist and nationalist governance, the president concluded that, in contrast to the ICC, 'America is governed by Americans. We reject the ideology of globalism, and we embrace the doctrine of patriotism.'[11]

Anxious reactions of US global counterparts have conveyed the sense of something unprecedented taking place in American foreign and IL policy. Jutta Brunnée concluded that 'compared to its predecessors, the Trump Administration's approach to international law is of another order altogether'. Specifically, the United States appears to challenge 'not only the content of specific legal norms and regimes, but the very foundations of an international rule of law'.[12] Yet, setting aside the haze of sometimes chaotic political outcomes,[13] the sets of beliefs underpinning the Trump administration's policy preferences confirm substantial continuity in the ideological structure of US IL policy, with ideas of 'populism' being pitted against those of 'globalism' and 'elitism'. The 'populist' label has become influential among opponents of President Trump, by which they identify a worldview encompassing ideas including 'nationalistic isolationism' and rejection of international cooperation.[14] In this view: 'Angry populist forces have to a large extent altered the U.S. political landscape ... In particular, existing liberal internationalist grand strategy is likely to be revised and gestured toward "neo-isolationism."'[15]

Supporters of Trump's position respond that it is elite 'globalists' who threaten US foreign policy interests, by subverting American national

[11] Donald J. Trump, 'Remarks by President Trump to the 73rd Session of the United Nations General Assembly, New York, NY', 25 September 2018, www.whitehouse.gov/briefings-statements/remarks-president-trump-73rd-session-united-nations-general-assembly-new-york-ny/.

[12] Jutta Brunnée, 'Keynote Speech Part III: Challenging International Law: What's New?', *Opinio Juris*, 19 November 2018, http://opiniojuris.org/2018/11/19/keynote-speech-part-iii-challenging-international-law-whats-new/.

[13] See Bob Woodward, *Fear: Trump in the White House* (Simon & Schuster, 2018).

[14] Ronald Inglehart & Pippa Norris, 'Trump, Brexit, and the Rise of Populism: Economic Have-Nots and Cultural Backlash' (August 2016) 26 *HKS Faculty Research Working Paper Series*, p. 7.

[15] Taesuh Cha, 'The Return of Jacksonianism: The International Implications of the Trump Phenomenon' (2016) 39 *The Washington Quarterly* 83, p. 84.

sovereignty to an alleged global common good.[16] For Mitchell, 'Republicans who think that globalism has not only been a disaster for the whole of . . . America but also that it is theoretically untenable will – or should – call what has happened a revolt in the name of national sovereignty, not populism'.[17] Relevantly to this book, the president is commonly characterised as an adherent of Mead's 'Jacksonian' tradition, with Trump himself seeking to associate himself with the anti-elitist populism of President Andrew Jackson.[18] The Jacksonian appellation matters substantively for IL policy precisely because international legal institutions and their proponents constitute core elements of the supposed elite targeted by the administration. Trump himself has distinguished between 'corrupt, power-hungry globalists' as a group that 'wants the globe to do well, frankly not caring about our country so much', and his own beliefs: 'I'm a nationalist.'[19] Moreover, a cross-cutting adherence to illiberal values is equally evident in Trump's articulation of commitment to a 'rule of law' and 'liberty' defined by particularistic American values. Rather than looking to universalism, American IL policy is instead informed by a 'culture built on strong families, deep faith, and fierce independence. We celebrate our heroes, we treasure our traditions, and above all, we love our country.'[20] The administration thus invokes the substantive ideological beliefs of illiberal nationalism that continue to underpin contestation between nationalist 'populism' and elitist 'globalism'.

The story of the Trump IL policy is thereby one of continuity in ideological structure – notwithstanding prominent disruptions being brought to global order. What may be new is not the type of underlying beliefs but the degree of dominance of illiberal nationalism. Although nationalist impulses have always formed a key pillar of US IL policy,

[16] On controversy surrounding the term's historical origins see Ben Zimmer, 'The Origins of the "Globalist" Slur', *The Atlantic*, 14 March 2018, www.theatlantic.com/politics/archive/2018/03/the-origins-of-the-globalist-slur/555479/.

[17] Joshua Mitchell, 'A Renewed Republican Party' (2017) 1 *American Affairs* 7.

[18] See Walter R. Mead, 'The Jacksonian Revolt: American Populism and the Liberal Order' (2017) 96 *Foreign Affairs* 2; Matteo Dian, 'Conclusions: US Foreign Policy under Trump, Years of Upheaval', in Marco Clementi, Matteo Dian & Barbara Pisciotta (eds.), *US Foreign Policy in a Challenging World* (Springer International Publishing, 2018), pp. 395–7.

[19] Aaron Blake, 'Trump's embrace of a fraught term – "nationalist" – could cement a dangerous racial divide', *The Washington Post*, 23 October 2018, www.washingtonpost.com/politics/2018/10/23/trumps-embrace-fraught-term-nationalist-could-cement-dangerous-racial-divide/.

[20] Trump, 'Remarks by President Trump to the 73rd Session of the UNGA'.

competing foreign policy ideologies have historically tipped toward internationalism. Even in this case, IL policy continues to be partially tempered by internationalist voices. Although the president has personally advocated torture of suspected terrorists and the killing of their families,[21] he conceded, following criticism from military experts, that the United States is 'bound by laws and treaties and I will not order our military or other officials to violate those laws'.[22] Nevertheless, the alignment of nationalist and illiberal impulses has fostered the most robust expression of illiberal nationalist legal policy in the modern era. Despite their ultimately irreconcilable differences, Bolton and Trump 'shared a deep skepticism of globalism and multilateralism' that drove withdrawal from a series of significant international legal instruments during Bolton's tenure.[23] Thus, although every element defining the Trump IL policy has its roots in established traditions of thought, the particular configuration of beliefs has never before been elevated so fully and unconstrained into the realm of legal policymaking. Stated differently, however: policy has not deviated from the structure of America's historical conceptions of the rule of law and, formally at least, does not seek to eliminate IL itself from global politics.[24]

That the Trump ICC policy confirms established patterns is not a reassurance that challenges to the court have a predictable outcome. Apart from the decline of counterbalancing beliefs, circumstances have changed since the mid-2000s, especially as regards more precarious global enthusiasm for an ICC that shows signs of institutional dysfunction combined with a disappointing track record of prosecuting core crimes.[25] Thus, for global advocates, the 'new rhetorical framing and

[21] Donald J. Trump, 'The Fox News GOP Debate Transcript, Annotated', *The Washington Post*, 3 March 2016, www.washingtonpost.com/news/the-fix/wp/2016/03/03/the-fox-news-gop-debate-transcript-annotated/.

[22] Damian Paletta & Nick Timiraos, 'Trump Reverses His Stance on Torture', *The Wall Street Journal*, 4 March 2016, www.wsj.com/articles/trump-reverses-his-stance-on-torture-1457116559.

[23] Peter Baker, 'Trump Ousts John Bolton as National Security Adviser', *The New York Times*, 10 September 2019, https://www.nytimes.com/2019/09/10/us/politics/john-bolton-national-security-adviser-trump.html.

[24] Jack Goldsmith & Shannon T. Mercer, 'International Law and Institutions in the Trump Era' (2018) 61 *German Yearbook of International Law* 12, p. 31.

[25] See the statement of four former presidents of the ICC's Assembly of States Parties: Prince Zeid Raad Al Hussein et al., 'The International Criminal Court Needs Fixing', *New Atlanticist*, 24 April 2019, www.atlanticcouncil.org/blogs/new-atlanticist/the-international-criminal-court-needs-fixing.

policy positions genuinely risk serious damage to the ICC and the rule of law around the world, and these steps will be difficult, if not impossible, to undo'.[26] Given that the beliefs of the Trump administration are themselves nothing new, Bosco sees the main achievement as 'pushing the ICC firmly into that category of international organizations . . . whose standing in U.S. officialdom will depend very much on U.S. presidential elections'.[27] For US global counterparts, there is now a disconcerting normalisation of American IL policy switching between opposing internationalist and nationalist tracks, each pegged to partisan electoral politics. Foreign policy ideology reveals more clearly why the first term of the Bush 43 administration never really marked an outer limit for possible and desirable policy divergence between the United States and ICC states parties. The invocation of exceptionalist beliefs in the Trump campaign slogan 'Make America Great Again' has translated into an IL policy that is nationalist-populist and led by values overtly illiberal and particularistic.

Understanding Contradictions in US International Law Policy

Analysing American ICC policy through foreign policy ideology does not dispel the criticism of frequent contradiction but, instead, redefines the nature of inconsistencies. The evidence suggests far greater coherence in legal principles, but greater political incoherence than is generally posited. Legal scholarship claims jurisprudential incoherence in American policy: that policymakers have pledged fidelity to the international rule of law, but that legal principle has been subverted to tactical political compromises in designing and developing the ICC. The conclusion from this book is that charges of hypocrisy do not stand up, with strong evidence that legal policymakers have been committed to the processes of the international legal system according to distinct and internally coherent conceptions of the rule of law. Policy outcomes were often revealed to be contradictory owing to domestic ideological competition, but decision-making processes were structured by multiple coherent legal commitments, rather than by an absence of them.

The process of ideological types competing within and between administrations demonstrates, however, that the *political* coherence of

26 Alex Whiting, 'Why John Bolton vs. Int'l Criminal Court 2.0 Is Different from Version 1.0', *Just Security*, 10 September 2018, www.justsecurity.org/60680/international-criminal-court-john-bolton-afghanistan-torture/.

27 David Bosco, 'Bolton Barked at the ICC, But With How Much Bite?,' *Lawfare*, 11 September 2018, www.lawfareblog.com/bolton-barked-icc-how-much-bite.

American IL policy cannot be assumed. Legal scholarship's standard explanation for contradictory outcomes is the consistent logic of US policy privileging 'considerations of self-interest above everything else'.[28] However, each ideology entails its own definition of the national interest and strategies for achieving it through IL. Owing to the same dynamic that establishes forms of legal coherence, American IL policy has exhibited contradictory outcomes over time by shifting between alternative definitions of interests. Incorporating the explanatory role of American foreign policy ideology precisely reverses the conclusions of legal analysis. Where legal scholars have seen contradictions in American fidelity to the international rule of law, they have tended to overlook underlying legal rationality. But, when they explain this as the rational process of national interests trumping law, they overlook fundamental contradictions in what policymakers believe interests are.

David Scheffer's recollection of the Rome Conference demonstrates the way that competing legal conceptions among American legal policymakers contribute to the appearance that American IL policy is bereft of any principled commitment to law. Scheffer was accompanied in the Rome negotiations by Senator Helms' staffers, whom he was expected to accommodate as a courtesy to the US legislature.[29] Unsurprisingly, Scheffer found himself correcting misperceptions among foreign diplomats that Helms' confrontational illiberal nationalist language represented the true US position, rather than the accommodating language in official communications.[30] Such internal conflicts signal to other states that official US statements mask a degree of hypocrisy, thereby increasing wariness toward making negotiated concessions. Clearer understanding by global counterparts of the competing legal commitments of US policymakers can facilitate more constructive engagement with dominant ideologies.[31]

Shifts between contradictory ideologies may also yield incoherent outcomes that fail to satisfy the interests of any legal policymaker. The aspirational Clinton decision to sign the Rome Statute was done with the strategic objective of bolstering US credibility and support for transnational legal development. Yet the Bush 43 reversal toward illiberal nationalism

[28] Johan D. van der Vyver, *The International Criminal Court: American Responses to the Rome Conference and the Role of the European Union* (Inst. für Rechtspolitik, 2003), p. 4.

[29] Scheffer, *All the Missing Souls*, p. 229.

[30] Ibid., p. 188.

[31] For a complementary study seeking to reduce US misunderstanding of European motivations see Caroline Fehl, *Living with a Reluctant Hegemon: Explaining European Responses to US Unilateralism* (Oxford University Press, 2012), pp. 7–8.

transformed the conspicuous act of signing into an especially potent symbol of the US exception once the statute was conspicuously unsigned. The comparatively muted response to the Trump administration reaffirming that act likely owes much to the Obama decision not to formally 're-sign' the Rome Statute in the interim period. Similarly, institutional obstructions such as 'hard-to-reverse consequences of path dependency' likely frustrated desired course changes by the Bush 43 and Obama administrations, who 'both violated and shaped' IL, yet were unable to fully realise 'starkly different goals for international law and institutions'.[32] These cases emphasise the limitation of drawing conclusions about legal principles or political interests from ICC policy outcomes, and the need to engage with ideological beliefs at the level of decision-making processes.

Contesting American ICC Policy

The significance of these arguments is to reconceive US disputes with the ICC as a battle *internal to* law rather than as an *external* battle against politics. Exhortations to honour formalised obligations, sovereign equality and the separation of international legal powers were not rejected by American policymakers merely as politically undesirable but as contrary to received understandings of an ICC designed in conformity with the international rule of law. Charges of hypocrisy in American ICC policy more often projected legalist beliefs on to American policymakers and then levelled the charge of incoherence when US policymakers failed to meet that imputed ideal.

ICC history reveals that the key to contesting American IL policy is instead understanding the structure of American foreign policy ideology and challenging contradictions on policymakers' own terms. The concern of legalist advocates was not that the United States was breaching international criminal law with impunity through these years, but that its proposals for the international rule of law rejected institutional constraints in favour of America's own good faith adherence to exceptionalist values. Bosco notes that US legal principles were 'competing with the narrative of accountability' throughout and thus remained unconvincing outside of American policymaking. Rather, these principles appeared as 'little more than an exercise in exceptionalism: the United States wanted international justice, but only if it could control how it would be

[32] Jack Goldsmith, '*The Trump Administration and International Law*. By Harold Hongju Koh. New York, New York: Oxford University Press, 2019. Pp. viii, 221. Index,' (2019) 113 *American Journal of International Law* 408, p. 414.

applied'.[33] The veracity of exceptionalism thus lay at the heart of divergence between legalist demands for more formalised legal relations and the American defence of more flexible and contextual arrangements. Challenging US legal policy required not pointing out contradictions with legalist principles, but demonstrating incoherence in exceptionalist assumptions.

The power of that strategy was demonstrated in the 2004 withdrawal of US demands for ICC immunity following the Abu Ghraib prisoner abuse scandal.[34] The passing of previous UNSC resolutions granting ICC immunity to US peacekeepers had been defended in terms of internationalist principles about the unequal US legal role in upholding liberal values and the merits of hegemonic privilege. The integrity of IL in both cases was assured by reference to exceptionalist beliefs in 'America as something different' and therefore its own check against abuse.[35] When the UNSC granted immunity in the 2002–3 resolutions, opposition had been expressed in terms of contravening the principle of sovereign equality and failed to resonate on each occasion.[36] In 2004, however, opponents pointed to the growing scandal as evidence that US privileges were no longer proportionate to any role in advancing international criminal justice. In American policymakers' own terms, the only means of avoiding hypocrisy became the equal application of internationally determined rights and duties to American military personnel.

The structure of exceptionalist beliefs emerges as the primary lever for influencing US responses in cases where the integrity of its own conduct is at issue. Such an opportunity seemed to be offered in the OTP's November 2017 request for authorisation to investigate the Afghanistan situation.[37] Previous ICC reports indicated alleged crimes to include

> [w]ar crimes of torture, outrages upon personal dignity and rape and other forms of sexual violence, by members of the US armed forces on the territory of Afghanistan and members of the CIA in secret detention

[33] David Bosco, *Rough Justice: The International Criminal Court's Battle to Fix the World, One Prosecution at a Time* (Oxford University Press, 2014), p. 179.

[34] See Chapter 6, *supra*.

[35] Committee on Foreign Relations, United States Senate, *Senate Committee on Foreign Relations, Nomination of Dr. Condoleezza Rice to be Secretary of State*, 1st Session 109th Congress (2005), p. 147.

[36] See SC Res 1422, UN Doc S/RES/1422 (12 July 2002); SC Res 1487, UN Doc S/RES/1487 (12 June 2003).

[37] Submitted to the ICC Pre-Trial Chamber pursuant to *Rome Statute*, Art. 15.

> facilities both in Afghanistan and on the territory of other States Parties, principally in the 2003–2004 period.[38]

In so proceeding, the OTP willingly entered uncharted territory by, for the first time, setting the authority and judicial credibility of the ICC against its most powerful and persistent critic. The ICC answered strident US objections by reiterating its character as 'an independent and impartial institution' that, 'as a court of law, will continue to do its work undeterred, in accordance with those principles and the overarching idea of the rule of law'.[39]

The entire history of US engagement with the ICC demonstrates the limits of such appeals to shared international rule of law principles. Even an ICC investigation maintaining complete integrity to the Rome Statute, including its inbuilt checks and balances, would remain a process disconnected from the ideological commitments of American legal policymakers. Bolton responded forcefully to the OTP request:

> If the ICC Prosecutor were to take the complementarity principle seriously, the Court would never pursue an investigation against American citizens, because we know that the U.S. judicial system is more vigorous, more fair, and more effective than the ICC. The ICC Prosecutor's November 2017 request of course proves that this notion, and thus the principle of complementarity, is completely farcical.[40]

This is a perverse argument from legalist conceptions, since the integrity of complementarity is said to be proven only by its inherent inapplicability to the United States. Yet the contest remains rooted in entirely different conceptions of the rule of law. Shortly thereafter, the ICC president appealed for the United States to support the Court, 'whose values and objectives are entirely consistent with the best instincts of America and her values'. This book has demonstrated why little traction was to be gained through the president's reassurances that complementarity 'does the very opposite of usurpation of national sovereignty. It actually prides and

[38] International Criminal Court, *Situation in Afghanistan: Summary of the Prosecutor's Request for Authorisation of an Investigation Pursuant to Article 15* (The Office of the Prosecutor, 20 November 2017), p. 6; International Criminal Court, *Report on Preliminary Examination Activities* (The Office of the Prosecutor, 14 November 2016), pp. 44 & 47.

[39] ICC, 'The ICC Will Continue Its Independent and Impartial Work, Undeterred', 12 September 2018, www.icc-cpi.int/Pages/item.aspx?name=pr1406.

[40] Bolton, 'Protecting American Constitutionalism and Sovereignty from International Threats'.

underscores national sovereignty.'[41] Each side remained segregated within their own ideological conception of IL.

Against widespread expectations, the Pre-Trial Chamber denied authorisation of the investigation in April of 2019 as contrary to the 'interests of justice' under the Rome Statute.[42] The decision met with speculation that the ICC had caved to US pressure but, more tangibly, echoed forms of policy-conscious legal reasoning long advocated by the United States. 'Interests of justice' were held to encompass a pragmatic assessment that successful and timely prosecution remained unlikely in circumstances of 'scarce cooperation' by concerned parties, including the United States.[43] Thus, although relevant jurisdiction and admissibility requirements were met, the geopolitical dimensions of an effective system of criminal justice were effectively rendered a legally relevant bar to proceeding. Unsurprisingly, the decision was both condemned by NGOs and legalist scholars, and praised by US legal policymakers, with each claiming the mantel of fidelity to the rule of law.

Nevertheless, the experience of the protracted investigation and the US responses reaffirms that genuine beliefs in American exceptionalism, and not appeals to ICC integrity, form the entry point for engaging the United States toward legal compromise. President Trump framed the decision not to investigate American personnel as 'a major international victory, not only for these patriots, but for the rule of law. We welcome this decision and reiterate our position that the United States holds American citizens to the highest legal and ethical standards.'[44] That assertion is contrary to the Pre-Trial Chamber finding that the United States failed to discharge its complementarity obligations[45] – an issue that would have been conspicuously examined had the investigation proceeded and may be still, should the OTP successfully appeal the

[41] Chile Eboe-Osuji, 'ICC President's Keynote Speech "A Tribute to Robert H. Jackson – Recalling America's Contributions to International Criminal Justice" at the Annual Meeting of American Society of International Law', 29 March 2019, www.icc-cpi.int/Pages/item.aspx?name=190329-stat-pres.

[42] *Decision Pursuant to Article 15 of the Rome Statute on the Authorisation of an Investigation into the Situation in the Islamic Republic of Afghanistan, Case No. ICC-02/17, 12 April 2019*, pars. [87]–[96].

[43] Ibid., par. [91].

[44] Donald J. Trump, 'Statement from the President', 12 April 2019, www.whitehouse.gov/briefings-statements/statement-from-the-president-8/.

[45] *Case No. ICC-02/17*, pars. [78]–[79].

decision.[46] Yet, even in his illiberal nationalist defence of the rule of law, the president was compelled to invoke US claims to implement superior prosecutorial and judicial power at the domestic level as a check on unconstrained US sovereignty. As with the Abu Ghraib case, contesting US policy ultimately resonates most powerfully by communicating not the ICC's institutional integrity but any gap between alleged US crimes and accountability on the one hand and exceptionalist conceptions of the international rule of law on the other.

The power of holding 'a mirror of conscience' up to American policymakers' own legal ideals is not a means for establishing the legalist international rule of law.[47] This is a reactive strategy that ameliorates only unambiguous cases of hypocrisy. The historical record, however, is that, in routine cases, discomfort with US policy has been a principled objection to the absence of support for independent institutions rather than recognition of actual lawlessness. Conversely, the greatest threat to the international rule of law, as conceived by any involved party, is precisely those more disruptive cases where US actions truly contradict not only legalism but American ideological commitments, too.[48] Engaging through foreign policy ideology will not align parties' conceptions of the international rule of law, but it can influence policies toward more acceptable compromises. In particular, this may entail strategically appealing to the ideas of liberal internationalism and internationalism more generally as the legal approaches having most common ground with legalism. Conversely, legal policymakers can work to delegitimise nationalist and specifically illiberal nationalist beliefs as the conceptions most incompatible with the legalist international rule of law.[49] Through this dynamic, it does ultimately matter that American legal policymakers from all persuasions are committed to dialogue over the

[46] See *Request for Leave to Appeal the 'Decision Pursuant to Article 15 of the Rome Statute on the Authorisation of an Investigation into the Situation in the Islamic Republic of Afghanistan', Case No. ICC-02/17*, 7 June 2019.

[47] Eboe-Osuji, 'ICC President's Keynote Speech'.

[48] The Congressional Research Service cites the example of the 1968 My Lai Massacre in this context: see Ellen Grigorian, *The International Criminal Court Treaty: Description, Policy Issues, and Congressional Concerns* (Congressional Research Service, 6 January 1999), pp. 11–12, n. 46.

[49] Schabas describes the shift away from the Bush 43 administration's illiberal nationalism as a 'great diplomatic defeat for the United States': William Schabas, *An Introduction to the International Criminal Court* (Cambridge University Press, 2011), p. 34.

meaning of the international rule of law, and that none identifies US interests in explicit lawlessness.

Contesting Power through the International Rule of Law

Beyond the ICC

Identifying the role of foreign policy ideology in the case of the ICC aspires to provide a framework capable of explaining American IL policy more generally. The beliefs shaping ICC policy are hardly confined to that court alone, with Congressional refusal to ratify the *Genocide Convention* (1948) for over forty years founded in fears that it would expose American citizens to international prosecutions. The objection was overcome only when reservations foreclosed that possibility.[50] Likewise, from 1946 to 1986, the United States accepted the compulsory jurisdiction of the ICJ subject to the 'Connally reservation', which allowed the United States to determine on a case-by-case basis whether any legal dispute was the sole province of domestic courts.[51] Where the United States was unable to rely on even this reservation to determine international legal power, it withdrew consent entirely to compulsory jurisdiction under Article 36(2), while defending its decision as 'commitment to the rule of law'.[52]

Beyond US policy toward international courts specifically, foreign policy ideology promises to shed new light on a range of puzzles in general post-Cold War IL policy. The legal policy of each president from Bush 41 onward in the 'long war with Iraq', lasting from 1990 to 2011 (and arguably longer),[53] has provoked voluminous analysis about implications for the international rule of law. Of particular interest are convergent legal justifications for the use of force against Iraq across the Clinton and Bush 43 administrations. The legality of airstrikes carried out under Clinton throughout the 1990s was based in part on implied and

[50] Michael J. Struett, *The Politics of Constructing the International Criminal Court: NGOs, Discourse, and Agency* (Palgrave Macmillan, 2008), p. 69.

[51] See Sean D. Murphy, 'The United States and the International Court of Justice: Coping with Antinomies', in Cesare P. R. Romano (ed.), *The Sword and the Scales: The United States and International Courts and Tribunals* (Cambridge University Press, 2009), pp. 65–6.

[52] US Department of State, cited in Marian N. Leich, 'U.S. Withdrawal of Proceedings Initiated by Nicaragua' (1985) 79 *American Journal of International Law* 431. See *Charter of the United Nations* (1945), Art. 36(2).

[53] Timothy J. Lynch, 'Obama, Liberalism, and US Foreign Policy', in Inderjeet Parmar, Linda B. Miller & Mark Ledwidge (eds.), *Obama and the World: New Directions in US Foreign Policy* (Routledge, 2014), p. 47.

revived authorisation of UNSC resolutions from the Persian Gulf War,[54] which became the explicit foundation for the 2003 invasion.[55] Yet, despite commonalities, there was a conspicuous contrast between intense criticism of the 2003 war, both domestically and externally, and moderate criticism of the Clinton airstrikes. Bellinger has argued that 'there was either legal authority to use force, or there was not . . . [and] if there was not legal authority to use force, then the legal problem did not begin in 2003 – it went all the way back through the 1990s'.[56] Focusing on ideology moves beyond doctrinal analysis to distinguish these periods according to broader systemic implications from competing conceptions of the international rule of law.

Another interesting question is whether the theorised ideological structure extends beyond the executive and legislative branches to the judiciary as 'legal policymakers': Do US judges' conceptions of IL exhibit the same ideological dimensionality and structure as general foreign policy? Within the US Supreme Court in particular, views on IL and its reception into the common law have animated intense disagreements that parallel beliefs within each administration.[57] There is some truth to Sands' description of certain members of the US Supreme Court refusing to follow IL pursuant to an 'exceptionalist and isolationist perspective that sees America as an island of law hermetically sealed off from the rest of the world'.[58] Associate Justice Anthony Kennedy's retirement during the second year of the Trump administration sparked a partisan battle shaped in part by the retiring justice's forceful advocacy for the integration of American law into transnational processes[59] and the opposing

[54] Gavin A. Symes, 'Force without Law: Seeking a Legal Justification for the September 1996 US Military Intervention in Iraq' (1997) 19 *Michigan Journal of International Law* 581, pp. 602–8.

[55] See William H. Taft IV & Todd F. Buchwald, 'Preemption, Iraq and International Law' (2003) 97 *American Journal of International Law* 557, pp. 559–60. Notably Taft conceded that this interpretation 'certainly did have a weakening effect' on the institution of the UNSC by likely increasing reluctance to pass future resolutions: see William H. Taft IV, Interview with Author (22 November 2011).

[56] John B. Bellinger III, 'Interview with John Bellinger', International Bar Association, 2011, www.ibanet.org/Article/Detail.aspx?ArticleUid=37f4f087-bc3a-4c21-a108-92f15391785c.

[57] Compare the divided views on application of Common Article 3 of the 1949 Geneva Conventions in *Hamdan* v. *Rumsfeld* (2006) 548 *U.S.* 557, at 633 per Stevens J & 718–19 per Thomas J.

[58] Philippe Sands, *Lawless World: Making and Breaking Global Rules* (Viking, 2006), p. 252.

[59] See Jeffrey Toobin, 'Swing Shift: How Anthony Kennedy's Passion for Foreign Law Could Change the Supreme Court' (2005) September 12 *The New Yorker* 42.

desire for a Republican nominee who agreed that 'reliance on foreign law or unratified treaties undermines American sovereignty'.[60]

Between Power and Transcendent Values

In 2005, Secretary of State Condoleezza Rice faced the task of redressing perceptions among allies that the early years of the Bush 43 administration signalled a retreat from the international rule of law. Rice reassured of America's

> strong belief that international law is vital and a powerful force in the search for freedom. The United States has been and will continue to be the world's strongest voice for the development and defense of international legal norms. We know from history that nations governed by the rule of law are nations that are just.[61]

The gesture, in the context of a turn from illiberal nationalism to internationalism, received a tepid response. In his concluding chapter entitled 'Window Dressing', Sands noted that these were 'important words, but they remain just that'.[62] This book has made the case that the very meaning of the international rule of law is contested such that statements of legal obligation, including that by Rice, are not mere rhetoric to mask a conscious repudiation of legal ideals but a manifestation of divergent political interests within the very meaning of the international rule of law. American legal policymakers' competing ideological commitments set the parameters of the possible in American IL policymaking and are united in accepting that the international rule of law 'cannot rest upon an unbridled faith in legalism'.[63] The political foundation of IL is confirmed by Sands' own position that he in contrast 'unashamedly makes the case for international rules' in the belief that they 'reflect common values, to the extent that these can be ascertained'.[64] Each side of this divide has the capacity to express good-faith commitment to legal principle, but the substance of those commitments remains indivisible from ideological context.

60 Republican National Committee, *2016 Republican Party Platform*, 18 July 2016, www.presidency.ucsb.edu/ws/index.php?pid=117718.

61 Condoleezza Rice, 'Remarks at Annual Meeting of the American Society of International Law', Lowes L'Enfant Plaza Hotel, Washington, DC, 1 April 2005, https://2001-2009.state.gov/secretary/rm/2005/44159.htm.

62 Sands, *Lawless World*, p. 253.

63 John M. Czarnetzky & Ronald J. Rychlak, 'An Empire of Law: Legalism and the International Criminal Court' (2003) 79 *Notre Dame Law Review* 55, p. 126.

64 Sands, *Lawless World*, p. xviii.

This book has equally emphasised that the task of defining legal principles to guide the design and development of international institutions should not be abandoned as futile. As Koskenniemi has argued, something must be built up beyond recognition that law is politicised: 'From the fact that law has no shape of its own, but always comes to us in the shape of particular traditions or preferences, it does not follow that we cannot choose between better or worse preferences, traditions we have more or less reason to hope to universalize.'[65] Intervening to argue that foreign policy ideology is ingrained in IL is done to sharpen analytical understanding, not to defeat the political project of lawyers such as Sands looking to an international rule of law based on 'common values'. That vision ultimately emerges as the core of contestation over the international rule of law: as a paradoxical quest to reconcile global power and transcendent values. Law is inevitably 'always part of a political project that connects the present via the past to a future "utopia"'.[66] The claim made by each of the ideological types, and by legalist advocates, is to have melded power and principles within law. Yet each formulation necessarily represents partial values and particularistic interests. The international rule of law is thus revealed as a commitment to the process of contesting the meaning of non-arbitrary global governance, equality under IL, and the integrity of international judicial power.

The value of legalism remains as a vehicle for contesting imperialistic global power and its ossification in IL. What is required is a consciousness that formalised legal rules, sovereign equality and the separation of international legal powers are harnessed to a common political purpose. Moyn cautions:

> [N]o one approaches international criminal law as a political enterprise. Its supporters, almost to a man and woman, appear to believe that the best way to advance it is to deny its political essence, as if talking about international criminal law exclusively as extant law would by itself convert passionately held ideals into generally observed realities. So long as no one interested in the topic openly discusses international criminal law as a political matter . . . the project will lack plausibility.[67]

65 Martti Koskenniemi, 'International Law in Europe: Between Tradition and Renewal' (2005) 16 *European Journal of International Law* 113, p. 119.

66 Friedrich Kratochwil, 'Legal Theory and International Law', in David Armstrong (ed.), *Routledge Handbook of International Law* (Routledge, 2009), p. 56.

67 Samuel Moyn, 'Judith Shklar versus the International Criminal Court' (2013) 4 *Humanity: An International Journal of Human Rights, Humanitarianism, and Development* 473, pp. 494–5.

Shklar recognised the power of legalism to translate political values into a more desirable international order if adherents freed themselves 'from the illusions of the "rule of law" ideologists'.[68] The role of foreign policy ideology in IL, once uncovered, makes a return to the neutral conception of the rule of law impossible. In these terms, Koskenniemi reasserts the value of legalism because of, rather than despite, its political foundation in opposing imperialism: 'You need to choose the law that will be yours; you need to vindicate a particular understanding, a particular bias or preference over contrasting biases and preferences. The choice is not between law and politics, but between one politics of law, and another.'[69]

On the other hand, American conceptions of the international rule of law remain central and indispensable to the dialogue. The evidence is incontrovertible that American power put in the service of commonly agreed legal objectives has great potential for realising an operational system of law. But it is also true that strands of American legal belief stray so far from the normative views of global counterparts that they will be seen as inherently threatening and a barrier to even pragmatic compromises on global institutions. Nevertheless, in cases where US IL policy becomes conspicuously arbitrary, unequal or imperial, the promised release valve for other states remains genuine belief in American exceptionalism. For Kagan, the belief that national values are universal values means that 'Americans have been forced to care what the liberal world thinks by their unique national ideology'. Through that mechanism, policy toward the international legal system can be directed back toward politically acceptable bounds by 'the steady denial of international legitimacy by fellow democracies'.[70]

The advancement of the international rule of law remains an iterative process between irreconcilable positions that will challenge each other, occasionally align, but never converge on the precise conception of legal ideals. Yet consensus cannot be the ideal for law. The end state of each concept of IL is a utopian vision that could be realised only by levelling the rich diversity of ideological commitments and values of the real people making up the international legal system: legal utopia presupposes a form of totalitarianism. The opposition of ideologies preserves the vision of reconciling power and transcendent values precisely because it is a contest that cannot be resolved.

[68] Shklar, *Legalism*, p. 142.

[69] Koskenniemi, 'International Law in Europe', p. 123.

[70] Kagan, *Of Paradise and Power*, pp. 151–2.

INDEX